STUDY TEXT

Advanced Certificate (Stage 2) New Syllabus

Marketing Communications

In this June 2003 edition

- New for the new syllabus examinable in December 2003
- Material supporting assignment based learning
- Plenty of activities and examples
- Question and answer bank
- Pilot paper

BPP Professional Education
June 2003

First edition June 2003

ISBN 0 7517 1097 0

British Library Cataloguing-in-Publication Data
A catalogue record for this book
is available from the British Library

Published by

BPP Professional Education
Aldine House, Aldine Place
London W12 8AW

www.bpp.com

Printed in Great Britain by W M Print
45-47 Frederick Street
Walsall, West Midlands
WS2 9NE

We are grateful to the Chartered Institute of Marketing for permission to
reproduce in this text the syllabus, tutor's guidance notes and past examination
questions. We are also grateful to Kate Machattie for preparing this text, and
to Karen Beamish for preparing the material covering Assignment Based
Learning.

(ii)

HOW TO USE THIS STUDY TEXT

Aims of this Study Text

To provide you with the knowledge and understanding, skills and applied techniques required for passing the exam

The Study Text has been written around the new CIM Stage 2 Syllabus, which is reproduced later in this introduction. Each topic is cross-referenced to the place in the text where it is covered.

- It is **comprehensive**. We do not omit sections of the syllabus as the Examiner may choose to examine any aspect of any part of it - and you do not want to be left high and dry.

- It is **on-target**. We do not include any material that is not examinable. You can therefore rely on your BPP Study Text as the stand-alone source of all your information for the exam.

To allow you to study in the way that best suits your learning style and the time you have available, by creating and following your personal Study Plan

You may be studying at home on your own until the date of the exam, or you may be attending a full-time course. You may like to (and have time to) read every word, or you may prefer to (or only have time to) skim-read and devote the remainder of your time to question practice. Whatever approach you select, you will find the BPP Study Text meets the needs of your personal Study Plan.

To tie in with the other components of the BPP Effective Study Package to ensure you have the best possible chance of passing the exam

Recommended period of use	Elements of BPP Effective Study Package
3-12 months before exam	**Study Text** Acquisition of knowledge, understanding, skills and applied techniques
1-6 months before exam	**Practice and Revision Kit (9/2003)** There are numerous examination questions to try, graded by topic area, along with realistic suggested solutions prepared by marketing professionals. There are two complete mock examinations, one of which is the official CIM Pilot Paper for your syllabus.
1 –6 months before exam	**Passcards (9/2003)** Handy, pocketsized revision notes you can take anywhere and use to refresh the essential knowledge you need.

Settling down to study

By this stage in your career you may be a very experienced learner and taker of exams. But have you ever thought about how you learn? Let's have a quick look at the key elements required for effective learning. You can then identify your learning style and go on to design your own approach to how you are going to study this text - your personal Study Plan.

Key element of learning	Using the BPP Study Text
Motivation	You can rely on the comprehensiveness and technical quality of BPP. You've chosen the right Study Text - so you're in pole position to pass your exam!
Clear objectives and standards	Do you want to be a prizewinner or simply achieve a moderate pass? Decide.
Feedback	Follow through the examples in this text and do the Action Programme and the Quick quizzes. Evaluate your efforts critically - how are you doing?
Study Plan	You need to be honest about your progress to yourself - do not be over-confident, but don't be negative either. Make your Study Plan (see below) and try to stick to it. Focus on the short-term objectives – completing two chapters a night, say - but beware of losing sight of your study objectives
Practice	Use the Quick quizzes and Chapter Roundups to refresh your memory regularly after you have completed your initial study of each chapter

These introductory pages let you see exactly what you are up against. However you study, you should:

■ **Read through the syllabus and teaching guide** - this will help you to identify areas you have already covered, perhaps at a lower level of detail, and areas that are totally new to you

■ **Study the examination paper section**, where we show you the format of the exam (how many and what kind of questions etc).

Key study steps

The following steps are, in our experience, the ideal way to study for professional exams. You can of course adapt it for your particular learning style (see below).

Tackle the chapters in the order you find them in the Study Text. Taking into account your individual learning style, follow these key study steps for each chapter.

Key study steps	Activity
Step 1 *Chapter Topic List*	Study the list. Each numbered topic denotes a **numbered section** in the chapter.
Step 2 *Setting the Scene*	Read it through. It is designed to show you **why the topics in the chapter need to be studied** - how they lead on from previous topics, and how they lead into subsequent ones.
Step 3 *Explanations*	Proceed **methodically** through the chapter, reading each section thoroughly and making sure you understand.
Step 4 *Key Concepts*	**Key concepts** can often earn you **easy marks** if you state them clearly and correctly in an appropriate exam.
Step 5 *Exam Tips*	These give you a good idea of how the examiner tends to examine certain topics – pinpointing **easy marks** and highlighting **pitfalls**.
Step 6 *Note taking*	Take **brief notes** if you wish, avoiding the temptation to copy out too much.
Step 7 *Marketing at Work*	Study each one, and try if you can to add flesh to them from your **own experience** - they are designed to show how the topics you are studying come alive (and often come unstuck) in the **real world**. You can also update yourself on these companies by going onto the World Wide Web.
Step 8 *Action Programme*	Make a very good attempt at each one in each chapter. These are designed to put your **knowledge into practice** in much the same way as you will be required to do in the exam. Check the answer at the end of the chapter in the **Action Programme review**, and make sure you understand the reasons why yours may be different.
Step 9 *Chapter Roundup*	Check through it very carefully, to make sure you have grasped the **major points** it is highlighting
Step 10 *Quick Quiz*	When you are happy that you have covered the chapter, use the **Quick quiz** to check your recall of the topics covered. The answers are in the paragraphs in the chapter that we refer you to.

Developing your personal Study Plan

Preparing a Study Plan (and sticking closely to it) is one of the key elements in learning success.

First you need to be aware of your style of learning. There are four typical learning styles. Consider yourself in the light of the following descriptions. and work out which you fit most closely. You can then plan to follow the key study steps in the sequence suggested.

Learning styles	Characteristics	Sequence of key study steps in the BPP Study Text
Theorist	Seeks to understand principles before applying them in practice	1, 2, 3, 7, 4, 5, 8, 9, 10 (6 continuous)
Reflector	Seeks to observe phenomena, thinks about them and then chooses to act	
Activist	Prefers to deal with practical, active problems; does not have much patience with theory	1, 2, 8 (read through), 7, 4, 5, 9, 3, 8 (full attempt), 10 (6 continuous)
Pragmatist	Prefers to study only if a direct link to practical problems can be seen; not interested in theory for its own sake	8 (read through), 2, 4, 5, 7, 9, 3, 8 (full attempt), 10, (6 continuous)

Next you should complete the following checklist.

Am I motivated? (a) ⬚

Do I have an objective and a standard that I want to achieve? (b) ⬚

Am I a theorist, a reflector, an activist or a pragmatist? (c) ⬚

How much time do I have available per week, given: (d) ⬚

- the standard I have set myself
- the time I need to set aside later for work on the Practice & Revision Kit
- the other exam(s) I am sitting, and (of course)
- practical matters such as work, travel, exercise, sleep and social life?

Now:

- take the time you have available per week for this Study Text (d), and multiply it by the number of weeks available to give (e). (e) ⬚
- divide (e) by the number of chapters to give (f) (f) ⬚
- set about studying each chapter in the time represented by (f), following the key study steps in the order suggested by your particular learning style.

This is your personal **Study Plan**.

BPP PROFESSIONAL EDUCATION

Short of time?

Whatever your objectives, standards or style, you may find you simply do not have the time available to follow all the key study steps for each chapter, however you adapt them for your particular learning style. If this is the case, follow the Skim Study technique below (the icons in the Study Text will help you to do this).

Skim Study technique

Study the chapters in the order you find them in the Study Text. For each chapter, follow the key study steps 1-2, and then skim-read through step 3. Jump to step 9, and then go back to steps 4-5. Follow through step 7, and prepare outline Answers to the Action Programme (step 8). Try the Quick Quiz (step 10), following up any items you can't answer, then do a plan for the illustrative question (step 11), comparing it against our answers. You should probably still follow step 6 (note-taking).

Moving on...

However you study, when you are ready to embark on the practice and revision phase of the BPP Effective Study Package, you should still refer back to this Study Text:

■   as a source of **reference** (you should find the list of Key Concepts and the index particularly helpful for this)

■   as a **refresher** (the Chapter Roundups and Quick Quizzes help you here).

Key Concepts

In order to help you transfer your learning to the real world, we use this feature to introduce you to some of the technical terms used by marketing professionals. These key concepts also appear in list form at the back of the text.

Marketing at Work

The syllabus specifically requires students to develop an awareness of what marketers are actually doing in their everyday professional lives: what new initiatives are being attempted; what is working and what is not; how different organisations tackle the same tasks. We encourage you to collect, examples of promotional techniques and articles on marketing organisation and campaigns from magazines such as Campaign, PR Week, Marketing Week and other relevant journals and newspaper Media sections. We also encourage you whenever possible (and when professional discretion allows) to swap stories of successes, failures and house styles with other students and practitioners. Our 'Marketing at Work' section will help - but it should only be a prompter to the kind of insatiable curiosity about other people's efforts that makes a good marketing professional.

Action Programme

You must get used to attempting a wide variety of marketing tasks and analysing your performance according to relevant criteria. Our Action Programme exercises help you step by step through this active learning process. They also assist you in reflecting on what you have learnt and applying it to the appropriate context.

Pilot paper and marking guide

We have included the CIM Pilot Paper at the back of the text as an indication of the kind of questions you could expect in the exam. We have provided a question-by-question analysis and brief notes on how you might tackle each one.

Examined dates

We show the dates of the exams under the old syllabus in which particular topics were examined. We think this is useful as it indicates those subjects that are potentially in the Examiner's mind.

A note on pronouns

On occasions in this Study Text, 'he' is used for 'he or she', 'him' for 'him or her' and so forth. Whilst we try to avoid this practice it is sometimes necessary for reasons of style. No prejudice or stereotyping according to sex is intended or assumed.

SYLLABUS

Aim

The Marketing Communications module provides the skills and knowledge that enable marketers to manage marketing communications and brand support activities within organisations. It provides participants with an understanding of the concepts and practice of promotional activity at an operational level. Although reference is made to relevant strategic issues in order to provide a relevant context for learning, the focus is primarily on creating applied coordinated promotional activities, campaign development and the management of relationships with a variety of stakeholders, particularly customers and members of marketing channels.

Related statements of practice

Cc.1 Create and build competitive brands.
Cc.2 Manage competitive brands.
Dc.1 Create effective communications plans.
Dc.2 Manage communications activities.
Gc.2 Manage and monitor support to channel members.
Hc.1 Establish and monitor activities and information for delivering effective customer relationships.
Hc.2 Manage and monitor provision of effective customer service.

Learning outcomes

Participants will be able to:

- Explain the role of marketing communications and advise how personal influences might be used to develop promotional effectiveness.

- Explain how the tools of the promotional mix can be coordinated in order to communicate effectively with customers and a range of stakeholders.

- Devise a basic media plan based on specific campaign requirements using both offline and online media.

- Develop marketing communication and brand support activities based on an understanding of the salient characteristics of the target audience.

- Explain the main elements, activities and linkages associated with the formulation and implementation of a marketing communications plan.

- Recommend a suitable marketing communications budget.

- Explain the importance of developing long term relationships with customers, channel members, agencies and other stakeholders and transfer such knowledge to the development of marketing communication activities.

- Suggest suitable methods to influence the relationships an organisation has with its customers, any marketing channel partners and other stakeholders, using marketing communications.

- Use the vocabulary of the marketing communications industry and be able to communicate effectively with other marketing practitioners.

Knowledge and skill requirements

Element 1: Understand customer dynamics (20%	
1.1	Explain how individuals can influence the effectiveness of marketing communications through word-of-mouth communications, as opinion leaders, as opinion formers or in multi-step models.
1.2	Describe the main concepts associated with buyer information processing and explain how marketing communications might be used to change or reinforce attitudes, alter perceptions and develop knowledge and understanding about a brand.
1.3	Describe the main concepts associated with the purchase decision process, including source credibility, involvement, perceived risk, and how they influence marketing communications.
1.4	Assess the principal differences between consumer and organisational markets and consider how they impact on marketing communications.
1.5	Summarise the importance for organisations of ethics and corporate responsibility, and their impact on brand reputation.

Element 2: Coordinated marketing communications (50%)	
2.1	Define and explain the roles of marketing communications to differentiate, remind or reassure, inform and persuade (DRIP).
2.2	Evaluate the effectiveness of each of the promotional tools using appropriate criteria such as cost, communication effectiveness, credibility, and control.
2.3	Explain the meaning of the terms above-, through- and below-the-line.
2.4	Explain the role of each of the promotional tools within a coordinated marketing communications mix.
2.5	Evaluate the effectiveness of coordinated campaigns.
2.6	Identify primary and secondary media (online and offline) and contrast their main characteristics.
2.7	Explain key media concepts (reach, frequency, duplication, GRPs, flighting) and describe the principal approaches used to measure media effectiveness.
2.8	Compare information and emotional based advertising messages and explain the concept of likeability.
2.9	Outline the key characteristics associated with push, pull and profile strategies.
2.10	Describe the main characteristics of key accounts and explain the stages and issues associated with key account management.
2.11	Describe how co-ordinated marketing communications can be used to develop key account relationships.
2.12	Explain how marketing communications can be used to launch new products, support brands, maintain market share, develop retention levels encourage customer loyalty, and support internal marketing within the organisation.
2.13	Draw and describe the main parts of a marketing communications planning framework and explain the principal linkages between the various elements.
2.14	Explain the main methods used to determine a marketing communications budget.
2.15	Discuss the main issues concerning the use of marketing communications in an international

BPP
PROFESSIONAL EDUCATION

	and global context, such as media availability, culture, religion, education and literacy.
2.16	Evaluate the effectiveness of marketing communications activities, tools, media and campaigns.

Element 3: Marketing channels (15%)	
3.1	Identify and explain how the promotional mix can be suitably configured for use in a range of marketing channels and business-to-business situations.
3.2	Explain, in terms of the impact on marketing communications within a relationship context, the structural concepts: interdependence, independence, disintermediation and reintermediation.
3.3	Explain the role of trust, commitment and satisfaction when developing marketing communication activities for use in the marketing channel and business-to-business contexts.
3.4	Identify the causes of conflict in trade channels and explain how marketing communications can be used to resolve such disagreements.
3.5	Explain how Internet- and digital-based technologies can been used to enhance marketing communications and relationships within channels and between business-to-business partners.

Element 4: Relationship management (15%)	
4.1	Compare the principles of transaction and relationship marketing.
4.2	Explain the characteristics of relationship marketing including the features, types, levels, development and implementation steps and communication issues.
4.3	Describe how marketing communications can be used to develop relationships with a range of stakeholders, based on an understanding of source credibility, trust and commitment.
4.4	Explain in broad terms the nature, structure, ownership and any key issues facing the marketing communications industry in any single country or region.
4.5	Describe how agencies manage their operations in order to meet client needs: pitching, briefing, structure, review, the role of account planners and managers, relationship management.
4.6	Explain how advertising agencies and marketing communication agencies use resources to meet the needs of clients with international and global requirements.
4.7	Describe in broad terms the regulatory and voluntary arrangements that are used to manage relationships between the public, customers, clients and agencies.

Related key skills for marketers

The syllabus covers the core knowledge and skills for marketing professionals. The .key skills for marketers. cover the broader business and organisational skills that marketing professionals should also possess. Participants will not be assessed specifically on their ability to perform key skills. However, as professionals working in organisations, they will be expected to demonstrate during assessment in the relevant modules their knowledge, understanding and competence in the areas defined by the key skills. Participants should be encouraged to develop and demonstrate the application of relevant key skills through activities, assignments and discussions during their learning.

■ Using ICT and the Internet

- Using financial information and metrics
- Presenting information
- Improving own learning and performance
- Working with others
- Problem-solving
- Applying business law

Assessment

CIM will normally offer two forms of assessment for this module from which centres or participants may choose: written examination and continuous assessment. CIM may also recognise, or make joint awards for, modules at an equivalent level undertaken with other professional marketing bodies and educational institutions.

Marketing journals

Participants can keep abreast of developments in the academic field of marketing by reference to the main marketing journals, a selection of which are listed in the Appendix to this document.

Press

Participants will be expected to have access to current examples of marketing campaigns and so should be sure to keep up to date with the appropriate marketing and quality daily press. A selection of marketing press titles is given in the Appendix to this document.

Websites

A list of websites that tutors and participants may find useful is shown in the Appendix at the end of this document.

Overview and rationale

Over the past few years there has been increased interest in the nature and form of the relationships organisations develop with a range of stakeholders. Of these, customers are regarded as central in many market sectors. The development of long-lasting, profitable relationships is now regarded as a requirement within organisations and often it is marketing people who are at the forefront of this activity.

In addition, one of the pivotal roles of marketing communications is to deliver the marketing plan to target audiences. Indeed a great part of marketing activity in organisations is consumed on communications-related activities. Communications also play a determining role in the development of successful marketing relationships. This module brings these two elements together and provides an exciting opportunity for participants to learn about and develop new skills and be able to make a significant contribution to an organisations in marketing communications operations and associated activities, both internally and externally with agencies and other outsourced providers.

Approach

The aim is to provide participants with the necessary conceptual frameworks and tools for determining and managing marketing communications in order to help form suitable relationships. In order to achieve this the unit will consider knowledge and develop understanding in the areas of customer information processing and purchase decision making, the management of the promotional mix and develop projects and activities associated with the management of relationships with a range of stakeholders.

The overall focus is upon the operational, medium-term management of marketing communication issues. It does not dwell on the strategic aspects of the subject although it is recognised that certain strategic topics will be encountered if only to put events into context. It is also recognised that the development of relationship marketing is a long-term strategic issue.

Participants will be expected to relate their knowledge and understanding to practical examples. To do this successfully, participants will need to understand certain concepts and theoretical frameworks and use examples to illustrate their understanding. To be successful at this level, participants will need to explain, describe and illustrate their knowledge through practical examples, rather than through evaluation, critical appraisal and discussion. They should be encouraged to develop simple communications plans, a skill that will be developed further in the Marketing Management in Practice module.

Syllabus content

This syllabus draws on a number of strands. The essence has been drawn from the Integrated Marketing Communications module in the Postgraduate Diploma module. However, this new syllabus deliberately avoids the word .integrated. for a number of reasons. The first is that the term 'integrated' is synonymous with strategy and this module sits just below that level. A new word 'co-ordinated' is introduced in order to focus attention on the promotional mix and the co-ordination of communications in developing relationships. The word also provides a point of Syllabus for Stage 2 Marketing Communications differentiation and to help provide clarity. A further reason is that the strategic issues concerning integrated marketing communications are considered throughout Stage 3.

The syllabus has four elements in order to segregate the core topics embedded in the module. Participants are expected to illustrate their understanding and knowledge of this syllabus through the application of examples.

Element 1: Understanding customer dynamics (20%)

This element introduces buyer behaviour in order that participants develop their marketing communications skills and knowledge on a customer focused foundation. These concepts and frameworks are concerned with how people process information and how they make purchase decisions. Marketing communications need to reflect this knowledge if they are to be successful. The emphasis in this element is upon participants being able to explain and demonstrate how these theories and frameworks are applied in practice, not on learning the theories themselves in isolation.

Element 2: Coordinated marketing communications (50%)

In terms of weighting, this is the most important element of this module. Here the syllabus concentrates on the tools and media used to communicate co-ordinated messages with target audiences. Participants will develop their understanding developed at Stage 1 about the characteristics of the promotional tools and consider them as part of a coordinated promotional mix designed to support a brand and other business activities. International marketing communications issues are introduced, as are budgeting techniques and evaluation methods concerning campaigns, tools and media.

Although key terms associated with marketing communications strategy, namely push, pull and profile strategies, are mentioned, these are only considered briefly in order to provide knowledge of the overall scope of activities.

Knowledge of the components of a marketing communications planning framework and the way the parts are linked together is developed. This is intended to provide structure and context for understanding the various parts of this subject and for developing plans for co-ordinated communications campaigns.

Again it is the use of practical examples to demonstrate understanding that is required.

Element 3: Marketing channels (15%)

For a long time marketing communications education has focused on b2c and b2b end user customers and have tended to marginalise members of marketing channels. This module helps correct this imbalance and introduces aspects of trade channel marketing communications. The mix of tools is obviously important but here the importance of relationships is considered and how marketing communications can play a crucial role in helping managers achieve channel objectives.

Element 4: Marketing relationships (15%)

This final element looks at relationship marketing concepts and at how trust and commitment through marketing communications can be developed. Inevitably there is a level of overlap with other elements in the syllabus, but that is useful since it should show the interaction between communications and relationship development.

This element is also important because it introduces the agency dimension and the relationships that develop between client and agency. By learning about how agencies are structured, operate and influenced by managers and the industry itself, participants are in a far better position to manage their employers. agency relationships more effectively.

Delivery approach

Ideally this module is delivered after participants have completed the Marketing Planning module where they cover planning processes and techniques.

The syllabus is quite extensive and requires a balance of theory and practical application through consideration of real life examples. Exam answers or continuous assessments need to demonstrate an excellent understanding of theory used effectively in the context of marketing communications and the relationships organisations have with a range of stakeholders.

It is unlikely that it will be effective to deliver this module on a lecture-only basis. The more appropriate role for the module leader is as a facilitator helping, guiding and encouraging participants to develop their own knowledge and skills through self-study. To help make this work, participants should secure a copy of the recommended textbook, supplemented by workbooks and other texts, and use these to develop their base knowledge. They should be encouraged to read more widely from marketing journals, marketing press and the quality newspapers.

Sessions should be used for presentations and small group work looking at cases and, perhaps, answers to short multiple-choice questions to test progress. Tutors should provide opportunities to develop simple plans and discuss implementation issues. All participants should develop a portfolio of materials based upon two brands from contrasting sectors. The portfolio should contain examples of marketing communications practice and relationship issues that are encountered by the organisation. It is through this form of work that effective learning develops.

The Marketing Management in Practice module will build on the theory and basic skills developed in this module by practising participants in the planning and implementation of communications activities to support marketing and wider business objectives.

Websites

The Chartered Institute of Marketing

www.cim.co.uk	The CIM site with information and access to learning support
www.cim.connectedin marketing.com	for participants.
www.cimvirtualinstitute.com	Full details of all that's new in CIM's educational offer
	specimen answers and Hot Topics.
www.cimeducator.com	The CIM site for tutors only.

Publications on line

www.revolution.haynet.co	Revolution magazine
www.marketing.haynet.com	Marketing magazine
www.FT.com	A wealth of information for cases (now charging)
www.IPA.co.uk	Need to register – communication resources
www.booksites.net	Financial times/Prentice hall Text websites

Sources of useful information

www.acnielson.co.uk	AC Neilson – excellent for research
http://advertising.utexas.edu/world/	Resources for advertising & marketing professionals, participants and tutors
www.bitzed.com	Case studies
www.esomar.nl	European Body representing Research Organisations – useful for guidelines on research ethics and approaches
www.dma.org.uk	The Direct Marketing Association
www.eiu.com	The Economist Intelligence Unit
www.euromonitor.com	Euromonitor consumer markets
www.europa.eu.int	The European Commission extensive range of statistics and reports relating to EU and member countries
www.managementhelp.org/research/research.htm	Part of the 'Free Management Library' – explaining research methods
www.marketresearch.org.uk	The MRS site with information and access to learning support for participants – useful links on ethics and code of conduct
www.oecd.org	OECD statistics and other information relating to member nations including main economic indicators
www.quirks.com	An American source of information on marketing research issues and projects
www.un.org	United nations publish statistics on member nations
www.worldbank.org	World bank economic, social and natural resource indicators for over 200 countries. Include over 600 indicators covering GNP per capita, growth, economic statistics etc

Case studies

Case studies

www.bluelagoon.co.uk	Case – SME website address
www.ebay.com	On-line auction – buyer behaviour
www.glenfiddich.com	Interesting site for case & branding
www.interflora.co.uk	e-commerce direct ordering
www.moorcroft.co.uk	Good for relationship marketing
www.ribena.co.uk	Excellent targeting & history of comms
www.sothebys.ebay.com	New service offered because of advances in electronic technology

The exam paper

Format of the paper

Section A

	Marks
Compulsory case study question	50

Section B

Two questions from a choice of four (25 marks each)	50
	100

Analysis of Pilot Paper

Part A (compulsory question worth 50 marks)

1   Established company making medium quality kitchen furniture. Steady sales growth to date, but facing increased competition from major national manufacturers,. and struggling with ole systems and procedures. Marketing plan seeks 15% growth per annum by attracting new customers – needs a marketing communications strategy but has limited resources.

    (a)   Evaluate current and future roles of marketing communications for the company

    (b)   importance of perceived risk, and how marketing communications could overcome it

    (c)   Use of Internet and digital based technologies

    (d)   Recommend and justify a suitable co-ordinated marketing communications mix

Part B (two questions, 25 marks each)

2   Promotional tools

    (a)   Sales promotion and public relations

    (b)   Use of promotional tools over the life of a product

    (c)   Improving trust between clients and agencies

3   Media concepts and opportunities

    (a)   Advantages and disadvantages of any two media

    (b)   Reach, frequency and opportunities-to-see

    (c)   Factors influencing international media choice.

4   Marketing channels

    (a)   Independence and interdependence

    (b)   Sources of conflict between members of marketing channels

    (c)   Factors influencing international media choice

5   Advertising agency

    (a)   Explain the role of account manager and the nature of the client brief

    (b)   Importance of adopting a relationship marketing approach

Assignment Based Learning: Marketing Communications

- Aims and objectives of this guide
- Introduction
- Structure and process
- Preparing for Assignments: general guide
- Presentation of the Assignment
- Time management for the Assignment
- Tips for writing Assignments
- Writing reports

Aims and objectives of this Guide to Assignment Based Learning

- To understand the scope and structure of the Assignment Based Learning process
- To consider the benefits of learning through Assignment Based Learning
- To assist students in preparation of their assignments
- To consider the range of communication options available to students
- To look at the range of potential assignment areas that assignments may challenge
- To examine the purpose and benefits of reflective practice
- To assist with time-management within the assignment process

Introduction

Assignment based learning is now a permanent feature of CIM's assessment strategy for its professional marketing qualifications Stages 1 and 2.

More and more study centres are offering the Assignment Based Learning option as an alternative to examinations. This change in direction, introducing the flexibility of assignment, was driven externally by industry representatives, students and tutors. All of them all of whom wanted a test of practical skills as well as a knowledge-based approach to learning.

At Stage 2, all modules are available via this Assignment Based Learning route. Assignment Based Learning is, however, optional, and examinations are still available. The choice of Assignment Based Learning or examination will of course depend upon the nature of delivery within your chosen Study Centre.

Clearly, all of the Stage 2 subject areas lend themselves to assignment based learning, due to their practical nature. The assignments that you will undertake provide you with an opportunity to be **creative in approach and in presentation.** They enable you to give a true demonstration of your marketing ability in a way that perhaps might be inhibited in a traditional examination situation.

Assignment Based Learning offers you considerable scope to produce work that provides existing and future **employers** with **evidence** of your **ability.** It enables you to develop a **portfolio** of evidence. This portfolio demonstrates your abilities and your willingness continually to develop your knowledge and skills. It will also, ultimately, help you frame your continuing professional development in the future.

It does not matter what type of organisation you are from, large or small, as you will find many benefits in this approach to learning. In some cases, students have made their own organisation central to their assignment and produced work to support their organisation's activities, resulting in subsequent recognition and promotion: a success story for this approach.

So, using your own organisation can be beneficial (especially if your employer sponsors you). However, it is equally valid to use a different organisation, as long as you are familiar enough with it to base your assignments on it. This is particularly useful if you are between jobs, taking time out, returning to employment or studying at university or college.

To take the Assignment Based Learning option, you are required to register with a CIM Accredited Study Centre (i.e. a college, university, or distance learning provider). **Currently you would be unable to take the Assignment Based Learning option as an independent learner**. If in doubt you should contact the CIM Education Division, the Awarding Body, who will provide you with a list of local Accredited Centres offering Assignment Based Learning.

Structure and process

The **assignments** that you will undertake during your studies are set **by CIM centrally** and not by the study centre. This standardised approach to assignment enables external organisations to interpret the results on a consistent basis. All assignments are validated to ensure a structured, consistent approach.

Each module at Stage 2 has one assignment, with four separate elements within it. This is broken down as follows.

■ The **Core Section** is compulsory and worth 40% of your total mark with a word limited on if of approximately 3,000 words.

■ The **Elective Section** has four options, from which you must complete **two**. Each of these options is worth 25% of your total mark. Please note here that it is likely that in some Study Centres the option may be chosen for you. This is common practice and is done in order to maximise resources and support provided to students. Each elective section allows a word limit of approximately 1,500 words.

■ The **Reflective Statement** is also compulsory. It is worth 10%. It should reflect what you feel about your learning experience during the module and how that learning has helped you in your career both now and in the future. The word limit for this section of the assignment is approximately 750 words.

All of these assignments have been designed to test the application of knowledge and understanding, and it will be insufficient to rely on theory alone for your assignment submissions. All assignments must be professionally presented, with arguments that are compelling and well reasoned. Any sources of information, definitions, methodologies and applications should be used where possible, but must be well referenced and well stated.

All of the Assignments clearly indicate the links with the syllabus and the assignment weighting (ie the contribution each assignment makes to your overall marks).

Once your Assignments have been completed, they will be marked by your accredited centre, and then **moderated** by a CIM External Moderator. When all the assignments have been marked, they are sent to CIM for further moderation. After this, all marks are forwarded to you by CIM (not your centre) in the form of an examination result. Your **centre** will be able to you provide you with some written feedback on overall performance, but **will not** provide you with any detailed mark breakdown.

Preparing for Assignments: general guide

The whole purpose of this guide is to assist you in presenting your assignment professionally, both in terms of presentation skills and overall content. In many of the assignments, marks are awarded for presentation and coherence. It might therefore be helpful to consider how best to present your assignment. Here you should consider issues of detail, protocol and the range of communications that could be called upon within the assignment.

Presentation of the Assignment

You should always ensure that you prepare two copies of your Assignment, keeping a soft copy on disc. On occasions assignments go missing, or second copies are required by CIM.

- Each Assignment should be clearly marked up with your study centre, your CIM Student registration number and, ultimately at the end of the assignment, a word count. The assignment should also be word-processed. <u>You should not put your name on your assignment</u>, as the assignment is treated as the same way as an examination in respect of marking.

- The assignment presentation format should directly meet the requirements of the assignment brief (ie reports and presentations are the most called-for communication formats). You **must** ensure that your assignment does not appear to be an extended essay. If it does, you will lose marks.

- The word limit will be included in the assignment brief. This limit is specified by CIM and must be adhered to and have already been referenced previously.

- **Appendices** should clearly link to the assignment and can be attached as supporting documentation at the end of the report. However failure to reference them by number (eg Appendix 1) within the report and also marked up on the Appendix itself will lose you marks. Only use an Appendix if it is **essential** and clearly adds value to the overall Assignment. The Appendix is not a waste bin for all the materials you have come across in your research, or a way of making your assignment seem somewhat heavier and more impressive than it is.

Time management for Assignments

One of the biggest challenges we all seem to face day-to-day is that of managing time. When studying, that challenge seems to grow increasingly difficult, requiring a balance between work, home, family, social life and study life. It is therefore of pivotal importance to your own success for you to plan wisely the limited amount of time you have available.

Step 1: Find out how much time you have

Ensure that you are fully aware of how long your module lasts, and the final deadline (eg 10 weeks, 12 weeks, 14 weeks). If you are studying a module from September to December, it is likely that you will have only 10-12 weeks in which to complete your assignments. This means that you will be preparing assignment work continuously throughout the course.

Step 2: Plan your time

Essentially you need to **work backwards** from the final deadline, submission date, and schedule your work around the possible time lines. Clearly if you have only 10-12 weeks available to complete three assignments, you will need to allocate a block of hours in the final stages of the module to ensure that all of your assignments are in on time. **This will be critical as all assignments must be sent to CIM by a set day. Late submissions will not be accepted and no extensions**

will be allowed. Students who do not submit will be treated as 'no shows' and will have to re-enter for the next period and undertake an alternative assignment. *Failure to submit your assignments on the due date could mean that your marks are capped at 50%.*

Step 3: Set priorities

You should set priorities on a daily and weekly basis (not just for study, but for your life). There is no doubt that this mode of study needs commitment (and some sacrifices in the short term). When your achievements are recognised by colleagues, peers, friends and family, it will all feel worthwhile.

Step 4: Analyse activities and allocate time to them

Consider the **range** of activities that you will need to undertake in order to complete the assignment and the **time** each might take. Remember, too, there will be a delay in asking for information and receiving it.

■ Preparing terms of reference for the assignment, to include the following.

1	A short title
2	A brief outline of the assignment purpose and outcome
3	Methodology – what methods you intend to use to carry out the required tasks
4	Indication of any difficulties that have arisen in the duration of the assignment
5	Time schedule
6	Confidentiality – if the assignment includes confidential information ensure that this is clearly marked up and indicated on the assignment
7	Literature and desk research undertaken

This should be achieved in one side of A4

■ A literature search in order to undertake the necessary background reading and underpinning information that might support your assignment

■ Writing letters and memos asking for information either internally or externally

■ Designing questionnaires

■ Undertaking surveys

■ Analysis of data from questionnaires

■ Secondary data search

■ Preparation of first draft report

Always build in time to spare, to deal with the unexpected. This may reduce the pressure that you are faced in meeting significant deadlines.

Warning!

The same principles apply to a student with 30 weeks to do the work. However, a word of warning is needed. Do not fall into the trap of leaving all of your work to the last minute. If you miss out important information or fail to reflect upon your work adequately or successfully you will be penalised for both. Therefore, time management is important whatever the duration of the course.

Tips for writing Assignments

Everybody has a personal style, flair and tone when it comes to writing. However, no matter what your approach, you must ensure your assignment meets the **requirements of the brief** and so is comprehensible, coherent and cohesive in approach.

Think of preparing an assignment as preparing for an examination. Ultimately, the work you are undertaking results in an examination grade. Successful achievement of all four modules in a level results in a qualification.

There are a number of positive steps that you can undertake in order to ensure that you make the best of your assignment presentation in order to maximise the marks available.

Step 1 – Work to the brief

Ensure that you identify exactly what the assignment asks you to do.

■ If it asks you to be a marketing manager, then immediately assume that role.

■ If it asks you to prepare a report, then present a report, not an essay or a letter.

■ Furthermore, if part of it asks for 2,500 words, then do not present 1,000 or 4,000 unless in both instances it is clearly justified, agreed with your tutor and a valid piece of work.

Identify if the report should be **formal or informal**, who it should be **addressed to**, its **overall purpose** and its **potential use** and outcome. Understanding this will ensure that your assignment meets fully the requirements of the brief and addresses the key issues included within it.

Step 2 – Addressing the tasks

It is of pivotal importance that you address **each** of the tasks within the assignment. **Many students fail to do this** and often overlook one of the tasks or indeed part of the tasks.

Many of the assignments will have two or three tasks, some will have even more. You should establish quite early on, which of the tasks:

■ Require you to collect information
■ Provide you with the framework of the assignment, i.e. the communication method.

Possible tasks will include the following.

■ *Compare and contrast.* Take two different organisations and compare them side by side and consider the differences ie the **contrasts** between the two.

■ *Carry out primary or secondary research.* Collect information to support your assignment and your subsequent decisions

■ *Prepare a plan.* Some assignments will ask you to prepare a plan for an event or for a marketing activity – if so provide a step-by-step approach, a rationale, a time-line, make sure it is measurable and achievable. Make sure your actions are very specific and clearly explained. (Make sure your plan is SMART.)

■ *Analyse a situation.* This will require you to collect information, consider its content and present an overall understanding of the actual situation that exists. This might include looking at internal and external factors and how the current situation evolved.

■ *Make recommendations.* The more advanced your get in your studies, the more likely it is that you will be required to make recommendations. Firstly **considering and evaluating your options** and then making justifiable **recommendations**, based on them.

- *Justify decisions.* You may be required to justify your decision or recommendations. This will require you to explain fully how you have arrived at this decision and to show why, supported by relevant information, this is the right way forward. In other words, you should not make decisions in a vacuum; as a marketer your decisions should always be informed by context.

- *Prepare a presentation.* This speaks for itself. If you are required to prepare a presentation, ensure that you do so, preparing clearly defined PowerPoint or overhead slides that are not too crowded and that clearly express the points you are required to make.

- *Evaluate performance.* It is very likely that you will be asked to evaluate a campaign, a plan or even an event. You will therefore need to consider its strengths and weaknesses, why it succeeded or failed, the issues that have affected it, what can you learn from it and, importantly, how can you improve performance or sustain it in the future.

All of these points are likely requests included within a task. Ensure that you identify them clearly and address them as required.

Step 3 – Information search

Many students fail to realise the importance of collecting information to **support** and **underpin** their assignment work. However, it is vital that you demonstrate to your centre and to the CIM your ability to **establish information needs**, obtain **relevant information** and **utilise it sensibly** in order to arrive at appropriate decisions.

You should establish the nature of the information required, follow up possible sources, time involved in obtaining the information, gaps in information and the need for information.

Consider these factors very carefully. CIM are very keen that students are **seen** to collect information, **expand** their mind and consider the **breadth** and **depth** of the situation. In your *Personal Development Portfolio*, you have the opportunity to complete a **Resource Log**, to illustrate how you have expanded your knowledge to aid your personal development. You can record your additional reading and research in that log, and show how it has helped you with your portfolio and assignment work.

Step 4 – Develop an Assignment plan

Your **assignment** needs to be structured and coherent, addressing the brief and presenting the facts as required by the tasks. The only way you can successfully achieve this is by **planning the structure** of your Assignment in advance.

Earlier on in this unit, we looked at identifying your tasks and, working backwards from the release date, in order to manage time successfully. The structure and coherence of your assignment needs to be planned with similar signs.

In planning out the Assignment, you should plan to include **all the relevant information as requested** and also you should plan for the use of models, diagrams and appendices where necessary.

Your plan should cover your:

- Introduction
- Content
- Main body of the assignment
- Summary
- Conclusions and recommendations where appropriate

Step 5 – Prepare draft Assignment

It is good practice to always produce a **first draft** of a report. You should use it to ensure that you have met the aims and objectives, assignment brief and tasks related to the actual assignment. A draft document provides you with scope for improvements, and enables you to check for accuracy, spelling, punctuation and use of English.

Step 6 – Prepare final document

In the section headed 'Presentation of the Assignment' in this unit, there are a number of components that should always be in place at the beginning of the assignment documentation, including **labelling** of the assignment, **word counts**, **appendices** numbering and presentation method. Ensure that you **adhere to the guidelines presented**, or alternatively those suggested by your study centre.

Writing reports

Students often ask 'what do they mean by a report?' or 'what should the report format include?'

There are a number of approaches to reports, formal or informal: some report formats are company specific and designed for internal use, rather than external reporting.

For Assignment Based Learning process, you should stay with traditional formats.

Below is a suggested layout of a Management Report Document that might assist you when presenting your assignments.

- A **Title Page** includes the title of the report, the author of the report and the receiver of the report

- **Acknowledgements** should highlight any help, support, or external information received and any extraordinary co-operation of individuals or organisations

- The **Contents Page** provides a clearly structured pathway of the contents of the report – page by page

- The **Executive Summary** is a brief insight into purpose, nature and outcome of the report, in order that the outcome of the report can be quickly established

- The **Main body of the report divided into sections, which are clearly labelled**. Suggested labelling would be on a numbered basis eg:

    - 1.0   Introduction
    - 1.1   Situation Analysis
    - 1.1.1 External Analysis
    - 1.1.2 Internal Analysis

- The **Conclusions** section draws the report to a conclusion, highlighting key points of importance, which will impact upon any recommendations that might be made

- The **Recommendations** section clearly outlines potential options and then makes final recommendations. Where appropriate justify recommendations in order to substantiate your decision

- **Appendices** should add value to the report. Ensure that they are numbered and referenced on a numbered basis within the text. If you are not going to reference it within the text, then it should not be there

- **Bibliography.** In a business environment a bibliography might not be necessary, but for an **assignment-based report it is vital**. It provides an indication of the level of research, reading and collecting of relevant information that has taken place in order to fulfil the requirements of the assignment task. Where possible, and where relevant, you could provide academic references within the text, which should of course then provide the basis of your bibliography. References should realistically be listed alphabetically and in the following sequence

  - Author's name and edition of the text
  - Date of publication
  - Title and sub-title (where relevant)
  - Edition 1st, 2nd etc
  - Place of publication
  - Publisher
  - Series and individual volume number where appropriate.

Resources to support Assignment Based Learning

The aim of this guidance is to present you with a range of questions and issues that you should consider, based upon the assignment themes. The detail to support the questions can be found within your BPP Study Text and the 'Core Reading' recommended by CIM.

Additionally you will find useful support information within the CIM Student website www.cim.co.uk -: www.cimvirtualinstitute.com, where you can access a wide range of marketing information and case studies. You can also build your own workspace within the website so that you can quickly and easily access information specific to your professional study requirements. Other websites you might find useful for some of your assignment work include www.wnim.com - (What's New in Marketing) and also www.connectedinmarketing.com - another CIM website.

Other websites include:

www.mad.com	– Marketing Week
www.ft.com	– Financial Times
www.thetimes.com	– The Times newspaper
www.theeconomist.com	– The Economist magazine
www.marketing.haynet.com	– Marketing magazine
www.ecommercetimes.com	– Daily news on e-business developments
www.open.gov.uk	– Gateway to a wide range of UK government information
www.adassoc.org.uk	– The Advertising Association
www.marketresearch.org.uk	– The Marketing Research Society
www.mintel.com	– Research Reports
www.statistics.gov.uk	– Detailed information on demographics
www.dma.org.uk	– The Direct Marketing Association
www.theidm.co.uki	– The Institute of Direct Marketing
www.hmtreasury.gov.uk	– Government Expenditure and policy
www.bankofengland.com	– Bank of England
www.moneyworlds.co.uk	– Investment News
www.eiu.com	– Economic Intelligence Unit
www.ech.int/	– Economic Intelligence Unit
www.europa.eu.int/comm/eurosta-	– Euro statistics
www.un.org/depts/unsd/social/main/htm	– United Nations Statistics
www.dti.com	– Department of Trade and Industry
www.tradepartners.co.uk	– View of international economic/cultural situation

Core and Optional Assignments

We are not at liberty to give you specific guidance on the core or optional elements of the Marketing Communications Assignment. However, it will be useful to consider possible assignment themes, and how you might approach the subject areas in terms of research, a questioning approach and meeting the requirements of the brief. The format is usually predetermined by CIM, and generally takes the form of a report or presentation.

Possible Assignment themes

Although we cannot publish the contents of the assignment, we can provide you with an indication of the **key themes** that the assignment and its elements will focus upon. Assignment themes and weightings will change with each sitting every six months. The purpose of this section will therefore be, to provide you with key questions and issues that you should consider based around potential subject areas. You must be clear that whilst these are valid points you may not need to use them all (or alternatively, you may be required to look much further a field.)

As you know there are two assignment sittings per year, to align with examination, and therefore we propose to cover the subjects for both December 2003 assignment submissions and June 2004 assignment submissions

For the purpose of Marketing Communications, the assignment themes include: -

Element 1 – Core

December 2003 Submission

Marketing communications mix
Buyer behaviour characteristics

June 2003 Submission

Marketing Communications Portfolio

- Public relations
- Use of technology
- Marketing communications

Optional Electives

December 2003 Submission

- Relationship marketing

- Role of Marketing Communications - Corporate and Ethical Responsibilities

- Public Relations - Press releases

- Interactive Marketing Communications – Evaluation between online and offline marketing communications.

June 2004 Submission

- Relationship Marketing

- Planning frameworks – Marketing Communications Planning and External Influences on Marketing Communications Planning

- Direct Marketing

- Media Mixes – Buyer Behaviour Characteristics and Different Classes of Media.

You will note that there is a lot of overlap at times. Although the subjects will be the same, the context of the questions will be different. As we are not at liberty to disclose those questions, we aim to give you a generic overview of the approach you need to take and some of the questions you will need to be able to answer in order to complete your assignments successfully.

Reflective Statement

You need to reflecting upon your learning experience, what you did well, how you did it and how it might influence and direct your future.

Before moving on to the detail of the assignment, it might be useful to focus your mind on the **learning outcomes** of the Marketing Communications module, as well as the **related skills** for marketers.

- By considering what the learning outcomes are for the module, you will understand the scope of the task ahead of you in terms of completing the Assignment Based Learning process.

- Key skills are undoubtedly something that most students will have come across by now. They demonstrate the importance of not just **acquiring knowledge**, but being able to **apply it** through the use of a range of related key skills for marketers. In undertaking Assignment Based Learning project work, you will find that the key skills are not only used, but also continually stretched and developed.

Possible Core Subjects for December 2003 Submission

Marketing communications Mix and Buyer Behaviour Characteristics

In order to successfully complete the assignment with consideration of the above assignment themes, you should consider the following:-

- What is the marketing communications mix?

- What are the various components that sit within it?

  - Advertising
  - Sales promotion
  - Public relations
  - Personal selling
  - Direct marketing

- You will need to understand the different characteristics of each element of the marketing communications mix, including breadth of coverage, cost, typical audience profiles, implications for delivery etc.

- You should consider how compatible each of these elements of the mix is with one another. If you had the job of preparing a co-ordinated communications mix, which elements would work together well and why?

- Think about the implications of co-ordinating a mix – what does this mean and why is co-ordination important?

- Why would buying behaviour be important and why would it be important to understand the different contexts of buying behaviour when developing a co-ordinated mix for a specific purpose?

- How would you use the marketing communications mix in different for different situations ie international, business-to-business or consumer goods. In other words how would you package the mix for each of these?

- Therefore you must establish which method is appropriate for which target audience.

- How do marketing communications models correlate with buying decision-making models and indeed the influences from different members of the decision making unit. This is particularly important in relation to both consumer and b2b marketing communications for industrial organisations.

- Think about issues such as:

  - Language
  - Culture and tradition
  - Legal and regulatory requirements
  - Buying habits and motivational factors
  - Standards of living
  - Media availability and usage
  - The competitive environment.

This core element contributes towards 40% of your assignment overall. However, ensure that when you are issued with your assignment you select the appropriate information and consider the appropriate points from above.

Possible elective Options for December 2003 Submissions

Optional Elective One – Relationship Marketing

This particular elective arises again for the June 2004 assignment submission, so will relate to both sessions.

- What is relationship marketing?

- Can you provide a range of diverse definitions of relationship marketing?

- Who does the organisation have relationships with?

- Is relationship marketing just about customers, or does it include the broader stakeholder audience?

- Relationship marketing includes four types of partnerships:-

  - Supplier partnerships
  - International partnerships
  - Lateral partnerships
  - Buyer partnerships

- Why will it be important to consider each of these relationships in a different way?

- What is the difference between transaction marketing and relationship marketing?

- What is the loyalty ladder and why is customer loyalty so important to organisations?

- What are the benefits of establishing relationships based on co-operation, commitment and trust and how can you use marketing communications tools to achieve this?

- Does the concept of relationship marketing vary in different markets i.e. consumer, organisational, not-for-profit and service marketing and if so are you able to highlight the differences ie compare and contrast different approaches. For example, for organisational markets the relationship is likely to be highly involved on a personal level and require large amounts of face-to-face contact – how does this differ to consumer markets?

- What is the link between quality and service in the context of relationship marketing?

- What is the link between relationship marketing and customer retention management?

- Why would a co-ordinated marketing mix be effective in the context of relationship marketing?

- How might key account management act as an aspect of relationship marketing, and why might a co-ordinated mix be imperative in this situation?

Optional Elective 2 - Role of Marketing Communications and Corporate and Ethical Responsibilities

This particular area is increasing in its profile over time and more and more you are seeing organisations not only state their vision and their mission, but also their ethical stance and corporate and social responsibilities. For examples of this go to www.marksandspencer.com and www.shell.com, both organisations clearly state their stance in these areas and you may find them valuable assets to your assignment.

- How can the marketing communications mix support and communicate corporate social responsibility and ethical issues?

- What are the implications for the communications mix when a company makes far reach statements in relation to their ethical stance and highlighting their corporate social responsibility to its target audience?

- What are the ethical dilemmas associated with marketing communications, that have impacted upon organisations such as Esso (see www.greenpeace.com and www.friendsoftheearth.com)

- How do organisations establish values that link with ethics and corporate social responsibility and establish them as an inherent part of the brand?

- What are the broader ethical considerations in marketing communications? Examples might include:

  - Advertising to children
  - Product labelling
  - Confusion pricing
  - Confusion marketing
  - The depiction of women in advertising
  - Environmental issues – i.e. promoting products such as products contain CFC gases?
  - Financial incentives

Kotler suggested that the "social marketing concepts hold that the organisations task is to determine the needs, wants and interests of the target markets and to then deliver as desired satisfactions more effectively and efficiently than competitors and in a way that maintains or improves the consumer's and the society's well being"

Kotler. P (2000) Marketing Management: the Millennium Edition – Prentice Hall

This is increasingly becoming a 'hot' topic in marketing and much is written about it. However, remember to provide some good and useful examples of this subject area to support your work. Also remember the constraints of your word limit which is 1500 words.

Optional Elective 3 – Public Relations and Press Releases

- Define public relations and its importance to the marketing communications mix?

- What are the benefits of public relations?

- What are the objectives of public relations?

- What level of compatibility does the function of public relations have with the rest of the communications mix?

- Who are the publics which organisations communicate with?

- Who are the opinion formers and opinion leaders who might shape or drive the function and even the necessity for PR to take place?

- Who is the likely target audiences involved in receiving PR in context of the organisation used for the assignment?

- Why is internal PR equally as important as external PR?

- What market information might you need to manage the PR function effectively?

- Public relations it often designed to change or influence the attitudes of customers – how and why?

- What are the various techniques used for public relations?

- How might you approach writing a press release?

- What are the uses of a press release?

- What are the benefits of using a press release process?

- What are the key characteristics of a press release?

- What makes a good press release?

This is a broad area, but again with a limited word count. Please note that the subject includes public relations and press releases, and it is possible that you may be required to write a press release, so be prepared. Undertake some research on key websites and see how they approach their press releases, look for good and bad practice examples. Use some of the websites shown earlier in this unit. However, also look at the two websites listed in the previous section: www.marksandspencer.com and www.shell.com.

Optional Elective 4 - Interactive Marketing Communications – Evaluation between online and offline marketing communications.

For this particular assignment, there is such a wealth of information out there to support it, that you will struggle to contain it within the word count. Therefore please ensure that you stay focused within the confines of the brief, but using a range of examples to support your case. Useful websites might include:

www.egg.com
www.easyJet.com
www.mytravelLite.com
www.johnlewis.com
www.virgin.com
www.savethechildrenfund.com

Critical considerations will include:

■   Define the differences between offline and online marketing communications.

■   What are the up and coming trends in online marketing communications?

■   What are the new technologies that are continually forcing online marketing communications into the market?

■   What is the conversion rate to online marketing communications by a range of different organisations, including:

  –   B2B – organisational marketing
  –   Not-for-profit sector
  –   Services sector
  –   Consumer sector

■   What are the advantages and disadvantages of online marketing versus the same in offline marketing?

■   Why will offline marketing always be important to all organisations?

■   What threats does online marketing pose to offline marketing?

■   What are the cost implications of developing a co-ordinated marketing mix to include both methods of communication?

■   Identify the benefits of online marketing as opposed of offline marketing for monitoring and controlling customer conversion and customer hits?

■   What are the limitations of online marketing as opposed of offline marketing?

■   What does the future hold for both?

Possible Core Subjects for June 2004 Submission

Marketing Communications Portfolio

You will probably gather from this heading that it is very much along the lines of the last core subject for the December 2003 submissions, in that it focuses upon the marketing communications portfolio, but with a particular emphasis on public relations, use of technology and developing a co-ordinated marketing communications mix.

For this particular area, we suggest that you look back at the coverage in the previous section for the core model and optional electives 4 and 5. However, you will need to rationalise how much of that information you use in context of the assignment, but the broader considerations are likely to be the same.

However, it is likely that there will be an emphasis on the co-ordination of the marketing mix and it would therefore be useful to consider the implications of co-ordinating the mix i.e. what does co-ordination of the mix mean.

- Ensure that you are fully able to define the term 'co-ordinated marketing communications'.

- Think about the implications of co-ordinating the mix and the benefits of costs associated with the co-ordination.

- What does taking a synergistic approach to marketing communications mean and how does it ensure more effective marketing communications?

- How could a co-ordinated marketing communications mix be used to deliver a competitive advantage through clearer positioning?

- How could a co-ordinated approach assist brand development both in terms of internal and external markets?

- What level of co-operation would this type of activity involve within the organisation?

- How can taking a co-ordinated approach to marketing communications assist in increasing the potential for employee participation and motivation?

- How can a co-ordinated marketing communications mix enhance the perception of the organisation in the minds of the customers?

Optional Elective 1 – Relationship Marketing

Please refer to the notes for Optional Elective 1 for December 2003 submission.

Optional Elective 2 – Planning Frameworks and External influences on Marketing Communications Planning.

- First consideration – what are the available planning frameworks that might impede the successful implementation of a co-ordinated marketing communications mix?

- Ensure you are familiar with frameworks such as SOSTAC?

- Are you familiar with the Marketing Communications Planning framework as defined by Chris Fill, Senior Examiner for this subject? This includes

    - **Context analysis** – What business are we in, what are the products and services, who are our competitors, what are the significant market trends, who are our customers, where are they and how can we segment them.

    - **Promotional goals and positioning – Setting** marketing communications objectives and identifying and forming positioning objectives.

    - **3 P's of Promotional Strategy** – Pull, Push and Profile Strategies.

    - **Co-ordinated Promotional Mix** – Using the marketing communications mix, as defined previously, advertising, selling, PR, sales promotions etc.

    - **Implementation, control and evaluation** – co-ordination of resources, physical, human, time and financial.

    This planning framework is the preferred planning framework as defined by the Senior Examiner.

- What are the external influences that affect the marketing communications planning framework and the way in which it is shaped? Here you might want to consider the following:

    Ethics and corporate social responsibility as being driven by external and governing bodies.

    - PESTEL factors.

- Emerging channels of communication.
- New and innovating Information Communication Technologies.
- Opinion Leaders and Opinion Formers.
- Competition.
- External Costs.
- σLegislation.

(Try and provide clear examples of each of these areas within the assignment.)

Optional Elective 3 – Direct Marketing

This is a very exciting area of marketing and evolving at a rapid rate, but there are increasing implications for organisations with the adoption of data protection acts and increasing pressure on legislation to support the control of junk mail. You may find CIM's website www.wnim.com a very useful resource in terms of this subject area.

- Define Direct Marketing.

- What are the different components and characteristics of Direct Marketing?

- What are the various methods of direct marketing?

- Which methods of direct marketing are most effective and why?

- What are the advantages and disadvantages of direct marketing?

- What are the new and emerging methods of direct marketing?

- How have Information Communications Technologies helped in more precise targeting of Direct Marketing?

- What legislation is underpinning direct marketing?

- What are the links between direct marketing and database marketing?

- What are the cost benefits of direct marketing?

- How could direct marketing underpin the co-ordinated approach of the marketing communications mix?

- Is direct marketing a successful way of reaching customers?

- What techniques can you use to directly measure and evaluate the success of failure of direct marketing?

- What do you think is the future for direct marketing?

- What are the limitations and restrictions upon direct marketing?

Try to find samples of good and bad practice of direct marketing to use within your assignment. Also look closely at new and innovative forms of direct marketing, particularly those of the online sort.

Optional Elective 4 – Media Mixes and difference Classes of Media

For this particular elective you should revert back to the information in the Core Section of the December 2003 element of the assignment, as the inherent themes here are similar. However, there are some additional considerations?

- This is a very broad area and it will require you to gain an understanding of the different forms of media that exist and how they can be targeted precisely to maximise access to and impact on customers.

- Think about the different forms of market segmentation strategies and how they will influence the types of media organisations use or that customers respond to.

- Consider the importance of demographics versus different forms of media.

- How do you establish the appropriateness of media types based on customer type?

- How can you successfully define the appropriate class of media to the appropriate class of customer?

- Why is lifestyle as important as a buyer behaviour characteristic in respect of responding to various forms of media?

- Identify and highlight the different characteristics, benefits, costs and limitations of different forms of media.

- What are the emerging trends in media types and media classes?

- Use BRAD to undertake research into typical uses of media versus customers. For example classic car magazines, music or photography magazines.

This is a very broad area, but it will be important to understand buyer behaviour characteristics, how we buy, what influences us to buy, which is why there is reference to areas such as market segmentation and demographics. There is clear evidence to suggest that lifestyle and class very much determine the nature of media that customers respond to, you must therefore be able to justify and argue such points.

Reflective statement

The final part of your assignment will ask you to prepare a 750 word reflective statement, where you will be required to reflect upon your **activities** and your **personal development** in the selected areas for the duration of your course. This is a much underestimated part of the assignment, and one many students fail to address effectively. It is this part of the assignment that actually brings all of your work together.

There are a number of **key components** that you should always include

- Where did you start off at the very beginning of this course? What were your particular strengths, weaknesses and knowledge gaps within Marketing Communications?

- What activities have you been involved in to achieve completion of your assignments?

- What did you do well?

- What could you have done better, and why?

- Do you feel that you have improved throughout the module?

- What value has this learning process added to your overall learning experience?

- Do you feel that the work undertaken will benefit you in your future personal development and organisational development?

- How will you continue to develop this area in the future? How do you anticipate you might use it?

One of the key considerations must be the future. Many people see reflection as 'thinking about something that has happened in the past'. Whilst this is true, we must also reflect upon 'how this will help us in the future'.

You may find that as a result of this learning process your **career aspirations** have completely changed. You may find that you have become more confident and ambitious, and that through consolidating your learning in this way you have considerably more to offer. If this is the case do not be afraid to say so, and demonstrate how the whole learning process has influenced you and how it will drive you forward.

Earlier in this guide you were provided with a range of skills in relation to approaches to assignments, research and report formation. With the above information and the approaches describe you should be able to produce a professional assignment. Refer back to the earlier part of the unit on how to present assignments and research if necessary.

Where appropriate provide relevant **examples** so that you can show your tutor and CIM what your organisation does. This will help to back you up in your evaluation and justifications.

Unit summary: Marketing Communications

You may have come to the end of the unit feeling that this is going to be hard work. Well you would be right in thinking this. But, as we suggested in the early part of this unit, it is likely to be one of the most beneficial learning processes you will embark upon, as you take your CIM qualifications.

The process of development prepares you to be a marketing professional in the future. It provides you with practical experience and an opportunity to apply the theory in a practical situation. You will demonstrate to your existing or future employer that you have the ability to learn, develop, grow progress and contribute significantly to the marketing activity within the organisation.

You have been provided with a range of hints and tips in presentation of assignments, development and approaches to your core and optional assignments.

Assignment Based Learning, like examinations, is a serious business, and you should consider the level of ongoing commitment that this process requires. The more you put in the more you are likely to get out of it. It will not be enough to leave all of your work to the end of the course as it destroys the ethos and benefit of the assignment. Use it as a continuous development tool for the duration of the course. A structured approach to the learning process will maximise its benefits to you.

We have tried to give you some insight into how to approach the core and optional assignments that you will embark upon. However, please ensure that you read the assignment carefully when it arrives, and address it directly. We have aimed to show you the level of detail you should enter into in order to produce an effective and professional piece of work.

The CIM qualifications are professional qualifications and therefore, to be successful you must take a professional approach to your work.

Part A

Understanding customer dynamics

Influencing customer decisions

1

Chapter Topic List	
1	Setting the scene
2	Understanding how communication works
3	Consumer buyer behaviour
4	Factors influencing consumer buying behaviour
5	The consumer decision-making process
6	Source effects influencing consumer behaviour
7	Perceived risk

Learning Outcome

☑ Explain the role of marketing communications and advise how personal influences might be used to develop promotional effectiveness

Syllabus References

☑ Explain how individuals can influence the effectiveness of marketing communications through word of mouth communications, as opinion leaders, as opinion formers or in multi-step models

☑ Describe the main concepts associated with buyer information processing and explain how marketing communications might be used to change or reinforce attitudes, alter perceptions and develop knowledge and understanding about a brand

☑ Describe the main concepts associated with the purchase decision process, including source credibility, involvement, perceived risk, and how they influence marketing communications

☑ Define and explain the roles of marketing communications to differentiate, remind or reassure, inform and persuade (DRIP)

Key Concepts Introduced

- Methods and media
- Exchange
- Noise
- Opinion leaders and opinion formers
- Innovation
- Diffusion
- Adoption
- Source credibility
- Consumer buying behaviour

- Culture
- Lifestyle
- Motivation
- Perception
- Belief
- Attitude
- Cognition, affectivity and conation
- Risk

1 Setting the scene: introduction to marketing communications

1.1 Most organisations, whether they operate in the private, public, not-for-profit or other sectors, all need to communicate with their customers. **Communications through promotional activities is an integral and essential part of the marketing mix**, part of an organisation's planned drive to satisfy their customers' needs.

Marketing communications might therefore be understood to be all forms of communication between an organisation and its customers and potential customers.

Action Programme 1

Make a list of the range of audiences that all organisations, large and small, need to communicate with in order to survive, grow and meet their various goals.

1.2 Therefore, marketing communications might involve **all communications** by an organisation with its **environment** and its various **stakeholders** who might influence it, **not just its customers**.

1.3 Marketing communications is one of the elements of the marketing mix and is responsible for the communications of the marketing offer to the target market. It is the task of a **planned** and **co-ordinated** set of communication activities to communicate effectively with each of the target customer groups, wherever in the world they may be. We must continually remind ourselves that we are not studying marketing communications strategies in isolation from the rest of the business or organisation. If they are to be successful, **marketing communications strategies must be co-ordinated with the overall planning process**.

Marketing communication methods

1.4 This is a very broad perspective and before we go any further we need to briefly consider the tools and methods of marketing communications.

The following diagram sets out the variety of promotional methods available to communicate with customers. These methods can be considered as a set of five, the **Marketing Communications Mix**.

Figure 1

1.5 These tools represent the deployment of **deliberate and intentional methods** calculated to bring about a favourable response in the customer's behaviour. The diagram represents the most obvious communication methods, though other parts of the marketing mix, including the product itself, pricing, policy and distribution channels, will also have decisive effects.

1.6 Choosing the correct tools for a particular promotions task is not an easy one. The process is becoming **more scientific** because of the access to consumer and media databases. Matching consumer characteristics with media characteristics can be rapidly carried out and promotional budgets evaluated for different mixes. In the final analysis however the expertise of the marketing manager is vital.

Key Concept

An obvious point, but remember that there are **five principal methods of marketing communication**. In addition there are a variety of media, which are the means by which advertising can be used to reach target audiences.

Methods and **media** are different and should not be confused.

Economic justifications for marketing communications

1.7 Marketing communications can be considered in the context of the **exchange process**. Exchanges, or transactions, are central to much modern thinking in economics: all activity undertaken by individuals or organisations can be seen as a series of exchanges.

Key Concept

An **exchange** requires the participation of two or more parties, each offers something of value to the other. They enter freely into the exchange process. The relevance to marketing is obvious: buy something and you will have experienced an exchange.

1.8 **Communication is central to the exchange process**. The DRIP model is often used to explain this point.

(a) **Differentiates** between competing offerings helping consumers to decide which exchanges to make, helping to prevent monopolies from developing, encouraging lower prices.

(b) **Reminds** customers of the benefits of past transactions and so convince them that they should enter into a similar exchange.

(c) **Informs** and makes potential customers aware of an organisation's offering.

(d) **Persuades** current and potential customers of the desirability of entering into an exchange relationship.

Action Programme 2

Think of a product/service or brand and consider how the DRIP factors can be applied.

Creative and social justification

1.9 Communication can itself be the object of an exchange. In return for the consumer's interest and loyalty, communication is provided:

- As **entertainment**
- As **information**
- As a **vehicle** for transferring values and culture to different groups

Marketing at Work

'Ethical advertising' by, say, the Government's anti drink/drive campaigns over the Christmas period, can help to raise awareness of important social, political and environmental issues.

Cadbury's Roses 'Thank you very much' campaign instilled values as well as selling the product.

Exam Tip

An exam question asked under a previous syllabus asked for a discussion of the comment 'Young people are threatened by the evil use of advertising techniques that stimulate the natural inclination to avoid hard work by promising the immediate satisfaction of every desire' (Pope John Paul II). Arguments can be put forward that advertising is manipulative, that it encourages consumerism and wastes resources, that it creates an unfair barrier to entry and so hinders competition. Some people find it irritating and intrusive: they would say it spoils other forms of entertainment or that it trivialises serious issues.

1.10 The main aim of this chapter is therefore to develop an understanding of the **various elements that influence the way individuals use information and make purchase decisions**. From this understanding it is possible to see how marketing communications can impact on customers and help them in the various decisions they need to make. We consider **organisational markets** in the following chapter.

2 Understanding how communication works

2.1 Kotler, *Marketing Management: Analysis, Planning, Implementation and Control* (1991), has put forward a simple **model of the communication process** to provide a framework. This is shown in the diagram below.

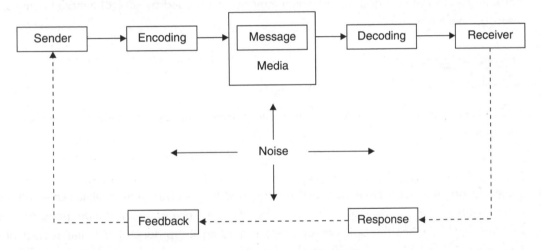

2.2 The elements of the model can be classified in the following way.

Element	Comment
Parties	
■ Sender	Sends the message to the other party
■ Receiver	Receives message
Communication tools	
■ Message	Content of communication
■ Media	Communication channels
Communication functions	
■ Encoding	Meaning is given in symbolic form (words etc) by sender
■ Decoding	Receiver translates and interprets message
■ Response	Receiver reacts to message
■ Feedback	Part of receiver's response is communicated back to sender

2.3 This model underscores many of the factors in effective communication. Senders need to understand the **motivation of their audiences** in order to structure messages that the audience will interpret correctly through the decoding process. The sender also has to ascertain the most **effective communication media** through which to reach the audience and must also establish effective **feedback channels** in order to find out the receiver's response to the message.

Action Programme 3

(a) Find some advertisements - watch TV for half an hour or flick through a newspaper or a magazine.

(b) Analyse each advertisement in the above terms. Consider who are the parties involved (*you* may not be the intended receiver), what communication tools are used, what sort of codes are used and how they will be decoded (for example by people in different income brackets or with different tastes), what form feedback will take, and so on.

2.4 This communication process is **not carried out in isolation**. There are many senders competing with their messages for the attention of the receiver. As a result there is considerable noise in the environment and an individual may be bombarded by several hundred commercial messages each day.

Key Concept

Noise is those factors that prevent the decoding of a message by the receiver, in the way intended by the sender.

2.5 **There is not just one receiver**, **but many**, and the receivers may communicate with each other regarding the sender's message. By virtue of experience or social standing one particular receiver may influence the opinions of others regarding the product that is the subject of the message. This is known as **opinion leadership** and may lead to a **two-step flow of communication**, whereby mass messages are filtered through opinion leaders to a mass audience. This can be represented diagrammatically below.

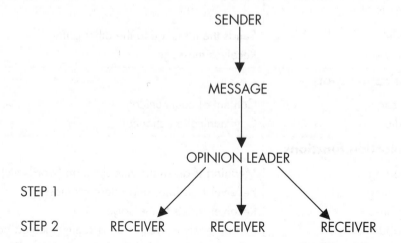

2.6   One of the marketer's tasks is to identify the relevant opinion leaders.

Key Concepts

- **Opinion leaders** are those who reinforce the marketing messages sent, and to whom other receivers look for information and advice.

- **Opinion formers** are people who are designated as knowledgeable about a subject: their advice is credible (eg pharmacists provide advice about medicines).

In addition, **opinion leaders** may communicate a marketing message to those members of the group who may have missed the **original message**. The marketer's task in identifying opinion leaders is made more difficult by the fact that **opinion leadership is dynamic**. At one time it was believed that opinion leadership was confined to a few prominent members of society, but increased understanding of the concept has shown that a person may be an opinion leader in certain circumstances but an **opinion follower** in others.

Opinion leader (eg hifi enthusiast)	Opinion former (eg pharmacists)
Interested in a topic	Part of job
Hobbyist	Objective
Enthusiastic (eg likes gadgets)	Easy to target, as often known (eg all pharmacists are registered)
Hard to target	

Exam Tip

Note the two issues likely to be covered by exam questions:

- Characteristics of opinion leader/former
- Different approaches to communicating with them.

This **'two-step'** approach contrasts to **Kotler's** simple model of communication identified earlier, which is a **'one-step'** model.

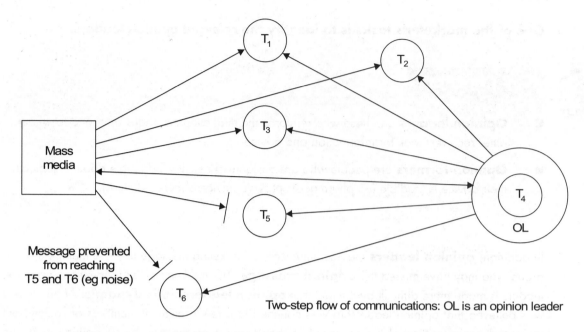

Two-step flow of communications: OL is an opinion leader

2.7 It is possible to conceive communications flowing in a multitude of directions, from a variety of people within communication networks. This is referred to as a **'multi-step'** approach.

The process of diffusion and adoption

2.8 An important contextual condition that affects marketing communication activity is the launch of new products and the propensity of consumers to respond to communication about new products.

Key Concept

An **innovation** refers to any good, service or idea that is perceived by someone to be new.

2.9 This is a subjective view, as a new product idea may have a long history but be an innovation to the person concerned. Innovations can be classified into three main groups.

Innovation	
Continuous innovation	The modification of an existing product rather than the invention of a completely new one. This causes the least disruption to established patterns of consumer behaviour.
Dynamically continuous innovation	Either the creation of a new product or the alteration of an existing product, but not significantly altering existing patterns of consumer buying or product use.
Discontinuous innovation	The introduction of a completely new product that alters existing consumer buying patterns in a radical way

Can you think of products that fit into each of these three categories?

Adoption

2.10 Adopters of new products have been observed to move through the following five stages.

Stage of adoption	Comment
Stage 1: **Awareness**	The consumer becomes aware of the innovation but lacks information about it.
Stage 2: **Interest**	The consumer is stimulated to seek information about the innovation.
Stage 3: **Evaluation**	The consumer considers whether to try the innovation.
Stage 4: **Trial**	The consumer tries the innovation to improve his or her estimate of its value.
Stage 5: **Adoption**	The consumer decides to make full and regular use of the innovation.

2.11 The progression suggests that the **marketer of the innovative product should aim to facilitate consumer movement through these stages**. The process of adoption of innovation described here bears a remarkable similarity to the 'core' process of consumer buying behaviour. Indeed, when considering the adoption process, all we are considering is the consumer buying behaviour process for a new rather than an existing product.

Diffusion

Key Concept

Diffusion can be defined as the process by which an innovation is communicated over time among the individuals within society who comprise the target market.

2.12 Four key elements significant to the process of diffusion

- The innovation itself
- The communication processes and channels used
- The time at which individuals decide to adopt the product
- The social systems involved

2.13 At the heart of the diffusion process is the decision by an individual to adopt the innovative product or service. This process of adoption focuses on **the mental processes through which** an individual passes from first hearing about the innovation to final adoption.

Key Concept

Adoption is the decision of an individual to become a regular user of a product.

Categories of adopters

2.14 It is a fact however, that people differ markedly in their readiness to try new products. There are five identified categories of adopters, which are often described diagrammatically in terms of a normal distribution curve (showing their relative numerical importance), as follows.

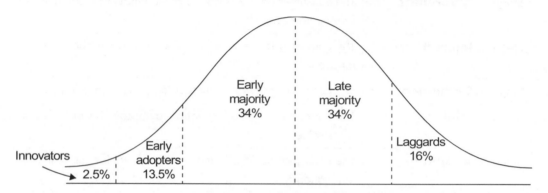

Time

2.15 **Characteristics of the various adopter groups.**

Measure	Comment
Innovators	■ Eager to try new ideas and products ■ Higher incomes ■ Self confident
Early adopters	■ Reliant on group norms ■ Oriented to the local community ■ Opinion leaders
Early majority	■ Deliberate more carefully ■ Process of adoption takes longer ■ Positioned between the earlier and later adopters
Late majority	■ Pressure to conform ■ Sceptical ■ Below average income and education
Laggards	■ Independent ■ Tradition-bound ■ Lowest socio-economic status

2.16 The **time dimension** to the process of diffusion and adoption is important. The diagram suggests that each group learns by observing the previous group's behaviours and then adopts the behaviour itself. The marketer should therefore have as clear an understanding of the dynamics of this process for his own industry as possible.

Encouraging adoption

2.17 It is a common assertion that **90% of new products fail**. How, therefore, can a marketer ensure that his new product stands the best chance of success in the market? There are five **characteristics associated with the success of new products**.

Characteristics	Comment
Relative advantage	The extent to which the consumer perceives the product to have an advantage over the product it supersedes
Compatibility	The degree to which the product is consistent with existing values and past experiences of the potential customer
Complexity	The degree to which a new product is perceived to be complex and difficult to use
Trialability	New products are more likely to be adopted when customers can try them out on an experimental basis.
Observability	A measure of the degree to which adoption of the product, or the results of using the product, is visible to friends, neighbours and colleagues. This process can be given added impetus if the product is seen to be used by celebrities or other role models. This factor obviously lends itself more to some products than others.

Action Programme 5

Apply this list of characteristics to the following innovations.

(a)   Mobile telephones
(b)   Banking by telephone or the Internet
(c)   Multimedia home entertainment (DVD)
(d)   Quorn (fungus based food products).

Communications and the product life cycle

2.18 The consumer adoption process describes the way in which new products and services become accepted by different types of consumer over time. The **product life cycle** concept describes the rate at which this process takes place for different types of product.

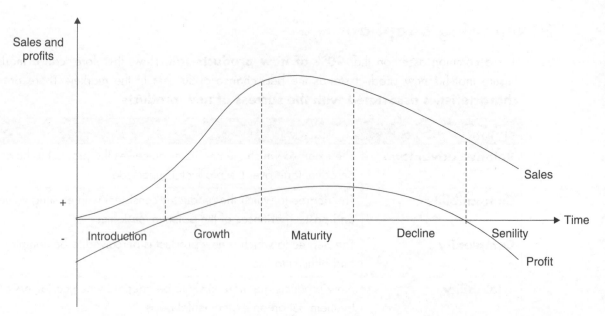

The diagram illustrates the different phases products and services pass through over time. The length of time products take to move through the stages will be dependent upon the type of product and a range of other marketing factors which determine how successful the product actually becomes.

2.19 Different kinds of communication will be appropriate at different stages

(a) Initially the objectives will be to **create awareness** and will involve advertising, particularly for fmcg products. Sales promotion may also feature to gain acceptance and encourage repeat purchase.

(b) In **growth phases**, advertising will still be important but at a reducing percentage of sales.

(c) At maturity, more active **segmentation and targeting** becomes significant as competition intensifies and positioning and repositioning come to the fore.

(d) Although in many cases products do not decline, **sales may reduce** significantly, and promotional activity will probably reduce.

(e) For products where sales continue to be healthy, promotion will still be a major element of the marketing mix as brands seek to maintain or improve their positions by encouraging **brand switching**.

2.20 Organisations have a number of strategies at their disposal to influence customers to adopt innovations and, among these, marketing communication is obviously very important. For example, in markets where **continuous innovation** is the norm, organisations can encourage trial through **free samples** and **price promotions**.

2.21 Encouraging adoption for a discontinuous innovation is more problematic because the product cannot be purchased on a trial basis. Advertising may have to be used to promote awareness and communicate product features.

3 Consumer buying behaviour

Key Concept

Consumer buying behaviour can be defined as, 'the decision processes and acts of individuals involved in buying and using products or services.' (Dibb *et al*, *Marketing: Concepts and Strategies* (1994)).

3.1 As Dibb *et al* say, the study of consumer buying behaviour by an organisation is important for a number of reasons.

(a) The **buyer's reaction** to the organisation's marketing strategy has a major impact on the success of the organisation.

(b) If organisations are truly to implement the marketing concept, they must examine the main influences on **what, where, when and how customers buy**. Only in this way will they be able to devise a marketing mix that satisfies the needs of the customers.

(c) By gaining a better understanding of the factors influencing their customers and how their customers will respond, organisations will be better able to predict the **effectiveness of their marketing activities**.

3.2 However, not all consumers behave in the same way. Decision making and purchase patterns of behaviour vary considerably within individuals and across product categories. This **complexity must be recognised** and **marketing communications adapted** to meet the needs of different customers.

Marketing at Work

From the unabashed artificiality of Mr Whippy to the erotic promise of Haagen-Dazs, ice cream – so we are led to believe – varies dramatically.

Now, however, that belief has been exposed as a fallacy by an academic's claim that commercial ice creams are much the same.

'There's a limit to which they can differ from each other,' said Peter Barham, a physicist at Bristol University. 'Yes, there is a variation in terms of quality due to the range of ingredients – top ice creams use fresh cream and eggs and the cheaper ones use milk powder – and of course there are differences in flavours. But they all have a problem of storage which means that there's a limit to how different their texture can be.'

His claim that there is little to choose between mass-produced ice creams will be reiterated by a consumer psychologist, who will argue that it is image rather than taste that determines which ice cream we buy.

'At its most basic, ice cream is little more than frozen emulsified fat with a flavour in it. There will be a difference in flavour but the real difference in quality for the price differential is relatively minimal,' said consultant psychologist Paul Buckley.

But these claims were dismissed last night by representatives of the UK's £1bn-a-year ice cream industry.

'We totally reject the idea that all ice creams are the same,' said Annette Low, spokeswoman for Ben and Jerry's. 'Premium ice-creams like Ben and Jerry's or Haagen-Dazs are partly defined by the amount of air in the ice cream and partly by the amount of butterfat. The less air, the more dense and rich it is. We also use premium ingredients, so our chocolate comes from Belgium rather than from the States, and our milk and creams from community farmed cows from Vermont.'

(Guardian, 4 June 2001)

4 Factors influencing consumer buying behaviour

4.1 The 'core' process of consumer buying behaviour described above will be influenced by a number of outside variables. These variables have been classified by Wilson *et al*, *Strategic Marketing Management: Planning, Implementation and Control* (1999), as follows, with the focus progressively narrowing.

- Cultural
- Social
- Personal
- Psychological

4.2 Each factor will be considered in more detail separately, but it is essential to remember that they are not **mutually exclusive**. Marketers must have a clear understanding of how the various factors interact and how they influence buyer behaviour, both separately and in their totality.

Cultural factors

4.3 These are the most fundamental of the influencing factors, and include culture, subculture and social class.

Key Concept

Culture comprises the values and attitudes in the life adopted by people that help them to interpret and communicate with others, as members of a society.

4.4 **Culture** is largely the result of a learning process. As we grow up we learn a set of values, perceptions, preferences and behaviour patterns through socialisation in the family and other institutions such as school and work.

4.5 This broad set of values is then influenced by the **subcultures** in which we develop. Subcultural groups can be defined in terms of religion, ethnic characteristics, racial characteristics and geographical areas, all of which further influence attitudes, tastes, taboos and lifestyle.

4.6 A third cultural influence is that of **social stratification**, that is social class. The key characteristics of social class have been highlighted as follows.

(a) People within a particular social class resemble each other more than they resemble those from other social classes.

(b) Social class is determined by a series of variables such as occupation, income, education and values, rather than by a single variable.

(c) Individuals can move from one social class to another.

Social factors

4.7 Within the context of culture, an individual is also influenced by a series of social factors, such as **reference groups**, family, social role and status, all of which can have a direct effect on buying behaviour.

4.8 Reference groups are groups 'with which an individual identifies so much that he or she takes on many of the values, attitudes or behaviours of group members' (Dibb *et al*). Four types have been identified.

(a) **Primary membership groups**, which are generally informal and to which individuals belong and within which they interact (family, friends, neighbours, work colleagues and so on).

(b) **Secondary membership groups**, which tend to be more formal than primary groups and within which less interaction takes place (trade unions, religious groups and professional societies are examples).

(c) **Aspirational groups**, to which an individual would like to belong.

(d) **Dissociative groups**, whose values and behaviour the individual rejects.

Action Programme 6

The CIM is, presumably, one of your own aspirational groups. What other reference groups do you have? Divide them according to the above classifications.

The family

4.9 Another major social influence is the family, particularly with regard to the roles and relative influence exerted by different family members. Research has indicated three patterns of decision making within the family.

(a) **Husband dominated**: life insurance, cars and television.
(b) **Wife dominated**: washing machines, carpets, kitchenware and furniture.
(c) **Equal**: holidays, housing and entertainment.

Marketing at Work

Changing behaviour

Not so long ago, a maternal seal of approval would have been the kiss of death for a product marketed at teenagers. However, unpublished research by advertising agency Ogilvy & Mather suggests that British teenage girls have open relationships with their mothers, share interests with them and admire what they have achieved.

The findings paint a picture of 13 to 18 year olds who want to be in control of their destinies and who are hard to shock.

They are independent and confident, though this confidence may sometimes be misplaced. Shopping is a frequent and social event, and they want access to brands even though they are on limited budgets.

At a more detailed level, the study highlights differences in how the younger and older girls related to brands and advertising.

Where younger girls seek security from brands that give them a sense of belonging and are a sign that they know what is fashionable, older teenage girls are more concerned with the 'integrity' of brands, looking for a sign of quality and a means of self-expression.

For advertising aimed at young girls to be effective, the most important elements are its final form and its display in magazines read by the target audience. For the older girls, however, the key to effectiveness seems more a matter of brand relevance.

Personal factors

4.10 Influencing factors that can be classified as personal include such things as age and life cycle, occupation, economic circumstances and lifestyle.

4.11 Individuals will buy different types of product depending on their age. This is particularly relevant to such products as clothes, furniture and recreation. However, consumption may also be shaped by the stage of the **family life cycle** within which an individual falls.

4.12 A person's occupation will influence consumption and the task for marketers is to identify the occupational groups that have an above average interest in their products and services.

4.13 Buying patterns are also heavily influenced by an individual's economic circumstances. Kotler states that an individual's economic circumstances consist of:

- Spendable income: its level, stability and time pattern
- Savings and assets, including the percentage that is liquid
- Borrowing power
- Attitude toward spending versus saving

However, people coming from the same subculture, social class and occupation may lead completely different lifestyles.

Key Concept

A **lifestyle** is an individual's mode of living, expressed by, amongst other things, his or her attitudes and activities.

Marketers will search for relationships between their products and lifestyle groups. There are many different lifestyle classifications; two examples, from McCann-Erikson and Taylor Nelson, are given in the table in Action Programme 7 below.

Marketing at Work

Advertisers are failing to notice the growing population of over 50 year olds, according to research by Datamonitor. By 2025 there are expected to be 177 million in this age group in Western Europe.

Three groups of over 50 year old consumers have emerged:

'Woofs': well off older folk
'Youthfully spirited': less financially secure then 'woofs', but willing to experiment
'Self preservationists': older, more conservative than the other groups.

Companies are obsessed with youth, and the staff in advertising agencies are predominantly under 30.

Psychological factors

4.14 The process of buyer behaviour is also influenced by four major psychological factors:

- Motivation
- Perception
- Learning
- Beliefs and attitudes

Motivation

Key Concept

Motivation has been defined as, 'an inner state that energises, activates, or moves, that directs or channels behaviour towards goals' (Assael).

4.15 Motivation arises from perceived needs. These needs can be of two main types - **biogenic** and **psychogenic**.

(a) Biogenic needs arise from physiological states of tension such as hunger, thirst and discomfort

(b)   Psychogenic needs arise from psychological states of tension such as the need for recognition, esteem or belonging.

4.16 Most needs are not intense enough to motivate an individual to act immediately, but when aroused to a sufficient level of intensity the individual will be motivated to act in order to reduce the perceived tension.

Theories of human motivation

4.17 **Maslow's** theory of motivation seeks to explain why people are driven by particular needs at particular times. Maslow argues that human needs are arranged in **a hierarchy** comprising, in their order of importance: physiological needs, safety needs, social needs, esteem needs and self-actualisation needs.

4.18 Maslow states that a person will attempt to **satisfy the most important need first**. When that need is satisfied it ceases to be a motivator and the person will attempt to satisfy the next most important need. For example, if you are hungry (a physiological need) you will venture out from the relative warmth and safety of your desk to get a sandwich.

4.19 **Herzberg** developed a 'two factor theory' of motivation that distinguishes between **factors that cause dissatisfaction and factors that cause satisfaction**. The task for the marketer is, therefore, to avoid 'dissatisfiers' such as, for example, poor after-sales service, as these things will not sell the product but may well unsell it. In addition the marketer should identify the major satisfiers or motivators of purchase and make sure that they are supplied to the customer.

Action Programme 7

(a)   Look at the two tables below. Have you moved, or are you about to move, from one category to another? What about the members of your family and your friends and colleagues at work?

(b)   See if you can think of five products or services that it would be easy to sell to a person in each of the lifestyle categories described.

(c)   For each product or service identified in (b), devise a communications strategy that would encourage the person in question to try your company's brand.

Life-style categories

McCann-Erikson Men	McCann-Erikson Women	Taylor Nelson
Avant Guardians. *Concerned with change and well-being of others, rather than possessions. Well educated, prone to self righteousness.*	Avant Guardians. *'Liberal left' opinions, trendy attitudes. But out-going, active, sociable.*	Self-explorers. *Motivated by self-expression and self-realisation. Less materialistic than other groups, and showing high tolerance levels.*
Pontificators. *Strongly held, traditional opinions. Very British, and concerned about keeping others on the right path.*	Lady Righteous. *Traditional, 'right-minded' opinions. Happy, complacent, with strong family orientation.*	Social resisters. *The caring group, concerned with fairness and social values, but often appearing intolerant and moralistic.*
Chameleons. *Want to be contemporary to win approval. Act like barometers of social change, but copiers not leaders.*	Hopeful seekers. *Need to be liked, want to do 'right'. Like new things, want to be trendy.*	Experimentalists. *Highly individualistic, motivated by fast-moving enjoyment. They are materialistic, pro-technology but anti traditional.*
Self-admirers. *At the young end of the spectrum. Intolerant of others and strongly motivated by success. Concerned about self-image.*	Lively ladies. *Younger than above, sensual, materialistic, ambitious and competitive.*	Conspicuous consumers. *They are materialistic and pushy, motivated by acquisition, competition, and getting ahead. Pro-authority, law and order.*
Self-exploiters. *The 'doers' and 'self-starters', competitive but always under pressure and often pessimistic. Possessions are important.*	New unromantics. *Generally young and single, adopting a hard-headed and unsentimental approach to life. Independent, self-centred.*	Belongers. *What they seek is a quiet, undisturbed family life. They are conservative, conventional rule-followers.*
Token triers. *Always willing to try new things to 'improve their luck', but apparently on a permanent try-and-fail cycle. Includes an above average proportion of unemployed.*	Lack-a-daisy. *Unassertive and easy-going. Try to cope but often fail. Not very interested in the new.*	Survivors. *Strongly class-conscious, and community spirited, their motivation is to 'get by'.*
Sleepwalkers. *Contented under-achievers. Do not care about most things, and actively opt out. Traditional macho views.*	Blinkered. *Negative, do not want to be disturbed. Uninterested in conventional success - in fact, few interests except TV and radio.*	Aimless. *Comprises two groups, (a) the young unemployed, who are often anti-authority, and (b) the old, whose motivation is day-to-day existence.*
Passive endurers. *Biased towards the elderly, they are often economically and socially disfranchised. Expect little of life, and give little.*	Down-trodden. *This group is shy, introverted, but put upon. Would like to do better. Often unhappy and pressurised in personal relationships.*	

Perception

Key Concept

Perception can be defined as a process by which people select and interpret stimuli into a meaningful picture.

4.20 The way consumers view an object could include their mental picture of a brand, or the traits they attribute to a brand. The way that a person perceives a situation will affect how they act. Possible differences in perception can be explained by three perceptual processes.

- Selective attention
- Selective distortion
- Selection retention

Selective attention

4.21 A receiver will not notice all the commercial messages that he comes into contact with, so the sender must design the message so as to **win attention** in spite of the surrounding noise. Repetition, size, contour, music and sexual attraction are features used to attract attention.

Selective distortion

4.22 In many cases receivers distort or change the information they receive if that information does not fit in with their existing beliefs. In other words, people hear what they want to hear. Selective distortion may take a variety of forms.

- Amplification (where receivers may add things to the message that are not there)
- Levelling (where receivers do not notice other things that are there).

The task of the sender is to produce a message that is clear, simple and interesting, what many refer to as **likeable**.

Selective recall and message rehearsal

4.23 A receiver will retain in memory **a small fraction of the messages** that are perceived and processed. The sender's aim, therefore, is to get the message into the receiver's **long-term memory**, because once in the long-term memory the message can modify the receiver's beliefs and attitudes. However, to reach the long-term memory the message has to enter the short-term memory, which has only a limited capacity to process information. The factor influencing the passage of the message from the short-term to the long-term memory is the amount and type of **message rehearsal** given by the receiver.

4.24 In message rehearsal the receiver elaborates on the meaning of the message in a way that brings related thoughts from the long-term memory into his short-term memory.

(a) If the receiver's initial attitude to the object of the message is positive and he rehearses support arguments then the message is likely to be accepted and have high recall.

(b)   If the receiver's initial attitude is negative and the person rehearses counter arguments against the object of the message then the message is likely to be rejected, but it will remain in the long-term memory.

Learning

4.25 Learning concerns the process whereby an individual's behaviour changes as a result of their experience. Theories about learning state that learning is the result of the interplay of five factors.

- Drives
- Stimuli
- Cues
- Responses
- Reinforcement

4.26 (a)   A **drive is a strong internal force impelling action**, which will become a motive when it is directed to a particular drive-reducing **stimulus** object (the product).

(b)   **Cues are minor stimuli** (such as seeing the product in action, favourable reactions to the product by family and friends etc) that determine when, where and how the person responds.

(c)   Once the product is bought, if the experience is rewarding then the **response** to the product will be **reinforced**, making a repeat purchase the next time the situation arises more likely.

Beliefs and attitudes

Key Concept

A **belief** is a thought that a person holds to be true about something.

4.27 Beliefs are important to marketers as the beliefs that people have about products make up the brand images of those products.

Key Concept

An **attitude** describes a person's 'enduring favourable or unfavourable cognitive evaluations, emotional feelings, and action tendencies toward some object or idea' (Kotler).

4.28 **Attitudes lead people to behave in a fairly consistent way towards similar objects**. Attitudes can be regarded as a short-cut in the thought process by ensuring that people do not have to interpret and react to every object in a fresh way. Attitudes settle into a consistent pattern, and to change one attitude may entail major changes to other attitudes.

Exam Tip

Since attitudes lead people to behave in a certain way (and so buy a certain product, as opposed to another), knowledge of these attitudes by marketing communicators can be used to influence the message that they send. This formed the topic of questions in both June and December 2002, under the old *Integrated Marketing Communications* syllabus.

How to change attitudes

4.29 In changing attitudes, we can change:

■ **Cognition**
■ **Affectivity**
■ **Conation**

Key Concepts

■ **Cognition**: what people know or believe about a product
■ **Affectivity**: what people feel abut a product
■ **Conation**: what people actually do; their behaviour

Changing the way people think

4.30 With regard to cognition, the aims of the marketing communicator would be:

■ To **change beliefs** entirely
■ To change the **relative importance** of existing beliefs
■ To develop **new beliefs**

Messages which change cognition should then have a 'knock on' effect on the other two components, leading to an overall change in attitude.

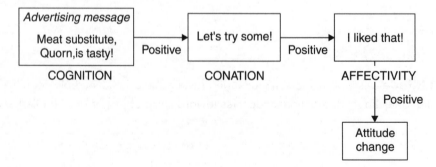

Changing the way people feel

4.31 Marketers can attempt to influence customers' feelings (**affectivity**) directly, before touching either beliefs or behaviour. The idea is to make the experience of using the product seem an enjoyable one (or a worthy, or exciting one).

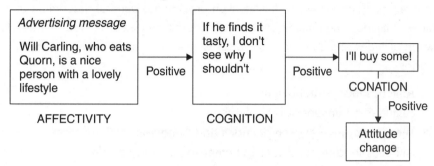

4.32 There are three main ways in which a message can change affectivity.

(a) **Repetition** of positive messages when the product is one in which the consumer is not much involved (eg washing up liquid).

(b) **Likeable advertising** means that the consumer is more inclined to like the product.

(c) **Classical conditioning** works by linking the product name with a stimulus that is liked by the consumer, such as music.

Changing the way people behave

4.33 Often a consumer will try or **experiment** with a product before either his beliefs or his feelings are changed, most usually because a product with fairly **low involvement** is reduced in **price**.

Exam Tip

Would you be able to describe the connections between attitudes and behaviour so far as customers are concerned, amplifying your arguments with relevant examples?

An answer could open with an introduction providing a general description of behaviour and attitudes. Attitudes and attitude components could then be considered in more detail. The links between attitudes and behaviour could subsequently be examined using the following four scenarios.

- Attitudes lead to behaviour
- Attitudes are influence by behaviour
- There is no link between attitudes and behaviour
- Attitudes lead to behaviour but other factors play a role

Finally you must draw a conclusion. It is at this point that it might be useful to introduce the impact of environmental issues. There is, of course, no right or wrong conclusion. Provided you justify yourself you may conclude that any of the four scenarios is an accurate reflection of reality.

5 The consumer decision-making process

5.1 As the main aim of marketing communications is to influence consumers with regard to a specific product or service offered, it is essential that the marketing communications practitioner has some understanding of the process by which consumers reach decisions to buy or not buy.

5.2 Steps in **the buying process**:

Step 1. Need recognition
Step 2. Information search
Step 3. Evaluation of alternatives
Step 4. Purchase decision
Step 5. Post purchase evaluation

Action Programme 8

Before reading on, think about a recent purchase of a fairly major item that you have made. Did you go through the stages listed above? Explain what the need was, how you searched for information and so on.

Step 1: Need recognition

5.3 The process begins when the buyer recognises a **need or problem**. This can be triggered by internal **stimuli**, such as hunger or thirst, or external stimuli, such as social esteem. If the need rises to a threshold level it will become a **drive**, and, from previous experience the buyer will know how to satisfy this drive through the purchase of a particular type of product. The task for the marketer is to identify the stimuli that trigger a particular need, and use this knowledge to develop marketing strategies that trigger consumer interest.

Step 2: Information search

5.4 Once aroused, the customer will search for more information. The information search stage can be divided into two levels.

(a) **'Heightened attention**, where the customer simply becomes more receptive to information about the particular product category.

(b) **'Active information search'**. The extent of the search will depend on the strength of the drive, the amount of information available, the ease of obtaining additional information and the satisfaction obtained from the search.

5.5 The task for the marketer is to decide which are the major information sources that the customer will use and to analyse their relative importance. According to Kotler **consumer information sources fall into four groups**.

- **Personal sources**: family, friends, neighbours, work colleagues
- **Commercial sources**: advertising, salespeople, packaging, displays
- **Public sources**: mass media, consumer rating organisations
- **Experiential sources**: handling, examining, using the product

5.6 A consumer will generally receive the most information exposure from commercial sources, but **the most effective information exposure comes from personal sources**. Each information source performs a somewhat different function, with consumers being informed by commercial sources and this information being legitimised (or not) by personal sources.

5.7 Through this information-gathering process the consumer will learn about **competing brands and their relative pros and cons**. This will enable the consumer to narrow down the range of alternatives to those brands that will best meet his or her particular needs: what has been called the **choice** or **evoked** set.

Step 3: Evaluation of alternatives

5.8 Trying to describe the process of evaluation of alternatives is not easy as there is no generally accepted single evaluation process. Most current models of evaluation are **cognitively** oriented: in other words they take the view that **the customer forms judgements largely on a conscious and rational basis**.

5.9 Kotler states that, as the consumer is trying to satisfy some need with the buying process, he will be looking for certain benefits from the product chosen and each product will be seen as a **'bundle of attributes'** with varying capabilities of delivering the benefits sought.

5.10 The consumer is likely to build up a set of **brand beliefs** about the position of each brand with regard to each attribute. The sum of these brand beliefs will make up the **brand image**. The consumer will most likely choose the brand that achieves the optimum balance between those attributes that are perceived to be the most important.

6 Source effects influencing consumer behaviour

Source effects influencing consumer behaviour

6.1 The source of the communication directly influences the consumer's acceptance and interpretation of a message. **Credibility** and **attractiveness** have been identified as the two major source factors influencing customers.

> ### Key Concept
>
> **Source credibility** is the level of expertise/trustworthiness customers attribute to the source of the message, where expertise/trustworthiness is the ability to make valid statements about the characteristics and performance of a product.

6.2 The two elements are interlinked. For example, some spokespersons may be regarded with high credibility in a particular field, but the trustworthiness of their product endorsements may be questioned because they are being paid by the advertiser.

6.3 **Source attractiveness** is determined by its likeability and its similarity to the consumer. Research has shown that when consumers perceive salespeople as similar to themselves, they are more likely to accept and be influenced by the sales messages.

Balance of the message

6.4 Our understanding of the level of involvement that may exist in the target audience can be used to determine the **overall balance of the message**. If there is **high involvement** then interested members of the target audience will **actively seek information**. Messages therefore tend to be **rational**, proclaiming product benefits and the key attributes.

6.5 Where there is **low involvement** the audience are not really interested and **need to be drawn to the communication message**. In these cases, image-based appeals tend to be more successful and the use of **emotion** rather than logic predominates.

6.6 The strategic implication is that if **coordination** and **consistency** is to be achieved, then adherence to an emotional or rational approach has to be maintained throughout all the promotional tools.

6.7 There are a number of ways in which the informational and emotional based messages can be presented to audiences. These are referred to as **message appeals**. We look at this in more detail in Chapter 6.

7 Perceived risk   (Specimen paper)

7.1 Allied to the concept of involvement is **perceived risk**.

Key Concept

Risk is hard to define as it has precise meanings in different contexts. In marketing, risk relates to the possibility that the outcome of a decision will not have the desired affect or may make the situation worse. The amount of risk perceived in purchases varies from individual to individual and across product categories. By identifying the dominant forms of risk present at any one time it is possible to design messages that can help to reduce levels of perceived risk.

Risk	Comment	Dealing with it
Performance risk	Will the product function properly?	Guarantees money back
Financial risk	Can I afford it, is it good value?	Emphasise value for money, quality
Physical risk	Will the product harm me or other people?	Emphasise safety
Ego risk	Will the product satisfy my needs for self esteem and self image?	Aspiration groups
Social risk	Will significant others disapprove?	Suggest psychological rewards
Time risk	Have I the time to go shopping to buy this product?	Importance or convenience of product

7.2 Most individuals will experience a number of these risks when making purchase decisions. It is unlikely that all these risks will present at any one time. Once the dominant risks are identified marketing communications can be used to transmit messages that seek to reduce these risks.

(a)   Should finance be an important factor, then interest free credit may help reduce this risk.

(b)   If social risk is high then pictures of people smiling and giving approval to the person using the product (eg children in Sunny Delight advertisements) will be effective.

7.3 Celebrity **endorsement**, the **approval** of opinion formers and **visual demonstrations** of the product/service in action are all important communication methods. Of course, one of the main methods is **branding**. Branding is a particularly powerful form of marketing communication as it allows individuals to assimilate product information quickly, identify levels of product quality and so reduce their levels of felt risk.

Exam Tip

We have begun this text with a consideration of buyer behaviour, since the syllabus indicates the importance for marketing communicators of developing a customer focus if they are to be successful. The theories need to be applied, rather than merely learned in isolation. For example, the December 2002 examination under the *Integrated Marketing Communications* syllabus asked a question about word-of-mouth *recommendation in the market for luxury watches, and why communicators in this market use sports stars and celebrities to endorse their products.*

Chapter Roundup

- Marketing communications fulfils a variety of roles within organisations. Principally it is used to **inform**, **remind**, **persuade** and **differentiate** an organisation and its products/services from those of its competitors.

- An **understanding** of the way communication works is an important part of building skills and knowledge about marketing communications.

- The **One-Step** model of communication depicts communication as a linear process but feedback and interaction, in order that a dialogue be developed, are important parts of real practical communications.

- The **Two-Step** and **Multi-Step** models reflect the influence of other people on the communication process. Opinion Leaders play important roles in bringing credibility, and hence conviction and belief, to the way people perceive and understand the communications they receive.

- In order to reach and influence members of the target audience it crucial to understand the **context** within which customers receive and understand marketing messages.

- Analysis of this contextual element revolves around the way in which information (marketing communication messages) is **processed**, **interpreted** and **acted upon**.

- Therefore, perception, **motivation**, **learning** and **attitudes** are key pyschological factors that need to be appreciated, as they apply to each target audience.

- The message to be delivered to target audiences must be perceived as **credible** if it is to be effective. The use of rational and/or image based appeals can assist the communication process.

- It is vital for marketers to have an understanding of the **processes** that customers go through when buying a product, whether this product is being bought by a consumer for individual consumption or by an organisation for production of other products or for resale. The thought processes of the buying process, both organisational and consumer, can be simply summarised as follows:

  - Recognition of problem/need
  - Information search
  - Evaluation of alternatives
  - Purchase decision
  - Post purchase evaluation

- **The extent to which a consumer engages in all these stages** will depend on the size, complexity and specific circumstances of the buying situation and a range of influencing factors can be identified that could possibly affect the process. Such factors need to be recognised by marketers so that they are taken into account in marketing and promotional activity.

Now try Question 1 in the Question Bank

Quick Quiz

1 What does the acronym DRIP refer to?

D.........

R.........

I..........

P.........

2 What does 'encoding' mean when referring to the communications process?

A Receiver translates and interprets message
B Part of receiver's response is communicated back to the sender
C Meaning is given in symbolic form by the sender
D Receiver reacts to message

3 Opinion leaders are often part of a two-step flow of communication

True ☐

False ☐

4 Diffusion can be defined as the process by which an .... is communicated over ....
among those within society who comprise the ....

5 Fill in the blanks in the statements below, using the words in the box.

When examining the various (1)........., we can identify five types. The first, (2).......,
demonstrate an eagerness to try new ideas and products, and they are followed by the early
adopters and early majority. The (3)........feel more pressure to conform, and so are a little
more sceptical. Those who adopt the latest tend to have the lowest socio-economic status and
are known as (4).......... Each group learns by observing the previous group's (5).......... and
then (6).......... the behaviour itself.

Adopts	Late majority	Behaviour
Laggards	Adopter groups	Innovators

6 Name the four core variables influencing consumer buying behaviour.

7 When thinking about changing attitudes, the marketer may seek to change:

■ *Cognition*: what people .... about a product
■ *Affectivity*: what people .... about a product
■ *Conation*: what people ....

8 There are six different types of perceived risk. What are they?

Action Programme Review

1   Your list may include any number of the following.

    (a)   **Customers**, users (of competitor products/services).

    (b)   **Non users**, suppliers, distributors (such as wholesalers, dealers and retailers).

    (c)   **Employees**, head office staff.

    (d)   **Financial service organisations**, trade unions, the local community, the wider national or international community, trade and professional associations, local or national government bodies, the media .... to name a few.

2   You could try applying this to your own organisation or look to apply to a specific market sector and compare the way in which different competitors approach each aspect.

3   As you develop your studies and examine more closely the use of different promotional tools, come back to this exercise and see how it applies to them eg direct mail or PR.

4   **Three suggestions**

    (a)   *Continuous innovation*: software packages such as Windows XP; these have to be similar enough to previous versions not to require extensive retraining by the user

    (b)   *Dynamically continuous innovation*: cheap electronic typewriters and PCs

    (c)   *Discontinuous innovation*: strictly speaking, this is more rare; the photocopier, or the fax machine or the video recorder are good examples

5   You might want to consider the role marketing communications could play in overcoming any perceived problem areas.

6   This list is likely to include groups which might be classified into business and personal categories. Can you identify any situations where these groups may have influenced your purchasing behaviour in either a business or personal context?

7   This exercise normally provides for an interesting discussion within a group situation. Try this with other members of your study group or some work colleagues.

8   When you have completed this, consider what were the major influencing factors on the purchase decision. Did reference group membership play a part?

Answers to Quick Quiz

1   **D**ifferentiates
        Reminds
        Informs
        Persuades

2   C

3   True

4   Diffusion can be defined as the process by which an innovation is communicated over time among those within society who comprise the target market.

5   (1) Adopter groups (2) Innovators (3) Late majority (4) Laggards (5) Behaviour (6) Adopts

6   ■   Cultural

- Social
- Personal
- Psychological

7
- Cognition: what people know or believe about a product
- Affectivity: what people feel about a product
- Conation: what people do

8   Performance; Financial; Physical; Ego; Social; Time

Organisational markets, ethics and social responsibility

2

Chapter Topic List	
1	Setting the scene
2	Organisational buying behaviour
3	The process of organisational buying behaviour
4	Influences on organisational buying behaviour
5	Ethics and social responsibility
6	Ethical codes
7	Social responsibility
8	Consumer and community issues
9	Green issues
10	Strategies for social responsibility

Learning Outcomes

☑   Explain the role of marketing communications and advise how personal influences might be used to develop promotional effectiveness

☑   Develop marketing communication and brand support activities based on an understanding of the salient characteristics of the target audience

Syllabus References

☑   Assess the principal differences between consumer and organisational markets and consider how they impact on marketing communications

☑   Summarise the importance for organisations of ethics and corporate responsibility, and their impact on brand reputation

Key Concepts Introduced

- Organisational buying
- Decision making unit
- Ethics
- Ethical issue

1 Setting the scene

1.1 This chapter continues the theme of understanding buying behaviour by describing the various elements that influence the way **organisations** use information to make their purchase decisions.

1.2 In this chapter we also focus on an area which is of increasing significance to marketers: the importance of **marketing ethics** and **social responsibility**. A lack of ethics can affect the purchasing decision process, and ultimately customer loyalty, both of which are central to successful marketing. In sections 9 and 10, we will develop the themes of social responsibility and the 'green' issue.

2 Organisational buying behaviour

Key Concept

Organisational (or industrial) buying has been defined as 'the decision-making process by which formal organisations establish the need for purchased products and services and identify, evaluate and choose among alternative brands and suppliers' (Webster & Wind, *Organisational Buying Behaviour*, 1972).

2.1 Kotler identifies a number of **differences between organisational and consumer markets** that mean that a modified approach needs to be taken when considering the process of buying behaviour.

(a) Organisational markets normally comprise **fewer buyers**, with those buyers often being very **concentrated** (a few buyers are responsible for the majority of sales).

(b) Because of this smaller customer base and the importance and power of larger customers there is generally a **close relationship between buyer and seller** in organisational markets, with a great degree of customisation and co-operation on product specification and other requirements.

2.2 A number of **demand factors** also influence the nature of organisational markets.

(a) Demand for industrial goods is ultimately **derived from the demand for consumer goods**. If the demand for these consumer goods slackens, then the demand for the industrial products that contribute to their production will also fall.

(b) The total demand for many industrial products is **inelastic**. In other words, it is not much affected by price changes.

(c)   Demand for industrial products may also be quite **seasonal** and more **volatile** than that for consumer products.

2.3   The specific characteristics of organisational markets may vary according to the **types of organisation** that comprise the market. Dibb *et al* identify four types of organisational market.

Market	Comment
Producer markets	Organisations that purchase products for the purpose of making a profit by using them to produce other products or by using them in their own operations. This may include buyers of raw materials and of semi-finished and finished items used to produce other products
Reseller markets	Intermediaries such as retailers and wholesalers who buy the finished goods in order to resell them to make a profit. Other than minor alterations, resellers do not change the physical characteristics of the products they handle.
Government markets	National and local governments who buy a variety of goods and services to support their internal operations and to provide the public services that are within their remit, normally making their purchases through bids or negotiated contracts.
Institutional markets	Organisations that seek to achieve charitable, educational, community or other non-business goals.

3   The process of organisational buying behaviour

3.1   This process follows the stages outlined below.

Stage 1. **Recognise the problem**: the stimulus may come from within or outside the firm

Stage 2. **Develop product specifications** to solve the problem. People participating in the buying decision assess the problem, and determine what will be required to resolve or satisfy it.

Stage 3. **Search** for products and suppliers. The third stage of the process is similar to that of **information search**, utilising trade shows, trade publications, supplier catalogues, and soliciting proposals from known suppliers. This should result in a list of several alternative products.

Stage 4. **Evaluate products** relative to specifications. These are evaluated in order to ascertain whether they meet the product specifications developed in the second stage.

Stage 5. **Select and order** the most appropriate product. In some cases an organisational buyer may select a number of suppliers in order to reduce the possibility of disruption. The order will then be made, often with specific details regarding terms, credit arrangements, delivery dates and technical assistance or after-sales service.

Stage 6. **Evaluate** the product and supplier performance against specifications regarding product quality and the performance of the supplier.

3.2 Again, as with consumer buying behaviour, the full buying process may not be applicable in all cases. **Three main types of organisational purchase can be identified**.

(a) **New task purchase**

The organisation is facing a need or a problem for the first time and the full organisational buying process will probably occur. As the problem has not been encountered before, the organisation will have to produce detailed specifications of both product and ordering routines. Given the fact that in many organisational markets there is a close and ongoing relationship between buyer and seller, these new task purchases can be important to sellers as they might be the start of a long relationship.

(b) **Modified re-buy**

Something about the buying situation has changed, but a lot still remains the same. Such situations may include circumstances where a buyer requires faster delivery, different prices or a slightly different product specification.

(c) **Straight re-buy**

The buyer routinely purchases the same products under the same terms of sale. In such situations the buying process will be truncated.

3.3 The implications of the types of buying situation for the stages of the organisational buying process have been summarised as follows.

	New task	Modified re-buy	Straight re-buy
Recognise problem	Yes	Yes	Yes
Develop specification	Yes	Possibly	No
Product/supplier search	Yes	Yes	Yes
Evaluate product	Yes	Possibly	No
Select product	Yes	Possibly	No
Evaluate performance	Yes	Possibly	No

The decision making unit (DMU)

3.4 One of the major differences between consumer and organisational buying behaviour is the fact that **organisational purchase decisions are rarely made by a single individual**. This obviously has a significant influence on the buying process in the organisational context. Normally, purchasing decisions are made by a number of people from different functional areas, possibly with different statuses within the organisation.

Exam Tip

This obviously complicates the process of marketing and selling the product and it is important that the marketer is fully aware of the composition of the buying group and the relative importance to the purchase decision of the individuals within it. This reflects the syllabus focus on a proper understanding of the customer (whether it be a consumer or an organisation).

3.5 A framework for considering these issues was provided by Webster and Wind, *Organisational Buying Behaviour*, with the concept of the **decision making unit (DMU)**.

Key Concept

The **decision making unit** is defined as 'all those individuals and groups who participate in the purchasing decision process, who share some common goals and the risks arising from the decisions.'

3.6 Webster and Wind suggested **six groups within the DMU**.

(a) **Users**, who may initiate the buying process and help define purchase specifications.

(b) **Influencers**, who help define the specification and also provide an input into the process of evaluating the available alternatives.

(c) **Deciders**, who have the responsibility for deciding on product requirements and suppliers.

(d) **Approvers**, who authorise the proposals of deciders and buyers.

(e) **Buyers**, who have the formal authority for the selection of suppliers and negotiating purchase terms.

(f) **Gatekeepers** who, by controlling the flow of information, may be able to stop sellers from reaching individuals within the buying centre.

Action Programme 1

Whenever you have the chance - when visiting clients, when browsing in the newsagents, at the dentist's or hairdresser's - browse through the trade magazines that you find (*Campaign, Farmer's Weekly, Banking World, Engineering Today* or whatever).

What do you notice about the way products and services are marketed in such publications? Is more technical language used? Are the ads less 'glossy'? What do you learn about price and place?

3.7 The size, structure and formality of the DMU will vary depending on the specific situation, however, as Wilson *et al, Strategic Marketing Management: Planning, Implementation and Control* (1992) state, the marketer has to consider five questions.

(a) **Who** are the principal participants in the buying process?

(b) In what areas do they exert the **greatest influence**?

(c) What is their **level of influence**?

(d) What **evaluative criteria** do each of the participants make use of and how professional is the buying process?

(e) To what extent is **buying centralised** in large organisations?

4 Influences on organisational buying behaviour

4.1 Kotler identifies four main forces influencing the organisational buyer, shown below in order of progressively narrowing focus.

- Environmental
- Interpersonal
- Organisational
- Individual

4.2 **Environmental forces** include such factors as the level of primary demand, economic outlook, the cost of money, the rate of technological change, political and regulatory developments and competitive developments. All these environmental forces must be monitored so as to determine how they will affect buyers.

4.3 Each organisation has its own **objectives**, policies, procedures, organisational structures and systems, which may constrain the freedom of action of organisational buyers and this may in turn affect the decision-making process. For example, an organisation may insist on long-term contracts or may require special credit arrangements.

4.4 **Interpersonal factors** are important where the buying decision may involve a number of people. Within the buying group, the use of power and the level of conflict could significantly influence organisational buying decisions.

4.5 **Individual factors** are the personal characteristics of the individuals in the buying group such as age, education, personality and position in the organisation. These will affect the decision-making process, and the seller must be aware of their potential influence.

Buyer's style

4.6 Marketers must ensure that they know as much as possible about their customers and the factors influencing them so that tactics can be adapted to the specific situation. Research in the United States by Dickenson, *Buyer Decision Making* (1967) on the issue of the buyer's style and its implications for marketing strategy identified seven different **types of buyers**.

Types of buyers	Comment
Loyal buyers	Remain loyal to a source for considerable periods
Opportunistic buyers	Choose between sellers on the basis of who will best further their long-term interests
Best deal buyers	Concentrate on the best deal available at the time
Creative buyers	Tell the seller precisely what they want in terms of the product, service and price
Advertising buyers	Demand advertising support as part of the deal
Chisellers	Constantly demand extra discounts
Nuts and bolts buyers	Select products on the basis of the quality of their construction

4.7 The approach of the marketer to each of these different types of buyers will have to be modified according to circumstances.

Organisational buyer behaviour matrix

4.8 An alternative framework for explaining the main influences and participants in the process of organisational buying behaviour has been put forward by the American Marketing Association, as shown below.

Departmental influences

Within the
organisation

Cell 1 Purchasing agent	*Cell 2* Buying centre
Cell 3 Professionalism	*Cell 4* Organisational environment

Within the
buying
department

In
other
departments

In other
organisations

4.9 **Cell 1: the purchasing agent**. This represents the buyer, located in the quadrant which is within the organisation and within the purchasing department. Various factors will influence the buyer, including social factors, price and cost factors, supply continuity and risk avoidance.

(a) **Social factors** include the relationships, friendships and antipathies that exist between buyer and suppliers and the extent to which these impinge on purchasing decisions. While in an ideal world such social factors should not influence decision making, they are, in reality, an important factor in the equation.

(b) **Price and cost factors** are obviously important and can include such things as the economic state of the buying organisation, the level of competition among suppliers, any cost/benefit analyses that might have been conducted, the purchasing budget and the personality and background of the purchasing agent (for example, an agent with an accountancy background may be more cost conscious).

(c) **Supply continuity** is a function of the number of suppliers that are available and the importance of the purchased item to the organisation.

(d) **Risk** avoidance is a common motivation for organisational buyers. Chisnall, *Strategic Industrial Marketing* (1989), states that the element of risk in the organisational buying decision can be considered along a continuum, ranging from the low risk of routine purchases to the high risk of new purchases involving high absolute or opportunity costs. Somewhere in the middle are reasonable risk situations, where the hazard involved with occasional purchases can be calculated to allow for reasonable risk minimisation or avoidance. **Buyers can typically cope with risk in a number of ways**.

(i) Exchanging technical and other information with their customers and prospects

(ii) Dealing only with those suppliers with which the company has previously had favourable experiences

(iii) Applying strict (risk reducing) rules

(iv) Dealing only with suppliers who have long established and favourable reputations

(v) Introducing penalty clauses, for example for late delivery

(vi) Multiple sourcing to reduce the degree of dependence on a single supplier

4.10 **Cell 2: the buying centre**. This cell equates to the decision making unit, where the focus is within the firm but between departments. Some of the influencing factors in this cell include organisation structure and policy, power, status and conflict procedures, and gatekeeping.

(a) With regard to **organisational structure and policy**, the place of the purchasing department within the organisation is very important as it will determine such matters as the level of influence and the reporting relationships.

(b) **Power, status and conflict procedures** relate to the degree to which the buyer or purchasing department wishes to change or maintain the status quo. For example, decentralisation and divisionalisation of the organisation may motivate outside departments to initiate their own buying decisions.

(c) Gatekeeping controls the **flow of information** in the organisation.

4.11 **Cell 3: professionalism**. This cell examines the influence of professional standards and practice in other organisations.

(a) **Specialist journals**, **conferences** and **trade shows** are likely to be the source of much professional knowledge. In addition, professional organisations usually attempt to set standards for professional conduct.

(b) **Word of mouth** communication can act as a potent force within the profession.

(c) **Supply-purchase reciprocity** refers to arrangements whereby two organisations reach an agreement to supply each other.

4.12 **Cell 4: the organisational environment**. This cell is concerned with factors outside the organisation, including economic, commercial and competitive forces, the political, social and legal environment, technological change, co-operative buying (through, for example, the formation of consortia), and the nature of the supplier.

Selection criteria

4.13 The issue of precisely **how** organisational buyers make the purchase decision, in terms of the selection criteria determining the choice of supplier, has been the subject of various pieces of research. For example, in a survey of purchasing managers it was found that the most important selection criteria were as follows.

- Delivery capability
- Quality
- Price
- Repair and after-sales service
- Technical capability
- Performance history
- Production facilities
- Help and advice
- Control systems
- Reputation

- Financial position
- Attitude toward the buyer
- Compliance with bidding procedures
- Training support
- Communications on the progress of the order
- Management and organisation
- Packaging
- Moral/legal issues
- Location
- Labour relations

5 Ethics and social responsibility

5.1 **Social responsibility** requires that organisations will not act in a way which harms the general public or which is thought to be socially irresponsible. It is because corporate decisions subsume marketing decisions that the **terms marketing ethics and social responsibility are often used interchangeably**.

The well-being of individuals and society

5.2 Critics of marketing argue that it is dedicated to selling products which are potentially damaging to the health and well-being of the **individual** or **society**. Examples include tobacco, alcohol, automobiles, detergents and even electronic goods such as computers and video recorders. It has been argued that even seemingly beneficial, or at least harmless, products, such as soft drinks, sunglasses or agricultural fertiliser, can damage individuals and societies. In traditional societies, new products can disrupt social order by introducing new aspirations, or changing a long established way of life.

Marketing at Work

Pampers Care Mats

Procter & Gamble has been forced to make an embarrassing U-turn on a newly-launched infant product, after fears were raised that it could suffocate young babies.

Pampers Care Mats, disposable mats on which infants can be placed while changing their nappies or to protect toddlers against bed-wetting, were launched last September. But P&G has been forced to put stickers on the packaging warning parents that they should not be used in cots for babies under 12 months old 'to avoid the risk of suffocation'.

P&G says it had to change the packaging because it had not realised parents would use the Care Mats in cots with young babies.

A spokeswoman says: 'We like to make sure our products are as safe as possible, which is why we stickered (the warning) as soon as we realised people were using them for cots.'

Marketing Week, 27 January 2000

Key Concept

Ethics are the moral principles and values which guide thinking, decision making and action. It is to our ethical framework that we must turn when making decisions which involve moral dilemmas.

Ethics and the law

5.4 Ethics deal with personal moral principles and values, but laws are the rules that can actually be enforced in court. However, behaviour which is not subject to legal penalties may still be unethical.

Marketing at Work

For example, is it acceptable for the RJ Reynolds Tobacco Company in the USA to target Afro-Americans for a new brand of cigarette, while public health statistics show that this group has a high incidence of lung cancer and smoking related illnesses? The company maintains that this is still within the law, but is it ethical?

5.5 We can classify marketing decisions according to ethics and legality in four different ways.

Marketing decisions according to legality and ethical status

Ethical but illegal	Ethical and legal
Unethical and illegal	Unethical but legal

A business may be operated on principles which are:

- **Ethical and legal** (eg the Body Shop)
- **Unethical and legal** (eg 'gazumping')
- **Ethical but illegal** (eg publishing stolen but revealing documents about government mismanagement)
- **Unethical and illegal** (eg employing child labour)

5.6 Surveys in both the UK and the USA show that the public think that business has poor ethical standards, and levels of trust are low. In the USA, 90% of respondents in a recent survey thought that white collar crime was 'very common', and more than three-quarters of the sample saw tumbling business standards as an important contributor to declining moral standards within society as a whole.

5.7 Different cultures view marketing practices differently. While the idea of **intellectual property** is widely accepted in Europe and the USA, in other parts of the world ethical standards are quite different. Unauthorised use of copyrights, trademarks and patents is widespread in countries such as Taiwan, Mexico and Korea. According to a US trade official, the Korean view is that ' ... the thoughts of one man should benefit all', and this general value means that, in spite of legal formalities, few infringements of copyright are punished.

Key Concept

An **ethical issue** can be defined as an identifiable problem, situation or opportunity requiring an individual or organisation to choose from among several actions that must be evaluated in terms of right and wrong.

Ethics in marketing

Product issues

5.8 Ethical issues relating to products usually revolve around **safety**, **quality**, and **value** and frequently arise from failure to provide adequate **information** in marketing communications to the customer. This may range from omission of uncomfortable facts in product literature to deliberate deception. A typical problem arises when a product specification is changed to reduce cost. Clearly, it is essential to ensure that product function is not compromised in any important way, but a decision must be taken as to just what emphasis, if any, it is necessary to place on the changes in product literature. Another, more serious, problem occurs when product safety is compromised. **Product recall** is the issue here.

Marketing at Work

When the French company Perrier discovered that its mineral water was in danger of contamination, they immediately withdrew all supplies, suffering huge losses. By acting ethically, the company's reputation was enhanced. Coca Cola dithered, played down the issue, denied liability and suffered a huge blow to its image.

Promotion issues

5.9 Ethical considerations are particularly relevant to **promotional practices**. Advertising and personal selling are areas in which the temptation to select, exaggerate, slant, conceal, distort and falsify information is potentially very great indeed. Questionable practices here are likely to create **cynicism in the customer** and ultimately to preclude any degree of trust or respect for the supplier. It was because so many companies were acting unethically with regard to marketing communications that the Trade Descriptions Act 1968 came into being. Even taking into account the protection afforded to the consumer by such legislation, many think that persuading people to buy something they don't really want is intrinsically unethical, especially if hard sell tactics are used.

Marketing at Work

Hoover and Dyson

Dyson Appliances has won the latest round in its advertising war with Hoover as the two companies prepare to do battle in the High Court over alleged copyright infringements. The Advertising Standards Authority (ASA) this week called on Hoover to drop claims that its bagless Vortex model was 'the most advanced vacuum cleaner on the market'. The ASA also rejected a claim made in brochure and national press ads that the Vortex would save customers £140 on dust filters over its lifetime. In a wide-ranging criticism of Hoover in the ASA's monthly report, the authority slammed the vacuum cleaner manufacturer for failing to co-operate with its investigations and taking too long to respond to inquiries. The authority even accused Hoover of trying to justify a particular performance claim by referring to a Dyson-commissioned report which, in the course of another ASA investigation, Hoover had rubbished. In all, seven complaints were upheld against Hoover, compared with two of Hoover's complaints against Dyson. The rulings will come as a severe blow to Hoover, which is preparing to defend itself in the High Court over claims that the design of its Vortex model infringed Dyson's copyrights. The case, which will begin next week, could result in the Vortex range being withdrawn from sale. The Committee on Advertising practice, which draws up ASA guidelines, is preparing a guidance note for the vacuum cleaner industry in an effort to cut down on time consuming performance disputes. Hoover plans to appeal against the ASA's rulings. Marketing director Joe Grech says: 'We believe the ASA itself could be guilty of misleading consumers. In some cases we have been ruled against because we were late with our submissions.'

Marketing Week 13 July 2000

5.10 Also relevant to this area is the problem of **corrupt selling practices**. It is widely accepted that a small gift such as a mouse mat or a diary is a useful way of keeping a supplier's name in front of an industrial purchaser. Most business people would however condemn the payment of substantial bribes to purchasing officers to induce them to favour a particular supplier. But where does the dividing line lie between these two extremes?

6 Ethical codes

6.1 **It is now common for businesses to specify their ethical standards. Some have even published a formal declaration of their principles and rules of conduct**. This would typically cover payments to government officials or political parties, relations with customers or suppliers, conflicts of interest, and accuracy of records. The Boeing Corporation has published such a code since 1964. Yet in 1990, it was charged with using inside information to win a US government contract and fined $5.2m.

6.2 Ethical standards may cause individuals to act against the organisation of which they are a part. More often, **business people are likely to adhere to moral principles which are 'utilitarian', weighing the costs and benefits of the consequences of behaviour. When benefits exceed costs, the behaviour can be said to be ethical**. This is the philosophical position upon which capitalism rests, and is often cited to justify behaviour which appears to have socially unpleasant consequences. For example, food production regimes which appear inhumane are often justified by the claim that they produce cheaper food for the majority of the population.

6.3 The American Marketing Association has produced a **statement of the code of ethics** to which it expects members to adhere.

Code of Ethics

Members of the American Marketing Association (AMA) are committed to ethical professional conduct. They have joined together in subscribing to this Code of Ethics embracing the following topics.

Responsibilities of the Marketer

Marketers must accept responsibility for the consequence of their activities and make every effort to ensure that their decisions, recommendations, and actions function to identify, serve, and satisfy all relevant publics: customers, organisations and society.

Marketers' professional conduct must be guided by

1   The basic rule of professional ethics: not knowingly to do harm.
2   The adherence to all applicable laws and regulations.
3   The accurate representation of their education, training and experience.
4   The active support, practice and promotion of this Code of Ethics.

Honesty and Fairness

Marketers shall uphold and advance the integrity, honor and dignity of the marketing profession

1   Being honest in serving consumers, clients, employees, suppliers, distributors and the public.

2   Not knowingly participating in conflict of interest without prior notice to all parties involved.

3   Establishing equitable fee schedules including the payment or receipt of usual, customary and/or legal compensation or marketing exchanges.

Rights and Duties of Parties in the Marketing Exchange Process

Participants in the marketing exchange process should be able to expect

1   Products and services offered are safe and fit for their intended uses.

2   Communications about offered products and services are not deceptive.

3   All parties intend to discharge their obligations, financial and otherwise, in good faith.

4   Appropriate internal methods exist for equitable adjustment and/or redress of grievances concerning purchases.

It is understood that the above would include, *but is not limited to*, the following responsibilities of the marketer.

In the area of product development and management

- Disclosure of all substantial risks associated with product or service usage.

- Identification of any product component substitution that might materially change the product or impact on the buyer's purchase decision.

- Identification of extra-cost added features.

In the area of promotions

- Avoidance of false and misleading advertising.
- Rejection of high pressure manipulation, or misleading sales tactics.
- Avoidance of sales promotions that use deception or manipulation.

In the area of distribution

- Not manipulating the availability of a product for purpose of exploitation.
- Not using coercion in the marketing channel.
- Not exerting undue influence over the reseller's choice to handle the product.

In the area of pricing

- Not engaging in price fixing.
- Not practising predatory pricing.
- Disclosing the full price associated with any purchase.

In the area of marketing research

- Prohibiting selling or fund raising under the guise of conducting research.
- Maintaining research integrity by avoiding misrepresentation and omission of pertinent research data.
- Treating outside clients and suppliers fairly.

Organisational relationships

Marketers should be aware of how their behaviour may influence or impact on the behaviour of others in organisational relationships. They should not demand, encourage or apply coercion to obtain unethical behaviour in their relationships with others, such as employees, suppliers or customers.

1   Apply confidentiality and anonymity in professional relationships with regard to privileged information.

2   Meet their obligations and responsibilities in contracts and mutual agreements in a timely manner.

3   Avoid taking the work of others, in whole, or in part, and represent this work as their own or directly benefit from it without compensation or consent of the originator or owner.

4   Avoid manipulation to take advantage of situations to maximise personal welfare in a way that unfairly deprives or damages the organisation or others.

Any AMA members found to be in violation of any provision of this Code of Ethics may have his or her Association membership suspended or revoked.

(Reprinted by permission of *The American Marketing Association*)

6.4   The CIM's code is as follows. How do you think it compares to the AMA's?

(a)   A member shall at all times conduct himself with integrity in such a way as to bring credit to the profession of marketing and The Chartered Institute of Marketing.

(b)   A member shall not by unfair or unprofessional practice injure the business, reputation or interest of any other member of the Institute.

(c)   Members shall, at all times, act honestly in their professional dealings with customers and clients (actual and potential), employers and employees.

(d)   A member shall not, knowingly or recklessly, disseminate any false or misleading information, either on his own behalf or on behalf of anyone else.

(e)   A member shall keep abreast of current marketing practice and act competently and diligently and be encouraged to register for the Institute's scheme of Continuing Professional Development.

(f) A member shall, at all times, seek to avoid conflicts of interest and shall make prior voluntary and full disclosure to all parties concerned of all matters that may arise during any such conflict. Where a conflict arises a member must withdraw prior to the work commencing.

(g) A member shall keep business information confidential except from those persons entitled to receive it, where it breaches this code and where it is illegal to do so.

(h) A member shall promote and seek business in a professional and ethical manner.

(i) A member shall observe the requirements of all other codes of practice which may from time to time have any relevance to the practice of marketing insofar as such requirements do not conflict with any provisions of this code, or the Institute's Royal Charter and Bye-laws; a list of such codes being obtainable from the Institute's head office.

(j) Members shall not hold themselves out as having the Institute's endorsement in connection with an activity unless the Institute's prior written approval has been obtained first.

(k) A member shall not use any funds derived from the Institute for any purpose which does not fall within the powers and obligations contained in the Branch or Group handbook, and which does not fully comply with this code.

7 Social responsibility

7.1 There is a growing feeling that **the concerns of the community ought to be the concerns of business** since businesses exist within society, and depend on it for continued existence. Business therefore has a moral obligation to assist in the solution of those problems which it causes. Businesses and businessmen are also socially prominent, and must be seen to be taking a lead in addressing the problems of society. In the short term, responsibility is a very valuable addition to the **public relations** activities within a company. As pressure for legislation grows, **self-regulation** can take the heat out of potentially disadvantageous campaigns.

7.2 Recent studies in the US have shown that between 25% and 40% of the financial community take a company's record on social responsibility into account when making investment decisions. More and more, it is being realised that it is necessary for organisations to develop a sense of responsibility for the consequences of their actions within society at large, rather than simply setting out to provide consumer satisfaction. **Social responsibility involves accepting that the organisation is part of society and, as such, will be accountable to that society for the consequences of the actions which it takes.** Three concepts of social responsibility are **profit responsibility**, **stakeholder responsibility** and **societal responsibility**.

Profit responsibility

7.3 **Profit responsibility** argues that companies exist to maximise profits for their proprietors. Milton Friedman asserts:

'There is one and only one social responsibility of business: to use its resources and engage in activities designed to increase its profits so long as it stays within the rules of the game - which is to say, engages in open and free competition without deception or fraud'.

7.4 Thus, drug companies which retain sole rights to the manufacture of treatments for dangerous diseases are obeying this principle. The argument is that intervention, to provide products at affordable prices, will undermine the motivation of poorer groups to be self-sufficient, or to improve their lot. Proponents of this view argue that unless the market is allowed to exercise its disciplines, groups who are artificially cushioned will become victims of 'dependency culture', with far worse consequences for society at large.

Stakeholder responsibility

7.5 **Stakeholder responsibility** arises from criticisms of profit responsibility, concentrating on the **obligations of the organisation to those who can affect achievement of its objectives**, for example, customers, employees, suppliers and distributors.

Marketing at Work

Social responsibility

Corporate power on the scale of today is unprecedented, Wally Olins (corporate identity expert) says. One man, Bill Gates, has more money than 135 of the United Nations' 185 members; Ford Motor Company has a greater global sales total than the combined gross domestic products of Greece, Ireland and Luxembourg. Consequently, companies must blend their public image with the governments whose wealth and power they dwarf. They must be accountable not just to shareholders, but to consumers and employees.

'Slogans like shareholder value are simply not good enough any more,' says Mr Olins. 'It is now incumbent upon companies to modulate their behaviour to recognise that economic value is insufficient. Consumers have enormous power. They will buy from organisations that match their expectations in both behaviour and product and will be able to destroy those that don't.'

Financial Times, 3 December 1999

Societal responsibility

7.6 **Societal responsibility** focuses on the responsibilities of the organisation **towards the general public**. In particular, this includes a responsible approach to environmental issues and concerns about employment. A socially responsible posture can be promoted by **cause related marketing**, when charitable contributions are tied directly to the revenues from one of its products. An example is Procter & Gamble's support for the Special Olympics when particular products are purchased.

Marketing at Work

Cause-related marketing

Charities face a constant struggle to get both corporations and the general public to support their cause, which many say has grown worse since the launch of the National Lottery.

Generally, individual giving in this country has ground to a halt. Levels of giving are not falling, but we are not getting any more generous. But it's not all bad news. Corporate Britain is becoming increasingly generous.

BPP
PROFESSIONAL EDUCATION

The nature of corporate giving has changed, however. Corporate donations used to be made on a purely philanthropic basis. Today, that philanthropy has been finely tuned to ensure the giver is able to bask in the glow of is own generosity – it's called **cause-related marketing**.

But, says Barnardo's director of marketing and communications Andrew Nebel, this is no bad thing.

'It used to be that the target of a company's philanthropy was the choice of the chairman's wife. Now the selection of a charity is analysed carefully, which means the links, when they are made, are much stronger.

It also enable charities to get access to larger budgets from, for example, companies' marketing departments or staff incentive schemes,' says Nebel.

Marketing Week, 16 December 1999

The social audit

7.7 Socially responsible ideas may be converted into actions through plans developed in the course of a **social audit**. Companies develop, implement and evaluate their social responsibility through a social audit, which assesses their objectives, strategies and performance in terms of this dimension. Marketing and social responsibility programmes may be co-ordinated.

Action Programme 2

What do you think a social audit might involve?

7.8 In the USA, social audits on environmental issues have increased since the Exxon Valdez catastrophe in which millions of gallons of crude oil were released into Alaskan waters. The **Valdez principles** were drafted by the Coalition for Environmentally Responsible Economics to focus attention on environmental concerns and corporate responsibility. They encourage companies to behave responsibly towards the environment.

(a) Eliminate pollutants, minimise hazardous wastes and conserve non-renewable resources

(b) Market environmentally safe products and services

(c) Prepare for accidents and restore damaged environments

(d) Provide protection for employees who report environmental hazards

(e) Appoint an environmentalist to their board of directors, name an executive for environmental affairs, and develop an environmental audit of their global operations, which is to be made publicly available

8 Consumer and community issues

8.1 The consumer movement can be defined as a collection of organisations, pressure groups and individuals who **seek to protect and extend the rights of consumers**. The movement originated in a realisation that **the increasing sophistication of products meant that**

the individual's own judgement was no longer adequate to defend against inappropriate marketing.

Marketing at Work

Four basic consumer rights were identified by US President John Kennedy.

(a) **The right to safety**. Consumers expect that the products they purchase will be inherently safe to use. This right is bolstered in many countries by extensive product liability legislation.

(b) **The right to be informed**. It is not acceptable for marketing communications to suppress important information or make false claims.

(b) **The right to choose**. Companies should not attempt to stifle competition or make comparisons difficult by, for instance, restricting the information they make available.

(d) **The right to be heard**. Complaints should be dealt with fairly, effectively and speedily.

8.2 The main consumer protection body in the UK is the **Office of Fair Trading**. The Director of Fair Trading has a number of roles.

- To promote competition
- To encourage the adoption of codes of practice
- To curb anti-competitive practices
- To issue licences under the Consumer Credit Act
- To administer the Estate Agents Act

8.3 As well as government bodies, there are voluntary associations. Chief of these in the UK is the **Consumers' Association** (CA).

(a) *Which?* magazine is published by the CA every month. It contains detailed reviews of products and services. Each product review features detailed breakdowns of the performance of competing products in a number of tests. Whilst readership of *Which?* magazine is limited, its findings are widely reported in the media.

(b) The CA provides its members with **legal advice**, even acting on members' behalf in some cases, against malpractice or poor service.

(c) **The CA also lobbies Parliament and ministers** on matters such as product safety, labelling, advertising honesty and so forth.

8.4 There are a number of other organisations and groups representing consumer interests.

- National Consumer Council (a government sponsored body)
- National Federation of Consumer Groups
- National Association of Citizen's Advice Bureaux

8.5 Some industries have panels of individuals appointed to represent the consumer interests. This is particularly true of utilities. There are consumer groups representing users of London Underground for example.

8.6 Consumer protection legislation

- Trade Descriptions Act 1968
- Fair Trading Act 1973
- Unfair Contract Terms Act 1977
- Food Act 1984
- Weights and Measures Act 1985
- Consumer Protection Act 1987

Marketing at Work

Product contamination

In 1982, the US healthcare products group Johnson & Johnson wrote the book on crisis management with its deft handling of the poisoned Tylenol affair. In 1999, Coca-Cola appeared to tear the book up in its response to an unfolding fiasco in Europe over sales of tainted Coke.

The partial withdrawal of Coca-Cola products from four European countries set a record for the biggest product recall yet by a packaged goods manufacturer. But a much greater cost arose from the damage done to Cola-Cola's brand, meticulously managed over the past 115 years.

The world's biggest soft drinks maker acknowledged that Coca-Cola products going mainly into the Belgian market had been tainted in two separate incidents. One involved the accidental injection of 'defective' carbon dioxide gas into some cola. In the other, the outside of soft drink cans was contaminated by a fungicide used to treat wooden shipping pallets.

But the admission came only after Coca-Cola had spent most of the preceding week assuring consumers that its products were safe. It made that claim as dozens of Belgian children were being taken to hospital, complaining of stomach cramps, vomiting and dizziness after drinking Coca-Cola products.

There were no confirmed reports of any serious illnesses directly attributable to Coca-Cola's products, and Coca-Cola said that no health or safety issues had been identified. But its proposed solution to the problem fell far short of what the authorities demanded.

Coca-Cola's plan was for a targeted withdrawal of the affected products. Instead, sales of nearly all Coca-Cola's canned and bottled products were banned by the governments of Belgium and Luxembourg. And in France, where only the affected products were banned, some retail chains such as Carrefour removed all Coca-Cola products from their shelves rather than risk confusion.

Coca-Cola also earned hostile headlines in much of northern Europe. In the countries affected, it became the butt of cartoon jokes - such as one showing its trade-mark polar bear writhing in pain, and another changing its name to 'Coca-Colic'.

In terms of the textbook method of dealing with crises such as these, Coca-Cola broke nearly all the basic rules. One is to act quickly to recall the affected products. Another is to be open with consumers about what went wrong, and a third is to show contrition.

The textbook was devised by Johnson & Johnson 17 years ago. It acted after an extortionist tried to wring money out of the company by lacing capsules of its Tylenol painkiller with cyanide, and seven people died.

While the government was still considering what to do, and before the media had time to put the company on the defensive, Johnson & Johnson recalled all Tylenol products. That cost about $100m and it lost short-term sales. But it emerged from the episode with consumer confidence at a higher level than ever, and quickly regained its leadership of the painkiller market.

Financial Times, 17 June 1999

Community issues

8.7 Marketers and organisations are members of a community which expects them to contribute to its well-being. Areas which the marketer might consider as suitable for supporting community growth, and increasing community satisfaction, include education, the arts and disadvantaged groups. The organisation also has a responsibility towards its own employees, which is recognised by modern employment protection legislation and health and safety regulations.

8.8 Recognition of community issues can also have a **long-term benefit** for the organisation. It can generate **goodwill and publicity** and perhaps **affect the attitudes** of potential customers.

Marketing at Work

'Met tackles 999 time wasting with email campaign'

The Metropolitan Police in London has selected interactive mobile services firm Buongiorno to handle an email marketing campaign aimed at cutting time wasting calls. Two million non-urgent calls are received each year, diverting resources from real emergencies.

The integrated campaign operates in two stages, and is the Met's first online marketing campaign. The first stage is an email encouraging 250,000 Londoners to consider several situations, and reinforces the idea that none are worthy of a 999 call. Says Nikki Redmond, head of publicity: 'Targeting Londoners via email and SMS offers an alternative way of reaching our audience. It provides awareness of the problem and an innovative approach to tackling issues around misuse of the 999 facility.'

The second stage enables Londoners who provide their mobile phone number to be sent the number of their local police station via SMS, for storing on their phone until needed. They can opt in to receive further information, and are encouraged to forward the email to family and friends.

Jonathyn Smith of Buongiorno says 'It is fulfilling to use our marketing and technical capabilities and experience on a project that has the ultimate objective of improving community life. The recognition of the power of new media is also very positive....delivering a fully integrated marketing campaign is an ideal way of reaching the target audience.'

Brand Republic, Revolution UK online, March 25th 2003

Exam Tip

When thinking about ethics in the context of a *Marketing Communications* exam question, think about how the marketing communicator can enhance his or her appeal to the ethical consumer. Here are some ideas.

Identify and position the product to a specific target audience

- Formulate and publish your policy for the benefit of both customers and staff. This announces to the world that "We are prepared to be judged against what we say we will do"

- Use third party endorsement, such as the Fairtrade Mark, supported by advertising and promotion

- Use public relations to reinforce the market position

There are risks associated with an avowedly ethical stance. You can make yourself a target for allegations of hypocrisy. Perhaps more significantly, ethical judgements may not be shared by the different cultures that international companies market to. Attitudes to animal welfare, for example, are not universal.

9 Green issues

9.1 **Public awareness of the connections between industrial production, mass consumption and environmental damage is higher than it has ever been**, with information flooding out through the mass media and sometimes generating profound public reaction. Modern marketing practice, then, needs to reflect awareness of these concerns, and is being changed by the issues that they raise. In particular, **food scares, when badly handled** (as in the case of BSE in the UK), **have caused great damage to primary producers and retailers**. When handled well (as, for instance, in the scare over the mineral water Perrier - see above), little damage to sales is caused, and the company or industry may even emerge with an enhanced reputation.

Green concerns

9.2 The modern Green Movement is animated by concerns over pollution, overpopulation and the effects of massive growth on the finite resources of the earth. A series of ecological disasters, notably at the Union Carbide plant at Bhopal, India; the Chernobyl nuclear reactor in Ukraine; the Exxon Valdez oil spill in Alaska; and the torching of the Kuwaiti oilfields at the end of the Gulf War highlighted links between business and environmental damage. According to green thinkers, conventional economics has failed to deal with the problems of overproduction. Green economists have tried to put together an **economics based on alternative ideas**.

- Monetary valuation of economic resources
- Promoting the quality of life
- Self reliance
- Mutual aid
- Personal growth
- Human rights

The impact of green issues on marketing practices

9.3 **Environmental impacts on business**

(a) **Direct**

- Changes affecting costs or resource availability
- Impact on demand
- Effect on power balances between competitors in a market

(b) **Indirect**. Examples are pressure from concerned customers or staff and legislation affecting the business environment.

Green pressures on business

9.4 Consumers are demanding a better environmental performance from companies. In recent surveys, it has been demonstrated that around three-quarters of the population are applying environmental criteria in many purchase decisions.

(a) **Green pressure groups** increased their influence dramatically during the late 1980s. Membership of the largest 13 green groups in the UK grew to over 5 million, with staff of over 1,500.

(b) **Employees** are increasing pressure on the businesses in which they work, partly for ethical reasons.

(c) **Legislation** is increasing almost by the day. Growing pressure from the green or green-influenced vote has led to mainstream political parties taking these issues into their programmes.

(d) **Environmental risk screening** has become increasingly important. Companies in the future will become responsible for the environmental impact of their activities.

Marketing at Work

Coca-Cola and Pepsi were recently fined $4,000 each by India's Supreme Court after painting advertisements on 'ecologically sensitive' rock faces along a highway through the Himalayas. Although such a site may have seemed an attractive idea in terms of generating awareness, the choice of medium backfired.

Head office of both companies claimed not to be aware of what their local franchisees were up to, but this lack of control did not constitute an acceptable excuse and the companies may have to tighten up their operations manuals.

9.5 **Sustainability** requires that the company only uses resources at a rate which allows them to be replenished and confines emissions of waste to levels which do not exceed the capacity of the environment to absorb them. **Policies based on sustainability have three aims**.

- To pursue equity in the distribution of resources
- To maintain the integrity of the world's ecosystems
- To increase the capacity of human populations for self-reliance

Green marketing

9.6 There are strong reasons for bringing the environment into the business equation. The green consumer is a driving force behind changes in marketing and business practices. Green consumption can be defined as **the decisions related to consumer choice which involve environmentally-related beliefs, values and behaviour**. There is extensive evidence that this is of growing importance to business.

- Surveys which indicate increased levels of environmental awareness and concern
- Increasing demand for, and availability of, information on environmental issues
- Value shifts from consumption to conservation
- Effective PR and marketing campaigns by environmental charities and causes

Segmenting the green market

9.7 Profiles of green consumers show that the force of green concern varies. Many consumers have not resolved the complex, confusing and often contradictory messages which are being sent out by various interest groups in this area. Broadly, females are more environmentally-aware than males, and families with children are more likely to be concerned about making green consumption choices. The evidence also shows that consumers are becoming both more aware and more sophisticated in their approach.

9.8 Marketing diagnostics has developed a **typology of green consumers which identifies four main groups**.

(a) **Green activists** (5 - 15% of the population) are members or supporters of environmental organisations.

(b) **Green thinkers** (30%, including the activists) seek out green products and services, and look for new ways to care for the environment.

(c) **Green consumer base** (45 - 60%) includes anyone who has changed behaviour in response to green concerns.

(d) **Generally concerned** (90%) claim to be concerned about green issues.

9.9 A behaviourally-based **psychographic typology** by Ogilvy and Mather involves a range of factors. Four categories of consumers are identified in terms of tendencies and characteristics going beyond environmental matters.

(a) **Activists** (16%)

- Aware of the issue
- Likely to buy green products
- Concerned for their children
- Optimistic about technological change
- People oriented
- Home owners with children
- Conservative voters
- Likely to be upmarket consumers

(b) **Realists** (35%)

- The youngest group - those with young children
- Worried about the environment
- Consider profit and environmental protection as conflicting

- Pessimistic about a solution
- Sceptical about a 'green bandwagon'
- Vote Labour

(c) **Complacents** (28%)

- Upmarket consumers with older children
- Optimistic about mankind, business and government
- Likely to see this as someone else's problem
- Not very conscious of green issues
- Right wing politically

(d) **Alienated** (22%)

- Less well educated, downmarket consumers
- Young families or senior citizens
- Unaware of green issues
- Likely to see greenness as a fashion or a fad
- Pessimistic about a solution
- Left wing politically

9.10 Studies show that consumer behaviour varies in greenness according to the information which is available about the product, the regularity of purchase, the price-sensitivity of the purchase involved, their degree of brand loyalty to existing brands, the availability of substitutes and the credibility of green products.

Exam Tip

Successful green marketing for the marketing communicator (at work, and in the exam!)

(a) Understand the environmental issues which are relevant to the company, customer, products and market environment.

(b) Evaluate the degree to which green product attributes fit consumer needs.

(c) Develop strategies which identify and effectively meet consumer needs and competitor challenges in relation to green issues.

Marketing planning

9.11 Marketing plans need to be reconsidered in the light of **new environmental priorities**. Certain areas will require redefinition.

- Strategic product/market objectives
- Markets
- Market share, customer satisfaction and competitor comparisons
- Performance and technical aspects of product performance and quality

All of these aspects will have to be fitted within **a view of the company's performance which takes account of environmental responsibilities**. In addition, the traditional criteria for evaluating success or failure, and the parameters within which they operate, may well have to be redrawn.

9.12 **Timescales** also have to be lengthened considerably, since products are now evaluated in terms of their long-term effects, as well as the impact of the processes by means of which they have been produced. Programmes designed to clean up environmental impacts often take a long time to become fully operational.

9.13 Getting marketing's 4Ps right leads to profit, according to orthodox ideas. Green marketing insists that the mix must be evaluated in the terms of **four Ss**.

(a) **Satisfaction** of customer needs

(b) **Safety** of products and production for consumers, workers, society and the environment

(c) **Social** acceptability of the products, their production and other activities of the company

(d) **Sustainability** of the products, their production and other activities of the company

The Green Marketing Process
(from Ken Peattie, *Green Marketing*)

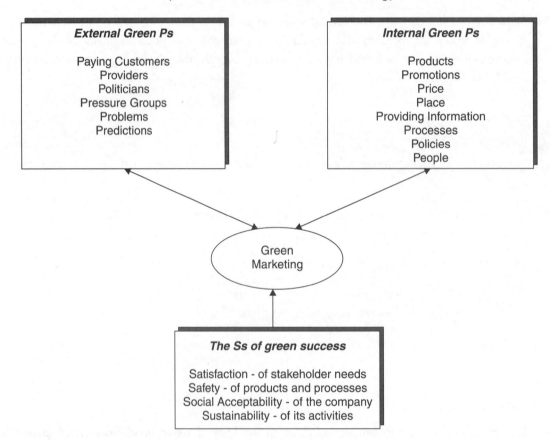

External Green Ps

Paying Customers
Providers
Politicians
Pressure Groups
Problems
Predictions

Internal Green Ps

Products
Promotions
Price
Place
Providing Information
Processes
Policies
People

Green Marketing

The Ss of green success

Satisfaction - of stakeholder needs
Safety - of products and processes
Social Acceptability - of the company
Sustainability - of its activities

Marketing at Work

Green marketing

Being able to predict problems can produce great strategic advantages, but also some odd results. The problem of CFCs from aerosols, and their effects on the ozone layer, was known about from the early 1970s, and Johnson & Johnson abandoned the use of them in their products back in 1976. Consumer reactions to the product began in the late 1980s, and, of course, the firm was well prepared, but found itself in a very strange position, having to attach 'ozone friendly' labels to products which had, in fact, been modified more than ten years before.

This illustrates green marketing problems very well. Action is vital at the time when public *perceptions* threaten a product, rather than the manufacturer simply dealing with the environmental dangers which the product may pose. Green marketing practices will have to deal with more and more of these problems, and the old assumption that these worries are simply a 'moral panic' which will run its course and disappear is surely now revealed as wishful thinking.

Nevertheless, resistance to green marketing within many companies is likely to remain strong. It may be necessary for marketers to market ideas internally for these changes. New products, new communications strategies and messages, new 'clean' plant and technology, new appointments of staff skilled in these areas, and very broad changes in organisational culture will all have to be 'sold' to powerful individuals and groups within organisations. Obviously, the internal politics of business organisations need to be taken into account by green practitioners.

Action Programme 3

What are the implications of green issues for services marketing?

9.14 The **not-for-profit (NFP) sector**, since the profit motive has been blamed for generating wasteful and environmentally damaging over-consumption, would seem to be intrinsically greener. Free market enthusiasts argue that not having to make a profit is more likely to promote waste and inefficiency, since the discipline of competition is absent. Even within the NFP sector, there are likely to be varying factors at work, for instance government departments are more likely to feel a responsibility for the environment than smaller organisations.

10 Strategies for social responsibility

10.1 An organisation can adopt one of **four types of strategy** for dealing with social responsibility issues.

Proactive strategy

10.2 A **proactive strategy** implies taking action before there is any outside pressure to do so and without the need for government or other regulatory intervention. A company which discovers a fault in a product and recalls the product without being forced to, for example, before any injury or damage is caused, acts in a proactive way.

Reactive strategy

10.3 A **reactive strategy** involves allowing a situation to continue unresolved until the public, government or consumer groups find out about it. The company might already know about the problem. When challenged, it will deny responsibility, while at the same time attempting to resolve the problem. In this way, it seeks to minimise any detrimental impact.

Defence strategy

10.4 A **defensive strategy** involves minimising or attempting to avoid additional obligations arising from a particular problem. There are several defence tactics.

- Legal manoeuvring
- Obtaining support from trade unions
- Lobbying government

Marketing at Work

During 2001, a group of large pharmaceutical companies initiated proceedings in the South African courts against the South African government. They wished to prevent the government from importing cheap, private copies of their anti-AIDS drugs. The pharmaceutical companies suffered predictable abuse for 'putting profits before people' and world-wide negative publicity. The companies were following a defence strategy in that they were attempting to prevent the financial damage that would follow the South African government's assumption of moral superiority. This is also an excellent example of the extremely hard choices that ethical considerations can impose.

Accommodation strategy

10.5 An **accommodation strategy** involves taking responsibility for actions, probably when one of the following happens.

(a) Encouragement from special interest groups
(b) Perception that a failure to act will result in government intervention

The essence of the strategy is action to **forestall** more harmful pressure.

10.6 It can be seen that **this strategy falls somewhere between a proactive and a reactive strategy**. McDonalds developed a nutrition-centred advertising campaign in an attempt to appease nutritionists and dieticians who were pressing for detailed nutritional information to be provided on fast food packaging. Action before the pressure arose would have been proactive; action after government intervention in response to the pressure would have been reactive.

Chapter Roundup

- As we saw in Chapter 1, it is vital for marketers to have an understanding of the **processes that customers go through when buying a product**. This applies equally when the customer is an organisation buying the product for use, further processing or resale. The organisational buying process can be simply summarised as follows:

  - Recognition of problem/need
  - Information search
  - Evaluation of alternatives
  - Purchase decision
  - Post purchase evaluation

- The **extent to which a consumer engages in all these stages** will depend on the size, complexity and specific circumstances of the buying situation and a range of influencing factors can be identified that could possibly affect the process. Such factors need to be recognised by marketers so that they are taken into account in marketing and promotional activity.

- **Ethics** are the moral principles and values which guide the thinking, decision making and actions of individuals and groups within society. Many of the most important ethical values form the basis for legislation which governs business activity in general including marketing. However, while ethics deal with personal moral principles and values, laws express the standards of a society which can actually be enforced in court. Ethics and legality are not necessarily congruent.

- Ethical issues can arise in relation to any of the elements of the marketing mix.

- Some businesses have **published ethical codes**, specifying the ethical standards to which they adhere and setting out the standards which they expect all their staff to meet. The AMA has also published a *Code of Ethics*.

- In the UK, there is a growing feeling that the **concerns of the community ought to be the concerns of business**. Social responsibility involves accepting that the organisation is part of society and, as such, will be accountable to that society for the consequences of its actions.

- Three key areas of social responsibility which have implications for marketers are **consumer issues**, **community issues** and '**green**' **issues**.

- **Green marketing** is founded on responsibility for the community and sustainability - the idea that we must be aware of the need for resources to be marshalled and monitored so that the environment can continue to provide inputs and absorb the products of consumption.

- An organisation can adopt one of a number of different strategies for dealing with **social responsibility issues**.

Now try Question 2 in the Question Bank

BPP
PROFESSIONAL EDUCATION

Quick Quiz

1   Define organisational buying.

2   Fill in this grid:

Type of organisational market	Characteristic
P.......................	Organisations that purchase products for the purpose of making a ....
R......................	.... such as retailers and wholesalers who .... the finished goods in order to .... them
G......................	Buy goods and services to support their internal operations and to provide ....
I.......................	Seek to achieve charitable, educational, community or other .... goals.

3   What are the six stages of the organisational buying process?

4   Match the six actors within the DMU (user, influencer, decider, approver, buyer, gatekeeper) to their respective roles:

   (a)   Help define the specification and evaluate the available alternatives: ....
   (b)   Control the flow of information to the buying centre: ....
   (c)   Initiate the buying process and help define purchase specifications: ....
   (d)   Authorise the proposals of deciders and buyers: ....
   (e)   Responsibility for deciding on product requirements and suppliers: ....
   (f)   Authority for the selection of suppliers and negotiating purchase terms: ....

5   When discussing ethics and marketing, there appears to be a .... : what is profitable for a .... may not be in the interest of the ....

6   Give an example of a business practice which is both unethical and illegal.

7   How does stakeholder responsibility differ from profit responsibility?

8   What are the four S's of the green marketing mix?

S............................	S.......................................
S............................	S.......................................

Action Programme Review

1   The result or answer to this activity will depend on items that you have chosen. You are likely to have concluded that while the advertisements will often continue to be 'glossy', they tend to be based ore upon satisfying needs for information on such issues as product functionality, price and distribution rather than more emotional, image-based appeals.

2   ■   Recognising society's expectations and the rationale for engaging in socially responsible activity

       ■   Identification of causes or programmes which are congruent with the mission of the company

       ■   Determination of objectives and priorities related to this programme

       ■   Specification of the nature and range of resources required

       ■   Evaluation of company involvement in such programmes past, present and future

3   Service providers have traditionally thought that green issues are less relevant to them than to other types of business enterprise. Although service enterprises typically do have less environmental impact than other types of business, they still consume resources and generate waste. They still face the same choices in their selection of suppliers, their investments and their contribution to the welfare of staff and customers. In fact, the very proliferation of green marketing practices is creating a growing demand for business services such as environmental auditing, green training, waste management and pollution control specialists.

Answers to Quick Quiz

1   The decision-making process by which formal organisations establish the need for purchased products and services and identify, evaluate and choose among alternative brands and suppliers'.

2

Type of organisational market	Characteristic
Producer	Organisations that purchase products for the purpose of making a profit.
Reseller	Intermediaries such as retailers and wholesalers who buy the finished goods in order to resell them.
Government	Buy goods and services to support their internal operations and to provide public services.
Institutional	Seek to achieve charitable, educational, community or other non-business goals.

3   *Stage 1.* Recognise the problem
      Stage 2. Develop product specifications to solve the problem
      Stage 3. Search for products and suppliers
      Stage 4. Evaluate products relative to specifications
      Stage 5. Select and order the most appropriate product
      Stage 6. Evaluate the product and supplier performance

4   (a)   Influencer
        (b)   Gatekeeper
        (c)   User
        (d)   Approver
        (e)   Decider
        (f)   Buyer

5   Conflict; business organisation/company; customer

6   Employing child labour

7   Stakeholder responsibility arises from criticisms of profit responsibility, concentrating on the obligations of the organisation towards all of those who can affect achievement of its objectives (for example, customers, employees, suppliers and distributors).

8

Satisfaction of customer needs	**S**afety of the products
Social acceptability of the products	**S**ustainability of the products

Part B

Co-ordinated marketing communications

The planning framework and budget

3

Chapter Topic List	
1	Setting the scene
2	The business context
3	Corporate strategy and business strategy
4	Marketing communication objectives
5	Marketing planning
6	Segmenting the market
7	Market targeting
8	How to decide budgets
9	Strategic considerations
10	Controlling the budget

Learning Outcomes

☑ Devise a basic media plan based on specific campaign requirements using both offline and online media

☑ Explain the main elements, activities and linkages associated with the formulation and implementation of a marketing communications plan

☑ Recommend a suitable marketing communications budget

Syllabus References

☑ Draw and describe the main parts of a marketing communications planning framework and explain the principal linkages between the various elements

☑ Explain the main methods used to determine a marketing communications budget

Key Concepts Introduced

- Corporate strategy
- Adstock effect
- Target marketing
- Market segmentation
- Positioning

- Market positioning
- Psychological positioning
- A/S ratio
- Share of voice

1 Setting the scene

1.1 As we have seen in the previous chapters, some basic principles apply to all types of co-ordinated marketing communications. Marketers must be aware of how these can be expected to work in the marketplace. They cannot control all the information that customers gather and process about products, but nevertheless marketing organisations must use these principles of communication in order to develop an effective **co-ordinated marketing communications plan**, and thereby exert some form of control.

1.2 Such plans are vitally important in the modern market, because the marketing mix variables on which marketers have traditionally relied to distinguish themselves from their rivals (product design, lower prices, distribution channels etc) have been changed by the march of technology (see Chapter 10 for more on this). Competitors can copy what is done quicker than ever before.

1.3 It could be that **marketing communications** is one area where it is still possible to differentiate your product or service – making the customer believe what you want him to believe about your company, product, brand or service.

1.4 **Major tasks facing those responsible for marketing communications**

- Who should receive messages
- What the messages should say
- What image of the organisation/brand receivers should retain
- How much is to be invested in the process
- How the messages are to be delivered
- What actions receivers should take
- How the whole process should be controlled
- Determine what was achieved

Marketing at Work

According to Schultz *et al* (*Integrated Marketing Communications – Putting it Together and Making it Work*, 1993):

'What exists in the mental network of the consumer or the prospect is truly where marketing value resides. [It] is what people believe, not what is true. [It] is what people want, not what is available; what people dream about, not what they know that really differentiates one product from another in a parity marketplace. That is why...communications is rapidly becoming the major marketing force of today and certainly tomorrow.'

So the proper co-ordination of all marketing messages becomes extremely important. What the marketer says about a product must fit with whatever information the customer has already collected.

1.5   The nature of the **prevailing market conditions** is an important **context** that needs to be considered when planning and developing marketing communications activities.

1.6   Like all other areas of business activity, marketing communications needs careful housekeeping. The **amount of money available** is the key constraint on marketing communications, and there is growing pressure on total communications expenditure. This is because of fluctuating world economies, increasing media costs and also because methods of measuring the effectiveness of spending have been improved, and wastefulness is more transparent.

1.7   So in the final part of this chapter we consider who sets the **budget** and how, and what can be done to control expenditure and get the best value for money.

2   The business context

2.1   An organisation's interaction with the various markets in which it operates is, of course, crucial. In order that its marketing communications be effective it is necessary to understand the conditions and elements that prevail in specific markets.

- Is the market **expanding or contracting**?

- What are the **values and beliefs** held by the target audience towards your products and those of your competitors?

- What are the attitudes of **intermediaries**?

- What is the nature of **competitive communications**?

2.2   These elements (and others) constitute the business context. An organisation's primary linkage with the market in which a product/brand is distributed is through the strategies and plans that it develops in order to articulate its intentions and manage its designated resources.

3 Corporate strategy and business strategy

Key Concept

Corporate strategy is concerned with identifying the scope of activities and markets with which the company wishes to be associated.

3.1 The direction in which a company will move forward will be dependent upon a number of factors.

- ■ The nature of the changing environment
- ■ The existing and future resource capabilities of the organisation
- ■ The strategies adopted by competitors
- ■ The expectations and values of the management and workforce
- ■ The maintenance of a competitive position within the market

The strategic triangle

3.2 One way of looking at this is from the perspective of the three main players, as in the 'strategic triangle', so called by Japanese management consultant Kenichi Ohmae.

The strategic triangle

3.3 Once the corporate strategy has been decided, this may then be translated into a **business unit strategy**. Business unit strategy is concerned with how individual strategic business units will compete within their chosen market.

3.4 **Functional strategies (or operational strategies)** encompassing marketing, finance, production and personnel will then be created to support the corporate or individual business unit strategy. As part of the marketing mix, a promotional strategy will be devised that will integrate into the strategic marketing plan and contribute to the fulfilment of business unit objectives.

3.5 The framework within which the promotional strategy operates is built upon prior decisions regarding product policy, segmentation and targeting (see sections 5 and 6). As a consequence, should any of these decisions be fundamentally flawed, then the promotional strategy is somewhat restricted by these decisions. Creative advertising may sell the product once, but should the product not meet customer expectations, it may not sell it again.

3.6 This example highlights the contribution that a promotional strategy makes **within the overall corporate strategy**. It also shows how corporate level or business level decisions provide the framework within which the promotional plan can function.

3.7 In the short term, marketing communications are directed against competitors because marketing communications are a type of 'noise'. Two examples are:

- Repositioning
- 'Knocking copy' (eg disputes on which is the cheapest air fare)

4 Marketing communication objectives

4.1 As we have already emphasised, the nature of marketing communications strategy has to be viewed within the context of an **overall marketing strategy**, since a promotional strategy cannot exist in isolation. Prior to the promotional strategy being decided, the company will make a series of **corporate** and/or **business unit** decisions that will determine the nature of the overall marketing strategy. It is this which will then lay down the parameters within which a promotional strategy will be developed.

4.2 Each level of the organisation has a **hierarchy** of:

- Objectives
- Strategy
- Tactics

4.3 **The tactics of the upper level then become the objectives of the next level** down in the organisation. The levels we can usually consider are:

- Corporate (and then business unit, if separately managed)
- Functional (including marketing)
- Activity (including marketing communications)

These relationships are shown in diagram below, Simon Majaro's Planning Hierarchy.

The planning hierarchy
by Simon Majaro

4.4 An organisation's mission statement is a description of long-term vision and values. Mission statements have become increasingly common because they can provide clear guidance to managers and employees on the future direction of the organisation. In particular the mission statement can be used to develop the hierarchy of objectives that link the long-term vision and values with specific objectives at each level of the organisation.

4.5 In order to deliver an effective plan, it is important to **establish marketing communications objectives**. These will involve variables such as perception, attitudes, developing knowledge and interest or creating new levels of prompted and spontaneous awareness.

4.6 It should be clear from the diagram below that for our purposes there are three different forms of objectives: corporate, marketing and marketing communications objectives. Collectively these are referred to as **promotional goals** or **objectives**.

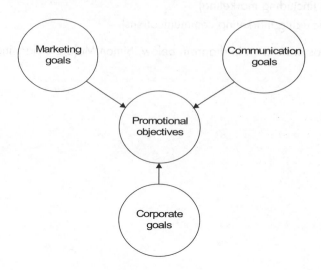

Promotional objectives

4.7 Objectives need to be **specific** in that they must be capable of communicating to a target audience *(who)*, a distinct message *(what)*, over a specified time frame *(when)*. Promotional objectives must therefore include:

- Identification of the **target audience**
- A **clear message**
- **Expected outcomes** in terms of trial purchase, awareness and so on
- A measurement of **results**
- Mechanisms for **monitoring and control**

4.8 The objectives need to be **measurable and therefore quantifiable**. Statements such as 'increase consumer awareness' are vague, whereas 'increase awareness of the 55 - 65 year age group from 40% to 80%' is more precise and capable of measurement.

4.9 Objectives need to be **achievable**. Purely from an internal company perspective, if sales are targeted to increase by 25% over a designated time period then manufacturing capacity will have to be secured to meet this target. Likewise, attempting to gain additional shelf space within a retail outlet will require that additional resources are devoted to the sales force, to sales promotions and to advertising.

4.10 Objectives need to be set with a degree of **realism** rather than on the basis of wild imagination. Otherwise, a company would be better off having no targets at all. An unrealistic target would tend to ignore the competitive and environmental forces affecting the company, the available resources at the company's disposal and the time frame in which the objectives have to be achieved.

4.11 **Finally, objectives need to be timed over a relevant time period**. Although a plan of action may be drawn up for a year, it will be the case that the plan will be reviewed against target, for example monthly or quarterly, so as to enable corrective action to be taken.

4.12 These principles of **SMART** (**s**pecific, **m**easurable, **a**chievable, **r**ealistic and **t**imed) apply not only to the overall communication strategy but also to the setting of objectives for each tool within the **promotional mix**. Once the overall communication strategy has been set then individual (yet co-ordinated) plans need to be devised for each of the five main promotional tools. Using the SMART principle, objectives can be set for advertising, sales promotion, public relations, direct marketing and personal selling.

Types of objectives

4.13 Earlier it was identified in the diagram that there were different types of objectives (or goals). These are **corporate objectives**, **marketing objectives** and **marketing communications objectives**. Each consists of one of two main components - they are either **sales** or **communication based**.

Action Programme 1

Select a television or print advertisement and think about the goals it attempted to achieve.

One of the first things that you might have thought of was that to increase sales was the main goal. What other elements might the advertisers be seeking to achieve?

Is it fair to expect marketing communications to achieve all the marketing plan's objectives?

Sales goals

4.14 If you ask most people what the goal of marketing communications is, then most will respond 'to increase sales'. Ultimately this (and profit) is an important outcome, but ask yourself this: are sales generated by marketing communications alone? What role does each of the other elements of the marketing mix play? How will sales vary if a competitor reduces its prices or you increase yours? What impact do marketing channel and product availability play in sales performance? **Marketing communications is important but it is not the sole contributor to marketing success or failure**.

4.15 One further difficulty associated with sales goals concerns the **impact of past promotional activities**.

Key Concept

This is referred to as the **Adstock effect**. Sales today might be the result of last year's (month's, week's) communications. It is just that the customer was not ready to buy then, but the significance of the communication enabled them to store salient messages and use them when they were ready. Setting sales-based goals fails to account for this important point.

4.16 Sales goals are important and performance can be determined in terms of sales volumes, sales value or revenue, market share, or profitability measures such as return on investment (ROI). They are a useful management aid as they are easy to comprehend and measurement is straightforward.

Communication goals

4.17 In earlier chapters we explored ideas about how marketing communications might work. The AIDA and other 'hierarchy of effects' models are no longer accepted as valid interpretations of the overall process. However, the essence of these **sequential models** is that in order to achieve a sale, each buyer must move, or be moved, through a series of steps. These steps are **essentially communication-based stages** whereby individuals learn more about a product and mentally become more disposed towards adjusting their behaviour in favour (or not) of purchasing the item.

4.18 Awareness is an important state to be achieved as without awareness of a product's existence it is unlikely that a sale is going to be achieved. To achieve **awareness** people need to see or **perceive** the product, they need to **understand** or **comprehend** what it might do for them (benefits) and they need to be **convinced** that such a purchase would be in their best interest and to do this there is a need to develop suitable **attitudes** and **intentions**.

Corporate communication goals

4.19 **Analysis of the organisational context** will have determined the extent to which action is required to communicate with members and non-members. Corporate communications, particularly with employees, and corporate branding to develop the image held by key stakeholders, should be integral to such co-ordinated marketing communication campaigns. These tasks form a discrete part of the communication programme.

4.20 In addition to this, it is the responsibility of the communication programme to **communicate the mission and purpose of the organisation in a consistent** and understandable form. In addition, the organisation needs to be able to listen and respond to communications from their stakeholders in order that they are able to adjust their position in the environment and continue to pursue their corporate goals.

5 Marketing planning

5.1 Marketing communication strategies are intended to support and deliver the marketing objectives. **Marketing objectives are prepared and articulated through a marketing plan**. This document acts as a cornerstone for the development of effective marketing communications.

Marketing communications planning framework

Exam Tip

This framework should ideally be learnt, as it can be applied to most questions about marketing planning. For example, a question in December 2002 under the old *Integrated Marketing Communications* syllabus asked how the use of a marketing communications planning framework might assist the development of a campaign to promote a range of motor oils. Mere recitation of the framework is not enough – you need to be able to extract the communication issues associated with it and discuss them in the context of the question.

It represents a structure whereby marketing communications plans can also be developed for use in your other studies, and in the workplace. Whether you work for a large multinational, a not-for-profit organisation, a medium sized service sector organisation or a small independent trading company, the structure is equally applicable.

Context analysis

5.2 It should be clearer now that **each marketing communications programme is developed in unique circumstances**. It is vitally important that the contextual conditions are analysed in order that any factor that may influence the content, timing or the way the audience receives and interprets information, be identified and incorporated within the overall plan.

5.3 In order to help provide for a systematic appraisal of the prevailing and future conditions, a context analysis is recommended when formulating a marketing communications programme. This consists of a review of the various sub-contexts.

Main sub-contexts:

Exam Tip

This framework is not prescriptive, and other frameworks and factors can be introduced, reflecting the organisation or brand and its particular conditions at any one moment. Students may wish to utilise this framework to help develop their understanding and familiarity with this concept.

The elements of context analysis

The business context

5.4 This part of the analysis involves a consideration of the markets and conditions in which the organisation is operating, which are of prime concern for the co-ordinated marketing communication programme.

5.5 **Competitors' communications**, general **trading conditions** and trends, the organisation's **corporate and marketing strategies**, a detailed analysis of the **target segment's** characteristics and a **brand audit** are the primary activities associated with this context.

The customer context

5.6 Here the emphasis is upon understanding **buyer behaviour** and the decision-making processes that buyers in the market exhibit. The objective is to isolate any key factor in the process or any bond that customers might have with the product/brand. This can then be reflected in any communication.

The stakeholder context

5.7 Co-ordinated marketing communications recognises that there are **audiences other than customers**, with whom organisations need to communicate. For example, members of the marketing channel, the media, the financial community, local communities and shareholders all seek a dialogue with the focus organisation. The strength and duration of the dialogue may vary but messages need to be developed and communicated and the responses need to be understood and acted upon wherever necessary.

The organisational context

5.8 The characteristics of the organisation can impact heavily on the nature and form of the communications they enter into. It is important, therefore, to consider the **culture and the strength of identity the workforce has with the organisation**. This is of absolute importance if truly co-ordinated communications are to be forged. In order to appreciate the strength of this sub-context think about the way the staff of different companies communicate with you as a customer. Internal and external audiences communicate with each other and this is a significant part of co-ordinated marketing communications.

The external context

5.9 Co-ordinated marketing communications is influenced by a number of factors in the wider environment. These political, economic, social and technological elements are largely uncontrollable by organisations, for example economic conditions or the laws and regulations. Nevertheless, they can shape and determine what, when and how messages are communicated to audiences.

Exam Tip

Marketing communications occur in particular contexts. It is very helpful when developing strategy and writing communication plans to understand the prevailing contextual conditions. It is also good exam practice to imagine the different forces and restraints operating on marketers. Consider for example the following circumstances.

- Launching new products
- Reviving a flagging brand
- Price competition
- Introducing a new variant
- A new competitor enters the market
- Regulations change
- Promotional budget is slashed

5.10 Linkages within the marketing communications planning framework (Fill, *Marketing Communications – Contexts, Strategies and Applications, 2002*)

	Derived from:
Objectives	The marketing plan (including the competitor analysis) in - The business context - The customer context - The stakeholder context - The internal context
Strategic balance (3Ps)	An understanding of the brand, the needs of the target audiences (including employees and other stakeholders) and the marketing goals.
Brand/product positioning	The perception, attitudes and motivations of users and non-users.
Message content and style	An understanding of the level of involvement, perceived risk, DMU analysis, information processing styles and positioning intentions.
Promotional tools and media	An analysis of the target audience and their media habits, involvement and preferences, media compatibility, competitor analysis and resource review.

Exam Tip

The examiner will test understanding of the planning process. This might be through the preparation of a marketing communication plan. However, you might be asked to explain the linkages between the various parts of the plan or asked to focus on the key strategic elements. Whatever the tasks required students are advised strongly to develop their understanding of this framework and to practise its application to mini-case questions

5.11 Summary

(a) The essence of the **marketing communications planning framework** (MCPF) is that the process begins with an attempt to understand the **context** within which the communications are expected to work. This is referred to as the **context analysis**. This leads to the determination of objectives or the particular desired outcomes from the marketing communications activities: for example, an increase in the number of people who are aware of a new product offering.

(b) From this point, a communication strategy is developed that is essentially a **determination** of the **overall focus** of the marketing communication activities. This is then supported by the development of suitable **messages** and the formulation of suitable **promotional mixes**.

(c) **Human and financial resources** need to be assessed before a schedule is determined and the plan implemented.

(d) The final part of the process is to **investigate what has been achieved** in the campaign and to use the knowledge as an input into the next context analysis as the cycle is repeated for the next promotional exercise.

6 Segmenting the market

6.1 Within this framework, an understanding of the **target audience** is fundamental to marketing communications.

Key Concept

The **target marketing process** (TMP) consists of segmenting the market, targeting particular segments and then positioning the offer in the selected segment in order to achieve the marketing goals.

6.2 We have included information about segmentation here as it is an important part of the promotional plan, although you will be familiar with much of this material.

Market segmentation

Key Concept

Market segmentation is the process of breaking down the total market into segments that share common properties, that is, customers who behave in a similar way and who can be reached by similar strategies.

6.3 The overriding requirement for modern marketing is **better targeting at specific segments**. This applies to a range of activities including the location of a new retail superstore, the stocking of a range of products, the placement of an advertisement in a newspaper and the launching of a new product into the market. The key aim is to communicate effectively with as many people as possible within a given market, while minimising the waste in communicating with those people in whom the organisation is not interested.

Bases for segmentation

6.4 The major issue surrounding the debate on market segmentation is the criteria upon which markets are segmented. There are five main **bases upon which markets can be segmented**.

- Geographics
- Demographics (including socio-economics, age, race, religion)
- Geodemographics
- Psychographics (including attitudes, interests, opinions and lifestyle)
- Behaviour (including benefits sought, brand loyalty/usage rates, situation specifics)

Geographic segmentation

6.5 **Geographic segmentation** is possibly one of the easiest forms of dividing markets into individual segments. This form of segmentation depends upon there being discernible disparities in consumer buying behaviour between one region and the next.

Demographic segmentation

6.6 **Demographics** encompass age, sex, education, income, occupation and family composition. Consumption of holidays and of clothing provide good examples of segmentation based upon age. An important element within this form of segmentation is the **family life cycle**. Wells and Gubar established the nine stage family life cycle outlined below.

Stage of life cycle	Characteristics
1 Bachelor stage: young single people living at home	Have limited or no financial commitments. Buy stereos, cars and fashion conscious.
2 Newly married couples. Dual incomes, no children	Financially well off, tend to buy consumer durables.
3 Full nest 1: youngest child under 6	Cash position is low, savings are minimal. Purchase toys, clothes, baby foods and some white goods.
4 Full nest 2: oldest child over 6	Returning to dual incomes, savings improving; purchasing bicycles, computers, holidays.
5 Full nest 3: older married couples with dependent children	Financially more secure, some children working, increased ability to purchase desirables and luxury goods.
6 Empty nest 1: children left home and head of household still in work	House ownership at a peak, savings at a maximum; purchase holidays and spend more on recreation and home improvements.

Stage of life cycle	Characteristics
7 Empty nest 2: older married, no children at home, husband and wife retired	Reduction in income, dependent upon pension, savings and investments. Health conscious and buy medical products.
8 Solitary survivor in the workforce	Income high.
9 Solitary survivor, retired, dependent	Income at its lowest, may sell home, may require attention.

6.7 The **changing political and social environment**, and altering attitudes and expectations are impinging upon this analysis. The traditional associations between age and life-styles are changing, requiring a new marketing focus. Some examples include:

(a) More women are having children later in life

(b) Older people are now more likely to engage in leisure and sports pursuits later in their lives, as well as embarking upon new challenges, such as education

(c) There is a rising incidence of divorce, and so there are more single parent families

(d) Many young couples are leaving it later and later to get married

(e) The need for increased financial awareness and planning at a younger age will affect disposable income in earlier years (ie stages 2 and 3), while improving financial spending power in later years (stages 6 and 7). This has been brought about because of the prospect of cutbacks in state pensions so that many more people have taken out their own pensions policies. This has provided the opportunity for financial institutions to promote a wide range of products to the younger age groups.

6.8 One of the more common means of demographic segmentation is by **socio-economic grading**. This involves characterising a market by occupational status, related specifically to the head of the household. Commonly referred to as the AB/C1/C2/DE classification, it is based upon JICNARS (Joint Industry Committee on National Readership Surveys) and assumes that buying behaviour is related to occupational types.

A: Upper middle class
B: Middle class
C1: Lower middle class
C2 Skilled working class
D: Manual workers
E: Those at the lowest level of subsistence

6.9 This approach has some major weaknesses.

(a) It tends to ignore income, especially dual incomes where both the husband and wife are in employment.

(b) Concentration on the 'head of household' occupation wrongly assumes that buying behaviour by other family members will be related to this.

(c) While comparisons between the highest and lowest categories may afford some benefits, comparisons between the middle groups are somewhat less useful.

6.10 Nonetheless, this basis is still widely used because the main newspapers present their readership profiles in this manner and because the information that supports this system is relatively easily obtained.

Geodemographics

6.11 **Geodemographics** (locality marketing) can be defined as the analysis of people according to where they live. It relies on the concept that people live in relatively homogenous neighbourhoods, and that these neighbourhoods are capable of classification.

Widely-used geodemographic systems

6.12 (a) *ACORN* (A Classification Of Residential Neighbourhoods) divides up the entire UK population in terms of the type of housing in which they live. For each of these areas, a wide range of demographic information is generated and the system affords the opportunity to assess product usage patterns, dependent upon the research conducted within national surveys. There are 54 separate groupings, including, the following examples.

- Wealthy suburbs, large detached houses
- Private flats, elderly people
- Gentrified multi-ethnic areas
- Rural areas, mixed occupations
- Council areas, residents with health problems

(b) *MOSAIC.* This system also analyses information from various sources including the census, which is used to give housing, socio-economic, household and age data; the electoral roll, to give household composition and population movement data; postcode address files to give information on post 1991 housing and special address types such as farms and flats; and the CCN files/Lord Chancellor's office to give credit search information and bad debt risk respectively.

Marketing at Work

Circular Distributors claims to be the leader in Britain in delivering advertising leaflets and free samples door to door: it claims to deliver to 19.5m of the UK's 22m households.

The company uses Mosaic, which splits UK residents into a number of consumer types, categorised by income levels, addresses (grouped into postcode areas) and tastes as indicated by certain products and services.

As a general rule, for instance, people in Merseyside spend 20 per cent more per head on toys and other products for children (such as prams) than people elsewhere in the UK. In Surrey, people are 20 per cent less likely to visit pubs regularly and only half as likely to go to wine bars as the average British citizen.

Using this type of data, split up into much smaller areas, comprising around 700 or so households, Circular Distributors can decide on which areas of Britain are most likely to be receptive to the specific promotional offers or adverts that one of its clients wants dropped through people's letterboxes on a targeted basis.

In this way, for example, literature related to special deals in a cut-price supermarket would find its way to poorer households in a run-down inner city area, while wealthier families in the suburbs might receive leaflets asking them to take expensive holidays.

Source: *Financial Times*

Behavioural segmentation: benefits sought

6.13 **Benefit segmentation** relates to the different benefits being sought from a product or service by customer groups. Individuals are segmented directly according to their needs. In this form of segmentation, it is usual for varying customer groups to obtain the same benefits from the product or service.

6.14 Individuals can be categorised by usage patterns, whether they are light, medium or heavy users of a product or service. The TGI (Target Group Index) helps to identify these groups for a wide range of products and services. This form of segmentation assists the marketer in developing distinct and personalised strategies aimed at specific users, based upon their existing consumption of a product or service. For example, banks and other financial institutions are introducing incentive schemes for customers when using their credit cards. This potentially allows heavy users of the service to amass points and convert them into gifts.

Behavioural segmentation: situation specific

6.15 Situation specific segmentation refers to the actual situation in which consumption of the product takes place. Dependent upon the situation, it would appear that a different form of the product may be appropriate, or even an alternative brand. For example, the purchase of ice cream may vary in relation to the following situations:

- A special occasion
- Everyday consumption by the family
- An outdoor picnic
- In a restaurant
- In groups or alone

6.16 In each of these situations the consumer will evaluate alternative product types and brand offerings. Where the evaluation of brands takes place, the attributes of each brand will also vary in importance depending upon the situation in which consumption takes place. Part of the communication process is to keep the brand at the forefront of the consumer's evoked set, and to emphasise the situation specific benefits of the product.

Action Programme 2

Nestlé manufacture a range of confectionery products that fit with this situation specific typology, these include Quality Street, After Eights and Kit Kat. For each of these products:

- Identify the situation for which they are purchased
- Identify the target groups
- Evaluate the communication techniques used for each product

Psychographics

6.17 An individual's activities, interests, opinions and values represent that person's lifestyle. Quantitative measures of lifestyle are known as psychographics.

6.18 **Psychographic segmentation** provides a richer analysis of the consumer than is provided by simple demographic segmentation. It does not replace demographic segmentation but enhances it, and in so doing provides the opportunity to target individual consumers more precisely within a specific geographic area.

6.19 **EXAMPLE**

A major tour operator in the UK recognised the difference between demographics and psychographics and the implications for developing a promotional strategy. Two families living next door to one another, with similar family life cycles and income profiles, demonstrated different attitudes to spending their holidays. One family was keen on package holidays abroad, while the other family preferred camping and walking holidays. **The two families have similar demographic profiles but contrasting psychographic lifestyles**. The consequence is a need for alternative communication strategies.

6.20 **Lifestyle segmentation** groups people in relation to how they spend their time and money. Traditional socio-economic groupings aggregate individuals in terms of their occupation. Recent lifestyle analysis deals with how people spend their money rather than how much they earn. Young and Rubicam, the international advertising agency, developed an alternative segmentation system, the Four Cs (Cross-Cultural Consumer Classification), which identified the following groups.

Group	Characteristics
Mainstreamers	■ Brand conscious ■ Seek security/reliability ■ Risk averse ■ Buy British
Aspirers	■ Image conscious ■ Seek individual recognition ■ Conspicuous consumption ■ Fashion oriented
Achievers	■ Career oriented ■ Achieved personal success ■ Like to be in control ■ Personal wealth

Group	Characteristics
Reformers	■ Value of life ■ Highly educated ■ Independent ■ Family oriented

6.21 The major problem with psychographics is that, unlike other segmentation approaches, it is difficult to assign any form of specific measures. Although it is possible to identify the number of males aged 24-35 in a given area earning £25,000 per annum, it is almost impossible to estimate how many are fun-loving, carefree and fashion-oriented. Nonetheless, this does not prevent advertising agencies portraying these and other characters as part of the communications message. Psychographics today within the advertising industry is inextricably tied in with other demographic and economic descriptions.

Action Programme 3

With reference to Young and Rubicam's Four Cs, identify recent advertisements on television that refer to each of the groups specified. For each one, evaluate to what extent the characteristics portrayed are similar and identify other factors that are indicated.

Criteria for effective segmentation

6.22 One of the **problems** of market segmentation is determining **to what extent definable market segments are worth pursuing**, especially when considering developing an individual promotional campaign. There are a number of criteria that need to be satisfied in order for a market segment to be deemed commercially viable.

6.23 **Size** or **substantiality**. One of the first questions to be asked concerns whether the market is of sufficient size to justify attention. Will the segment generate sufficient demand and hence sales to help create the required return from the sector? This will depend to some extent on the resources at the disposal of the company. Many small segments can be identified but they are not seen as being worthy of any further attention. Morgan, the family run car manufacturer, which produces fewer than 10 cars a year, finds the segment in which it competes lucrative, while Ford and GM would undoubtedly find this market unprofitable.

6.24 **Measurability**. The market segment needs to have characteristics that will assist in measuring the market potential both for the producer and the consumer. It is necessary to establish whether there are discrete groups of people with relatively homogeneous buying habits.

6.25 **Access**. A necessary prerequisite is that the market is capable of being accessed both from the point of distribution and promotion. A fairly scattered market segment in terms of geographic penetration would lead to wasted promotional expenditure if it appealed to only 10% of the market. Modern direct marketing techniques, however, reduce the potential waste, especially if the market segment can be easily identified.

6.26 Uniqueness in response. The market segment identified must exhibit similar behavioural characteristics in as much as the individuals making up the segment would all respond in a similar way to a targeted marketing strategy.

6.27 Stability. For any company to divert resources to a particular market segment that has been identified, it must reassure itself that the segment will remain fairly stable over a long enough time period to warrant specific marketing attention.

6.28 Actionability. This is the degree to which marketing programmes can be formulated for attracting and servicing segments.

Marketing at Work

A marketing programme to expand the volume of sales for existing Rolls Royce models by attracting people on only average incomes is obviously *not* actionable. If Rolls Royce chose to expand its targets, a new product would need to be developed.

7 Market targeting

7.1 Once the market has been segmented along the relevant bases, the marketing manager must decide which market to target. The target market decision relates to the selection of the specific segment or segments towards which the promotional effort will be focused. The firm has four options:

- **Undifferentiated** marketing
- **Differentiated** marketing
- **Concentrated** marketing
- **Customised** marketing

7.2 **Undifferentiated or mass marketing** occurs where an organisation tends **to ignore the differences that exist within a market, and aims to provide a standard product or service to a wide variety of customers**. It is more appropriate for some product forms (for example, Intel computer chips) than others.

7.3 **Differentiated marketing** acknowledges the differences that exist in customer tastes and a **separate marketing mix is developed for each identifiable market segment**. This strategy is quite **common in large companies**, as is reflected in a trend towards multiple product offerings. **Kellogg's**, the breakfast cereal manufacturer, adopts multiple marketing strategies to accommodate the requirements of a diverse market, including children, adults, families, the health conscious, and weight watchers.

7.4 **Concentrated marketing focuses attention solely upon a distinct customer group** to the exclusion of all others. The aim is to concentrate on one segment and focus resources on excellence. Examples include Ferrari (car manufacturer) and Steinway (piano manufacturer), where the company targets individuals and/or groups on one or a combination of characteristics, such as income or age. The danger of concentration is that a market can dry up with amazing rapidity.

7.5 **Customised marketing** refers to the extent to which organisations will move towards individually-tailored products to meet individual customer needs. Some car manufacturers are working towards computer-generated cars which will reflect the personal whims and desires of the customer. Financial products offered by the banking and financial sector are increasingly reflecting the need for tailoring to individual financial circumstances.

7.6 The fundamental basis on which the marketer selects one of these approaches to the segments available is a **cost/benefit analysis**. The marketer expects to generate additional revenue from a segment by satisfying the needs of that group, and by developing effective promotional activities that better match that segment. In doing so, the marketer incurs additional costs for new advertisements, promotions, sales force activities, public relations campaigns and so on. The marketer will only choose to develop a new segment if the **incremental revenues generated exceed the incremental costs of serving that segment**.

Effective positioning

7.7 According to the basic principles of marketing, products and services are created to solve customer 'problems' (that is, to satisfy needs and wants) and provide benefits. Thus, to be effective, **positioning must promise the benefit the customer will receive**, create the expectation, and offer a solution to the customer's problem. If at all possible, the solution should be different from and better than the competition's solution, especially if the competitors are already offering their own solution.

Key Concept

Positioning is about how the target market perceives the presentation of the product/service relative to competing products. It is what is in the minds of the target audience.

7.8 Positioning should be a single-minded concept, an umbrella from which everything else in the organisation flows. Perhaps the most important aspect of positioning is that **a company should not try to be all things to all people**. A company that tries to be the high quality service provider to all niches while offering an array of special capabilities at a low price is likely to fail.

7.9 Properly targeted, single-minded positioning affects everything a product does or stands for, not only advertising, but also all its promotions. Positioning also affects policies and procedures, employee attitudes, customer relations, complaint handling, and the myriad of other details that combine to make up the customer's experience.

7.10 There must be a consistency among a company's various offerings and it is the positioning statement that guides this consistency.

7.11 Tests of effective positioning

- The position must be **believable** in the customer's mind.
- The **product must deliver that promise** on a consistent basis.

There is no point in implementing a particular positioning strategy just because a market analysis reveals that an **opportunity exists**. For instance, if an analysis reveals a potential opportunity for a high-quality premium-priced positioning strategy, the first thing to ask is **whether your company** is suited for such an approach.

7.12 It is imperative that everyone in the company 'buys into' the strategy. In other words, the positioning strategy should permeate the entire organisation, from the CEO to the sales force to the delivery driver. **The biggest positioning mistake a company can make is to create a false impression that it cannot live up to in the marketplace**.

Developing a successful positioning strategy

7.13 The positioning process consists of the various steps needed to develop an effective positioning strategy. This process must be continuous to keep up with changes in the environment, including the changing needs of the customer and the competitors' tactics.

Market positioning

7.14 Market positioning is the first step.

Key Concept

Market positioning is defined as the process of identifying and selecting markets or segments that represent business potential, to determine the criteria for competitive success.

This must be based on a thorough knowledge of the needs, wants, and perceptions of the target market, along with the benefits offered by the company's products or services.

(a) What is **important** to the target market?
(b) How does the target market **perceive the product**?
(c) How does the target market **perceive the competition**?
(d) What **attributes** should a product use to **differentiate** itself?

7.15 The reality is that if the target market does not perceive the image, the image does not exist. If the target market does not believe that what the product has to offer is a benefit, it is not a benefit. If the target market doesn't believe that the benefit can be delivered, promises are meaningless. If the benefit isn't important to the target market, it isn't important. If the benefit is not perceived as being different from that of the competition, then differentiation has not succeeded. **In short, images, benefits, and differentiation are solely the perception of the customer, not the perceptions of production managers or marketers**.

Psychological positioning

7.16 This step utilises communications to convey a product's identity and image to the target market. It converts customer needs into images and positions a product in the customers' minds.

Key Concept

Psychological positioning is a strategy employed to create a unique product image with the objective of creating interest and attracting customers.

7.17 **There are two kinds of psychological positioning**: **objective positioning and subjective positioning**.

(a) **Objective positioning**

　(i) **What is it?** Objective positioning is concerned, almost entirely, with the objective attributes of the physical product. It means creating an image about the product that reflects its physical characteristics and functional features.

　(ii) **How is it used?** If a product has some unique feature, that feature may be used to position the product objectively, to create an image, and to differentiate it from the competition.

　(iii) **Drawbacks**. Less successful objective positioning occurs when the feature is not unique. This is why many product promotions fail to create a distinct image or successfully differentiate the product. One of the first rules of effective positioning is uniqueness.

(b) **Subjective positioning**

　(i) What is it? Subjective positioning is concerned with subjective attributes of the product. Subjective positioning is the **image, not of the physical aspects of the product, but of other attributes perceived by the customer** (that is, attributes that do not necessarily belong to the product but to the customer's mental perception). These perceptions and the resulting images may not necessarily reflect the true state of the product's physical characteristics. They may simply exist in the customer's mind and not all customers' imaginings will agree with a particular perception or image. What the marketer hopes is that the people in the **target market will agree on a favourable image** whether or not the image is true.

Positioning strategies

7.18 Marketers may decide to select the most appropriate of the following strategies, depending on the information gathered during market and psychological positioning. (There is some overlap between the strategies: for instance superb after-sales service could be offered simply as a customer benefit or as something that a competitor does *not* offer).

- Attribute, feature or customer benefit
- Price and quality
- Use or application
- Product user
- Product class dissociation
- Competitor

Action Programme 4

For each of the positioning strategies mentioned below, identify a product and/or a service that fits into the category.

7.19 Positioning by **attribute or feature** involves positioning the product by clearly identifying it **with a distinct set of attributes which distinguish the product within the market**. BMW, the German car manufacturer, while positioned within the luxury end of the car market, make constant reference to the engine performance and design as part of their positioning statement. Likewise, Volvo the Swedish car manufacturer have for many years positioned themselves on safety features incorporated into the design of the car.

7.20 Another way to differentiate yourself from the competition is by providing **a unique range of services**. Depending on the characteristics of your local market, unique capabilities could include 24-hour operations, free pickup and delivery, or electronic commerce (online file transfer and on-demand output).

7.21 **Exceptional customer service** can be another differentiator. For obvious reasons, customers prefer vendors who follow their instructions and offer a simple ordering system, on-time delivery, easy problem-resolution, timely and accurate invoicing, and personalised service.

Marketing at Work

Positioning and differentiation strategies online

It has been suggested that, in an online context, retailers can position their products relative to competitor offerings according to four main variables: product quality, service quality, price and fulfilment time.

(These positioning options have much in common with Porter's competitive strategies of cost leadership, product differentiation and innovation.)

The aim of positioning is to develop a perceived advantage over rivals' products. In an e-marketing context the advantage and positioning can be communicated by developing an **online value proposition (OVP)**. For maximum effectiveness the OVP should clarify:

- A clear differentiation of the online proposition compared to the conventional offline proposition.

- A clear differentiation of the online proposition from competitors based on cost, product innovation or service quality.

- Target market segment(s) that the proposition will appeal to.

- How the proposition will be communicated to website visitors, and in all marketing communications.

- How the proposition is delivered across different parts of the buying process

- How the proposition will be delivered and supported by resources.

Price and quality

7.22 **Price and quality** are becoming increasingly important as companies attempt to offer more features, better value and improved quality at competitive prices.

7.23 **Price**. Some companies go for the bottom line: they attract customers by being the lowest cost service providers in the market. They do this by having highly efficient operations, so their cost-per-unit (eg per square foot, per page, etc) of output is the lowest. This does not necessarily mean those businesses spend less money than their competitors. For example, the price leader in a given market will probably do the most advertising, but because of the high volume of work the advertising helps bring in, the business will achieve the lowest cost per unit. However, a low-price positioning strategy always requires a high volume of business.

7.24 **Quality**. A company that provides exceptional quality to its customers can command a higher price for its services than its less quality-conscious competitors. However, quality is a variable that customers may take for granted after a while. When a competitor offers those customers a lower price, some of them might give the competitor a try, and may find out they 'get what they pay for'.

7.25 If a company intends to sell its quality programme in order to charge higher prices for its services, then it must be willing to invest the time and money required to live up to the higher expectations of its customers. If it creates expectations of superior quality but fails to deliver, few customers will give the company a second chance.

Use or application

7.26 In the third case, the company attempts to position its product or service by deliberately associating it with a specific **use or application**. Kellogg's, the cereal manufacturer, in striving to defend their market position and increase sales, have positioned their main product Corn Flakes as an 'any time of day food', and not just to be eaten at breakfast.

Product user

7.27 Positioning by virtue of product user associates the product with a particular class of user. SmithKline Beecham have positioned 'Lucozade Sport' with the sporting fraternity, and have strengthened this through endorsement advertising using major sporting personalities.

Product class dissociation

7.28 It is possible to position a company brand against a product class or an associated product class, claiming that yours is different from the rest. Heinz, who produce a range of 'Weight Watcher' foods, are positioning these against normal but more calorific foods.

Competitors

7.29 A **competitor's position** within a market may be used as a frame of reference in order to create a distinct positioning statement. Avis car rental used the slogan 'We're number 2, so we try harder'. Here the market leader is being used as a reference point to create a competitive statement. The key determinant for the marketer is whether claims made within a promotional campaign which use blatant comparisons can be substantiated through better quality, service, value, cost and so on.

7.30 This approach is used when it is necessary to meet the competition head-on; to bring out differences between products. For example, Visa credit cards competed with American Express by showing examples of places from around the world that do not accept American Express but do accept Visa.

Marketing at Work

Ice cream success is in the difference

The premium ice cream sector had been dominated by the sophistication of the Haagen-Dazs brand, and previous challenges had come to ground after challenging head on with similar approaches to branding and communications. Having established brand presence via limiting distribution and selective use of PR, Ben and Jerry's finally took on Haagen-Dazs but chose a very different approach. Rather than promote luxuriousness via sexual connotations which had been the Haagen-Dazs theme, B&J's built a position based on humour.

The communications aim to remain true to the original brand positioning of the niche, loveable underdog. The success of the brand led to its acquisition by the giant food group Unilever.

From *Marketing Business*, July/August 2000.

Perceptual product mapping

7.31 Part of the positioning strategy involves **mapping the competing products** within a defined product class so that specific gaps may be identified into which the company may place a new product offering. These perceptual product maps identify the attributes that are strongly associated within a given product class. For example, below is shown a hypothetical product map that may be appropriate for the shampoo market.

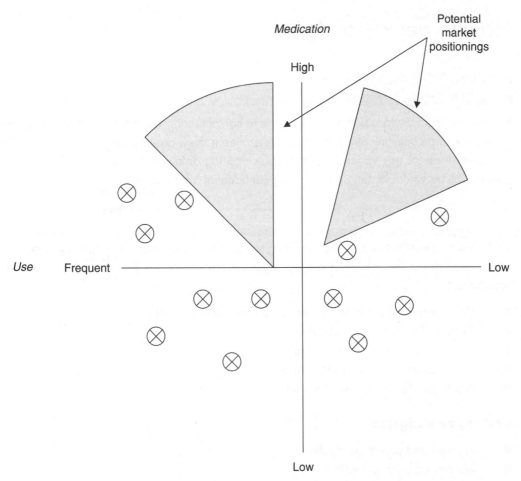

Hypothetical product positioning map 'Hair shampoo'

7.32 By plotting the competing products on this map, it would be possible to identify the gaps that exist within the market, and enable new products to be positioned accordingly in the mind of the consumer. Since the map illustrated is only two dimensional, it must be remembered that other factors will need to be taken into consideration, such as price, which will undoubtedly affect the optimal marketing mix employed for the new product.

 Exam Tip

When considering the importance of marketing planning for the exam, remember that the ultimate success of any promotional strategy will be dependent upon a number of inter-related factors, such as the creative stance adopted, choice of media, sales training and so on.

However, these issues are dependent upon two main strategic choices, made at the planning stage:

The chosen segment in which the company will compete

The nature of the positioning statement, which will influence consumer choice.

These two issues will determine to what extent the company is able to create for itself a definite competitive edge within its chosen market.

8 How to decide budgets

For several organisations with which you are in contact, carry out a review of how they decide their marketing communications budgets. Determine if there are any similarities and decide what the reasons are for any variety in methods. Comparing data with friends and colleagues at college will be valuable, but don't give out confidential information.

8.1 There is no one uniform method of deciding what to spend on marketing communications. This is not so surprising. The following are some of the considerations that can affect the amount of expenditure.

- What variety of marketing communications is to be used?
- What tasks are to be undertaken?
- How competitive is the market place?
- How well known is the organisation?
- Are there any special requirements?

8.2 Costs to be budgeted

- Air time and broadcast media
- Space and printed media
- Production costs
- Staff salaries
- Overheads and expenses

Theoretical approaches to budgeting

8.3 Theoretical approaches to setting budgets, for example by marginal costing approaches, have not found favour in industry because the effects of **any marginal increase on expenditure are likely to be swamped**, or at least hidden, by many other marketing variables. The effects of any expenditure will have both long-term and short-term effects. It is worthwhile emphasising the view here that **marketing communications should be treated as an essential long-term investment**.

Marketing at Work

Marketing Metrics

The total amount spent on marketing in the UK last year was £20bn - probably. But it could have been £25bn or even £30bn, no one really knows.

This uncertainty is evidence of a curious paradox. On the one hand, marketing is vital to business and accounts for truly staggering sums of money; on the other, much of it is ill-defined and unaccountable.

There is little understanding, outside the discipline, of how marketing budgets are arrived at, even though they are sometimes the largest single company expenditure.

There is no standard vocabulary and no agreement on how to measure the effectiveness of these vast budgets. There isn't even an agreed definition of what constitutes 'spending on marketing'.

It probably includes advertising, direct marketing, promotions and public relations. But what about price maintenance and a host of other activities?

Now the professional bodies concerned with marketing in the UK have decided enough is enough and have quietly formed a coalition to finance a research programme that could finally nail those issues.

'Marketing Metrics' is a 30-month project funded by the Marketing Council, the Marketing Society, the Institute for Practitioners in Advertising and the London Business School.

It aims to set common standards for terminology and develop models of best practice, particularly in the important area of measuring effectiveness.

If successful the project will shed much needed light on the arcane processes by which huge marketing appropriations are arrived at. For although no company will admit that the setting of marketing budgets amounts to little more than guess work, there is consensus among commentators that the process leaves much to be desired.

Financial Times

8.4 **Methods of deciding budgets** have been developed over a period of time and, in the absence of clearer guidance, are useful in approaching a budget decision for the first time. After several years' operations it is possible to use experience to make decisions. One, or a combination of more than one, of the following methods can be used to approach the problem.

- Completely arbitrarily
- All you can afford
- Historical basis
- Matching the competition
- Percentage of sales
- Experiment and testing
- Modelling and simulation
- Objective and task method

Recent research has indicated a growing trend towards database methods and especially favours the objective and task method.

Completely arbitrarily

8.5 There are many examples of budgets being set in an apparently **arbitrary way by senior management**. There may be a link between the **personality** of the **decision maker and the level of expenditure**. This link may not be obvious to people elsewhere in the organisation. Subsequent arbitrary cuts in expenditure if trading becomes difficult and the profit margins begin to suffer are more worrying.

All you can afford (usually a minimum)

8.6 This often applies to a new company starting up or to an existing company advertising for the first time. The conscious decision has to be taken to forgo immediate profits or to forgo an investment in another area in favour of an investment in marketing communications. This often means investing at a minimum level. This will necessarily limit the scope of the work, however, and limit the results to be achieved.

Historical basis

8.7 We have already indicated that with experience managers are able to form their own judgement of the effectiveness or otherwise of particular expenditure levels and different promotional methods. Year-on-year figures provide the basis for following trends and making decisions accordingly.

(a) The **danger of inertia**: a temptation just to keep it the same, in which case all the elements of the environment and the costs associated with the task facing the organisation are ignored.

(b) A slight improvement is to use a **media multiplier**, which at least recognises that **media rate card costs** may have increased.

Matching the competition

8.8 In many cases an organisation is trying to reach exactly the same customers through exactly the same channels. In order to obtain a certain market share it is then necessary to match the competition and particularly the market leader.

Percentage of sales method

8.9 The percentage of sales is a commonly used method of determining a marketing communications budget because:

- It is easy to calculate
- It is precise
- It can be quickly monitored
- It can be varied in progressive steps
- It appears logical
- It is financially safe

However, the percentage chosen should be conditioned by all the variables listed earlier (not least by whether the market is a consumer or industrial one) and it should be dependent upon how competitive the market is. The following figures are suggested based on experience of different accounts.

Percentage of sales on total communications budget

State of competition	Consumer markets	Industrial markets
No competition	1%	0.5%
Little competition	2%	1%
Average competition	5%	2%
Heavy competition	10%	3%

Action Programme 6

Use the above table to determine the approximate marketing communications budget for a number of market situations with which you are familiar. Include consumer and industrial markets.

Action Programme 7

What do you think is the logical flaw associated with the percentage of sales method as an effective technique for budget allocation?

8.10 If all companies in an industry use a similar calculation then expenditure will approximate to market share positions. However, it must be clear that the real position is very complex and sales are the result of marketing communications and not the other way round. The method is in reality over-simplistic but does form a good basis of calculation.

8.11 Once a sales forecast has been made then the approximate budget level can be obtained. It can then be moderated for special circumstances such as the degree of competition experienced in the previous year or expected in the next year.

Experiment and testing method

8.12 This method involves selecting a set of matched markets. Different final promotional budgets can be set for each of these markets and the results carefully monitored. The resulting levels of awareness and sales delivered can be compared. For example, this method can be used to evaluate alternative media schedules. Problems associated with this method include:

- The cost of conducting the experiment
- The time it takes to get results
- The premature informing of competitors
- The fact that markets can never be completely matched

Modelling and simulation method

8.13 With advancing use of computer databases and more precise promotional media it is possible to build models to forecast the likely performance of different media schedules. There are likely to be an increasing number of PC-based modelling programs available which will allow a number of business variables to be examined including:

- Sales levels
- Purchase frequency
- Awareness levels
- Profits achievable

Problems associated with modelling include time and cost and the validity of the chosen model.

The objective and task method

8.14 The objective and task method is probably the one which is most **logical and appropriate** to the complex situation found in planning marketing communications programmes. Basically the logic of the method is as follows.

```
┌─────────────────────────────┐
│   Determine the marketing   │
│  communications objectives  │
└─────────────────────────────┘
               ↓
┌─────────────────────────────┐
│  Determine tasks necessary to │
│   achieve these objectives  │
└─────────────────────────────┘
               ↓
┌─────────────────────────────┐
│   Determine the cost of cash │
│           element           │
└─────────────────────────────┘
```

8.15 This approach is simple to understand and it embodies some elements of the marginal cost approach, but this time in conjunction with carefully considered and linked objectives and tasks. It is necessary to be realistic about the objectives and accurate in the costing of the tasks.

Action Programme 8

To demonstrate the logic and difficulty of this method choose a marketing communications problem with which you are familiar:

> Define the precise marketing communication objectives.
> Determine the tasks necessary to achieve these objectives.
> Cost out the problem both in terms of the individual tasks and in total.

8.16 A systematic approach to applying the objective and task method will pay dividends because of its rigorous nature. Although it will not necessarily produce perfect results it will lead to disciplined thinking and provide an excellent communication and decision device.

Ten steps in applying the objective and task method

Step 1. Define marketing and promotion objectives

Step 2. Determine the tasks to be undertaken

Step 3. Build up expenditure by costing the tasks

Step 4. Compare the results against industry averages

Step 5. Compare the results as a percentage of sales

Step 6. Reconcile differences between steps 3, 4 and 5

Step 7. Modify estimates to meet company policies

Step 8. Specify when expenditures are to be made

Step 9. Maintain an element of flexibility

Step 10. Monitor actual results against these forecasts

Action Programme 9

Compare the advantages and disadvantages of the various methods that can be used to determine the appropriate levels of marketing communication budgets.

9 Strategic considerations

9.1 You may notice, say, that you see British Telecom ads far more frequently than ads for most of its competitors such as the cable companies' telephone services. BT is, of course, the largest player in the market. But then, French car ads are more often to be seen than ads for Japanese cars, yet the Japanese have a larger share of the market. How can we analyse these strategies?

Advertising to sales ratios (A/S Ratios)

9.2 One of the important factors that always needs to be considered is the amount spent on communications by competitors. It can be difficult determining the amount spent by competitors on **below-the-line** activities, although accurate guesstimates can often be made by those actively involved in the market.

9.3 **Above-the-line** activities can be measured (data bought from various marketing research agencies) and can be used to gain an insight into possible strategies.

9.4 The A/S ratio for an industry provides a benchmark against which it is possible to determine how much should be spent or stimulate consideration of why certain amounts have been spent.

Key Concept

The **A/S ratio** is different for each market sector. It is calculated by working out the total amount spent on advertising (usually at rate card cost) as a proportion of the sales in the market. Therefore, if sales in a market are valued at £150 million per year and the amount spent on advertising is £14 million then the A/S ratio is said to be 9.33%.

9.5 Part of the strategic decision is to decide whether an individual company's A/S ratio should be higher or lower than, or the same as (at equilibrium with) the industry average.

(a) **Reasons to spend more** might be that a **new product or variant** is being introduced to the market so greater effort is require to **develop awareness** (reach) and then perhaps knowledge and/or establish brand values.

(b) **Reasons to underspend** the industry average might include trying to maintain an established market position or **directing spend to other products** in the portfolio or deciding to **put more work below-the-line**.

Share of voice

Key Concept

Share of voice. Within any market the total of all advertising expenditure (adspend), that is, all the advertising by all the players, can be analysed in the context of the proportions each player has made to the total.

9.6 If one advertiser spends more than any other then more of their messages will be received and therefore stand a better chance of being heard and acted upon. If a brand's **share of market (SOM)** is equal to its **share of voice (SOV)** an equilibrium can be said to have been reached.

9.7 It is possible that organisations can use their advertising spending either to maintain equilibrium (SOV = SOM) or to create disequilibrium.

9.8 The following matrix shows how different spending strategies are appropriate depending on your competitors' share of voice and your own share of market.

9.9 Note that careful monitoring of the fortunes of competitors is needed: if you know that a competitor is spending large sums on restructuring, say, they may not be in a position to retaliate to a sudden advertising burst by your company.

10 Controlling the budget

10.1 Marketing communication budgets may be very substantial and have a major effect on profitability. Controlling the effectiveness of the budget may be difficult if not impossible. What is possible is to use normal budgetary control techniques in marketing expenditure, and to review its effectiveness regularly, even if this is only by means of informed judgement.

Controlling the budgets and effectiveness

Chapter Roundup

- In order to be effective the development of marketing communications must take place within the context of the prevailing **corporate, business and marketing strategies**.

- **Promotional objectives** need to be stated in such a way that it is easy to understand what is to be achieved and what was achieved. Using the **SMART** approach enables this clarity to be achieved.

- The determination of promotional objectives is an important part of **co-ordinated marketing communications**.

- The goals to be achieved take three main forms. These are **sales**, **communication** and **corporate communication objectives**.

- There are **five** main contextual areas that need to be considered when developing marketing communication campaigns. These are the **business**, **customer**, **stakeholder**, **organisational** and **external contexts**.

- The overriding requirement for marketing in today's modern markets is better **targeting**, and this means aiming at the proper segment of the market. Common criteria for market **segmentation** are geography, demographics, geodemographics, behaviour and psychographics.

- To determine whether a segment is worth pursuing, the market needs to consider the **size**, **measurability, access, uniqueness of response, stability and actionability** of the segment.

- The basic options in targeting are **undifferentiated** or **mass** marketing, **differentiated** marketing, **concentrated** marketing and **customised** marketing. The approach is selected on the basis of **cost/benefit** analysis.

- **Positioning** of a product is concerned with how it creates and establishes an image in the minds of consumers and how it is evaluated against competing products. Positioning may be according to attribute, price and quality, use or application, product user, product class or competition.

- The use of **perceptual maps** can assist the positioning decision.

- **Methods of budgeting**.

  - Spending an arbitrary amount
  - Spending all you can afford
  - Determining the spend on a historical basis
  - Matching competitors' expenditure
  - The percentage of sales method
  - By experiment and testing
  - By modelling and simulation
  - The objective and task method

- The **objective and task method** is the most rigorous. As its name suggests this entails determining the marketing communications objectives, determining the tasks necessary to achieve those objectives and determining the cost of each element.

- Special cases in budgeting include **corporate advertising**, **co-operative advertising**, **new product launches** and **dying products**.

- **Budgetary control** is essential because of the large sums involved. In essence this involves establishing satisfactory measures of the effectiveness of the marketing communications process.

Now try Question 3 in the Question Bank

Quick Quiz

1   'In order that its marketing communications be effective it is necessary to understand the conditions and elements that prevail in specific markets' – this statement refers to an organisation's customer context.

   True ☐

   False ☐

2   Which three C's make up the 'strategic triangle'?

   C..........

   C..........

   C..........

3   Which one of the following statements is correct?

   A   Marketing communications are a type of 'noise'
   B   Marketing communications should never be directed against competitors
   C   The promotional plan is totally independent of the overall corporate strategy
   D   Creative advertising will always be able to sell a product

4   Pick the correct four words from the six options given.

   Prior to the promotional (1) .... being decided, the company will make a series of (2) .... decisions that will determine the nature of the overall (3)........... It is this which will then lay down the parameters within which a (4) .... strategy will be developed.

Promotional	Marketing strategy	Customers
Strategy	Noise	Corporate

4   Promotional objectives need to be specific. What 'W' word can be used to summarise each of these?

   ■   Capable of communicating to a target audience: **W**.....

   ■   A distinct message: **W**.....

   ■   Over a specified time frame: **W**.....

6   What are the five elements of context analysis?

7   What does 'MCPF' stand for?

8   Match these definitions to the processes they describe – positioning, target marketing process or segmentation?

   (a)   Breaking down the total market into segments that share common properties

   (b)   How the target market perceives the presentation of the product/service relative to competing products.

   (c)   Segmenting the market, targeting particular segments and then positioning the offer in the selected segment in order to achieve the marketing goals.

9   List three ways of setting a marketing budget

10   If total sales in a market are valued at £300 million and the amount spent on advertising is £25 million, what is the A/S ratio?

BPP
PROFESSIONAL EDUCATION

Action Programme Review

1   Marketing communications can most effectively be expected to achieve objectives related to increasing awareness levels, changing attitudes and behaviour patterns. Increasing sales or market share is dependent on other marketing factors such as product acceptability, price and distribution.

2   Another example you could have considered is Cadbury's Roses, where the buying situation in advertisements has involved a sense of guilt or obligation on the part of the giver. Many products in this category are purchased as gifts for differing reasons rather than for personal consumption. You may also consider here the role of point of sale displays as an influencing factor in the purchase decision process.

3   Try undertaking this task by examining advertisements for products in the same category eg alcoholic drinks or cars. You can identify which brands are being promoted to the different classifications.

4   Try and further identify similar kinds of products or services from competing companies. How does their approach to positioning vary? A skim through one of the Sunday newspaper supplements will show a range of different advertisements for motor cars that are all aimed at the same target audience but from a variety of positioning platforms.

5   Having identified the different approaches to budgeting, what are the significant differences in the way in which the budget is spent? It will be interesting to compare the different kinds of businesses and the way in which different kinds of communication tools are used.

6   You will be able to identify sales turnover figures from company Annual Reports. Also look at market sector reports from Mintel or Keynote.

7   The main deficiency of the percentage of sales method is that it turns the traditional cause and effect relationship on its head.

Promotion causes sales. Hence, the amount of sales is a function of the amount spent on promotion. The strict implementation of the percentage of sales method means that the promotional spend becomes a function of the level of sales. Therefore, if sales decrease, then the amount spent on promotion is also decreased, whereas it might be wiser to keep the promotional spend constant in the face of declining sales.

The problem in forecasting future sales is the uncertainty of knowing what resources will be available to achieve the sales targets. Hence, this method should only be used to determine how much needs to be spent if conditions remain static. Beyond that, the budget needs adjusting in view of the new objectives.

8   This could involve looking at your own organisation or use a past examination paper mini case study.

9   This can be achieved by checking back to the points made in this chapter.

Answers to Quick Quiz

1   False. This statement describes the business context.

2   Company, customers, competition

3   A

4   (1) Strategy; (2) Corporate; (3) Marketing strategy; (4) Promotional

5   ■   Capable of communicating to a target audience: Who
    ■   A distinct message: What
    ■   Over a specified time frame: When

6   Business, customer, organisational, stakeholder, external

7   Marketing Communications Planning Framework

8   (a) Segmentation
    (b) Positioning
    (c) Target marketing process

9   Check your answer against paragraph 8.4

10 8.33%

Promotional tools 4

Chapter Topic List	
1	Setting the scene
2	An overview of the promotional tools
3	Primary and secondary roles
4	How to co-ordinate the tools
5	Advertising
6	Personal selling
7	Sales promotion
8	Public relations
9	Direct marketing
10	The Internet and e-commerce

Learning Outcomes

☑ Explain how the tools of the promotional mix can be co-ordinated in order to communicate effectively with customers and a range of stakeholders

☑ Explain the main elements, activities and linkages associated with the formulation and implementation of a marketing communications plan

Syllabus References

☑ Evaluate the effectiveness of each of the promotional tools using appropriate criteria such as cost, communication effectiveness, credibility and control

☑ Explain the meaning of the terms above-, through- and below-the-line

☑ Explain the role of each of the promotional tools within a co-ordinated marketing communications mix

Key Concepts Introduced

- Above-the-line
- Below-the-line
- Advertising
- Personal selling
- Sales promotion

- Public relations
- Direct marketing
- E-commerce
- Internet marketing

1 Setting the scene

1.1 There are a variety of tools that can be used to communicate with audiences. This chapter will remind you of the salient points about each tool.

Exam Tip

An understanding of the promotional tools and the ways in which they work is essential. What is most important is an appreciation of the way in which the tools can be co-ordinated in order that consistent and meaningful messages be presented to target audiences.

This knowledge can be examined in a number of ways. One of the more obvious approaches is through the preparation of a marketing communications plan. Other ways include direct questions on co-ordination or the effectiveness of promotional tools.

Read *Campaign, Marketing Week, Marketing* and other trade journals on a regular basis and look out for case histories that track the use of a selection of promotional tools.

2 An overview of the promotional tools

2.1 In this part of the Study Text the aim is to make you more familiar with the very broad range of promotional tools and to provide some guidelines for **choosing the most appropriate promotional mix**. With promotional tools this is not an easy job because usually it is not just one tool that is required but a combination.

2.2 Having chosen a suite of promotional tools, and even allocated them as either **primary** or **secondary**, it is important to be able to **co-ordinate** them in a comprehensive and **cost effective** whole.

The range of promotional tools

2.3 The range of promotional tools continues to grow. The variety of media that can be used for **above-the-line** campaigns has expanded, both in the printed advertising field and in the broadcast field. There are literally thousands of publications aimed at different target groups. In the broadcast field the number of television stations steadily increases through satellite, cable and digital television and the number of commercial radio stations has also grown considerably.

Key Concepts

Above-the-line campaigning is advertising placed in paid for media, such as the press, radio, TV, cinema and outdoor sites. The 'line' is one in an advertising agency's accounts, above which are shown its earnings on a commission basis, from the buying of media space for clients.

Below-the-line promotion involves product-integral and negotiated sales incentives, such as packaging, merchandising, on-pack discounts and competitions and so on. (Agency earnings on a fee basis are shown below the 'line' in their accounts.)

2.4 The diagram on the next page shows the range of tools that can be used to influence a customer or potential customer. These tools represent the use of **intentional methods calculated to bring about a favourable response in the customer's behaviour**. The diagram represents the most obvious promotion methods, though other parts of the marketing mix, including the product itself, pricing, policy and distribution channels, will also have decisive effects.

Action Programme 1

(a) Actually read your junk mail, wander around the supermarket, read the paper, watch TV, and start collecting those leaflets that are constantly posted through your letterbox. How many examples of the tools shown on the next page can you find? Be on the alert constantly for real-life examples and illustrations that you could use in your examination answers.

(b) Were you influenced by any of the examples that you found? Did you respond? You should be able to analyse your reasons.

(c) Can you think of (or better, find examples of) any other promotional tools, not shown in the diagram above?

2.5 There have been **major changes** in the way organisations communicate with their audiences. New technology, new media and changes in the way that people spend their time (working from home, shopping habits and leisure patterns etc) have meant that companies have to find new ways to reach people. **Direct marketing** (see section 9) is now a more significant part of the marketing plan for many products, along with interactive forms such as the Internet (see section 10).

2.6 The traditional emphasis on heavy mass above-the-line advertising has given way to more highly targeted campaigns. Below-the-line, and even what Fill (*Marketing Communications – Contexts, Strategies and Applications*, 2002) terms **'through-the-line'** promotion is now far more common. To quote Fill:

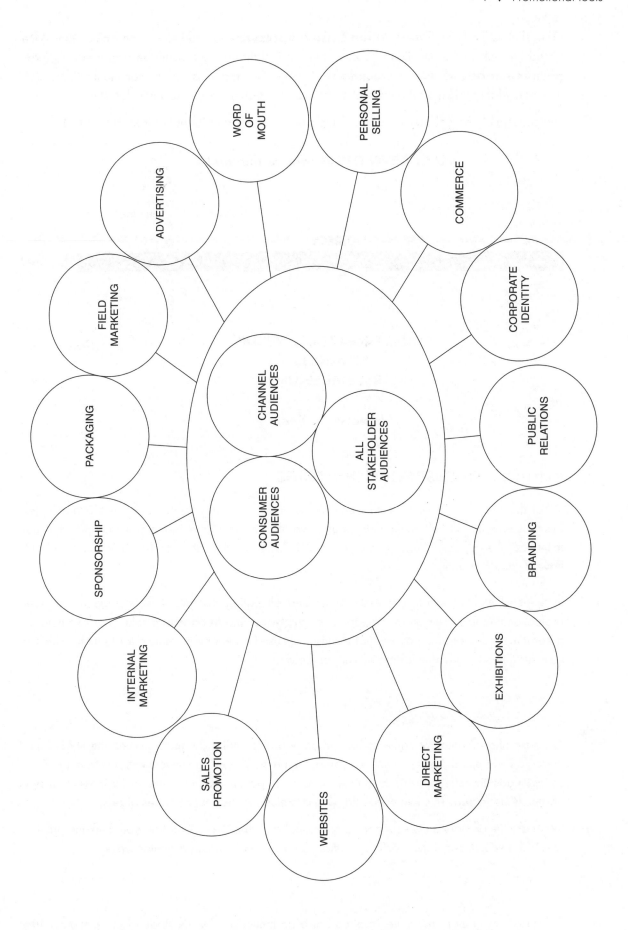

"The shift is from an **intervention-based approach** to marketing communications (one based on seeking the attention of a customer who might not necessarily be interested), towards **permission-based communications** (where the focus is upon communications with members of an audience who have already expressèd an interest in a particular offering)."

The concept of 'through-the-line' can be depicted on a diagram (adapted from Fill, 2002).

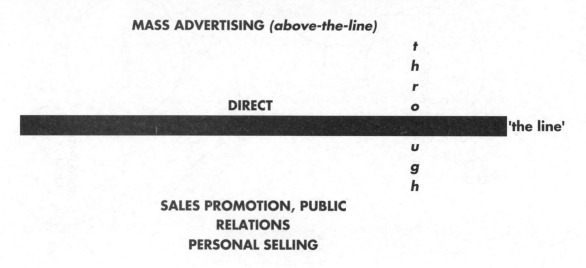

MASS ADVERTISING *(above-the-line)*

DIRECT

t
h
r
o
'the line'
u
g
h

SALES PROMOTION, PUBLIC RELATIONS PERSONAL SELLING

(below-the-line)

3 Primary and secondary roles

3.1 What should already be clear is that influencing customers and potential customers is a complex business. Discussions of buyer behaviour have shown that there is not just one process that influences the customer but a whole series. It follows therefore that each promotional tool will have a variety of roles.

3.2 In terms of making management decisions and allocating budgets it is possible to consider promotional tools in two broad categories of **primary** and **secondary** roles. For example, in a consumer campaign it may be that television is used as the main vehicle for launch, which is then sustained by a longer-lasting poster campaign.

Action Programme 2

A mobile phone company, ran a campaign of TV ads featuring a romance along the lines of the Nescafé Gold Blend couple. Then they ran a competition showing viewers extracts from the first series of ads and offering a prize to those who could put the extracts in the order in which they originally appeared. This (we were told) was a prelude to the second series of ads.

What are the primary and secondary promotional activities here? What do you think the prize was? Can you classify other campaigns that you have witnessed in a similar way?

3.3 The choice of primary promotion tool can also be influenced by the stage of the **product life cycle (PLC)**.

3.4 The PLC and developing promotional strategy

According to the PLC model, each of the stages from introduction to decline have different strategic requirements from their promotional activities.

Promotional Activities	Introduction	Growth	Maturity	Decline
Strategic focus	Strong push then pull for awareness	Pull to differentiate	Pull and push to sustain loyalty and exposure through reassurance	Some pull to remind core users
Public relations	x			
Advertising	x	x	x	
Direct marketing		x	x	x
Personal selling	x	x	x	x
Sales promotion	x		x	
			x	

3.5 The table above sets out the **strategic focus for each phase,** and the main promotional activities to be considered. What the table does not show is the way the promotional tools are used to support a push as opposed to pull approach. One particular benefit of the PLC is that it is possible to overlay the various stages of the process of **diffusion**. Through this it is possible to identify the **different types of buyer** involved with the product at each stage and through this fine tune the appropriate message and media.

3.6 Introduction

For consumer brands this phase is critical as the primary need is to **secure trade acceptance** (and hence shelf space) and then build **public (target audience) awareness**. Sunny Delight was developed by Procter & Gamble in consultation with major multiple grocers. When the product was launched the multiples accepted the brand as it had been developed partly to their specification on price, ingredient and packaging/size.

3.7 Growth

During growth, promotional activity is used competitively to **build market share**. Customers are normally willing to buy, having been made aware, but their problem becomes one of **brand choice**. Marketing communications should therefore be used to **differentiate and clearly position** product such that it represents significant value for the customer.

3.8 Maturity

Once the rapid growth in a market starts to ease, the period of maturity commences. The primarily characteristic of this stage is that there is little or no growth. The battle therefore is to **retain customer loyalty**, and to do this sales promotions are often used, to encourage trial by non-users of a brand and as a reward for current users.

Marketing at Work

Hoover have had to reposition themselves due to the market entry by Dyson with a technically superior product. Sales promotions alone therefore may not be sufficient, and a whole repositioning programme may be necessary to sustain a brand in competitive conditions.

3.9 Decline

As sales start to decline it is normal practice to withdraw a great deal of promotion support. **Direct marketing** and a little well targeted advertising to **remind** and **reassure** brand loyals is the most commonly used.

Exam Tip

Use of the tools of the promotional mix over the life of a product features on the Specimen Paper, so it is worth thinking about which tools may be appropriate at which stage of the life cycle.

4 How to co-ordinate the tools

4.1 Promotion work is exciting because the aim is to influence customers favourably towards your organisation's products or services. It is not an exact science. It is necessary to co-ordinate all the promotional elements to achieve the maximum influence on the customer.

4.2 Having recognised the need for co-ordination, it is now necessary to consider some more **practical steps to ensure that co-ordination** occurs. The following diagram shows that co-ordination can be a conscious choice **during the planning process**, and it can also be a necessary part of the review and revision process.

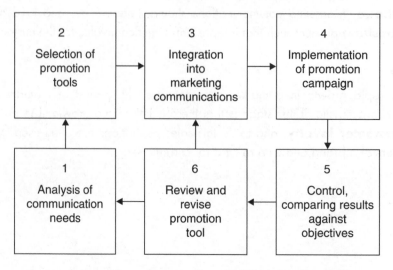

Integration of promotional tools into planning

4.3 The diagram below demonstrates the use of measures that can be taken to ensure co-ordination. The first three involve asking questions about the **effectiveness**, **economy** and **efficiency** of the promotion tools. The efficiency can be forecast in the pre-campaign phase and then measured by means of tracking studies during the campaign. This will lead to a review, revision and further co-ordination of the promotion tools.

Criteria for integrating promotion tools

5 Advertising

Key Concept

Advertising may be defined as non-personal paid-for communications targeted through mass media with the purpose of achieving set objectives. Advertising is a means of reaching large audiences in a cost-effective manner. Personalised feedback from an advertising message is not usually obtained.

5.1 **The purpose of advertising is to achieve set objectives**. These objectives will vary depending on the following factors.

- The result of the context analysis
- The nature of the product or service to be advertised
- The stage it has reached in its life cycle
- The marketplace in which it operates
- The role advertising is to play

Action Programme 3

Choose some television or print advertisements and try to work out what each one might be trying the achieve. What type of goals might there be?

5.2 It is not the purpose of advertising to win awards for creativity (though winning any sort of award is good publicity). In this chapter we are concerned with the practicalities of arranging for advertising to be used as a promotional tool.

6 Personal selling

Key Concept

Personal selling has been defined as 'the presentation of products and associated persuasive communication to potential clients, which is employed by the supplying organisation. It is the most direct and longest established means of promotion within the promotional mix' (Baron *et al*, *Macmillan Dictionary of Retailing* 1991).

6.1 All organisations have employees with responsibility for contacting and dealing directly with customers and potential customers. These employees, known as the **sales force**, provide a vital function to the organisation as they form a direct link to the buyers.

6.2 An organisation has a choice as to how it **organises itself for selling**.

(a) Employ a direct sales force, consisting of full- or part-time paid employees who work exclusively for the company. This type of sales force may, in turn, consist of two groups: **inside sales personnel** who conduct their business from the company premises via the telephone, or **field sales personnel** who travel and visit customers.

(b) An organisation could employ a **contractual sales force**, which could comprise sales agents, dealers or brokers who are paid a commission on the sales they generate.

6.3 Irrespective of the type of sales force a company may use, the sales force needs the support of other groups within the organisation if it is to operate efficiently and effectively. The activities of the following groups impact upon the effectiveness of the sales force.

(a) **Top management** who can be increasingly involved in the selling process, particularly with big orders or key accounts.

(b) **Technical sales personnel** who supply technical information and service to the customer before, during or after the sale of the product.

(c) **Customer service representatives** who provide installation, maintenance and other services to the customer.

(d) **Office staff** including sales analysts, administrators and secretarial staff.

Selling should increasingly be regarded as a **team effort** involving all these groups.

The tasks in the selling process

6.4 Personal selling is probably the area of the promotional mix that has the most stereotypes attached to it. The image of the 'travelling salesman' is an enduring one. However, the term sales representative covers a broad range of positions, which vary tremendously in terms of tasks and responsibilities.

Role	Comment
Order collector	The salesperson's job is predominantly to deal with routine orders normally through telemarketing.
Order taker	The salesperson passively takes orders from the customer. This can be further divided into *inside* order takers, such as shop assistants, or *outside* order takers, such as those salespeople who call on regular customers to take an order periodically. The customer has already been persuaded to use the product, or has been using the product in the past.
Pre-order caller	The salesperson is not expected or permitted to take an order but is expected to build goodwill or educate the customer in the use of the product. Medical representatives from pharmaceutical companies may fall into this category
Order supporter	The salesperson's main skill is the application of his technical knowledge relating to the product.
Order getter	The salesperson has to stimulate demand and creatively sell tangible or intangible products.

6.5 The 'degree of difficulty' of the salesperson's tasks increases the nearer the person gets to being an order getter. However, the art of 'selling' in its narrowest sense is only one of a number of tasks that the salesperson could perform. A salesperson could perform as many as seven different activities.

Activity	Comment
Prospecting	Gathering additional prospective customers in addition to sales leads generated by the company on his behalf.
Communicating	Communicating information to existing and potential customers about the company's products and services can take up a major proportion of the salesperson's time.
Selling	'The art of salesmanship', encompasses approaching the customer, presenting, answering objections and closing the sale.
Servicing	A salesperson may provide various services to the customer, such as consulting about their problems, rendering technical assistance, arranging finance and expediting delivery.
Information gathering	The salesperson can be a very useful source of marketing intelligence because of his or her links with the end customer. Many salespeople are responsible for supplying regular reports on competitive activity within their particular sales area.

Activity	Comment
Allocating	The salesperson may assist in evaluating customer profitability and creditworthiness, and may also have to control the allocation of products to customers in times of product shortages.
Shaping	An increasingly important role is to help build and sustain relationships with major customers.

6.6 While a salesperson may engage in all these tasks from time to time, **the mix of tasks will vary according to the purchase decision process, company marketing strategy and the overall economic conditions of the time**. For example, the skills needed for a straight rebuy situation (where the customer has bought the same product in the same way in the past) will be totally different from those required to develop a new account.

6.7 **Sales force activity must also be undertaken within the context of the organisation's overall marketing strategy**.

(a) For example, if the organisation pursues a **'pull'** strategy, relying on massive consumer advertising to draw customers in to ask for the brand, then the role of the sales force may primarily be a servicing one, ensuring that retailers carry sufficient stock, allocate adequate shelf space for display and co-operate in sales promotion programmes.

(b) Conversely, with a **'push'** strategy, the organisation will rely primarily on the sales force to sell the brands to intermediaries, who will then assume the main responsibility for selling on the brands to the end customer.

6.8 **The mix of a salesperson's tasks may vary with the prevailing economic conditions**. For example, in times of product shortage the art of selling may not be as important. However, such a view neglects the other roles of the salesperson that will be of greater importance in such circumstances, such as allocating, counselling customers, communicating company policy to customers and perhaps selling other products that are not in short supply.

7 Sales promotion (Specimen paper)

Key Concept

The Institute of Sales Promotion (ISP) defines **sales promotion** as 'a range of tactical marketing techniques, designed within a strategic marketing framework, to add value to a product or service, in order to achieve a specific sales and marketing objective.'

7.1 (a) Sales promotion encompasses a range of techniques appropriate for targeting **consumers**, for instance via price reductions, competitions or gifts with purchases. However, **trade and sales force incentives** are also implied under the general heading of sales promotion.

(b) Sales promotion is viewed by the ISP as a tactical promotional tool. The majority of companies will use sales promotion as a means of achieving a short-term objective, for instance to gain short-term sales volume or to encourage trial and brand switching by a rival manufacturer's consumers.

(c) Although it is used as a tactical tool, sales promotion works within a strategic marketing framework. Sales promotion should start with due regard to the strategic objectives for the brand.

(d) Sales promotion always seeks to add value to a product or service. Thus consumers are offered something extra for their purchase, or the chance to obtain something extra.

7.2 Sales promotion includes the notion of both **sales pull** and **sales push** techniques. As we have seen, sales pull techniques incentivise the consumer to buy. Sales push techniques ensure that the distribution pipeline is well loaded, and sales are pushed along the distribution chain.

Exam Tip

Be aware of the potential for confusion between the terms promotion (used as a synonym for communication techniques in general) and sales promotion (which is a specialist term reserved for the specific techniques described in this chapter). In examinations some candidates read the question paper very quickly and mistake a question on sales promotion for one on promotional techniques in general. This unfortunate slip can result in a candidate scoring virtually no marks.

To reinforce this point, the Specimen Paper for the new syllabus features a question asking for a comparison between sales promotion and public relations.

Sales promotion objectives

7.3 Examples of consumer sales promotion objectives.

- **Increase awareness** and interest amongst target audiences
- Achieve a **switch in buying behaviour** from competitor brands
- **Incentivise consumers** to make a forward purchase of your brand
- **Increase display space** allocated to your brand in store
- **Smooth seasonal dips** in demand for your product
- Generate a **consumer database** from mail-in applications

7.4 Sales promotion objectives will link into overarching marketing and marketing communications objectives.

Marketing objective	To increase brand X market share by 2 percentage points in the period January to December 2003
Marketing communications objective	To contribute to brand share gain of 2% in 2003 by increasing awareness of X from 50% to 70% among target consumers.
Sales promotion objective	To encourage trial of brand X among target consumers by offering a guaranteed incentive to purchase.

Action Programme 4

Tesco and Sainsbury issue a type of loyalty card which shoppers present when they reach the check-out. Points are awarded for sums spent over a minimum amount and these are added up each quarter. Money-off vouchers to be used against future grocery bills are sent to the shopper's home. What do you think is the value of this?

8 Public relations   (Specimen paper)

Definitions

Key Concept

The Institute of Public Relations has defined **public relations (PR)** as 'the planned and sustained effort to establish and maintain goodwill and mutual understanding between an organisation and its publics'.

8.1 The Public Relations Consultants Association (PRCA) says that:

'Public relations is the name given to the managed process of communication between one group and another. In its purest form it has nothing to do with marketing, advertising or "commercialism". It will, however, often promote one group's endeavours to persuade another group to its point of view and it will use a number of different methods, other than (although often alongside) advertising to achieve this aim'.

The scope of PR

8.2 The scope of public relations activity is very broad.

- Government - national, local, international
- Business and industry - small, medium, large
- Community and social affairs
- Educational institutions, universities, colleges

- Hospitals and health care
- Charities and good causes
- International affairs

8.3 Whilst the specific practice of the discipline of public relations will vary from sphere to sphere (and indeed, from organisation to organisation) there are numerous separate types of activities that the PR practitioner may carry out at some time.

- Counselling based on an understanding of human behaviour
- Analysing future trends and predicting their consequences
- Research into public opinion, attitudes and expectations and advising on action
- Establishing and maintaining two-way communication
- Preventing conflict and misunderstandings
- Promoting mutual respect and social responsibility
- Harmonising the private and public interest
- Promoting goodwill with staff, suppliers and customers
- Improving industrial relations
- Attracting good personnel and reducing labour turnover
- Promoting products and services
- Projecting a corporate identity

8.4 From this list of activities it can be seen that the scope of **public relations activity**, if implemented effectively, should **embrace the whole organisation**. A number of criteria have been put forward in an attempt to define what constitutes 'excellent' public relations within an organisation.

- Programmes should be managed strategically
- There should be a single integrated public relations department
- Public relations managers should report directly to senior management
- Public relations should be a separate function from marketing
- The senior public relations person should be at board level
- Communication should adhere to the 'two-way symmetrical model' (see below)

Four models of PR

8.5 This last factor relates to the way in which public relations is practised. Given the diversity of the role of PR as emphasised above, it is logical to consider different ways in which PR could be practised. A framework for considering this has been propounded by Grunig and Hunt, *Managing Public Relations* (1984), who suggest that there are four models of public relations practice. Each model will be considered in turn.

Press agency/publicity

8.6 The role of PR is primarily one of **propaganda**, spreading the faith of the organisation, often through incomplete, half-true or distorted information. Communication is one-way, from the organisation to its publics: essentially telling the publics the information the organisation wants them to hear.

Public information

8.7 In this model the role of PR is the dissemination of **information**, not necessarily with a persuasive intent. As Grunig and Hunt state, 'the public relations person functions essentially as a journalist in residence, whose job it is to report objectively information about his organisation to the public'.

Two-way asymmetric

8.8 Grunig and Hunt describe the main function of the two-way asymmetric model as scientific persuasion, using social science theory and research about attitudes and behaviour to persuade publics to accept the organisation's point of view and to behave in a way that supports the organisation. The aim is to achieve the maximum change in attitudes and behaviour.

Two-way symmetric

8.9 In the two-way symmetric model the **PR practitioner serves as a mediator between the organisation and its publics** with the aim of facilitating mutual understanding between the two. If persuasion occurs it is as likely to persuade the organisation's management to change its attitude as it is to persuade the publics to change theirs.

8.10 Public relations is, therefore, the **management of an organisation's reputation with its publics** and this management involves a close consideration of the relationships involved. The organisation can be either reactive or proactive in its management of these relationships.

(a) **Reactive PR** is primarily concerned with the communication of what has happened and responding to factors affecting the organisation. It is primarily defensive, with little or no responsibility for influencing policies.

(b) In contrast, **proactive public relations practitioners** have a much wider role and thus have a far greater influence on overall organisational strategy.

8.11 Inevitably some techniques will be more appropriate in certain circumstances with certain types of publics than others. It is possible, therefore, to classify the different types of techniques or media according to the type of project areas in which they appear to be most effective. The most frequently used techniques are as follows.

(a) **Consumer marketing support area techniques**

- Consumer and trade press releases
- Product/service literature
- Promotional videos
- Special events (in-store competitions, celebrity store openings
- Consumer exhibitions
- In-house magazines for sales staff, customers and/or trade
- Salesforce/distributor incentive schemes
- Sport, and to a lesser extent, arts sponsorships

Marketing at Work

Sports sponsorship was worth £460 million in the UK at the end of 2002. This figure is still a long way from that spent on conventional advertising, but it is a sign of a resilient sector. It is no longer the 'poor relation' of other marketing initiatives, nor is it necessarily the first activity to be axed in an economic downturn.

The public has a high level of acceptance of sponsorship, with many recognising that if there is no sponsorship, there will be no event at all. Spiralling costs have meant that sponsors are increasingly prepared to consider involvement at the grass roots level rather than the higher cost, 'glamour' events. This in turn encourages the development of sport over the long term, and appeals to today's socially responsible consumer who is looking for genuine involvement to overcome his cynicism about corporate motives. The Football Association in the UK, for instance, now has a limited number of sponsorship partners, who are expected to get involved at all levels of the game. To quote Martin Cannon of the Institute of Sports Sponsorship:

"Perhaps the one certainty of the coming year is that the growth of auditing and evaluation services that have been developed in the recent past will continue apace. To survive, sponsorships will not just have to be seen to be successful, they will have to be clearly and unequivocally proven successes with a measurable impact on the achievement of sponsors' objectives."

Adapted from What's New in Marketing, online, 2003

(b) **Business-to-business communication area techniques**

- Corporate identity design
- Corporate literature
- Corporate advertising
- Trade and general press relations, possibly on a national or international basis
- Corporate and product videos
- Direct mailings
- Sports and arts sponsorships
- Trade exhibitions

(c) **Internal/employee communications area techniques**

- In-house magazines and employee newsletters
- Employee relations videos
- Formal employee communications networks and channels for feedback
- Recruitment exhibitions/conferences
- Speech writing for executives
- Company notice boards
- Briefing meetings

(d) **Corporate, external and public affairs area techniques**

- Corporate literature
- Corporate social responsibility programmes, community involvement
- Trade, local, national and possibly international media relations
- Issues tracking
- Management counselling
- Local or central government lobbying
- Industrial lobbying
- Facility visits
- Local/national sponsorships

(e) **Financial public relations area techniques**

- Financial media relations on both a national and international basis
- Design of annual and interim reports
- Facility visits for analysts, brokers, fund managers, etc
- Organising shareholder meetings
- Shareholder tracking research

8.12 While this is not a comprehensive list it does give an indication of the many types of PR techniques that can be used in various circumstances and how certain techniques will re-occur in various settings. Media relations, for example, is used in virtually all areas of activity.

9 Direct marketing

9.1 The aims of direct marketing are to **acquire and retain customers**. Here are two further definitions.

Key Concept

The Institute of Direct Marketing in the UK defines **direct marketing** as 'The planned recording, analysis and tracking of customer behaviour to develop relational marketing strategies'.

The Direct Marketing Association in the US define direct marketing as 'An interactive system of marketing which uses one or more advertising media to effect a measurable response and/or transaction at any location'.

9.2 It is worth studying these definitions and noting some key words and phrases.

	Comment
Response	Direct marketing is about getting people to send in coupons, or make telephone calls in response to invitations and offers.
Interactive	It is a two-way process, involving the supplier and the customer.
Relationship	It is in many instances an on-going process of selling again and again to the same customer.
Recording and analysis	Response data are collected and analysed so that the most cost-effective procedures may be arrived at. Direct marketing has been called 'marketing with numbers'. It aims to take the waste out of marketing.
Strategy	Direct marketing should not be seen merely as a 'quick fix', a 'one-off mailing', a promotional device. It should be seen as a part of a comprehensive plan stemming from clearly formulated objectives.

9.3 Direct marketing helps create and develop direct relationships between you and each of your prospects, between the consumer and the company on an individual basis. It is a form of direct supply, embracing both a variety of alternative **media channels** (like direct mail), and a choice of **distribution channels** (like mail order). Because direct marketing removes all channel intermediaries apart from the advertising medium and the delivery medium, there are no resellers, therefore avoiding loss of control and loss of revenue.

Components of direct marketing

9.4 Direct marketing encompasses a wide range of media and distribution opportunities.

- Television
- Radio
- Direct mail
- Direct response advertising
- Telemarketing
- Statement stuffers
- Inserts

- Take-ones
- Electronic media
- Door to door
- Mail order
- Computerised home shopping
- Home shopping networks

9.5 In developing a comprehensive direct marketing strategy, organisations will often utilise a range of different yet complementary techniques.

9.6 **Direct mail tends to be the main medium of direct response advertising**. It has become the synonym for it. The reasons for this is that other major media, newspapers and magazines, are familiar to people in advertising in other contexts. Newspaper ads can include coupons to fill out and return, and radio and TV can give a phone number to ring (DRTV is now very common). However, direct mail has a number of strengths as a direct response medium.

(a) The advertiser can target down to **individual level**.

(b) The communication can **be personalised**. Known data about the individual can be used, while modern printing techniques mean that parts of a letter can be altered to accommodate this.

(c) The medium is good **for reinforcing interest stimulated by other media** such as TV. It can supply the response mechanism (a coupon) which is not yet available in that medium.

(d) The opportunity to use **different creative formats** is almost unlimited.

(e) **Testing potential is sophisticated**: a limited number of items can be sent out to a 'test' cell and the results can be evaluated. As success is achieved, so the mailing campaign can be rolled out.

9.7 The cornerstone upon which the direct mailing is based, however, is **the mailing list**. It is far and away the most important element in the list of variables, which also include the offer, timing and creative content.

9.8 A **database** is a collection of available information on past and current customers together with future prospects, structured to allow for the implementation of effective marketing strategies. Database marketing is a customer-oriented approach to marketing, and its special power lies in the techniques its uses to harness the capabilities of computer and telecommunications technology. Building accurate and up-to-date profiles of existing customers enables the company to

- Extend help to a company's target audience

- Stimulate further demand

- Stay close to them. Recording and keeping an electronic database memory of customers and prospects and of all communications and commercial contacts helps to improve all future contacts

Marketing at Work

Database applications

Computers now have the capacity to operate in three new ways which will enable businesses to operate in a totally different dimension.

'Customers can be tracked individually. Thousands of pieces of information about each of millions of customers can be stored and accessed economically.

Companies and customers can interact through, for example, phones, mail, E-mail and interactive kiosks. ... for the first time since the invention of mass marketing, 'companies will be hearing from individual customers in a cost-efficient manner'.

Computers allow companies to match their production processes to what they learn from their individual customers - a process known as 'mass customisation' which can be seen as 'the cost-efficient mass production of products and services in lot sizes of one'.

There are many examples of companies which are already employing or experimenting with these ideas. In the US Levi Strauss, the jeans company, is taking measurements and preferences from female customers to produce exact-fitting garments. The approach 'offers the company tremendous opportunities for building learning relationships'.

The Ritz-Carlton hotel chain has trained staff throughout the organisation to jot down customer details at every opportunity on a 'guest preference pad'.

The result could be the following: 'You stay at the Ritz-Carlton in Cancun, Mexico, call room service for dinner, and request an ice cube in your glass of white wine. Months later, when you stay at the Ritz-Carlton in Naples, Florida, and order a glass of white wine from room service, you will almost certainly be asked if you would like an ice cube in it.'

(Financial Times)

9.9 **Telemarketing** is the planned and controlled use of the telephone for sales and marketing opportunities. Unlike all other forms of direct marketing it allows for immediate two-way communication.

Telemarketing as an co-ordinated marketing activity

9.10 Role of telemarketing

(a) **Building, maintaining, cleaning and updating databases.** The telephone allows for accurate data-gathering by compiling relevant information on customers and prospects, and selecting appropriate target groups for specific product offerings.

(b) **Market evaluation and test marketing**. Almost any feature of a market can be measured and tested by telephone. Feedback is immediate so response can be targeted quickly to exploit market knowledge.

(c) **Dealer support**. Leads can be passed on to the nearest dealer who is provided with full details.

(d) **Traffic generation**. The telephone, combined with postal invitations, is the most cost effective way of screening leads and encouraging attendance at promotional events.

(e)   **Direct sales and account servicing**. The telephone can be used at all stages of the relationship with the prospects and customers. This includes lead generation, establishing buying potential for appropriate follow-up and defining the decision-making process.

(f)   **Customer care and loyalty building**. Every telephone contact opportunity can demonstrate to customers that they are valued.

(g)   **Crisis management**. If, for example, there is a consumer scare, immediate action is essential to minimise commercial damage. A dedicated hotline number can be advertised to provide information and advice.

10 The Internet and e-commerce

Exam Tip

You can count on exam questions coming up which cover the case for Internet-based marketing communications.

10.1 The Internet is the name given to the technology that allows any computer with a telecommunications link to send and receive information from any other suitably equipped computer. Terms such as 'the net', 'the information superhighway', 'cyberspace', and the 'World Wide Web (www)' are used fairly interchangeably, although technically the 'web' is what makes the 'net' user friendly (rather as Windows did for MS-DOS).

10.2 Access to the Internet is becoming easier and easier: most new PCs now come pre-loaded with the necessary software and developments in telecommunications networks will eventually render modems unnecessary. The decision to use the **Internet and related digital technologies** for either the whole or as a part of the business operations is a **strategically significant decision**.

10.3 The Internet can be used by organisations for business-to-consumer and/or business-to-business purposes. In the UK some 80% of Internet activity is **business-to-business related**, although as more members of the public get on line and telephone and access costs reduce, so this divide should narrow.

Websites

10.4 Most companies of any size now have a 'site' on the Net. A site is a collection of screens providing information in text and graphic form, any of which can be viewed simply by clicking the appropriate button, word or image on the screen. The user generally starts at the site's 'home page', which sets out the contents of the site. For instance, Penguin Books have a home page which includes the following options.

Marketing at Work

The Penguin Home Page

Preview	Read about our brand new titles, including sample extracts
Penguin direct	Order books here
World of Penguin	Search or browse our unique database. It contains over 10,000 Penguin titles
Penguin press	Browse through our whole range of academic titles
Features	The latest news and events from Penguin
Penguin history	Find out why we've been world famous since 1935
Competitions	Win some great prizes
Penguin search	Search the whole Penguin site by author, title or keyword

If you click on, say, *Penguin direct* you are taken to a page that allows you to fill in your name and address and credit card details and then enter details of the titles you want (perhaps obtained from browsing among the Penguin database or in response to a news feature). You then click on a button to submit your order directly over the telecommunications link to Penguin and receive the books by post a few days later.

Audience profile

10.5 The Internet is reckoned to be currently the fastest growing communications medium in Britain. It is thought that use is growing at between 10% and 15% per month. Estimates of the number of Internet users vary widely: one survey found that 4.6m adults in Britain (10%) of the population had Internet access. Many net users use it both at work and at home.

Internet Service Providers (ISPs)

10.6 Connection (if not available through a user's organisation) is made via an Internet Service Provider (ISP). The user is registered as an Internet subscriber and pays a small monthly fee together with local telephone call charges, even if contacting other users on the other side of the world.

10.7 ISPs such as America Online (AOL) and Microsoft Network (MSN) provide their own services, in addition to Internet access and e-mail capability. For instance, AOL also offers a main menu with options such as Life, Travel, Entertainment, Sport, Kids. It is rather like a quality Sunday newspaper, except that the sections are updated at least daily, and it provides much larger information resources (one option in the travel section, for instance, is to find out about train and plane timetables throughout the UK or worldwide).

10.8 There are many ISPs offering a combination of cost and performance.

Browsers and search engines

10.9 Most people use the net through interface programs called **browsers** often provided by the ISP. Internet Explorer and Netscape Navigator are two examples. Surfing the net is done using a **search engine** such as Yahoo!, Excite and AltaVista. These guide users to destinations throughout the world: the user simply types in a word or phrase such as 'beer' to find a list of thousands of websites that contain something connected with beer.

Promotion: banner advertising

10.10 Companies such as Yahoo! make money by selling advertising space. For instance if you type in 'beer', an advertisement for Miller Genuine Draft will appear, as well as your list of beer-related sites. If you click on the advertisement you are taken to the advertiser's website, perhaps just to be told more about the product, perhaps to be favourably influenced by the entertainment provided by the site, or perhaps even to buy some of the product. The advertiser may get you to register your interest in the product so that you can be directly targeted in future. At the very least advertisers know exactly how many people have viewed their message and how many were interested enough in it to click on it to find out more.

Marketing at Work

Banners to get bolder

Typically, advertising on the Internet has meant squeezing messages into thin rectangular strips that appear across the top of the screen. Compared to TV and print advertising, these formats have failed to generate sufficient revenues to meet costs. The sizing of the banner advertising has failed to attract customer interest as they have been more focused on website content than the peripheral advertising.

Publishers are hoping that moves to new bolder and bigger formats will both increase revenues and lead to greater consumer interest. The Internet Advertising Bureau, a trade group of web publishers have announced voluntary guidelines for seven new formats that will be closer to traditional print based formats. It is hoped these formats will be more attractive to the larger advertising agencies who have shunned banners previously as they fail to allow the creative execution required by their clientele.

The new formats are also intended to overcome the effects of ad-blocking software which has been developed to eradicate annoying banner style advertisements. If consumers can be persuaded that on screen advertising adds value and is interesting, they will be less inclined to use such software.

From an article in Financial Times 2 March 2001

E-mail as a promotional tool

10.11 E-mail is cheap, targeted and can be sent to millions of people at relatively little cost, and therefore can be used in a number of different ways.

- To advertise a product/service, usually with a link to a website.
- To update a subscriber to a product/service with useful information
- To confirm an order
- To invite users to write in or to respond to a helpline

10.12 Unsolicited e-mail is probably more intrusive than traditional 'junk mail', though less so than the telephone. However, bad use of e-mail can have the habit of upsetting large numbers of people, to the extent that in Europe regulation is felt to be needed.

Curbing the cost of junk e-mail

10.13 The European Commission have published a report entitled 'Unsolicited Commercial Communications and Data Protection', which highlights the significant issues of concern surrounding the use of e-mail for consumer targeting. The report estimates that in future the cost of downloading unsolicited e-mails could reach £6.4 billion a year. Regulations covering the use of direct mail are relatively clear in most countries with opt in/out clauses and mail preference services. The situation online is far from clear. Issues surrounding costs to recipients present a different aspect to this form of communication. Unwanted direct mail can be thrown away whereas e-mail incurs costs in viewing and downloading from the Internet.

10.14 'Spamming' – the process of sending millions of unsolicited messages at one go - creates major problems for recipients imposing high costs. E-mailing is an attractive form of communication for marketers, being both cheap, fast and effective.

10.15 In Europe, four separate directives cover unsolicited e-mail but are considered to be unclear and inconsistent. To date five countries (Austria, Denmark, Finland, Germany and Italy) have legislated for opt-in systems which allow for e-mail to be sent to consumers who have indicated they want to receive them. However the 'policing' of this issue is complex and will take some time to arrive at any kind of international agreements.

Internal communication: intranets

10.16 The idea behind an 'intranet' is that companies set up their own mini version of the Internet, using a combination of the company's own networked computers and Internet technology. Each employee has a browser, and a server computer distributes corporate information on a wide variety of topics and also offers access to the global net.

10.17 Potential applications include daily company newspapers, induction material, online procedure and policy manuals, employee web pages where individuals post up details of their activities and progress, and internal databases of the corporate information store.

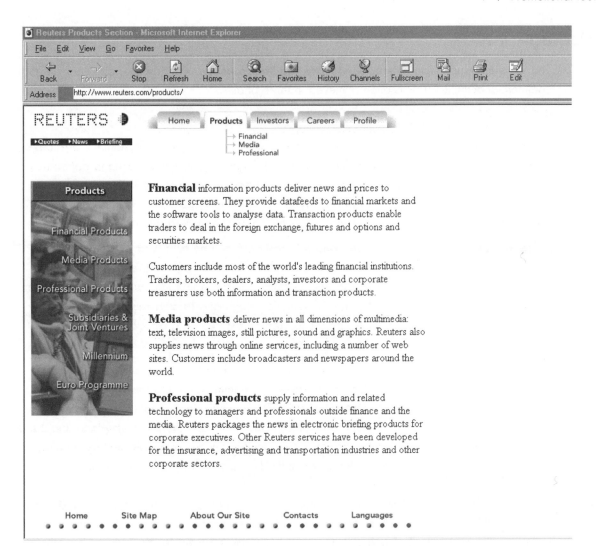

Marketing and e-commerce

10.18 Before we look at some of the strategic issues associated with marketing communications and the Internet, it is important to establish what is meant by some key terms, namely, **e-commerce** and **Internet marketing**.

Key Concepts

- **E-commerce** is about transactions involving the exchange of goods and services, for payment, using the Internet and related digital facilities.

- **Internet marketing** is about the application of the Internet and related digital facilities to help determine and satisfy marketing objectives.

10.19 Although Internet marketing is not concerned with the mechanics associated with payments and security the boundaries between e-commerce and Internet marketing are becoming blurred. As a result of this these phrases will be used interchangeably.

Strategic issues

10.20 The development of an interactive facility requires a major shift away from conventional commercial activities. This is often achieved in three phases.

	Comment
Presentation	The use of a website to enable visitors/customers to **access information**, provides an opportunity to stand out from competitors and **enhance corporate image**. It is an opportunity to illustrate the organisation's products and services. This facility is often referred to as brochureware.
Interaction	This phase is characterised by **two-way communication**. Questions and answers flow between the system and the user. Visitors to the site are able to enquire more deeply than at the presentation stage and **information about the visitor** is logged and stored on a **database** for future reference and for both on and offline communications.
Representation	When this phase is reached the organisation will have replaced parts of its commercial activities with **full online transactions**. The organisation's traditional commercial trading methods and channels may still be in place and the new interactive facility provides a complementary and/or alternative method for particular market segments.

10.21 It should not be assumed that all organisations move through each of these phases and if they do, it is a different speeds. Those that do migrate do so according to a number of variables, including, the **nature of the markets in which they operate**, their strategy, technical resources, attitude to risk and competitive pressures.

10.22 Internet technology can also be used strategically to enable communication with particular audiences.

(a) The **Internet** itself enables public access to an organisation's website.

(b) An **intranet** refers to a private internal network which is normally used to enable communication with employees.

(c) **Extranets** allow particular external audiences such as distributors, suppliers and certain customers access to an organisation's facilities.

10.23 The Internet offers two main marketing opportunities, namely **distribution and communication**. The ability to reach customers directly and so avoid many channel intermediaries reduces transaction costs and is a prime goal for most organisations.

10.24 The use of the Internet as a communications medium is equally attractive. It is more than a medium as it **facilitates interactivity and a two-way dialogue** that no other method of communication can support. Unlike other forms of communication, dialogue is induced by the customer, the speed and duration of the communication is **customer controlled** and the intensity of the relationship (with the online brand), is again customer managed. All the traditional tools of the promotional mix can be deployed over the Internet, with varying degrees of success, but it appears that **offline marketing communications are**

required to support the online communications and facilities. A combination of off and online communications need to be determined if the overall communications are to fulfil the **DRIP** roles that we discussed earlier in this Study Text.

10.25 The use of the Internet can perhaps be best observed when set alongside the purchase decision process. See the table below.

Use of the Internet to support stages in the Buying Process

Awareness

Not very effective at generating awareness and needs the support of offline communications to drive visitors to the site.

Positioning

As a means of presenting features and benefits the web is very good once a prospective customer has determined a need for a supplier search and is looking to compare offerings.

Lead generation

Once an active search commences leads can be obtained and used to reach prospects in the future.

Purchase decision support

By carrying vast amounts of information at low cost websites provide good opportunities to impress visitors and build credibility.

Facilitate purchase

Through the provision of basic transaction facilities (credit card payment) sales should not be lost once a decision to buy has been made.

Post purchase support and retention

Through the provision of free customer support and advice, levels of cognitive dissonance in customers can be reduced. Feedback from customers, e-mail updates about product developments and the use of sales promotions to stimulate repeat site visits can improve reputation, enable cross selling and promote favourable word of mouth recommendations.

E-commerce and website management

10.26 Management need to attend to three main decisions concerning their Internet and digital related facilities. These are their **development, maintenance and promotion**. All of these use resources and management need to be clear about the level of support that is appropriate. One of the key concerns is the website itself. To be successful the website should do the following.

(a) **Attract visitors** – with online and offline methods

(b) **Enable participation** - interactive content, and suitable facilities to allow for transactions

(c) **Encourage return visits** - design targeted at needs of particular segments, free services and added value facilities

(d)   **Allow for two-way information sharing** - personalisation reflecting visitor preferences, direct marketing and information retrieval provide visitors with the information they are seeking

Marketing at Work

Brand or business?

"It is all very well spending millions on marketing so every person in the country knows about your company. But if none of them are actually buying your products or services, it is money down the drain."

It has been suggested that the brief flourish of the "dotcom" revolution ended largely because those responsible for marketing concentrated too many resources on "brand blazing" rather than looking after customers. Few dotcom businesses bothered to analyse, profile or even contact their website visitors.

Adapted from *Marketing Business* October 2001

Business-to-business e-commerce

Exam Tip

This is a likely exam topic, as the use of Internet based technology in the business-to-business context is more highly developed and globally significant than in the consumer field.

10.27   Many observers are taking the view that the future of Internet marketing lies in the **business-to-business** (B2B) sector. The belief is based on the premises that:

(a)   Selling low value items to consumers requires significant spending on advertising and promotion and costly back up systems.

(b)   Consumers expect free content

(c)   Businesses which look for quotes can massively increase their source of suppliers, nationally and globally

(d)   Suppliers have a wider market to appeal to

B2B is therefore expected to break down barriers and enhance supply chain management.

Marketing at Work

Worldwidetender.com is an online B2B marketplace which allows businesses to buy and sell excess stock. Customers include retail chains, supermarket chains, convenience store groups, bulk catering companies and restaurant chains. Average sales are around £10,000 but can reach £250,000. With these higher value transactions, communications rely on the telephone and e-mail to encourage trading.

Many similar middle market companies are following the worldwide tender approach. The E-Business Report published recently by Birmingham Business School shows only some 25% of middle market firms are using the Internet for marketing and sales to consumers and almost 50% involved in B2B activity. Surveys by Forrester Research suggest the online market will account for approximately one third of all B2B sales by 2005.

Other significant issues that will determine the success of such activity include the co-ordination of Internet services with traditional marketing communications tools including the telephone, creating the web-enabled call centre.

From an article in the *Sunday Times* 27 May 2001

Marketing at Work

Otis

Otis is the world's largest company in the manufacture, sales and service of people moving products such as elevators, escalators, shuttle systems and moving walkways. They have taken a dynamic and innovative approach to e-business.

Services include 24-hour access to maintenance records, an Internet-enabled flat-panel display elevator communication and entertainment system and the facility for customers to plan, price and track new equipment projects online. The global website can be accessed in more than 51 countries and in 26 languages. These initiatives have led to a re-evaluation of customer relationships and generation of new business. The process for ordering a new elevator had previously been based on the completion of 300 technical questions taking one to three months to complete. This now consists of 15 questions and an online ordering system that can be completed in 20 minutes. These changes now allow sales people to deliver excellent customer service.

From an article in *The Times* 11 April 2001

10.28 Benefits of using the Internet in e-commerce

Benefit	How generated
Loyalty	Faster response
Productivity	Better management of the supply chain
Reputation	Depends on competition, and ability of web-based strategies to offer real customer benefit
Costs	Generally lower; easier for customers to obtain information

BPP PROFESSIONAL EDUCATION

Exam Tip

Students are required to understand how Internet marketing can (and should) impact on marketing communications. Ideas about the Internet, intranets and extranets will be tested, normally through the mini-case questions. Individual specific knowledge about banner advertisements or the role of portals for example is not required. It is necessary to understand the strategic significance of Internet technologies, the impact they may have on current commercial systems and marketing activities and the role traditional marketing communications will continue to have in the strategic promotional activities of organisations.

There are two sides to this topic. A question in December 2002 turned the issue on its head by asking students why luxury goods markets tend *not* to rely on online sales activity.

Chapter Roundup

■ There is an enormous **range of promotional tools** that the marketer can choose from. The skill is not so much choosing the right tools, but choosing the right **combination** of tools.

■ The choice should be made within the overall context of the **promotional objectives** and the strategies that have been determined.

■ Promotional tools have a **primary** or **secondary** role. The product life cycle model might be helpful in choosing which tool plays the primary role.

■ All the promotional elements must be **co-ordinated** if the maximum effect is to be achieved.

■ The **Internet** is the name given to the technology that allows any computer with a telecommunications link to send and receive information from any other suitably equipped computer.

■ Most Internet activity in the UK is **business-to-business** related.

■ A lot of the advertising on the Internet takes the form of **banner ads**.

■ **E-mail** is cheap, targeted and can be sent to millions of people at relatively little cost. It is therefore of great interest to marketers, but there is increasing concern at the prevalence of 'junk' e-mail.

■ The idea behind an **intranet** is that companies set up their own mini version of the Internet, using a combination of the company's own networked computers and Internet technology, to facilitate internal communications and hence shared knowledge.

■ **E-commerce** is about transactions involving the exchange of goods and services, for payment, using the Internet and related digital facilities.

■ **Internet marketing** is about the application of the Internet and related digital facilities to help determine and satisfy marketing objectives

The Internet **facilitates interactivity and a two-way dialogue** that no other method of communication can support.

The Internet can be used to support stages in the **buying process**.

To be successful a **website** should do the following.

- **Attract visitors**
- **Enable participation**
- **Encourage return visits**
- **Allow for two-way information sharing**

Now try Question 4 in the Question Bank

Quick Quiz

1   What range of promotional tools is available?

2   What is through-the-line promotion?

    A   Advertising placed in paid-for media
    B   Communication with an audience which has already expressed an interest
    C   Any form of advertising which reduces profits
    D   Sales incentives such as packaging and merchandising

3   Suggest promotional strategies (pull and/or push) for the different phases of the product life cycle:

Phase	Strategy
Introduction	
Growth	
Maturity	
Decline	

4   Choose the most appropriate words from the grid to fill in the gaps:

    Sales promotion includes the use of both pull and push techniques. Sales pull techniques (1) .... the (2).......... to buy. Sales push techniques ensure that sales are pushed along the (3) ....

Direct selling	Incentivise	Advertising
Distribution chain	Consumer	DMU

5   Direct marketing encompasses a wide range of opportunities. How many can you recall from the list in paragraph 9.4?

6   What are three advantages of e-mail as a promotional tool?

7   What are we talking about here?

    (a   .... is about transactions involving the exchange of goods and services, for payment, using the Internet and related digital facilities.

    (b)   .... is about the application of the Internet and related digital facilities to help determine and satisfy marketing objectives.

8   How might Internet marketing generate increased customer loyalty?

Action Programme Review

1   You will find it useful to maintain files of these examples. Try and find examples relating to differing market sectors including consumer products, services, public sector and not for profit. At your place of work collect examples based on business-to-business marketing communications. Collect examples for the same companies over a period of time. This will illustrate different use of communication tools and identify changes in strategy and tactics over time.

2   How does this approach differ from other companies in this sector? How was this co-ordinated with other communications activities by One-to-One?

3   Consider the goals in relation to business, marketing and communications strategies.

4   On the launch of its 'Clubcard' Tesco said that it was a way of saying thank you to customers and that it wanted to 'recreate the kind of relationship that existed between consumers and local shops half a century ago'.

In practice, however, the schemes give supermarkets the chance to build up a massive database containing customers' names, addresses and detailed information on individual shopping habits. But did they really encourage loyalty? No. Safeway decided that the considerable expenditure in the loyalty card scheme could be better spent on sales promotions targeted at local level (eg leafleting of local households). Safeway reported substantial increases in sales – but this has to be set against the fact that Tesco, still using the Clubcard, is the UK's most successful retailer.

Answers to Quick Quiz

1   Check your answer against the diagram following paragraph 2.4

2   B

3
Phase	Strategy
Introduction	Strong push, then pull for awareness
Introduction	Pull to differentiate
Maturity	Pull and push to sustain loyalty
Decline	Some pull, to remind core users

4   (1) Incentivise (2) Consumer (3) Distribution chain

5   Check your answer against paragraph 9.4

6   ■   Cheap
     ■   Targeted
     ■   Can be sent to millions of people quickly

7   (a)   E-commerce
     (b)   Internet marketing

8   It may lead to faster response times, that encourage customers to visit your website again and again in the expectation of superior service.

Pull, push and profile 5

Chapter Topic List	
1	Setting the scene
2	Pull based communication strategies
3	Branding and customer retention
4	Push based communication strategies
5	Profile based communication strategies

Learning Outcomes

☑ Explain how the tools of the promotional mix can be co-ordinated in order to communicate effectively with customers and a range of stakeholders

☑ Develop marketing communication and brand support activities based on an understanding of the salient characteristics of the target audience

Syllabus References

☑ Outline the key characteristics associated with push, pull and profile strategies

☑ Describe the main characteristics of key accounts and explain the stages and issues associated with key account management

☑ Describe how co-ordinated marketing communications can be used to develop key account relationships

☑ Explain how marketing communications can be used to launch new products, support brands, maintain market share, develop retention levels, encourage customer loyalty and support internal marketing within the organisation

Key Concepts Introduced

- Pull strategy
- Brand
- Push strategy
- Key account
- Profile strategy

1 Setting the scene

1.1 The focus of this part of the marketing communication process is to consider the emphasis of the marketing strategy - the balance between the need to communicate with consumers, with distributors and with all other stakeholders.

Type of Audience	Message Focus
1. Consumers and business-to-business customers	Products and Services
2. Members of the marketing channel, such as dealers	Products and Services
3. All stakeholders, in order to raise the visibility of the organisation	The Organisation

These approaches are referred to as the **3Ps of Marketing Communication**:

1. **Pull** communication strategies
2. **Push** communication strategies
3. **Profile** communication strategies

Exam Tip

Communication strategy is a reflection of the objectives and positioning requirements set earlier in the marketing plan. 'Push', 'Pull' and 'Profile' strategies are not exclusive to each other and it is perfectly acceptable to choose an element of all three or just two approaches, depending upon what needs to be achieved. Do not forget that they can all be used in the international context.

Marketing at Work

Continental, the German tyre group uses a combination of 'push' and 'pull'.

- **Push to**: the OE (original equipment) market, by supplying tyres to the big car manufacturers
- **Pull via**: replacement tyres, with consumers tending to opt for the same brand

The tyre-fitting trade plays a large role in the route to the customer. Continental carries out a lot of 'push' activity here, with incentive programmes, training and education to make sure that the fitters understand the brand segments (premium, quality, economy, budget, own-label). A greater challenge was to get consumers to think about tyres as more than those black things attached to their cars. TV and press advertising in Europe sought to change this perception.

Adapted from *Marketing Business*, January 2002

2 Pull based communication strategies

Key Concept

A **pull strategy** is used to generate and sustain a dialogue with end user customers.

2.1 These might be consumers or they might be business-to-business customers where the customer is the end user and does not move the product on through the marketing channel. **Pull strategies encourage end-users to demand the product from the distributors**, pulling the product through the distribution network.

2.2 Where a pull strategy is specified, then the promotional mix and the message and media combination will need to be co-ordinated. This will be explored later.

2.3 Typical strategies are to create higher levels of **product awareness** (spontaneous or prompted).

Action Programme 1

In order to ensure that the target market develops appropriate **attitudes** towards the brand so that it has the best chance of being selected, the marketer has a range of options. Fill in the table below with your ideas as to what these options could entail.

Option	What does this mean?
Modifying the brand	
Altering beliefs about the brand	
Altering beliefs about competitors' brands	
Altering the importance of attributes	
Calling attention to neglected attributes	
Shifting the buyer's ideals	

2.4 A particular pull strategy that has been developed and refined over many years is **branding**.

3 Branding and customer retention

3.1 Branding originated as a means of differentiating products from commodities but it has come to be of major importance for reasons far wider in power and implication, especially since the introduction of mass media. In many markets it has taken over the role previously held by the direct selling operation.

What is a brand?

3.2 The following is a useful definition of a successful brand.

Key Concept

A successful **brand**:

■ Is an identifiable product, service, person or place
■ Augmented so that the buyer or user perceives
■ Relevant, unique, added values, which
■ Match the buyer's/user's needs closely

3.3 It is possible to depict this definition in diagram form. **The brand contributes the added value** and can be seen as adding 'clothes' to a naked product.

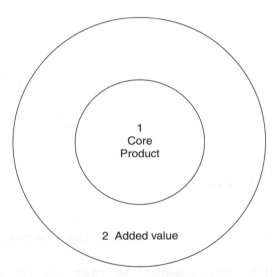

Added value concept

3.4 The **augmented product concept** takes this a stage further.

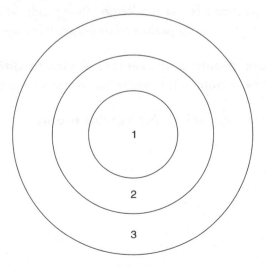

1 Core Product
2 Actual product
3 Augmented product

Augmented product concept

The **core product** satisfies the **basic need** of the customer, which is then built upon with **actual product** features and the **augmented product** 'embellishments'.

Action Programme 2

Apply this model to a Jaguar car. What are the core, actual and augmented elements of this particular product?

3.5 Another simple way of describing the difference between **commodities** and **brands** is the following diagram.

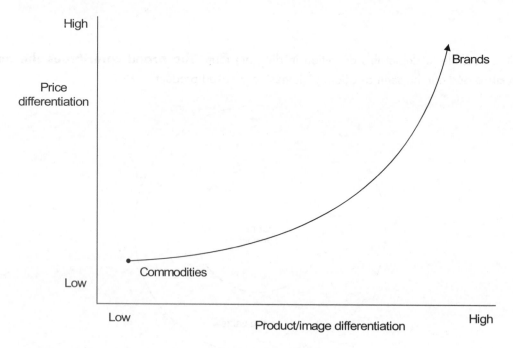

3.6 **Branding encourages the consumer to associate certain attributes with a product**. It differentiates very similar products into distinct segments of the market.

3.7 **The process of differentiation through branding allows the marketer to establish a unique position for a package**. Thus goods which in fact have very close substitutes, as in fmcg markets, can be positioned as though there was very limited competition.

3.8 **Brands are no longer simply a convenient device to differentiate, they are of importance in their own right**. It is often the brand that is bought, not the product.

3.9 The underlying justification for a brand is that it **builds profits**.

3.10 Types of brand

Type of brand	Comment
Individual brand name	This is the option chosen by Procter & Gamble, for example, who even have different brand names within the same product line, eg Bold, Tide.
Blanket family brand name for all products, eg Hoover, Heinz	This has the advantage of enabling the global organisation to introduce new products quickly and successfully. The cost of introducing the new product in terms of name research and awareness advertising will be reduced.
Separate family names for different product divisions	This is the option for the global organisation with 'inconsistent' product lines where a single brand name is not appropriate.
The company trade name	(For example, Kelloggs Corn Flakes, Rice Krispies). This option both legitimises (because of the company name) and individualises (the individual product name). It allows new 'names' to be introduced quickly and relatively cheaply.

Branding strategies

3.11 There are three main elements associated with successful branding: **differentiation, added value** and **integration**.

Differentiation

3.12 Through branding it is possible to differentiate a product from its competitors, make it distinguishable and **readily identifiable**. It has been suggested that differentiation is a four part process as shown below.

Product	Comment
Generic Product	Core product, nothing added (functional aspects only)
Expected Product	Minimal value expected by buyer (features, design, packaging and price)
Augmented Product	Value that surpasses a buyer's basic expectations (service, guarantees, add-ons, delivery and availability)
Potential Product	Binding buyers to the branded item (brand name, quality and value perceptions, reputation)

Added value

3.13 Branding needs to add value so that the consumers perceive a **meaning** in a brand that is **relevant** to them. This can be achieved through the way buyers perceive the performance of the brand, the psychosocial meanings attached to a brand and the level of **brand name awareness**.

	Comment
Perceived Performance	A function of the overall perceived quality and presence of important or significant attributes (eg Dyson).
Psychosocial meanings	A deduction of the social implications of brand ownership (eg Marlboro cigarettes and the differences between German/French cars).
Level of brand awareness	This can range from a state of unawareness through passive, active and Top-of-Mind awareness levels. This last stage is reached when the brand name becomes **synonymous** with the product category as with Walkman and Hoover.

Integration

3.14 For a brand to survive, the communications underpinning it must be consistent, uniform and reinforcing, so that it is very clear what it stands for.

Marketing at Work

Inmarsat is a satellite communication company which has expanded over the years beyond maritime communications into aeronautical, broadcasting, energy, emergency and aid relief sectors. Its nine satellites, positioned 36,000 km above the earth, give coverage everywhere apart from the North and South Poles.

Inmarsat wants to position itself by convincing companies that satellite communications are "neither too rarefied nor too expensive", and that it is able to deliver high speed global mobile data solutions. Its campaign, which ran in November 2001, aimed to show companies what they could do (positioning the brand in the market).

The advertisements, using the analogy of a 4x4 utility vehicle (which can be used both off road and in the city), looked like car advertising posters and ran in broadsheets and international business titles. The image was also used in public relations, direct marketing and channel marketing.

Because it operates through a range of distributors and service providers, Inmarsat helped to fund the marketing by these parties. The company also developed a range of initiatives to help employees understand the new branding (briefings, videos and competitions). Stephen Rogen, director of marketing communications, says that "The sense of positioning and brand values, how we talk, the tone of voice we use and how we communicate the message - this has changed quite substantially to show that we are far more 'real world' than many people expect."

Adapted from *Marketing Business*, October 2001

Branding and marketing communications

Exam Tip

In the December 2002 exam under the old syllabus, branding was an important issue in a Section A question, on marketing strategies in luxury goods markets (watches in particular).

3.15 The main idea behind branding is that **a basic product can be converted with marketing communications into a brand**. These communications can take one of two main approaches.

Approach	Comment
Functional	The aim is to provide information about the **attributes and benefits** associated with brand ownership. This is common where **persuasion** is important and where involvement and levels of perceived risk are also high.
Expressive	Emotions and feelings are central to the message and the prime goal is to develop audience **likeability** for the communication. Where involvement is low and perceived risk is minimal, it is common practise to try to engage the audience on an **emotional level**.

Brand strategies

3.16 Brand strategies may be summarised as follows.

Branding strategy	Description
Line extensions	Use of the same brand name to introduce new flavours, forms, colours and package sizes.
Brand extensions	Use of an existing brand name to launch new products in other categories (eg Mars into Mars Ice Cream, Honda into lawn mowers).

Branding strategy	Description	
Multibrands	The introduction of additional brands into a particular market (eg Electrolux owns Frigidaire, Kelvinator, Westinghouse, Zanussi, White and Gibson).	
New brands	The development of a new product into a market where none of the company's current brands would be applicable (eg Kellogg's entry into sportswear).	
Co-brands	Occurs where two (or more) established brands combine together to generate increased impact. There are a number of variants:	
	Ingredient co-branding	Volvo advertises that it uses Michelin tyres, Intel and Nutrasweet are other brands which are promoted within a brand.
	Same-company co-branding	When a company promotes two or more of its own brands in the same sector.
	Joint Venture co-branding	Microsoft sponsorship of the NSPCC charity.

3.17 The relevance of branding does not apply equally to all products.

(a)   The cost of intensive brand communications, principally advertising to project a brand image nationally, may be prohibitively high.

(b)   Goods or services which are sold in large numbers, on the other hand, promote a brand name by their existence and circulation.

3.18 Where a brand image promotes an idea of quality, a customer will be disappointed if his or her experience of a product fails to live up to expectations. **Quality control** is therefore an important element in branding policy. It is especially **a problem for service industries** (eg hotels, airlines, retail stores) where there is less possibility than in a manufacturing industry of detecting and rejecting the work of an operator before it reaches the customer.

Customer retention

3.19 Arguably, this is another 'pull-based strategy' predicated on the notion that 20% of customers provide 80% of profits.

3.20 New customers cost more because of advertising costs, sales administration costs, joining discounts etc, hence some firms enact customer retention programmes. Retention is not loyalty (which is 'emotional'), but it can be bought.

3.21 **Impact on marketing communications**

■   Customer retention requires internal and external marketing

■   Development of reward packages (eg Air Miles) and communication of these

■   More use of direct marketing (perhaps the Internet) with known customers as opposed to above-the-line advertising, relationship marketing

■   The main communications burden may therefore be carried out by service staff

Exam Tip

Exam questions will require you to use examples. We could cite Tesco as one where, in the long run, customer retention is a virtuous circle; if less money need be spent attracting new customers this represents a significant advantage over competitors and frees financial resources for other marketing activity (such as price cut).

Customer retention and loyalty was tested in the December 2002 sitting under the old syllabus – the role of schemes such as those described above, and the use of the tools of the promotional mix to develop customer retention. This area will continue to be highly examinable in the new Marketing Communications syllabus.

4 Push based communication strategies

Push based communication strategies

4.1 Communication with members of the marketing channel, such as **dealers and retailers**, is absolutely vital if sufficient **exposure and visibility** are to be obtained for the product. Without suitable distribution it is unlikely that the marketing objectives will be met.

4.2 It is therefore important to determine a promotional strategy to reach channel members in order to maximise the impact of a co-ordinated marketing communications approach. This strategy is referred to as a **Push Communications Strategy**.

Key Concept

A **push communications strategy** requires the identification of distributor needs and, through a combination of elements, an attempt to meet and satisfy these needs in order that both the supplier and the distributor are able to achieve their respective goals. The focus is on the intermediary.

4.3 **Members of a marketing channel** might be **independent** organisations and have their particular goals, but they choose to work together and are therefore **interdependent** and share a common goal: consumer/customer satisfaction.

4.4 Understanding the needs of the people who make up the decision making unit and then communicating effectively is an essential aspect of the push approach. Partnership success is achieved through co-ordination, trust, participation and the quality of information shared.

Key account management (KAM)

4.5 **Key account management** is an approach to determining which customer accounts are strategically important. These may be large revenue-driven accounts or they might be accounts that offer access to new markets or new technology, be competitively significant or represent a geographic advantage.

Key Concept

Key accounts are perceived to be strategically meaningful and the communications (primarily personal selling) are geared to sustaining and developing the relationship between the two parties.

4.6 Relationships with key accounts unfold and develop through a series of phases.

Stage	Activity
Pre KAM	Identification of potential key accounts
Early KAM	Tentative agreements and probing
Mid KAM	Account review and senior management involvement
Partnership KAM	Joint problem solving and sharing of sensitive information
Synergistic KAM	Synergy of shared values and a one entity perspective
Uncoupling KAM	A positive move recognising that there is no further value in the relationship

4.7 There is more on key account management in Chapter 11 in the context of **relationship marketing**.

5 Profile based communication strategies

5.1 The context analysis may have uncovered issues concerning the way the organisation is perceived by a range of stakeholders, perhaps as a result of an **ethical issue or crisis that has struck the company** and the associated **media comment**. In these circumstances, one of the objectives of the marketing communications strategy will be to correct or adjust the perception held by influential stakeholder audiences.

5.2 The extent of the perception gap will have been uncovered during the analysis of the organisation context. This in turn should have been articulated as a corporate communication objective.

Key Concept

A **profile communication strategy** addresses how the corporate entity is perceived by a range of stakeholder audiences. For example, it is quite common for an organisation to develop a communications campaign that is targeted at the financial markets and the stock market in particular. This is referred to as investor communications.

Corporate identity

5.4 Corporate identity and corporate image are two different facets of the profile development strategy. Increasingly organisations are adopting the phrase **corporate branding** as a substitute for corporate identity.

5.5 Corporate identity is about the way an organisation communicates with its audiences. There are two main forms of communication, those that are planned and pre-determined by the organisation, and those that are unplanned and unexpected.

5.6 The individual communication methods that make up these planned and unplanned communications are referred to as cues.

(a) Examples of **planned cues** are letterheads, logos, signage, product quality and the behaviour and level of knowledge of its employees.

(b) Examples of **unplanned cues** are media comment, the cleanliness of the company's vehicles and any actions taken by competitors and consumer groups that may reflect or directly relate to the organisation.

Action Programme 3

Identify three corporate communication campaigns and the cues used by each to communicate with the different audiences.

5.7 The way in which these cues are perceived frames the way an individual sees and understands an organisation and helps form the image they have of an organisation.

Marketing at Work

Monsanto developed a strong corporate campaign in order to raise the social and scientific arguments related to genetically modified foods. This attempt at being perceived as fair minded and concerned about these issues was articulated using two-sided arguments and invited comment and discussion. This has backfired spectacularly in Europe with huge opposition to GM foods.

5.8 **Corporate identity therefore is about how an organisation presents itself**. Corporate image is what an audience believes an organisation to be as a result of their understanding of the cues. Sometimes the perception of these cues is correct and sometimes it is not correct. This may be because of the quality of either corporate communications or corporate performance. **Corporate reputation** is an extension of corporate image.

Marketing at Work

'No Logo' by Naomi Klein is anti-branding and 'anti-multinational'. She considers that by their very nature multinationals aim to destroy difference and impose a homogeneous culture on the world. Corporate ethics is therefore seen as a cynical, halfhearted exercise. For example, oil companies trading on their green and ethical intentions have been undermined by allegations of human rights abuses.

Corporate communication strategy

5.9 As well as communicating about its individual products and services, the company may wish to pursue a corporate communication strategy. This can take either of two forms.

(a) First, it can be a simple corporate communication campaign aimed at improving the company's identity and subsequently its image.

(b) Secondly, it may be a campaign whereby the company associates itself with a current and topical social issue.

Action Programme 4

Identify two major companies which have developed corporate campaigns related to social issues. What do you consider to be the benefits and potential problems associated with such a strategy?

Crisis communications

5.10 Closely allied to corporate identity is the field of **crisis management** (communications). Company image and reputation can be severely tarnished or even ruined if a response to a crisis is deemed inappropriate.

Mercedes

The initial response by Mercedes when its then prototype vehicle the A-Class turned over when driven by journalists was to deny that there was a problem. That denial, which lasted eight days, turned into a crisis as 3,000 orders were lost and the media refused to let go of the problem. The reputation of Mercedes was dented for the first time in a long time and only the acceptance of the problem, and a public statement about the actions the company was to take with regard to production and design, alleviated the pressure on the company.

5.11 Some crises can be anticipated, perhaps because of the nature of the business environment in which an organisation operates. For example, hospitals can plan for bed shortages caused by epidemics or local accidents. Airlines plan meticulously to cope with air accidents although their incidence is relatively rare. However, the kidnapping of a senior executive cannot be anticipated with such clarity and neither can product sabotage and other seemingly unprovoked attacks on an organisation.

5.12 The following table sets out the phases through which most crises pass. The duration of each phase will vary, depending upon the nature of the disaster and the quality of the management and planning processes.

Disaster phase	Actions
Scanning	Scanning of the environment to pick up signals that might herald a disaster. Many signals fail to materialise but those that do not surprise the organisation.
	Identify the nature of different crises that might hit the organisation. Where and when will it affect the organisation?
	Devise alternative crisis programmes for differing disasters. Establish appropriate communication channels, internally and externally. Chief Executive to formalise the programme and establish its significance throughout the organisation.
Pre-impact	Preparation of a specific crisis plan accompanied by the deployment of crisis teams in order to minimise the effects, and to inform stakeholders of the proximity of the crisis.
	Select key senior personnel and delegate responsibility. Instigate training programmes as necessary.
Impact	Implementation of the plan and continued communication with key stakeholder groups. The aim is to neutralise and localise the affect of the crisis but not to hide or diminish its significance. Maintain close contact with the media and provide stakeholders with access to specific personnel.

Anticipate questions, do not speculate, use facts when answering questions and track media comment.

Readjustment   The speed of recovery is partly dependent upon the strength of the company's image/reputation before the crisis struck. However, internal and external (media, police) investigations characterise this phase. The organisation's attitude must remain consistent, positive and concerned.

Chapter Roundup

- It is possible to identify **three approaches to communication strategy**, based upon the general markets and audiences that are to be targeted.

- These three, **pull**, **push** and **profile strategies** are not mutually exclusive. In practice, all three strategies are used, it is just that the balance between the three strategies will vary, according to the needs of each programme.

- **Pull based programmes** are targeted at **end user consumers** and **business-to-business customers**. **Branding** is often used as pull strategy as it is possible to convey a great deal of information in a concise way.

- **Push based programmes** are directed at **members of the marketing channel** where trust and commitment are essential ingredients for effective communications. **Key account management** techniques serve to help communications with strategically important accounts.

- **Profile strategies** aim to influence the **way the organisation, as a whole, is perceived** by either a small or large range of stakeholders. These strategies serve to develop the visibility and credibility of an organisation. **Crisis management techniques** are an aspect of this, as are corporate branding and associated image activities.

Now try Question 5 in the Question Bank

Quick Quiz

1   What are the 3P's of marketing communications?

2   Pull strategies encourage end-users to demand the product from the distributors.

    True ☐

    False ☐

3   Fill in the gaps in this definition, using the words from the grid below.

    A successful brand:

-    is an (1) ………. product, service, person or place

-    (2)………. so that the buyer or user (3)……….

-    relevant, unique, (4) ………., which

-    (5)………. the buyer's/user's (6) ………. closely

Needs	Perceives	Added value
Identifiable	Matches	Augmented

4   What are the three main elements associated with successful branding?

5   Branding is appropriate for all products in all circumstances.

    True ☐

    False ☐

6   It is important to determine a promotional strategy to reach channel members in order to maximise the impact of a co-ordinated marketing communications approach. This strategy is referred to as a …….. communications strategy.

7   Which statement is correct? Key account management:

A   Justifies managers in ignoring those customers who only order small amounts
B   Is an approach to determining which customer accounts are strategically important
C   Is not important in industrial markets
D   Only really happens in advertising agencies

8   A profile communication strategy addresses how the corporate entity is perceived by a range of stakeholder audiences.

    True ☐

    False ☐

Action Programme Review

1

Option	Comment
Modifying the brand	Redesigning the product so that it offers more of the attributes that the buyer desires.
Altering beliefs about the brand	Pursued if the consumer underestimates the qualities of the brand.
Altering beliefs about competitors' brands	Would be appropriate if the consumer mistakenly believes that a competitor's brand has more quality than it actually has.
Altering the importance of attributes	Persuade consumers to attach more importance to the attribute in which the brand excels.
Calling attention to neglected attributes	Where the brand excels in these attributes. ('Have you forgotten how good they taste?').
Shifting the buyer's ideals	The marketer would try to persuade consumers to change their ideal levels for one or more attributes.

2 For a Jaguar car, the 'core' is transport from A to B. The 'actual' product is a mechanical/electrical/electronic machine in certain colours built with certain features such as leather seats. The 'augmented' component adds the history and tradition of the Jaguar name and heritage.

3 Look for campaigns from companies involved in similar fields and examine how they differ. Give some consideration to the possible differences in the objectives set.

4 Financial services companies such as the Cooperative Bank have developed campaigns based on their ethical investment strategy. Tesco, the food retailer, has been involved in promotional activity aimed at raising funds to provide computers in schools. Such strategies may find favour with different stakeholder groups and enhance corporate image. Drawbacks may include criticism if, for example, the Cooperative Bank is seen to be investing in an area or in a company where negative issues have been raised by pressure groups.

Answers to Quick Quiz

1 Pull communication strategies
Push communication strategies
Profile communication strategies

2 True

3 (1) Identifiable
(2) Augmented
(3) Perceives
(4) Added value
(5) Matches
(6) Needs

4   Differentiation, added value and integration

5   False. For example, the cost of intensive brand communications, such as advertising to project a brand image nationally, may be prohibitively high.

6   Push

7   B

8   True

Key Media – concepts and effectiveness

6

Chapter Topic List
1   Setting the scene
2   Media selection
3   Press
4   Radio
5   Television
6   Other media
7   Advertising on the Internet

Learning Outcomes

☑   Explain how the tools of the promotional mix can be co-ordinated in order to communicate effectively with customers and a range of stakeholders

☑   Develop marketing communication and brand support activities based on an understanding of the salient characteristics of the target audience

Syllabus References

☑   Identify primary and secondary media (online and offline) and contrast their main characteristics

☑   Explain key media concepts (reach, frequency, duplication, GRPs, flighting) and describe the principal approaches used to measure media effectiveness

☑   Compare information and emotional based advertising messages and explain the concept of likeability

Key Concepts Introduced

- Advertising
- Reach
- Frequency
- Ratings

- Advertising on the web
- Banner advertising
- Online and offline promotion

1 Setting the scene

Key Concept

Advertising is 'any paid form of non-personal presentation and promotion of ideas, goods or services by an identifiable sponsor'. (American Marketing Association)

1.1 In this chapter, we look at primary and secondary advertising media.

(a) We will start by outlining the general criteria involved in **media selection**

- **Criteria** by which the effectiveness and efficiency of media can be evaluated
- How the major media can be **compared** with each other

(a) We will then look at the characteristics of each of the **major media** (online and offline) in turn, and at how opportunities to advertise in each can be evaluated.

Exam Tip

With this chapter we are still concerned with the most heavily weighted (50%) area of the syllabus, covering *Co-ordinated Marketing Communications*. There is a concentration on 'the tools and media used to communicate co-ordinated messages to target audiences'. This is a development of your knowledge of the marketing planning framework from Chapter 3.

The Specimen Paper contains a question on media opportunities and key concepts.

2 Media selection (Specimen paper)

Marketing at Work

The advertising budget of your organisation 'can be an **investment**, producing a profit; or it can be an **expense**, producing nothing'. (Drayton Bird, *Marketing News*, 2001)

Bird lists some lessons:

(1) Advertising **does not have to be clever** to succeed

       (i)   People rarely concentrate when they look at advertising.

       (ii)   Most customers are not very clever.

       (iii)   You will waste your money on people who do not understand your message.

       (iv)   Whether clever or not, their money looks the same.

(2)   For advertising to succeed, you must **offer a benefit**

(3)   Advertising that **tells the truth** works better than lies. (Lies actively put people off)

(4)   It pays to be **consistent**

(5)   You **do not have to be original** to succeed, just find the most appropriate message for your product (eg Coca-Cola has concentrated on selling 'refreshment' for over a century)

(6)   Never make the mistake of **boasting** – nobody likes it

Bird also quotes some simple principles ('what works and work doesn't') gleaned by Gallup research in America.

(1)   The best advertisements command **attention**, communicate a **message** and **persuade** through illustrations, headlines and copy

(2)   A successful ad rewards the reader by providing **news or information**, solving a **problem**, or appealing to the **emotions**

(3)   You should **repeat the message** three times, in illustration, headline and copy

(4)   **Illustrations** which relate directly to the message work better

(5)   If you don't illustrate either the product or the idea, the ad is less effective than average

(6)   **Stereotyped pictures** – chatting people, loving couples, smiling sippers and ecstatic eaters kill ads

(7)   **Specific headlines** work best. Vague headlines reduce impact. The most damaging headlines are brag and boast

(8)   **Short headlines** perform just as well as very long ones

(9)   **New** ideas, products, new ways to use a product, can add to performance

(10)   **Humour** only adds a bit to the effectiveness of the ad, and then only when used carefully

(11)   **Celebrities** can add credibility. But if the celebrity is not relevant to the product, he or she does more harm than good.

(12)   **Coupons** do not add much impact, but boost persuasion.

Bird concludes: 'If you know all the things I have mentioned above about what makes advertising work, there is a very strong chance you know more than your advertising agency'.

2.1   The general criteria for selecting a medium to convey the promotional message to the appropriate audience are as follows.

- The advertiser's specific **objectives** and plans
- The **size of the audience** which regularly uses the medium
- The **type of people** who form the audience of the medium
- The **suitability** of the medium for the message
- The **cost** of the medium in relation to its ability to fulfil the advertiser's objectives
- The susceptibility of the medium to **testing** and **measurement**

2.2 The planning of an advertising campaign

(a) The identification of the **target audience**: Who are they? Where are they? Which demographic group do they fall in? What are their interests, media consumption habits, buying patterns, attitudes and values?

(b) The specification of the **communication** or promotional message. What do you need to say, and in what way, in order to impact on the audience in such a way as to achieve your marketing goals?

(c) The setting of **targets**: What is the marketing goal to which the advertising can contribute? What do you expect the ad to achieve and at what cost? What aspects of the audience's thinking or behaviour do you wish to change, and how will you recognise and measure that change if and when it occurs?

Balance of the message

2.3
As we first saw in Chapter 1, our understanding of the level of involvement that may exist in the target audience can be used to determine the **overall balance of the message**. If there is **high involvement**, messages tend to be **rational** (or **information based**), proclaiming product benefits and the key attributes. Where there is **low involvement** the audience are not really interested and the use of **emotion** (or **image**) predominates.

2.4
There are a number of ways in which these **information** and **emotional based messages** can be presented to audiences. These are referred to as **message appeals** and some of the more common approaches are outlined below.

2.5 Information based appeals

Issue	Comment
Factual	The benefits are presented using reasoned, factual arguments (eg nicotine patches).
Slice of life	Allow the target customer to identify with the characters and a common problem. Brand X is then perceived as a suitable solution (eg washing powders).
Demonstration	Show the audience how the product solves a problem (eg floor cleaners, before and after use).
Comparative	Through comparison it is possible to achieved enhanced status and superiority (eg credit and charge cards).

2.6 Emotional based appeals

Issue	Comment
Fear	The suggestion of physical danger or social rejection might be alleviated through use of the brand (eg life assurance, drink driving, anti-dandruff shampoo).
Humour	Attention and mood can be maintained by relaxing the target audience (eg Batchelors Super Noodles).

Issue	Comment
Animation	For low interest products/services animation can attract attention and convey complex products/issues in a novel manner (eg Inland Revenue Self Assessment, Tetley Tea Bags).
Sex	Used primarily to attract attention and to be salient (eg Diet Coke, Wonderbra, Citroen Xsara).
Music	Provides campaign continuity and a degree of differentiation through recognition (eg Ford Cougar, Peugeot 406).
Fantasy	Used to engage an audience and to encourage the question 'what is going on here?' (eg Bristol & West Building Society, Silk Cut, Ericsson).

Action Programme 1

Using a variety of media, identify two examples of all the message appeals listed above. Can you identify anything that is common to your selections?

2.7 When an **emotional approach** to advertising is used, the aim is that the consumer will develop positive feelings about the product being advertised. The role of what is termed **likeability** becomes paramount. People need to enjoy the advertisement at the same time as finding it credible. According to Fill (*Marketing Communications,* 2002) those advertisements that are remembered have certain characteristics. These characteristics add up to making an advertisement 'likeable'.

(a)   The **product is different** or new

(b)   The **advertisement itself is 'different'** or interesting

(c)   The message proclaims something that is **personally significant and relevant** to the consumer (Fill gives the example of a car advertisement seen by someone who is already planning to go out and buy a car the next day)

2.8 Researchers have isolated likeability as the only meaningful indicator of the success of advertising. Likeable messages are more likely to be **stored in the long term memory**, and retrieved when the customer is ready to make a purchase.

2.9 In an online context, the concept of likeability can also be applied to **websites**. Those that are enjoyable to visit and use are more likely to be remembered and revisited. In conclusion, according to Pelsmacker *et al* (*Marketing Communications,* 2001):

> 'Ad likeability might be an important factor because of its ability to **attract attention** and **facilitate information processing**. Peripheral cues such as humour, music, animals and children may attract attention, **induce curiosity** which leads consumers to watch the whole ad, and induce a favourable attitude towards the ad, which can lead to a **favourable brand attitude**.'

The size and type of the audience

2.10 Each medium reaches a certain number and 'type' (demographic group, market segment, interest group) of people. There is a trade-off between the size and relevance of the available audience.

(a) General-interest, national mass-market medium (such as a national newspaper or television) will have the largest **circulation figures**, but may not reach the highest percentage of a particular market segment.

(b) **Segmentation** may be possible through the scheduling and placing of ads in large-scale media (for example, in special-interest sections or supplements in the press, or by programme preference in TV).

(c) **Targeted media** may reach a smaller population, but a higher percentage of the target audience.

  - **Local or regional media** (in the catchment area)
  - **Specialist magazines** and journals related to the target audience
  - Media which fit the **'media habits'** of the target audience

Action Programme 2

Brainstorm a list of media which might be suitably targeted (by factors in the media themselves, or in the media habits of the target audiences) for advertising the following products/services.

(a) A local garage offering car service, maintenance and parts
(b) An up-market restaurant
(c) A software package for use by accountants (based on UK law and regulation)
(d) A new brand of washing powder
(e) A microchip for use in engineering applications

2.11 James Hearne *(Advertising Management)* suggests that the effective audience of a medium and therefore the competitiveness of different media is influenced by the following factors.

(a) **Opportunity to use the medium**. The potential audience will not be able to use TV during working hours, or magazines while driving, or cinema over breakfast. Radio in the morning and TV in the evening have bigger effective audiences.

(b) **Effort required to use the medium**. People usually use the medium that will cost them least effort. Print media require the ability to read and concentrate: television is comparatively effortless.

(c) **Familiarity with the medium**. People consume media with which they are familiar: hence the survival of print media, since the education system is still predominantly print-orientated. Electronic media are however gaining ground.

(d) **Segmentation by the medium**. The print media currently has the greatest capacity for segmentation into special-interest audiences. Commercial television segments to a limited extent through programming, and cable/satellite television to a greater extent, through the proliferation of channels. Some media only charge in proportion to the segment you are targeting, which is more cost effective than paying for the full circulation.

Action Programme 3

What opportunity, effort and familiarity issues might you consider when appraising the following media?

(a)   A newly launched radio station
(b)   Daytime television
(c)   Posters on buses
(d)   Web pages

2.12 **Media research** is designed to provide advertisers with detailed information on the size and composition of the audience for relevant media and the reading and viewing habits of the different types of people and so on. Media planners (the people in advertising agencies who plan how to deploy the main-media advertising budget) use as much reliable research data as they can obtain. Here are some examples.

(a)   The National Readership Survey or JICNARS (Joint Industry Committee for National Readership Surveys) for major newspapers and magazines

(b)   BARB (the British Audience Research Bureau) for television

(c)   RAJAR (Radio Joint Audience Research) for radio

(d)   JICPAS for posters

(e)   The Screen Advertisers' Association for cinema

A marketing organisation may wish to commission or carry out its own research into the media habits of its customers and potential customers.

The suitability of the medium for the message

2.13 Certain media 'do' certain things better than others. You might bear this in mind.

(a)   **The technical characteristics of the medium**. The success of a medium depends on its ability to identify and offer the benefits which its technical characteristics are best suited to provide: television for images and demonstrations, cinema for fantasy, visual impact, radio for music and participation, print for detailed information.

(b)   **The perceived function of the medium**. Media users look to different media to perform different functions in their lives: information/education (world news, local events, specialist instruction) or entertainment (music, sport, escapism, community contact). These perceptions of a medium's functions and strengths will influence the orientation of its audience towards advertising messages.

(c)   **The impact/realism of the medium**. One of the strengths of television is the impact to be derived from its realistic merging of sight and sound.

Cost and value for money

2.14 Cost in itself is not a helpful criterion (unless it rules out a medium by virtue of its exceeding the spending budget). What advertisers need to know, in order to compare and evaluate media meaningfully, is the following.

- How many relevant people are reached?
- How many times and how effectively?
- For how much?

2.15 The conventional criteria of value for money measurement is: **cost per thousand people reached** by a medium. If an advertisement in a newspaper with a circulation of 2 million readers costs £7,000, the cost per thousand is £3.50.

2.16 'Cost per thousand' is a common **inter-media comparison**-measuring device. However, it is only a crude measure, which does not take everything into account.

(a) The **targeting or relevance** of the audience reached by different media (or in different issues or time slots)

(b) The **potential impact** of an advertisement in different media (its size or length, colour or black and white, positioning in the publication or programme schedule, proximity to competing ads)

(c) **Extended or repeated exposure** to the ad (if people use the medium frequently, or pass it on to friends)

(d) **Selective exposure** to the ad (for example, people may not read the whole paper or magazine, or may leave the room during TV commercials)

2.17 The different media have their own methods of allowing for these factors when promoting their effectiveness to advertisers, and we will look at some of them – such as television ratings – later in this chapter.

Susceptibility to testing and measurement

2.18 **Testing**, or measuring the effectiveness of advertisements is the only sure way to know what 'works' in terms of gaining a response. The same ad run in different media can demonstrate the comparative effectiveness of the media, while different ads (size, position, timing, layout, response methods, headlines) in the same media can indicate the most effective form of the promotional message.

2.19 Some media are better for testing ads than others and if this is important to you, you will need to ask yourself the following questions.

(a) How **quickly** do I want our tests to yield results? (A daily publication produces response more quickly than a weekly.)

(b) How **effectively** does the medium allow me to elicit direct responses? (Will it carry a direct-response coupon, or memorable telephone number?)

(c) Will I be able to **attribute** increased enquiries/sales to their source in a particular ad? (Coded coupons, tracking for example).

A general comparison of major media

2.20 The next two pages show some of the ways in which you might usefully evaluate advertising media.

Medium	Advantages	Disadvantages
Newspapers (daily metropolitan/ national)	■ 'Mass' medium: large audience in single exposure ■ Targeted sections (auto, home, computers etc) ■ Reader navigation: seeking news, information ■ Short lead time for production: accept ads 24-48 hours before publication ■ Flexibility of ad size ■ Tangibility of ad (can be torn out and kept) ■ Multiple readers/users ■ Allows detailed information (prices, phone numbers etc) ■ Allows (still) images ■ Allows response mechanisms (eg captions)	■ Circulation does not mean readership: wasted circulation paid for ■ Print/image reproduction of variable quality ■ No exclusivity: ad may be next to competitor's ■ Costs loaded for preferred positions ■ Short life-span of news
Newspapers (local/free)	■ Low cost ■ Geographical targeting ■ High local readership ■ Special sections (especially local real estate, entertainment etc)	■ Circulation of free papers/weeklies not always monitored/audited ■ Variable editorial content ■ Subject to weather and junk mail rejection if letterbox dropped
Magazines	■ High circulation (major titles) ■ Targeted audiences (special) ■ High quality reproduction (colour photography etc) ■ Potential high prestige ■ Reader motivation (selection, subscription) ■ Long shelf life and multiple use/readership ■ Tangibility, detail, images, response mechanisms (see newspapers)	■ High costs of production ■ Hyper-segmentation (by interest and geography, may be insufficient circulation to support local outlets) ■ Long lead times: copy/artwork required 1 – 3 months before publication, can be inflexible
Television	■ 'Mass' medium: large audience at single exposure, almost universal ownership/access ■ Detailed monitoring of exposure, reach, viewer habits ■ Allows for high degree of creativity ■ Realism: impact of sound + sight + movement ■ High-impact visual images reinforce retention ■ Allows demonstration ■ Flexibility as to scheduling ■ Allows association with desirable products	■ Most expensive of all media costs ■ High production costs ■ Lack of selectivity (except via programming) of audience ■ Lack of opportunity: does not reach commuters/workers ■ Long lead times for booking and production: penalties for withdrawal: inflexibility ■ Passive, unmotivated audience: 'zapping' by video fast-forward and remote controls erodes reach

Medium	Advantages	Disadvantages
Radio	■ 'Mass' medium: wide coverage/access ■ Audience selectivity (local/regional) programme style/variety/content) ■ Opportunity: radio is portable – in-home, in-car, on public transport, shops, offices – even jogging ■ Function: high usage for morning news, home 'companionship', background ■ Personal (and potential for participation) ■ Highly competitive costs of air time and production ■ Can be backed by personal DJ promos	■ May be passive 'background' noise: low attention, retention ■ May be 'cluttered' by announcers/DJ promotions ■ Sound only: no tangibility (pressure on retention of message), no shelf-life or 'pass on' circulation, no demonstration, no coupons, limited details
Outdoor media (poster sites bus stops, buildings etc)	■ Flexible: sites, duration of lease ■ Comparatively low cost ■ Opportunity: exposure to commuters, shoppers	■ Difficulty of verification of exposure/response ■ Subject to weather ■ Opportunity: site specific ■ No audience selectivity (except by site)
Cinema	■ Glamorous ■ High impact (large size, highly visual, loud sound, high quality) ■ Captive audience (no TV 'zap' factor) ■ Can segment by local area	■ High cost ■ Opportunity: site/time specific ■ Poor verification of response ■ Limited number of people reached per exposure
Internet	■ Principally sight, but with sound and colour further possibilities are developing ■ Interactive, permitting direct response ■ Able to track audience movements ■ Message permanent, and can be down-loaded	■ Generally poor viewership ■ Consumer confidence in security low (but improving) ■ Possible to direct audience to information, but can be difficult to gain large audience without support from other media ■ Not yet a mainstream media with broad customer appeal ■ Speed of access depends on sophistication of technological link ■ No universal computing language yet agreed

2.21 The following is a broad SWOT analysis comparing some of the major media.

Medium	Applications	Targeting	Testing	Cost per contact	Response speed	Response %	Response volume
Press	– Lead generation – Direct sales – General awareness – Support for other activities – Boost store traffic	Medium	Medium	V low	Fast	Low	High
Radio	– Awareness – store and event traffic boost – lead generation (high ticket business-to-business)	Medium to poor	Poor	High	Medium	V Low	Low
TV - general	– Awareness – Store traffic boost	Medium to poor	Poor	High	Fast	Low	Low
TV – direct response	– Lead generation (high ticket items) – Direct sales (low ticket items) – Support for other activities	Medium	Poor	Low	Fast	Low	Medium
Posters	– Awareness – Store traffic boost	Poor	Nil	V low	Slow	Nil	Nil
Inserts	– Lead generation – Direct sales (especially non cash-with-order sales	Good	V Good	Low to medium	Fast	Medium to low	High
Direct Mail	– All (weakest where prospects 'cold', no suitable list available)	V Good	V Good	V High	Medium	High	Medium

2.22 **When** are the messages to be communicated to the target audience? This depends on a number of factors.

(a)　**Objectives** of the campaign. If these are short term, then a concentrated burst will be best. Longer-term objectives can probably be satisfied by a less intense campaign.

(b)　It is important to reach the consumer at or very near the **point of purchase**.

(c)　The **level of involvement** is important. For high involvement purchases, less repetition is needed than for low involvement, where the message needs to be more frequent.

(d)　The **characteristics of the target audience** will also dictate scheduling times – when their favourite programmes are on television, for instance.

(e)　The size of the promotional **budget** is also a key factor.

2.23 The following **scheduling options** have been identified.

Continuity patterns

2.24 These represent **regular and uniform** presentation of advertisements for **reminder** purposes, generally on mature products and fmcg's, where no additional information is needed by the customer prior to purchase. The danger with this type of scheduling is that where the budget is limited, resources may be spread too thinly over the period during which the advertisement is running.

Flighting patterns

2.25 Flighting means **concentrating advertising in only a few periods**, allowing advertisers to spread resources over a longer period of time. No campaign is run at all in some months, in order to be able to spend more during times of peak demand. For that reason it is appropriate in situations where there is a **varying demand** for the product, or there is likely to be a sudden requirement for some kind of competitive response. Other situations where flighting may be appropriate include:

- Major sales promotions
- A response to adverse publicity
- One-off market opportunities
- Seasonality (such as tour operators advertising summer holidays in the depths of winter)
- Launch of new products
- Promotion of a particular event

Pulsing

2.26 The disadvantage of a flighting pattern is that the target customers can easily forget messages during times of no advertising. A **pulsing** pattern represents a combination of both flighting and continuous presentation. A certain level of advertising takes place during the whole period, with levels increased at certain times of the year. This is a 'safe' pattern, but is also likely to be comparatively **expensive**. The key advantage of pulsing stops target customers from forgetting, building awareness and providing a barrier in the customer's memory against competitor advertising.

3 Press

3.1 Press or print media

- **Newspapers**: daily and weekly, morning and evening, national and regional
- **Magazines**, periodicals and journals: general appeal, special interest and trade

Circulation and readership figures

3.2 The **Audit Bureau of Circulation (ABC)** provides audited figures of the actual circulation of major newspapers and magazines. This figure is often the basis of advertising rates. It offers only partial information.

(a) There may be many **more readers than purchasers**. People may pass a publication on to others to read, or it may be perused by many people in dentists' waiting rooms or hairdressers. It is the estimated **readership** that interests the advertiser. The **Readership Survey** publishes the average readership per issue.

(b) Readership data is also available on what **types of reader** consume various publications, with what frequency and in what manner (all the way through or some sections only).

Types of press ads

3.3 Print media offer different types of advertising.

(a) **Classified advertising**. The classified sections of publications offer small spaces for text-only ads. The advantage is that classified space is very cheap, and the publication usually typesets the ad for you. The disadvantage is the difficulty of attracting attention with so much competition and so little space: icons, headline, styles and impactful/incentive copy are required to make an ad stand out.

(b) **Semi-display advertising** allows you to use borders, typographic features and illustrations to attract attention (although on a crowded page, white space and simplicity may be more effective). Small ads in the Yellow Pages are a good example.

(c) **Display advertising** offers further opportunity for creativity: the advertisers design and provide their own artwork or film, constrained only by the technical specifications (size, colour) of the publication. Full-colour magazine ads are a good example. 'Long copy' advertisements break the usual simple visual style of display advertising by including lots of detailed information.

(d) **Advertorials** are advertisements presented as edited copy, in order to take advantage of the perceivably objective authority of editorial matter. Features on health and beauty, advice, house and garden are often advertisements for the products and services 'reviewed' or 'recommended'.

(e) **Loose inserts or 'drop outs'** are printed leaflets (produced by the advertiser) inserted into magazines and newspapers. They usually work out 4 or 5 times more expensive than advertising space – but draw up to 5 or 6 times as many responses as a full-page advertisement.

Marketing at Work

Car manufacturers often use long copy display ads for their cars. Full-page advertisements include detailed technical specifications and engineering drawings of the cars' driving and safety features. Such extensive copy is often effective for very expensive products, because it provides sufficient information to support an expensive purchase decision – and to justify or rationalise the purchase as a 'good' decision, not merely based on desire or snobbery.

Contrast this with purely visual display ads – often with no copy at all.

Press ad rates

3.4 Print media is bought in **column inches** (or centimetres) or standard **page divisions** (quarter, half or full page, or 'junior' page). The cost/rate differs.

- The **size** of the ad
- The number of **colours** in the ad and the production quality of the publication
- **Position** of the ad for which a premium may be charged
- The **readership** number of the publication
- The **potential for readership** targeting or niche marketing
- The **prestige** of the publication and the spending power of its readership.

Positioning press ads

3.5 Media research into **'traffic per page'** (the reading and noting of different pages in a print publication) suggests the following.

- **Early pages** are read more than late pages (depending on editorial content)

- **Right-hand pages** have higher noting scores than left-hand pages

- **Pages opposite relevant or popular editorial content** do better than pages opposite other advertising and less read editorial content.

3.6 **Cover space** is particularly sought after because of its high visibility, and usually also because the covers are printed on better quality paper for colour production. The outside front cover is likely to be most expensive, followed by outside back, inside front (especially if opposite the contents page) and inside back.

Scheduling of press ads

3.7 The approach to **scheduling** requires a combination of the following concepts.

- **Reach or exposure** - how many of the right type of people see the ad

- **Frequency** - how many times people see the ad. It does not cover the quality of the exposure or whether any impact was made on the audience.

3.8 With press advertising, in some circumstances it is generally advisable to repeat an ad more often.

(a) if the ad is **small** (and may not be noticed by all readers at one exposure)
(b) if the publication is **high circulation** (so the ad may not be noticed by all readers)
(c) if the product or ad is **interesting** (and will therefore continue to attract attention)

3.9 Even so, the **law of diminishing returns** operates with repeated exposure. As the ad reaches a higher proportion of the relevant audience, more often, the rate of response levels off. Awareness of the company or offer increases with repetition, but the rate of direct response to individual ads (via coupon or response line) falls: the 'easiest' prospects have already been reached.

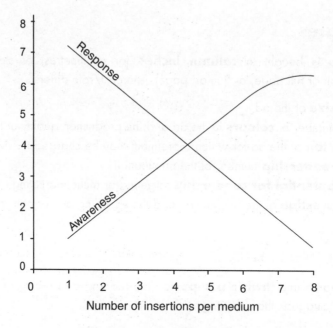

(*Source:* The Institute of Direct Marketing, quoted by Ros Jay, *The Essential Marketing Sourcebook*)

4 Radio

4.1 The perceived function and image of **radio** is an important factor in the response to radio advertising. Radio is a personal and 'intimate' medium which encourages relationship and trust: according to the Radio Advertising Bureau (www.rab.co.uk), people are more likely to believe what they hear on radio than what they see on television. **Local radio** has a particularly close 'community' image. National radio stations are aimed more at a particular type of listener.

4.2 Radio tends to form the **background** to other activities. This enables it to have a wide reach (since it can be listened to while driving, working, jogging), but also lessens listeners' attention to and retention of advertising messages. The lack of visual images is also a disadvantage, but can be overcome by different techniques: the use of dialogue, mood, drama, humour and curiosity.

4.3 Radio ads are usually bought in series of 15 second or 30 second '**slots**'. Because of the high 'portability' of radio, there may be a wider range of off-peak scheduling opportunities.

Marketing at Work

The **Radio Advertising** Bureau highlights these terms on its website (www.rab.co.uk).

TSA	Total Survey Area: the area covered by a station's signal.
Campaign reach	The number of listeners who hear at least one ad in a particular campaign – either expressed in thousands, or as a percentage of the population.
Frequency (Opportunities to Hear or OTH)	The average number of times a listener will hear a campaign ad, usually during a week.
RAJAR	Radio Joint Audience Research. The official measurement system for both BBC and Commercial radio audiences.
Listening	Listening to a station may be measured either in terms of how many listeners tune in each week (reach), or in terms of how much listening there is in each week (hours).
Weekly reach	The number of listeners who tune in to a station at some point during a week, expressed as a percentage of the TSA.
Weekly hours	The total amount of listening (measured in hours) that a station accounts for. So, if Commercial Radio has a 51% share, 51% of *all* radio listening is to a commercial station.

Listenership figures

4.4 **RAJAR (Radio Joint Audience Research Ltd)** release quarterly reports showing what percentage/volume of the population listens to commercial radio, at what times and for how long, with breakdowns for each radio station. Around 25% of the UK population listen to national commercial radio, and 50% to local commercial radio, in the course of a week, for an average 15 hours per week. Over 70% of 15 – 34 year olds listen to commercial radio and almost the same proportion of business people and housewives with children.

4.5 Although such figures do not indicate whether people hear or take in any ads that may air during their listening hours, there are several positive indicators that radio can perform well in this respect.

- **Prompted recall of radio ads** is 80% of that of TV ads
- Radio listeners report that they **do not generally switch stations** when ads come on
- An average weight campaign on radio will reach each consumer **four times a week**
- **Talk-back radio** has a high response rate, even late at night

5 Television

5.1 The **Independent Broadcasting Authority (IBA)** controls commercial TV (and radio) in the UK, and licenses a number of regional companies.

5.2 Because of the **high exposure**, **glamour** and **audio-visual impact** of television, it has become the favoured medium for launching new products, raising brand awareness and building brand loyalty, re-positioning brands and also motivating the employees and supply chain partners of the advertising organisation. (This perception is encouraged by advertising agencies, whose **commission** on TV airtime is many times higher than on print space and other media.)

5.3 A major recent trend is in the development of **direct response TV advertising**, in which the viewer is given a telephone number and invited to call for more information or to place an order. This used to be perceived as down-market and American, but research now shows that it promotes an image of the organisation as organised, financially sound and willing to be readily accessible to customers. Direct response advertising has also enabled detailed measurement of the effectiveness of ads on different stations, at different times, in different formats.

Viewership figures

5.4 As with radio, it is a complex matter to access not just how many sets are owned and switched on at particular times, but how many people are actually watching – let alone consciously taking in what is being transmitted.

5.5 The size of the television audience for a given programme (and advertising) is measured in **ratings**: rating points, or **TVRs**. One TVR point represents 1% of all homes which have a TV set in the region to which the programme is broadcast. Ratings are used by TV stations to monitor the popularity of their programmes, and to set advertising rates. The advertiser pays for the number of TVRs allocated to given advertising spots.

(a) A programme with 20 TVRs is seen by 20% of homes with a TV. This is the number of people who will (in theory) see an ad once.

(b) If you placed an ad in four programmes, each with a rating of 20 TVRs, you would achieve 80 TVRs. However, some homes might have seen the ad all four times, while others may have missed it altogether. You need to distinguish between **reach** and **frequency** (the number of times the ad is run, and therefore the number of **opportunities to see it, or OTS**).

(c) **Gross Rating Points (GRPs)** are a measure of probable reach multiplied by probable frequency. If you buy 280 GRPs, about 70% of households should have 4 opportunities to see your ad.

(d) **Target Audience Rating Points (TARPs)** measure reach and frequency against specific demographic audiences, across a wide range of criteria (geographic, gender, age, socio-economic bracket). These are the most effective guide for advertisers, since they allow the media planner to devise a schedule which will deliver the largest relevant audience for the available budget: the gross cumulative exposure of the campaign to the target audience can be assessed on the standard cost-per-thousand basis.

Key Concepts

Reach refers to the size of the audience which is exposed to an ad, both net (number of people reached) and gross (including cumulative multiple exposures)

Frequency refers to the number of times an ad is run, opportunities to see (OTS) the ad; or 'impacts'

Ratings are measurements of television audiences, which multiply reach by frequency (or OTS) to give the probable coverage and repetition of an ad, with (TARPS) or without (GRPs) breakdown by demographic criteria.

Exam Tip

These key concepts (reach, frequency and opportunities to see) are featured in a question on the Specimen Paper.

5.6 The lowest cost per thousand is not necessarily the best schedule: One recommendation is the purchase of at least 250 – 300 TVRs, giving 70% coverage and a minimum of three OTS, in order to make a TV campaign worthwhile.

5.7 Statistically valid and helpful for comparison as ratings are, they still give only limited information: they count 'pairs of eyes' not responsiveness to ads. Detailed **qualitative media research** is required to indicate people's media habits.

- **Leaving the room** during commercial breaks
- Using the **remote control** to change channel to avoid ads
- **Videoing** TV programmes and fast-forwarding through commercial breaks

Further testing will be required to gauge **awareness and recall** of specific ads.

Scheduling TV ads

5.8 In addition to TARPs, which suggest where and when to schedule ads in order to reach an optimum number of target viewers an optimum number of times, the advertiser should consider the following.

(a) **Daytime audiences** are more responsive. Direct responses to TV ads are greatest between 12 noon – 2pm and 2pm – 4pm on weekdays.

(b) Audiences show greater recall of ads at the **beginning** of a long commercial break. The more ads they see, the lower the recall of each.

(c) Audiences tend to watch through commercial breaks in the **middle of TV programmes**, because they do not want to miss any of the programme. However, viewers are reluctant to take action in response to ads during the programme, so direct-response ads are more successful during **end breaks.** (Most people respond within 15 minutes of the ad spot.)

(d)   Advertising guru David Ogilvy suggests that while most advertisers use 30-second ads, 90-second or even two minute ads can be more effective (as with long-copy press ads) especially for complex or expensive products.

(e)   Very short (10-second) ads can also be effective, and offer much higher TARPs for the available budget, since you can get more exposures. However, the greater impact of longer commercials usually offsets the reduced TARPs which longer ads deliver.

(f)   Repetition of ads increases TARPs, but is subject to the law of **diminishing returns**. It is essential for the message to sink in, but people easily become habitual and cease to notice or be motivated by the ad. One strategy is to have a **set of related ads** which can be rotated, reinforcing but varying the message.

Duplication

5.9   As part of the consideration of the effectiveness of a media plan, and related to the concept of **frequency**, it is important to think about how many times a message should be repeated. This goes back to point (f) above. There is general agreement that there should be at least three OTS.

   ■   First viewing: "What is this?" (seeking **understanding**)
   ■   Second viewing: "What does this mean to me?" (**recognition**)
   ■   Third viewing: "Oh, I remember" (**prompting action**)

5.10 Members of a target audience buy several magazines, and watch more than one television programme. They are exposed to many media vehicles. Those who are exposed to an advertisement only once are said to provide **unduplicated reach**. When a target is exposed to two or more overlapping advertisements, this is referred to as **duplicated reach**.

5.11 Duplicated reach is obviously more expensive than unduplicated reach, and so any media plan needs to specify how much of each type of reach is required.

Digital television

5.12 In the UK, it is predicted that digital TV will reach 13 million homes by 2004. Digital TV allows viewers to obtain in-depth information about products and services, via their remote control.

5.13 Digital television also offers opportunities for better targeting and segmentation. In theory, TV companies will be able to target particular advertisements to particular areas. However, this type of interactivity is still in its early stages. There is wariness by some marketers about becoming too intrusive.

Exam Tip

The impact of digital based technologies on marketing communications is a specific syllabus topic. As an indication of how it may be examined, a question set in June 2002 under the old *Integrated Marketing Communications* syllabus asked candidates about the use of interactive TV, and how customers might be encouraged to use it again and again.

Marketing at Work

The advent of digital television, where the viewer is in control, not only of the programmes he or she watches, but also their level of involvement with the content, may offer vast opportunities for marketers.

Broadcasters need material to fill their programmes, and specialist PR agencies are starting to emerge, dedicated to producing TV coverage which promoted brands via tailored footage of, for example, motor shows and fashion shows.

The first interactive TV ad in the UK was aired on 29 March 2000 by Van den Bergh foods for its Chicken Tonight cook-in sauce.

Action Programme 4

All other things being equal, and subject to detailed research, at what time of day, or in what kind of programme, might you advertise the following products on TV?

- Shoe polish
- Home disinfectant
- Car repairs
- Chat/introduction lines

6 Other media

Outdoor media

6.1 **Poster advertising** is one of the oldest media for consumer goods advertising. Sites on walls, hoardings and bus shelters can be leased for a fee per calendar month. In addition, many vehicles (buses, trucks and taxis) now carry external advertising, and some are tailor-made to do so (advertising 'floats'). Trains and buses also offer internal advertising positions. Size and visibility of the sites are the main consideration.

Cinema

6.2 Cinema advertising takes advantage of high audio-visual impact and a captive audience but still requires a high quality and entertainment value.

Cinema advertising best suits 'lifestyle' products.

- **Branded consumer goods** with high style and profile, aimed mainly at young adults (such as jeans and alcohol)

- **Local services** in the area of the cinema (particularly restaurants)

New media

6.3 Technology has widened the range of advertising media to include the following.

(a) **Videos** including informational instructional videos and advertising accompanying entertainment videos

(b) **Teletext** (usually via sponsoring of relevant types of information which the target audience might access)

(c) **Enhanced CD and CD-ROM** (especially for selling merchandise related to the information or entertainment contained on the CD)

(d) **Websites**. Internet shopping and other transactions are on the increase, as issues of payment security are sorted out. Websites with product/service information and related links vary in sophistication, but can provide an attractive **audio-visual and interactive** experience of promotional messages. In addition, they offer an opportunity for customers to access basic information which they might be reluctant to ask about over the phone.

Marketing at Work

Prices are falling in advertising media. According to an article in *Marketing Business* (January 2002) space costs are falling in newspapers, magazines and posters. In TV, the cost of a typical slot is around 12% lower than last year.

7 Advertising on the Internet

Key Concept

Advertising on the World Wide Web is generally acknowledged to be when an advertiser pays to place advertising content on another website.

7.1 The opportunities to reach target audiences are now many and varied, but **just because they exist, that does not mean that they have to be used**. The purpose of advertising is to 'inform, influence or persuade' (CIM), regardless of the media used. To quote from the CIM again:

> 'Matching medium to audience demands that the marketer consider a number of criteria, some of which will be more important than others depending on the campaign aims and objectives. These include cost, ability to reach the audience and creative ability of the medium.'

Marketing at Work

Online advertisements are becoming ever more attention seeking. Animation, video and audio are moving the field beyond the normal banner advert. A company called *Eyeblaster.com* has facilitated the development of brash and noisy online advertising. The new formats are giving scope for greater creativity.

Newspapers, which invested heavily in putting their content online, are at the forefront of experimenting with the new formats to attract advertising revenue to their sites.

The use of interactive banner adverts is also increasing, adding value to the advertisement by providing services such as:

■ Entering a destination to show the cheapest fare
■ Filling in an e-mail address to receive further information

7.2 So the Internet has become a medium for carrying advertising in its own right. The same principles that we have already discussed in this chapter, centred around **matching medium to audience**, still apply. Companies need to be sure that the web provides the right environment and audience profile to meet marketing objectives.

7.3 The most common form of web advertising occurs when the advertiser uses a range of sites to drive visitors to a corporate site.

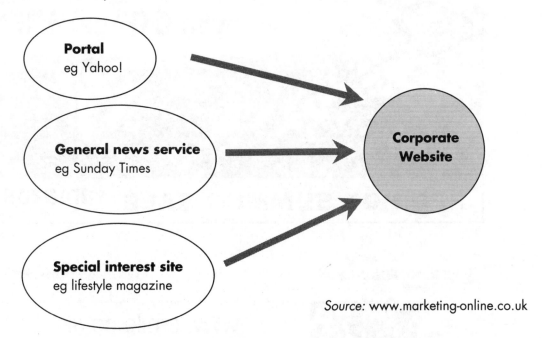

Source: www.marketing-online.co.uk

7.4 Companies are still learning what works with web advertising, and what does not. There are two basic types of promotion associated with the Internet, **online** and **offline**.

Key Concept

Online promotion uses communication via the Internet itself to raise awareness. This may take the form of links from other sites, targeted email messages or banner advertisements.

Offline promotion uses traditional media such as TV or newspaper advertising to promote a website address (URL).

Key Concept

A **banner advertisement** is "a typically rectangular graphic displayed on a web page for purposes of brand-building or driving traffic to a site. It is normally possible to perform a click through to access further information from another website. Banners may be static or animated". Banner adverts can be targeted at a particular audience.

Source: www.Marketing-online.co.uk

Here are some examples of banner advertisements.

Marketing at Work

There are some tricks to offline promotion that can be used to help the customer in finding the information they need on a website. When advertising in traditional media such as a newspaper or magazine, it is beneficial to highlight a specific page that is related to the offline promotion and the interests of the audience. For example:

■ In an American magazine: www.jaguar.com/us

■ In a phone advert from a company that sells other products: www.ericcsson.com/us/phones

■ For a specific digital camera: www.agfahome.com/ephoto

By doing this, the user will be sent directly to the relevant information without having to navigate through the corporate site.

A similar technique is to use a different sub-domain to the main domain, or register a completely different domain name which is in keeping with the campaign:

■ www.drivehonda.com rather than www.honda.com

■ www.fireandwater.com rather than Harpers and Collins Publishers

■ www.askntl.com to highlight that the site has the answers to questions such as: Who are NTL? What are their services?

Increasingly, promotion of the website in the offline media is not simply flagging the existence of the website as an afterthought via including the URL at the bottom of the advert, but highlighting the offers or services available at the website, such as special sales promotions or online customer service. Amazon commonly advertises in newspapers to achieve this.

Placing and paying for banner advertising

7.5 Banner advertising can generally be placed through a traditional agency. It is typically paid for according to the number of users who view the web page. Cost is calculated as **cost per thousand ad impressions**. The following table shows some figures from 1999 for banner advertising costs.

Site name	Type of site	Banner cost per 1,000
Yahoo home page (www.yahoo.co.uk	Portal	£21-£70
New Musical Express (www.mne.com)	Special interest	£30
Virgin Radio (www.virginradio.com)	Special interest	£25
Vogue magazine	Special interest	£39
AOL (www.aol.uk.com)	Portal	£60

(*Source:* Marketing-online.co.uk)

Action Programme 5

Who are the likely target audiences for each of the sites listed in the table above?

Measuring the effectiveness of Internet advertising

7.6 This is based upon the behaviour of web users. When using the Internet, users will go through several stages:

- **Be exposed** to a message (for example, through a banner advertisement)
- Look for **more information** by clicking on the banner
- **Go to the web page** of the advertiser

7.7 Based on this sequence, different types of ad effectiveness have been identified (listed by Pelsmacker *et al* (*Marketing Communications*, 2001). These can be measured for different online advertisements of the same advertiser, on a daily basis if required, to monitor web ad effectiveness.

- Total **ad impressions** (number of contacts made by the ad)
- **'Click throughs'** (contact by a user with advertisement)
- **Ad transfer** (successful arrival of a user at the advertiser's website)

Other online advertising methods

7.8 These include:

(a) **Promotion in search engines and directories** (such as Yahoo!). Your company may want to have its company website listed when a user types in a specific keyword, such as 'office equipment'. To achieve this, your website should be registered with each of the main search engines (Yahoo!, MSN, Infoseek, Netscape, Excite, for example).

Marketing at Work

Research shows that most users will only bother looking at the first 10 listings thrown up by their search.

(b) **Links from other sites**. This involves making sure that your site is linked to as many related sites as possible.

(c) **Using e-mail** for advertising new products directly to customers.

Chapter Roundup

■ **Media selection** should be made in accordance with the organisation's **advertising objectives** on the following criteria

- The size of the audience/circulation
- The type of audience (in relation to the target audience)
- The opportunity of the audience to use the medium
- The effort required to use the media
- The audience's familiarity with the medium
- The selectivity/segmentation allotted by the medium
- The suitability of the medium's technical characteristics for the message
- The suitability of the medium's perceived function for the message
- The cost-effectiveness of the medium
- The medium's susceptibility to testing and measurement

■ **Media research** is designed to provide data on circulated audience reach and media habits.

■ **Cost comparisons** are usually made on the basis of 'cost per thousand' (people reached, or impacts).

■ The **advantages and disadvantages of the major media** can be found in the table in 2.20.

■ Possible scheduling options include **continuity**, **flighting** and **pulsing**.

■ **Reach** refers to the size of the audience which is exposed to an ad, both net (number of people reached) and gross (including cumulative multiple exposures).

■ **Frequency** refers to the number of times an ad is run; opportunities to see (OTS) the ad.

■ **Ratings** are measurements of television audiences, which multiply reach by frequency (or OTS) to give the probable coverage and repetition of an ad, with (TARPS) or without (GRPs) breakdown by demographic criteria.

■ Those who are exposed to an advertisement only once are said to provide **unduplicated reach**. When a target is exposed to two or more overlapping advertisements, this is referred to as **duplicated reach**.

■ **Online promotion** uses communication via the Internet itself to raise awareness. This may take the form of links from other sites, targeted e-mail messages or banner advertisements.

■ **Offline promotion** uses traditional media such as TV or newspaper advertising to promote a website address (URL).

Now try Question 6 in the Question Bank

Quick Quiz

1   Fill in the gaps using the words in the grid below:

The general criteria for selecting a medium to convey the promotional message to the appropriate audience are as follows.

■   The advertiser's specific (1) ....
■   The (2) .... of the audience which regularly uses the medium
■   The (3) .... who form the audience of the medium
■   The (4)........ of the medium for the message
■   The (5).......... of the medium in relation to its ability to fulfil the advertiser's objectives
■   The susceptibility of the medium to (6) ....

Testing & measurement	Type of people	Size
Cost	Objectives	Suitability

2   What are the two types of message appeal?

3   Researchers have isolated 'likeability' as one of the most meaningful indicators of advertising success.

True   ☐

False   ☐

4   The conventional criteria of value for money measurement is: cost per thousand people reached. If an advertisement in a newspaper with a circulation of 3 million readers costs £21,000, the cost per thousand is:

A   £6.30
B   £3.50
C   £7
D   £21

5   Give one advantage and one disadvantage of the use of a national newspaper for advertising.

6   Fill in the gaps using the grid below:

(1)   .... refers to the size of the audience which is exposed to an ad

(2)   .... refers to the number of times an ad is run

(3)   .... are a measure of probable reach multiplied by probable frequency.

(4)   .... measure reach and frequency against specific demographic audiences, across a wide range of criteria (geographic, gender, age, socio-economic bracket).

Target audience rating points (TARPs)	Reach
Gross rating points (GRPs)	Frequency

7   What is duplicated reach, and why is it important to the process of media scheduling?

8   'Click throughs' are measures of:

A   The number of contacts made by an Internet advertisement
B   The direct contact by a user with an advertisement
C   Successful arrival of users at an advertiser's website
D   The number of banner advertisements seen by a use

Action Programme Review

1   Include these examples in the files you are keeping of differing communications activities.

2   (Suggestions only)

(a)   Local radio (in car), bus stop, poster sites (driver visibility), local paper 'Auto' section.

(b)   Local cinema (evening session, adult-appeal film), local paper 'Food' section, Good Food Guide (regional listing), local radio (classical music/news programmes?)

(c)   UK Accountancy journals (various), Underground Station posters in financial districts, direct mail.

(d)   Commercial TV (especially daytime for housewives, poster sites (shopper visibility), women's and household magazines. (Assuming mainly female buyer decision.)

(e)   Trade (engineering journals, Research/home Website of inventor

3   (a)   Opportunity and effort are good with radio: effortless background, portable etc. Familiarity may be a constraint where station newly launched: listeners may not want to switch from old favourites, may not be able to recall frequency.

(b)   Daytime TV: minimal effort and good familiarity with regular users, but limited opportunity if target audience includes workers/school-age commuters.

(c)   Bus posters: minimal effort (depending on size, length of copy, sight lines: can be a strain to read bus posters), good familiarity, good opportunity because moving around (outside posters) but limited by bus users only (inside).

(d)   Web pages: high effort (to search, wait, use hypertext queries etc, requires technological know-how) improving familiarity (biased towards young computer-literate), limited opportunity by virtue of technology, access and expertise required.

4   (a)   Assuming mainly professional male buyers, next to business news, news or evening/weekend sports.

(b)   Assuming mainly female buyers/decision makers, daytime (cost effective), home/lifestyle programmes, prime time soaps (eg for launch).

(c)   Assuming car-owner buyers, not during commuting hours: driving/car programmes, motor sports, home/lifestyle (women buyers).

(d)   Assuming single buyers, late-night television.

5

Site name	Target audience
Yahoo! home page	All web users
New Musical Express	18-30 year old males
Virgin Radio	Age 20-44, male and female, ABC1
Vogue magazine	Women, 18-34, ABC1
AOL	All web users

Answers to Quick Quiz

1   (1) Objectives (2) Size (3) Type of people (4) Suitability (5) Cost (6) Testing & measurement

2   Information and emotion-based appeals

3   True. Likeability seems to lead directly to favourable brand attitudes.

4   C.   (£21,000 divided by 3,000)

5   *Advantage*: mass medium to reach lots of people

   Disadvantage: short life span (generally only one day) so your ad may be missed

6   (1) Reach (2) Frequency (3) Gross rating points (4) Target audience rating points

7   When a target is exposed to two or more overlapping advertisements, this is referred to as duplicated reach. Duplicated reach is more expensive than unduplicated reach, and so any media plan needs to specify how much of each type of reach is required.

8   B.

The international context

Chapter Topic List	
1	Setting the scene
2	Cross border marketing communications
3	Cultural considerations
4	Media considerations
5	Legal considerations
6	Standardisation vs adaptation
7	International communications alternatives
8	Multinational communications agencies

Learning Outcome

☑ Develop marketing communication and brand support activities based on an understanding of the salient characteristics of the target audience

Syllabus Reference

☑ Discuss the main issues concerning the use of marketing communications in an international and global context, such as media availability, culture, religion, education and literacy

Key Concept Introduced

■ Globalisation

1 Setting the scene

1.1 In this book we are restricted to one chapter on the topic of **international communications**, and so we are really only scratching the surface. Different viewpoints exist concerning the **globalisation of markets**. On the one hand, there is the argument that consumers are converging in tastes (aided by global technological advances such as the Internet) and that companies have an opportunity to market standardised products worldwide. An alternative view is that consumer markets are fragmenting and that products and services need to be adapted to individual preferences.

Key Concept

'Globalisation of markets' is an expression which relates to:

- *Demand*: tastes, preferences and price-mindedness are becoming increasingly universal.

- *Supply*: products and services tend to become more standardised and competition within industries reaches a worldwide scale.

- *Multinational* corporations (ie those with operations in more than one country), trying to design their marketing policies and control systems appropriately so as to provide global products for global consumers.

1.2 This chapter begins by addressing a key question: to globalise or not to globalise? Then we go on to discuss various aspects of national differences.

2 Cross border marketing communications

A global village?

2.1 **Factors contributing towards the globalisation of markets** include the following.

(a) More **sophisticated consumers** who holiday outside their home country and are willing to experiment with non domestic products and services.

(b) The trend towards **elimination of political, trade and travel barriers** worldwide.

(c) The **internationalisation of broadcast and print media** (for example, cross border satellite transmission means consumers receive common programming).

(d) The **saturation of domestic markets**, leading companies to search for growth for their goods and services in new markets.

Vive la difference?

2.2 **Standardisation may suit companies, but may not be what consumers are seeking**. An alternative view is that **consumer markets are fragmenting rather than converging**. Consumers are seeking to express themselves as individuals and do not want to be treated as part of a homogeneous mass. Products and services should therefore be **adapted** to individual country markets.

2.3 These two conflicting opinions provide a starting point for any consideration of international marketing management.

(a) It is unlikely that the majority of companies competing outside their own home market will be able to standardise their marketing mix completely.

(b) Nor is it likely that they will choose to adapt their marketing mix totally for each country in which they operate.

(c) The nature of the product or service, consumer buyer behaviour and competitive market environment will all dictate the appropriate strategy to adopt.

Marketing at Work

Consumers in India are acutely price sensitive. They will think nothing of spending an entire morning scouting around to save five rupees. As a result, India has the largest 'used goods' market in the world. Most washing machines in the Punjab are used to churn butter, and the average washing machine (conventionally deployed) is over 19 years old.

"What many foreign investors don't understand is that the Indian consumer is not choosing between one soft drink and another; he's choosing between one soft drink and a packet of biscuits, or a disposable razor" says Suhel Seth of Equus Red Cell, an advertising company.

What this means for foreign investors is that they must price cheaply, and therefore source almost everything locally, to keep costs down.

There are other problems. Standard refrigeration becomes pretty useless when acute power shortages occur. Most consumable goods perish pretty quickly in the climate. And the country's fragmented regional culture means advertisers have to focus on common ground (such as music, Bollywood and cricket).

Is it worth the effort? Investors say that overcoming such obstacles has equipped them for success in any market in the world.

Adapted from the *Financial Times*, April 2002

3 Cultural considerations

3.1 Companies operating outside their home markets have to be aware of the implications of **cultural differences** for all aspects of the marketing mix. Marketing communicators need to be particularly sensitive to culture if messages are to work in global markets.

3.2 **We absorb the culture of our home society as we grow up**. Our family, our religious institutions, and our education system all play a part in passing culture from one generation to the next. Some behaviours and customs learned early in life are likely to remain resistant to the best marketing or promotional efforts. For instance, attitudes and behaviour with respect to particular foodstuffs can be culturally ingrained. Raw fish may be seen as a special treat in Japan, but is unacceptable to the majority of European markets.

3.3 **Culture evolves**. Although core cultural precepts are passed from one generation to the next, the values of society do change. Before the second world war, a 'marriage bar' existed in white collar occupations such as clerical work and teaching. When a single working woman married, she was expected to give up her job to look after her husband. This social norm seems inconceivable to us today.

3.4 Various dimensions of culture are relevant to the international marketing communicator

- Verbal and non verbal communications
- Aesthetics
- Dress and appearance
- Family roles and relationships
- Beliefs and values
- Learning
- Work habits

Verbal and non verbal communication

3.5 Common-sense dictates that care must be taken when translating copy from one language to another. A catchy phrase in the home market may not work so well elsewhere. A literal translation of an advertising slogan, 'as American as apple pie' would be meaningless in many countries.

3.6 Usually, agencies will aim to interpret and adapt in order to capture the spirit of a communication message, rather than relying on a mechanical word for word translation.

3.7 Most agencies will buy in the services of a translation house when required. This will usually ensure that translation is carried out by someone who speaks the vernacular language of the country in question, an important point given that languages are in constant evolution. If an agency subsidiary or local company office exists in the overseas market, it can also be helpful to incorporate their advice. Back translation, where the copy is translated back into English, can be a final precaution.

3.8 It may be difficult to decide exactly which language to choose for translation purposes. The official language of China is Mandarin, but a large proportion of Chinese living in the south of the country have Cantonese as their native tongue. In Canada, although the majority of the population speak English, packaging must include a French translation.

3.9 An additional consideration is that of the **space required for foreign language text**.

3.10 **Brand and product names** must be assessed for their suitability in international markets. Mars changed the name of their Marathon chocolate bar to Snickers in 1990 to facilitate their global communications strategy. A different approach is demonstrated by companies who choose to go with different names in different markets. For instance Ford's Mondeo name works well in European markets, where the 'world' association comes across powerfully. In the US market however, the car is called the Contour.

3.11 Sometimes the phonetic sound of names can cause a problem. The French soft drink Pschitt would have obvious disadvantages in the English-speaking world.

3.12 People communicate both by using language and by their use of **non verbal signals**. A shake of the head to British people, means no and a nod yes. This convention is reversed in some cultures.

3.13 Spatial zones can communicate. In Western societies, we give work colleagues or acquaintances a large zone of personal space. Only family and close friends will enter an individual's near zone. If a colleague comes too close, our reaction is to back off, as our personal space is being invaded. This is not so in some Far Eastern countries, where space is at a premium and people have far less privacy. There, it is acceptable to stand far closer to others.

Aesthetics

3.14 Attitudes towards different design and colour aesthetics vary around the world. A fragrance or toiletries carton decorated with chrysanthemum flower graphics would not be a success in France, where the flowers are traditionally associated with funerals. Similarly, the colour white, which carries connotations of freshness, purity and fragility in the UK is the colour of mourning in China.

3.15 Different cultures will have grown up with their own rules about visual representation. The idea of showing a figure partially out of frame is well known in Europe. In much of Africa by contrast, figures that go over the edge of their frame transgress the cultural rule about how pictures should look. Similarly, a bird's eye view of a sail boat in a Gilbey's Gin advert was not understood by any of the 600 consumers interviewed in a West African project exploring how advertising was decoded.

Dress and appearance

3.16 Dress, be it formal or social, is very much constrained by culture. Advertisers need to be aware of cultural dress codes when deciding if an execution prepared in one market will be acceptable in another. In Europe, for instance, adverts for shower and bath products will often depict a semi-nude model. Such executions would be out of the question in the Middle East, where women can only appear in advertisements if carefully attired.

Family roles and relationships

3.17 Family has always been the dominant agent for transmitting culture. However, it may be that family influences are on the decline, at least in Westernised societies. It is now the norm to talk about the nuclear family, geographically isolated from grandparents and other relatives. Single parent families are also on the increase. This contrasts with many third world countries, where the extended family lives in a tight knit community.

3.18 Family roles can differ greatly from country to country. Recent television adverts in the UK have shown fathers shopping in the supermarket with their children (Bisto); fathers washing children's clothes while their wives are out (washing powder commercial); and men cooking happily in the kitchen (Sainsbury's). In countries with more rigid gender codes, these executions might be either absurd or offensive.

Beliefs and values

3.19 Beliefs and values evolve from religious teachings, family structures and the pattern and nature of economic development in that society. In our culture, material well being is important, people tend to be defined (and define themselves) by their work roles, individualism and equal opportunities are held dear and time is a precious commodity. Different cultures may put a different emphasis on these values. Any communications imagery designed to be used internationally should therefore be scanned for underlying values or beliefs that are culture specific.

Learning

3.20 The level of education within a culture is an important factor for the international marketing communicator. Low literacy levels will mean that verbal methods of communication take precedence over visual ones. Press advertising and direct marketing may have to be ruled out. Packaging may need to be simplified, and point of sale and sales promotion techniques handled with care.

3.21 In some societies, education emphasises the value of rote learning. In others, critical thinking is encouraged. This may affect the way in which information is transmitted within a market.

Work habits

3.22 Not all societies conform to the Monday to Friday, 9.00am till 5.00pm work routine. In Hong Kong, the working week extends until Saturday lunchtime. In some parts of South Europe, it is usual to work from very early in the morning until early afternoon. Workers then go home for a siesta.

Advertising culture

3.23 In addition to being sensitive to a country's culture in general, **marketers should be aware of the level of a country's advertising literacy**. She argues that advertising in any national culture develops in a predictable way, and according to its position on this development curve, it can be described as having either high or low advertising literacy. Thus, imported advertising can be inappropriate because the advertising of country A is at a different stage of development from that of country B.

3.24 **Five levels of advertising development**

Level	Comment
Least sophisticated	The emphasis is on the manufacturer's description of the product. Messages are factual and rational with much repetition. Product or pack shots take prominence.
Unsophisticated	Consumer choice is acknowledged so emphasis switches to the product's superiority over the competition (eg products that wash whiter, feel softer).
Mid point	Consumer benefits are emphasised, rather than product attributes. Executional devices may include the use of celebrity endorsements or role models may give demonstrations, for example a dentist endorsing toothpaste products.

Level	Comment
More sophisticated	Brands and their attributes are well known, so need only passing references (perhaps by way of a brief pack shot or logo). The message is communicated by way of lifestyle narrative (eg Gold Blend couple; Bisto family).
Most sophisticated level	The focus is on the advertising itself. The brand is referred to only obliquely, perhaps at a symbolic level (eg Silk Cut; Benson & Hedges). Consumers are believed to have a mature understanding of advertising, and are able to think laterally in order to decode messages.

Action Programme 1

Choose a country which is quite dissimilar to your own. You could perhaps choose somewhere that you have visited on holiday, or that a friend, relative or colleague has visited and told you about. Using the headings listed in paragraph 3.4, compile a list of similarities and differences between the culture of the foreign country and that of your own.

Ideally, this should be conducted as a class exercise, so that you can pool your experiences.

4 Media considerations   (Specimen paper)

Exam Tip

Media is a complex, highly specialised area within marketing communications. International media is even more of a minefield and therefore the CIM does not expect students to have expert knowledge within this field. What can be expected however, is a grasp of the factors influencing media choice in overseas markets (this is the subject of a question on the Specimen Paper), and some understanding of the practical problems which may be experienced when planning the use of media.

4.1 The UK is a media rich country which offers a great variety of choice to the advertiser. Press is a well segmented sector with over 6,000 consumer and trade and technical magazines, as well as the national and regional newspaper titles. Commercial television now includes terrestrial and satellite channels. Radio as a sector is strengthening, with both local and national stations. Cinema and outdoor are mature mediums.

4.2 This diversity is not always mirrored in overseas markets. **Media availability can vary greatly from country to country**.

4.3 Trying to gain a perspective on the international media scene is a frustrating task. Different sources give conflicting information because of different definitions and different methods of data collection that have been used. Any facts that are collected tend to become dated very quickly because of the dynamic nature of the media sector. Whatever information is gained from secondary sources will always need to be double checked for accuracy in the home market itself.

Press

4.4 The first point to check when contemplating press as a media option, is the **literacy levels prevailing within the country**. The majority of European nations have literacy rates of 98% or 99%. By comparison, the literacy levels quoted for Hong Kong is 77%, for Egypt 44% and for India 41%.

4.5 In the UK, there are a large number of national newspaper alternatives (24 at the last count). Although some countries are similarly well served with national papers from which to choose (eg Germany, Finland), others have more of a tradition of reading strong daily regional papers.

4.6 The UK has one of the world's largest **trade and technical press sectors**, with business-to-business advertisers being particularly fortunate in the choice available to them. A strong trade press sector however, tends to go hand in hand with a strong economic industrial base. Less developed nations may have few, if any, trade media vehicles.

4.7 It is wise to preview any candidate title before going ahead with a decision to include it on the media schedule. This will help in gaining an understanding of the editorial stance of the publication and give an impression about the calibre of the competitive advertising. It also allows the intending advertiser a chance to gauge the quality of media reproduction.

4.8 There is some debate about whether truly international press options exist. Serious business journals such as *Time*, *Newsweek*, and the *Economist* are widely available, as are women's titles with different national editions (eg *Marie Claire*, *Cosmopolitan*, *Elle*). General interest magazines such as *Reader's Digest* and in-flight magazines reach many markets. However, such publications are likely to be read by only a niche business and professional or lifestyle group. To reach the less wealthy, less well travelled wider population, other local media will have to be accessed.

Action Programme 2

In Germany, where more advertising money is spent in magazines than in any country other than in the USA, the main classifications are supplements, 'ad mags', consumer magazines, customer magazines, and trade and technical journals. Supplements are loose inserts in newspapers or periodicals with a magazine format and with many pages printed in four-colour. The principal types are programme, quality, special topic, and trade and technical. Programme supplements, the most widely read, are published once a week and carried in daily newspapers. Editorial content is largely concentrated on previews of radio and television programmes. Quality supplements are found in some of the major newspapers and are largely read by males in managerial and professional positions. Special topic supplements come out at irregular intervals with various carriers. Trade and technical supplements focus on topics of interest to readers of the specialised journals in which the supplements are placed.

Imagine you are a media buyer and have, say, six different products or services that you want to advertise in German magazines. What products/services would you place where?

Television

4.9 Before TV can be included on the media options list, two important questions need to be answered.

- How extensive is television ownership?
- Do commercial stations exist?

4.10 In the UK, 98% of households have a television. In India, by comparison, television ownership is low, as purchase of the cheapest set is beyond the means of the majority. However, television watching may be a group activity and so while ownership is low reach might be higher.

4.11 The opportunities for television advertisers seem overwhelming in Italy, where there are several licensed national TV channels and several hundred local TV stations. Advertisers face a different sort of problem in Norway. The first terrestrial commercial channel started broadcasting in September 1992. Before that date, the only television advertising seen by Norwegians was on satellite stations.

4.12 Satellite television is perceived to offer good opportunities for reaching wide audiences across national boundaries. MTV, the pan-European music station, targets 16 - 34 year olds and is received in 27 different countries.

Outdoor

4.13 The UK lags behind many European countries in its use of posters as an advertising medium. Outdoor offers a good opportunity to communicate to international target groups, as copy tends to be minimal and visuals are key.

Cinema

4.14 Cinema may not always be experienced in the same way around the world. In some countries, cinema is viewed in outdoor theatres. There can also be dramatic variations in the quality of the films which are screened. Both these factors may affect how advertising is received by cinema goers.

Radio

4.15 While the cost of purchasing a television set is prohibitive in some nations, radio ownership seems to be ubiquitous around the world. In most countries, radio plays the role of support medium.

Media planning and buying

4.16 As well as the usual media planning considerations (campaign objectives, target markets, media availability, budgets), there may be specific factors which need to be taken into account when planning in international markets. For a food product, media scheduling will need to take account of climatic and seasonal characteristics of individual countries.

4.17 Some international print media may be purchased from the home country market via international media representatives. Other media may have to be bought by a local country agent, acting for the advertiser.

4.18 Media buying practices can vary from country to country. In the UK, published ratecard costs tend to be negotiable downwards. Other countries may be less flexible in negotiations.

Marketing at Work

MTV

MTV potentially faces strong competition from the BBC and Virgin since the launch of digital television. It needs to reinforce its position by raising awareness, but this is a problem because audience perceptions of MTV vary widely across Europe.

MTV's Europe Music Awards ceremony was targeted mainly at the Netherlands, Switzerland and the UK, but research indicated that it needed to adopt different approaches in each country.

(a)   In the UK its tactic was to highlight how many superstars were coming to the awards and play up the competitive aspect. One poster showed stars like George Michael and Bryan Adams; another featured rival Britpop acts Oasis and Pulp.

(b)   In the Netherlands young people like to see MTV as a reassuringly familiar part of their lives. The marketing had a softer more subdued feel, and consists of magazine ads with soft images of domestic situations.

(c)   In Sweden MTV's viewers tend to be more politically disaffected and an anti-establishment image is more appealing. The campaign focused on newspaper ads consisting of replica newspaper pages with graffiti style slogans such as 'Join Our Party'. MTV also placed Join Our Party toilet rolls in the toilets of bars and nightclubs, to achieve the desired subversive effect.

5   Legal considerations

5.1   Laws and regulations governing marketing communications must obviously be observed. Each country will have its own set of restrictions which apply to advertising, packaging, sales promotion or direct marketing.

5.2   **In the EU alone, there are a number of significant differences regarding the regulation of advertising between member states**. A recent Gossard TV commercial came under scrutiny in the UK for its risqué execution. In France, the problem was not the generous display of cleavage, but the fact that the advert was set in a bar where alcohol was being consumed. There is a ban on TV alcohol adverts and the Gossard ad needed to be re-edited to fall in line with French restrictions.

5.3   In some countries, restrictions apply to the use of non native models and actors. This can mean that advertising has to be reshot for specific countries.

5.4 **Packaging regulations** can vary. In a number of European markets, the push towards environmentally-friendly packaging has resulted in far more stringent rules than apply in the UK. In Denmark, soft drinks may not be sold in cans, only in glass bottles with refundable deposits.

5.5 Direct marketing is an area under threat from EU legislation. In the UK, direct marketers must offer consumers the choice of opting out of receiving further mailings. Recent European proposals suggest the idea of allowing consumers the choice of opting into direct mailings. This seems to imply that companies would have to write to consumers in advance of a direct mail campaign, asking consumers if they wanted to receive mail.

Cross border advertising

5.6 The **European Commission** maintains that there must be overriding reasons relating to the public interest for imposing additional national rules on communications, and these rules must be 'proportionate' to the public interest objectives. However, to test the validity of current national restrictions on commercial communications through the courts takes several years for each case. Many regard national advertising restrictions as thinly veiled protectionism.

Marketing at Work

National restrictions

'Sweden forbids all advertising aimed at children under 10; Greece bans TV toy advertising between 7am and 10pm; some countries require ads for sweets to carry a toothbrush symbol; others have rules intended to curb advertisers from encouraging children to exercise 'pester power'.

The same maze of national rules exists when it comes to promoting alcohol, tobacco, pharmaceuticals and financial services'.

There are proposals to set up a new body to deal with these issues, which are felt to be significant barriers to cross border trade.

Early meetings of the new body would examine national differences in sales promotions and sponsorship regulations ... On sponsorship, for example, the Netherlands was singled out as having particularly restrictive curbs on events sponsorship, while the UK and Denmark were seen to impose strict rules on broadcasting.

Price advertising and discounting is another area likely to get early attention. Measures are so disparate that cross-border campaigns using discounts are all but impossible ... In Germany, cash discounts are limited to 3% and the advertising of special offers is also restricted. Austria, Belgium and Italy also have strict regimes. In contrast, in Scandinavia, where the advertising law is more closely linked to consumer protection rather than unfair competition considerations, price advertising is encouraged – Swedish law, for example, promotes comparative price advertising between traders '

Source: Financial Times

6 Standardisation vs adaptation

6.1 **Strategies appropriate for companies operating in international markets** (Keegan).

(a) **Standardise** product/standardise communication (for example, Coca-Cola).

(b) **Standardise product/adapt communication** (Horlicks is promoted as a relaxing bedtime drink in the UK and as a high protein energy booster in India).

(c) **Adapt product/standardise communication** (washing powder ingredients may vary from country to country depending on water conditions and washing machine technology. However, the communication message of clean clothes is the same).

(d) **Adapt product/adapt communication**.

(e) **Invent a new product** to meet the needs of the market.

Action Programme 3

Over the next few months as you work towards the exam, scan the marketing and advertising trade press alongside the quality papers for examples of products and services which adopt the different strategies listed above. You will be able to generate your own list of current examples to illustrate points you make in the examination. Examiners welcome up-to-date relevant examples which demonstrate that you keep abreast of current practice.

6.2 **Advantages of standardising communications** include the following.

(a) **Economies of scale** can be generated. A single worldwide advertising, packaging or direct mail execution will save time and money.

(b) A **consistent and strong brand image** will be presented to the consumer. Wherever users see the brand, they will be reassured because the messages received will be the same.

(c) A **standardised communications policy** allows for **easier implementation** and control by management.

(d) Good **communications ideas are rare** and should be exploited creatively across markets.

Marketing at Work

Pirelli

A Pirelli ad featured Marie-Jo Perec, a double Olympic gold medal winner, outrunning an avalanche, a tidal wave and a river of volcanic lava. The ad is thought to have cost over £1m to make, but it ran in up to 40 countries from China to South Africa. This needs to be compared with the cost of making multiple commercials, a different one for each country: it is thought to cost at least £250,000 to make a decent 30-second ad.

'There are certain clues which showed that this ad was designed to run internationally. There was no dialogue, as that would mean expensive and potentially difficult translation. And the images were universally recognisable - human against nature. The only potential problem was that Perec's sprinting costume could be considered too skimpy for some Islamic countries'.

Source: Financial Times

6.3 **Arguments against standardising communications** include the following.

(a) Any standardisation policy **assumes consumer needs and wants are identical** across markets.

(b) Centrally-generated communications concepts may prove to be **inappropriate for the specific culture** of the local market (or indeed any market that may see the advertisement and take offence, as the example below illustrates.)

(c) **Media channel availability and infrastructure varies** widely from country to country.

(d) A country's level of **educational development** may prevent a standardised approach. For instance, a press campaign featuring detailed copy would be a non starter if literacy levels were low.

(e) **Legal restrictions** may prove to be a stumbling block. For example, France does not allow any advertising of alcohol on television; cashback sales promotion offers are not allowed in Italy or Luxembourg.

(f) Standardisation may encourage the **'not invented here' syndrome**, so that local management become lacklustre about creative ideas and communications policies imposed from above.

(g) Different countries have economies which may be much more or much less developed than others. Factors that need to be considered are as follows.

- What is the level and trend in per capita income?
- Is the balance of payments favourable or unfavourable?
- Is inflation under control?
- Are the exchange rates stable?
- Is the currency easily convertible?
- Is the country politically stable?
- How protectionist is the country?
- Who controls distribution channels?

Marketing at Work

Diageo's blunder

An advertisement on the London Underground in December 2002 for Smirnoff offended the Taiwanese. It showed a picture of an item with the label "Made in Taiwan" and the caption "Warning – this gift will break down on Christmas morning". Taiwan, so long a byword for inferior manufacturing quality, is now one of the leading high-tech manufacturers in the world. The Taiwan government was considering an outright ban on Diageo products.

Diageo was trying to achieve distinctiveness in a 'noisy' market, but this must never come at the expense of social responsibility and international awareness. This is a difficult line to tread – to appeal to one segment, you might risk offending others. Joking is always risky!

So Diageo found itself plunged into crisis management, despite the fact that its marketing code includes the provision: 'Don't use anything likely to be considered gratuitously offensive or demeaning to either gender, or to any race, religion, culture or minority group.'

Exam Tip

In addition to the compulsory mini-case question, which often has an international perspective, there has usually been at least one other 'international' question in the old Integrated Marketing Communications exam.

7 International communications alternatives

7.1 It is all too easy to focus on advertising and packaging as the prime communicators in international campaigns. However, sales promotion, public relations, sponsorship, exhibitions, direct marketing and personal selling can all play a part.

Sales promotion

7.2 Sales promotion encompasses a range of techniques appropriate for targeting consumers, for instance via price reductions, free gifts, or competitions. Trade and sales force promotions are also implied under the general heading of sales promotion.

7.3 Different countries have their own **local restrictions** concerning different sales promotional devices. For instance, collector devices are a familiar method of encouraging repeat purchase in the UK. However, they are not allowed in West Germany, Luxembourg, Austria, Norway, Sweden and Switzerland. Petrol forecourt promotions are very familiar to drivers in the UK, but following a vicious sales promotions battle between petrol companies in 1989, the Malaysian Government banned sales promotion of petrol.

7.4 Sales promotions that are to run across a number of different countries must tap into common tastes, interests and activities. As has been seen from the section on culture, this may not be an easy task.

Public relations

7.5 The UK's Institute of Public Relations describe public relations as, 'the planned and sustained effort to establish and maintain goodwill and mutual understanding between an organisation and its publics'. Publics can include:

- Customers
- Shareholders
- Employees
- Suppliers
- Trade intermediaries

- The local community
- Media
- Government
- Pressure groups

7.6 The importance of any one group will vary from country to country, which will mean that **public relations campaigns are unlikely to be completely standardised** across markets.

7.7 There is some debate as to whether public relations can be standardised at all. There is wide disparity in the sophistication of PR from country to country, as well as the usual list of cultural, language, media and legal barriers. The **political context** of individual countries may also affect the extent to which different public relations techniques can be used.

Sponsorship

7.8 Sponsorship seems a particularly appropriate means of communicating internationally. Internationally televised sporting events have an appeal that crosses borders and cultures, as football, rugby and cricket matches often show.

Exhibitions

7.9 Trade fairs and exhibitions are an effective means of initial business-to-business contact, providing an opportunity for producers, distributors, customers and competitors to meet. Where specialist exhibitions take place, rival companies from across the globe are likely to gather under one roof, offering an excellent opportunity for international buyers to compare offerings and place orders.

7.10 Exhibitions allow companies to display goods and mount demonstrations and trials. They can be good as a mechanism for image building, especially in new markets. Exhibitions provide a means for supporting local distributors and agents and allow direct contact with customers. There is also the chance to conduct competitor and customer market research.

7.11 Detailed evaluation of exhibition results should be carried out in order to fine tune future plans.

Direct marketing

7.12 International direct marketing has been growing slowly over the last decade. Factors driving the move to international direct marketing include the following.

(a) The growth in sophistication of computer and **database technology**

(b) The increasing availability of suitable **consumer or business listings**

(c) Growth of **international media**, which can be used for direct response advertising

(d) The perceived **accountability** of direct marketing campaigns compared with other communications campaigns

(e) The ease with which direct marketing campaigns can be **tested in advance** in order to maximise their effectiveness

(f) Improving **skills** of direct marketing agencies

(g)   Increasing **willingness of the consumer** to purchase items directly

(h)   Increasing use of **internationally accepted credit cards**

7.13   On the other hand, there are a number of factors restraining the move to international direct marketing.

- Lack of telephone and postal **infrastructure**
- Lack of road and rail penetration to facilitate **distribution**
- Lack of **suitable media** to use to target consumers
- Lack of **consumer and business lists** in some countries
- The threat of increasingly strict **legislation** concerning the use of consumer information
- **Consumer backlash** against what is seen as junk mail

Personal selling

7.14   Many of the communications tools described above will rely on integration with the personal selling function. For instance, certain types of consumer sales promotion will require **sales force support** to gain trade acceptance. Likewise, direct marketing campaigns will create sales leads that require follow up. Personal selling is therefore a likely requirement of most markets.

7.15   Companies may use **agents or distributors** to act in a sales capacity. Alternatively, a company may establish its own branch offices abroad with a team of local salespeople.

7.16   **Personal selling will be particularly important in industrial markets**, where products are high value and complex, or in markets where purchasing is controlled by government agencies.

Exam Tip

Students answering exam questions on international aspects of communications tend to focus on advertising and packaging as the prime promotional vehicles. Examiners welcome answers that demonstrate that other options such as sales promotion, public relations, sponsorship, exhibitions, direct marketing and personal selling have been considered.

8   Multinational communications agencies

8.1   When selecting an agency to handle communications on an international basis, any decision would take into account the differences in approaches to communications discussed in this chapter.

8.2   Often the decision making process will be influenced by the structure of the client company and how far they **devolve** marketing responsibility on a regional basis. Some elements of the communications strategy and branding may be handled centrally, whereas implementation is dealt with 'locally', where more detailed knowledge with regard to media and other context issues can be applied.

8.3 For many of the larger multinational and global companies such as Coca Cola, Heinz or Procter & Gamble there is a need to deal with agencies who have sufficient resources of their own to handle the size of budgets being allocated. As there has been consolidation taking place among multinational businesses through acquisition and merger, this has also been happening among communications businesses. Between them, companies such as WPP handle a significant share of the world's advertising billings. These agencies have grown partly by success in winning new business but also through the acquisition of other agencies in different parts of the world.

8.4 Other agencies offer multinational services to clients by being part of networks. They maintain independence as individual companies but via informal and sometimes formal collaborations, they can provide client services in different geographic markets. Sometimes clients may appoint a 'lead' agency who will hold ultimate responsibility for planning and co-ordination of agencies in different markets.

8.5 Advances in new technologies make the process of handling the communications needs of sophisticated multinational clients more straightforward but may not always replace the need for 'local' knowledge.

Chapter Roundup

- The international marketing communicator needs to decide **whether or not it is appropriate to standardise** communications across markets.

- Companies operating outside their home markets need to be aware of the implications of **cultural differences** for all aspects of the marketing mix. Verbal and non verbal communications, aesthetics, dress and appearance, family roles and relationships, beliefs, learning and work habits are dimensions of culture of particular relevance to communications.

- **Planning and buying media across borders can be a complex task**. Media availability can vary greatly from country to country. Media conventions which apply in a home market may not apply elsewhere.

- **Laws and regulations** governing marketing communications must obviously be observed. Each country will have its own set of restrictions which apply to advertising, packaging, sales promotion and direct marketing.

- **Research** should be used to support decision making before a campaign is planned. Research can also help evaluate whether objectives have been met at the conclusion of a campaign. However, obtaining accurate, unbiased, up-to-date information can be difficult. Conducting primary research on an international basis requires the help of experts.

Now try Question 7 in the Question Bank

Quick Quiz

1   One aspect of globalisation concerns the efforts by multinational corporations to design (1)............ which provide global (2)......... for global (3).......... . Fill in the gaps.

2   The internationalisation of broadcast and print media is one of the factors driving the internationalisation of markets. Is this true, and if so, why?

3   Various dimensions of culture are relevant to the international marketing communicator. See if you can recall them from paragraph 3.4.

C..........

A..........

D..........

F..........

B..........

L..........

W..........

4   Which of the following statements is true? (There may be more than one)

A   Literacy levels only vary to a small extent between countries, so using the press is always going to make sense

B   Literacy levels are important when considering press as a media option

C   Media availability varies greatly from country to country

D   In flight magazines reach many people in many markets and so are an invaluable mass advertising media

5   List some advantages of standardising communications.

6   Why might sponsorship be a particularly effective form of international marketing communications?

7   Which one of the following statements is true?

A   It is not necessary to research every international market, as some will be very similar to the domestic market

B   Research can help with the evaluation of the success of a campaign

C   Laws and regulations change so often that it is impossible, and unnecessary, for a marketer to keep up with them

D   Standardised marketing communications will always be better than adapted ones, because they are cheaper

8   Fill in the gaps using the words from the grid below:

Some advertising agencies offer (1)........... services to clients by being part of (2).......... They maintain (3).......... as individual companies, but via collaborations they can provide client services in different (4).......... markets.

Geographic	Contact	Account management
Multinational	Networks	Independence

Action Programme Review

1   Once you have completed this, consider the implications for differences in approach to marketing communications.

2   What differences would there be if you were promoting these products or services in the UK or another market?

3   Your own research.

Answers to Quick Quiz

1   (1) Marketing policies; (2) Products; (3) Consumers

2   True. For example, cross border satellite transmission means consumers in different countries receive common programming. Also, consumers are now more sophisticated and have increased exposure to other cultures via the broadcast and other media. This expands their tastes and preferences and makes 'international' products more attractive.

3   **C**ommunications (verbal and non-verbal)
Aesthetics
Dress (and appearance)
Family roles and relationships
Beliefs and values
Learning
Work habits

4   B and C

5   Check your answer against paragraph 6.2

6   International sporting events, such as the 2003 Cricket World Cup for example, attract audiences from many different cultures.

7   B

8   (1) Multinational; (2) Networks; (3) Independence; (4) Geographic

Evaluating marketing communications activities

8

Chapter Topic List	
1	Setting the scene
2	Understanding communications effectiveness
3	Consumer communication case studies
4	Business-to-business communications strategies
5	Marketing communications for service organisations
6	Marketing communications for non profit organisations
7	Marketing communications for small businesses

Learning Outcome

☑   Explain how the tools of the promotional mix can be co-ordinated in order to communicate effectively with customers and a range of stakeholders

Syllabus References

☑   Evaluate the effectiveness of co-ordinated campaigns

☑   Evaluate the effectiveness of marketing communications activities, tools, media and campaigns

1 Setting the scene

Exam Tip

In the exam, you will frequently be asked to provide examples of and evaluate campaigns of different kinds with which you are familiar. The module requires an understanding of marketing communications relating to different marketing sectors and types of business. Many of the cases used will relate to consumer situations as these are the ones most candidates will be most familiar with.

2 Understanding communications effectiveness

A summary of marketing communication effectiveness

2.1 Ultimately communications are designed to meet three objectives.

Awareness	Increase brand **awareness** and establish brand **recognition**
Trial	Stimulate **trial purchase**
Reinforcement	Stimulate and **reinforce** brand **loyalty**

2.2 To succeed in achieving these goals, communications must:

- Gain attention
- Communicate a message
- Improve attitude to the brand
- Reinforce the already positive attitude to the brand
- Obtain the readers'/listeners'/viewers' liking for the message and its execution

2.3 How to assess the effectiveness of communications campaigns

Principle	What it means
Value linkage	Communication must represent the value of the brand.
Sense making	Communications must be meaningful and relevant.
Simplification	Strict simplification is necessary in view of the avalanche of information.
Acceleration	The message must be transmitted in a few seconds.
Visualisation	We must communicate visually first and foremost.
Humanisation	Communication must relate to the lives and dreams of real people.
Emotionalisation	Communications should activate the receiver's feelings more.
Conditioning	Effective use requires strong, unambiguous, vivid stimuli.

BPP
PROFESSIONAL EDUCATION

Principle	What it means
Refreshment	Receivers can become bored or tired of campaigns.
Branding	The brand has to be a co-ordinated part of communications.
Entertainment	Entertainment can be extremely effective in some cases.
Consistency	Consistency has been the mainstay of major brands.

2.4 The difficult part is measuring the effectiveness of the marketing communications process. The following are some possible techniques.

Marketing communications methods	Examples of measurements
Personal selling	Sales targets
Public relations	Editorial coverage
Direct marketing	Enquiries generated
Advertising	Brand awareness
Sales promotion	Coupons redeemed
Exhibitions	Contacts made

2.5 Engel, Warshaw and Kinnear's book on *Promotional Strategy* contains a substantial chapter on the 'Measurement of Promotional Effectiveness' from which the following table is taken. This shows possible advertising effectiveness and control methods.

Classification of advertising effectiveness measures

Type of measure	Advertising related	Product related
Laboratory measures (Respondent aware of testing)	*Pretesting panels* ■ Consumer panels ■ Portfolio tests ■ Readability tests ■ Physiological measure eg eye movements	*Pretesting* ■ Theatre tests ■ Hall tests ■ Laboratory scores
Real world measures (Respondent unaware of testing)	*Pretesting* ■ Dummy advertising ■ Inquiry tests ■ On air tests *Post testing* ■ Recognition ■ Recall tests ■ Association measure:	*Pre and post procedures* ■ Sales tests ■ Test markets

Exam Tip

Candidates should be able to use suitable examples to demonstrate the points they are making. The age of an example is not important, nor is the culture or country from where the examples are drawn. What you must do is give more than a description. You should show your understanding through a structured interpretation and evaluation of a campaign.

Action Programme 1

For a campaign of your choice answer the following questions. (You might have to do this in an exam.)

(a)   Describe the organisation concerned and its competitors.
(b)   What factors and issues have shaped the campaign?
(c)   What are the marketing communications objectives?
(d)   What are the main elements of the communication strategy?
(e)   How can you measure the effectiveness of the campaign?

3 Consumer communication case studies

3.1   You are encouraged to keep up-to-date by reading the business press and, in particular, trade magazines such as *Marketing*, *Marketing Week* and *Campaign*. These contain regular reviews of marketing communications activities including varying campaigns from different types of organisations. You are also encouraged to obtain and study cases histories in more detail than you would normally find in such sources.

3.2   The IPA cases used here are presented in a format which would provide a framework for marketing communications planning:

- ■   Situation analysis
- ■   Communications objectives
- ■   Marketing communications strategy
- ■   Communications tactics – promotional mix
- ■   Action – implementation
- ■   Control – measurement and evaluation

Marketing at Work

Walker's Crisps: Gary Lineker

Situation

In 1989 Walkers and Smiths Crisps moved under the umbrella of PepsiCo Foods International. In 1993, the two brands were merged. With a turnover in the region of £300 million, Walkers Crisps had become the biggest single food brand in the UK.

By August 1994, Walkers had experienced two years of double-digit growth, and the brand's share had reached 22%, over three times that of its nearest branded rival. However, there were several clouds looming on the horizon:

- Plateauing distribution
- Success of promotions
- Advertising uncertainties.

Marketing communications objectives

To maintain volume and share growth on a par with that achieved in the previous two years, primarily through ROS (rate of sales) growth. In particular it needed to do this in two ways:

(a)   Theme advertising that would work harder than before and would generate ROS increases in its own right.

(b)   Through promotional advertising that would be part of the same campaign and hence more strongly branded than before, and that would generate even more pronounced short-term ROS uplifts than the previous promotional advertising.

Marketing communications strategy

In March 1993 Walkers had embarked on a successful series of 'Instant Win' promotions, producing unprecedented uplifts in volume and ROS. 'Instant Win' promotions were seen as another engine for dynamic growth. But it was unclear how important the novelty factor was to their success, and whether repetition would see declining effectiveness over time, and it seemed inevitable that competition would try to copy them.

There was little doubt that the promotional advertising had been successful in boosting sales. However, to protect the salience of Walkers' own promotions in the face of copying by competitors, stronger branding of the 'Instant Win' promotions was felt desirable, best achieved by a single brand umbrella bringing promotional and theme advertising together.

When Walkers put the advertising account out to pitch in mid 1994, it was to develop an co-ordinated brand campaign incorporating new theme and promotional advertising.

It was decided to create advertising that would appeal to a mass audience of adults as well as children. From qualitative research conducted amongst crisp-lovers of all ages, 'irresistibility' was identified as the quality that embodied everything they most enjoyed about snacking. It was shorthand for the perfect crisp. A creative vehicle that would generate PR and media coverage was desired. Given the importance of fame and the need for a mass audience, TV was chosen as the main medium.

The idea for the campaign can be summarised as 'Walkers are so irresistible they make even nice guys turn nasty when it comes to crisps'.

What set the idea apart was the thought of casting ex-England and Leicester footballer Gary Lineker as the nice guy turned nasty.

As the ambassador and genuine 'nice guy' of the game, Gary was as attractive to mums as to kids. His well-publicised return from playing in Japan offered unique PR opportunities. Most important of all, his down-to-earth personality and roots in Walkers' Leicester heartland provided a seamless fit with the desired brand personality and the unpretentious values to be established.

Tactics

Prior to the 1996 IPA Awards five TV executions had been produced in the series including two for further 'Instant Win' promotions:

Execution	Airdate	TVRs	Objective
'Welcome home'	Jan 95	472	Launch improved cheese & onion
'Nun'	Mar 95	520	Support 'Instant cheque' promotion
'Garymania'	May 95	451	Launch Crinkles range
'Dial-a-Prize'	Sept 95	361	Support 'Dial-a-Prize' promotion
'Salt & Lineker'	Jan 96	553	Launch improved S&V flavour

Action

From the outset, the Lineker campaign generated an amount of TV and press coverage much in excess of anything previously seen in the market. TV coverage ranged from News at Ten to Fantasy Football League, The Big Breakfast and How Do They Do that? Press coverage appeared in all national press, from *The Times, The Independent* and *Daily Telegraph*, to the *Daily Mail, Daily Mirror* and the front page of *The Sun* ... twice.

Control

Analysis of growth in different advertised varieties of Walkers crisps, showed that the advertising clearly influenced consumer behaviour. Two econometric models showed directly that the advertising was responsible for a large proportion of the brand's growth. The part played by other variables showed no other activity could have been responsible for the effect claimed for advertising.

The marketing objectives of sustaining volume and increasing market share growth were successfully exceeded.

Volume grew by 22.5% in the year following Gary Lineker's appointment.

Walkers continue to use Gary Lineker in their ads.

Action Programme 2

This is an co-ordinated campaign. Identify as many features of integration as you can, both from the above or from your own experience of the Walker's brand.

Marketing at Work

Dulux reveals true colours

Situation

Historically, Dulux the paint manufacturer had used advertising to associate the brand with white and 'Natural Hints' ranges. If they were to achieve ambitious targets for 1999, focus on the coloured paint sector was also required. Paint sales were expected to grow at the expense of wallpaper and the coloured sector was important as it was the most profitable sector and likely to see a significant proportion of the forecast growth. Brighter colours were more fashionable as a result of programmes such as Changing Rooms, which particularly appealed to a younger target audience. The image of Dulux was safe and respected but irrelevant to the younger market.

Target Audience

Focus was placed on the under 35s for a number of reasons. Unless younger customers could be attracted this would lead to longer-term loss of share as these were the customers of the future. First-time house purchase was on the increase fuelled by lower interest rates creating younger home owners. It was also the sector where Dulux had the lowest share and therefore most opportunity for growth. Further segmentation targeted females who were seen to be the decision makers and to seek consumers with a more adventurous mindset in order to move away from the 'safe' image.

Promotional mix

A TV campaign spearheaded the repositioning efforts, demonstrating the range of colours available and the consumer need this range met. The theme was bright, bold and controversial, very different to the gentle and romantic execution of earlier advertising.

A website allowed consumers to test different paint mixes and advise on suitability for different surfaces and calculate the quantity required. PR included a challenge to personalities to dye their hair for a day in aid of charity. Further media coverage arose from a body-painted naked lady visiting key media offices with the famous Dulux dog to deliver specially created paint mixes.

Measuring Effectiveness

Tracking studies four months into the campaign showed a 12% increase in the numbers agreeing that Dulux 'had the widest range of colours' and a 15% rise in those agreeing that Dulux 'always has the right colour for you'. As a result of the campaign, over 80% of those recalling the ads remembered the key message that Dulux can 'match the colour you want'.

In February 2000, Dulux volume share topped own label (Homebase /B&Q)sales for the first time.

Dulux was one of the winners of the CIM/Marketing Week Marketing Effectiveness Awards 2000.

From an article in *Marketing Business*, February 2001

Marketing at Work

Last laugh for Skoda

Situation

For years the butt of jokes based on the car's unreliability, the success of the brand over the last two years, provides a remarkable example of how to turn a brand around. Even after motoring journalists began praising the improvements made in product design and engineering, sales hardly moved. The advertising was doing little to overcome brand prejudice and although drivers might have recognised that the product had improved, they would still not want to be seen driving a Skoda. It was further recognised that the pan-European approach that had been taken did not reflect the fact that the brand meant something different in each market.

Budget constraints

A reduced promotional budget compared to earlier launches made the task even more of a challenge when launching the new Fabia model. £4.5 million was half of the £9 million Toyota spent on launching the Yaris and little more than a third of the £17 million spent by Renault on relaunching the Clio.

A risky approach

There was little doubt that it would take something different to change consumer attitudes toward the brand not made easier by the low budget available. The Fallon advertising agency created a campaign with the strapline 'It's a Skoda. Honest'. This centred on reducing the gap between consumer expectations and reality using self-deprecating humour in seeking revaluation of the brand. Research of the concept proved positive.

Promotional mix

£2.85 million was spent on a TV campaign, supported by £600,000 spent on posters and £274,000 in colour press. PR was used to extend and amplify the message and further activity included retail staff training and high profile location product placement.

Measuring effectiveness

In addition to improving sales of most models and creating a waiting list for the new Fabia, significant changes in attitude toward the brand were achieved.

Before the campaign 54% of people agreed that Skodas were better than they were commonly perceived. This increased to 79% after the campaign. Only 20% said they could imagine themselves driving a Skoda before the campaign with this increasing to 33% after.

The success of the communications has prompted Skoda to seek further improvements by building their database and nurturing customers (who may currently be warming to the brand), closer to point of purchase.

This campaign won the Grand Prix in the CIM/Marketing Week Marketing Effectiveness Awards 2000.

From an article in *Marketing Business*, December/January

---

4 Business-to-business communications strategies

4.1 Although the principles of marketing communications are the same for both consumer and industrial markets, there are significant differences in the details of how promotion is carried out. We saw this in earlier chapters.

4.2 In particular, the targets in industrial markets are usually more specific and promotional budgets are usually more limited. In order to understand these differences it is valuable to look again at the major differences between industrial (or business) marketing and consumer marketing.

Major differences between industrial and consumer marketing

	Area	Industrial marketing	Consumer marketing
1	Purchase motivation	Multiple buying influences Support company operations	Individual or family need
2	Nature of demand	Derived or joint demand	Primary demand
3	Emphasis of seller	Economic needs	Immediate satisfaction
4	Customer needs	Each customer has different needs	Groups with similar needs
5	Nature of buyer	Group decisions	Purchase by individual or family unit
6	Time effects	Long term relationships	Short term relationships
7	Product details	Technically sophisticated	Lower technical content
8	Promotion decisions	Emphasis on personal selling	Emphasis on mass media advertising
9	Price decisions	Price determined before Terms are important	Price substantially fixed Discounts are important
10	Place decisions	Limited number of large buyers, short channels	Large number of small buyers Complex channels
11	Customer service	Critical to success	Less important
12	Legal factors	Contractual arrangements	Contracts only on major purchases
13	Environmental factors	Affect sales both directly and indirectly	Affect demand directly

Business decision-making process

4.3 Perhaps the most significant differences are the nature of the **buying motivation** and the linked nature of the buying decision process. In industrial buying there are many motivations. These stem partly from the technical use of the product but also from financial, security of supply and, to a lesser degree, emotional reasons.

Decision makers and buying motivation

Decision makers	Buying motivation
1 Operations Manager	Uses the product in the organisation's processes - wants efficiency and effectiveness.
2 Technical Manager	Often has to test and approve the product – wants reliability.
3 The Managing Director	May approve major expenditure or change of supplier.
4 The Purchasing Manager	Approves conditions of purchase. Monitors supplier performance.
5 Legal Manager	Draws up or approves legal contracts with supplier.
6 Finance Manager	Approves expenditure and controls debt payment.
7 Health and Safety Manager	May have a role to play with hazardous supplies.

Implications for marketing communications strategy

4.4 It will be obvious that marketing communications strategy for industrial marketing must reflect this considerably more complex decision-making process.

Strategic importance

4.5 Business or industrial marketing can be regarded as involving more strategic decisions in its implementation. Consumer products, by definition, are mass market products often purchased in a routine and habitual manner. This is unlikely to be the case in industrial marketing. Business customers have differing needs and in some cases these needs may be conflicting within the organisation. Identifying business needs is complicated by having to deal with different decision makers within the company.

Impact of time

4.6 The length of time involved for the purchase evaluation and for the life of the product is much greater in industrial markets. Consumers often make buying decisions on the spur of the moment. Industrial buying decisions may take over one year. This then alters both the type of marketing communications and the relationships between the buying and selling organisations.

The buying organisation

4.7 Business buyers have several different methods of organising purchasing, and this can affect communication strategy. Some firms purchase on a highly centralised basis. This allows for maximum price advantage and negotiation strength because of economies of scale. Other organisations allow decentralised purchases, which leads to local needs being better met. In these cases, two different forms of selling organisation are needed and the communication strategy needed to reach the right person will be different in each case.

Variety of products and services

4.8 The variety of products in business markets is extremely large. Business products vary from product inputs to items for resale. They can be broken down into three main types.

- Capital equipment (major purchases of fixed assets)
- Production inputs (becoming part of the buyer's process)
- Business supplies/services (ongoing use by the buyer)

Again, each type of purchase will need a different communications strategy.

The business-to-business communications mix

4.9 The chart below shows the relative importance of differing elements of the promotional mix between consumer and industrial markets. These differences are reflected in developing marketing communication strategies for industrial markets.

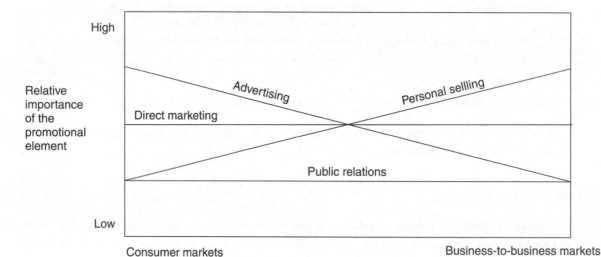

Relative importance of promotional elements

4.10 The clearest difference is the importance of personal selling in industrial markets because of the complexity of the decision-making process, the differing industrial needs and the higher value of individual purchases. Advertising, though still important in industrial marketing, is less so than for consumer marketing.

4.11 The diagram also shows that both public relations and direct marketing have important continuing roles in both consumer and industrial marketing. It is clear from the above list that the methods to communicate with industrial markets will be of a much greater variety than for consumer markets. This in turn means that industrial marketing decisions can be really challenging and **the need for effective co-ordinated marketing communications is important**.

4.12 The range of promotional methods is described below.

Method	Comment
Personal selling	This is a major component of industrial marketing because of the need to deal with technical and other issues on a face-to-face basis.
Internal selling	Increasingly it is recognised that a salesperson has an internal role to play in representing his customers' needs to the company.
Internet	The use of the Internet for e-commerce is perhaps more highly developed in industrial marketing than in the consumer sector. Advertising and online catalogues are just two of the ways that it can be used. Many companies have also set up electronic links with suppliers and customers for such functions as automatic ordering.
Advertising	A wide variety of publications exist which can be used to target individual market sectors including: (i) trade journals (ii) business press (iii) directories Advertising is used to create awareness, provide information, generate leads, assist channel members and sometimes to sell off the page.
Telemarketing	Telemarketing has been proved to be a very cost effective method of order processing, customer service, sales support and account management.
Direct mailing	Direct mail, another form of direct marketing, has been used by industrial marketers for a long time but its use has substantially increased. It can be used to provide information and generate enquiries. It can be tailored to individual customer needs.
Public relations	Sometimes in industrial markets this is referred to as publicity. It often focuses on getting editorial coverage in appropriate magazines but it has a wider role of building customer relations.
Sales promotion	Sales promotion is an important area of communication in industrial markets. There are a wide range of methods that are of well established use in industrial campaigns. ■ Literature ■ Exhibitions ■ Videos ■ Discounting ■ Events ■ Business gifts ■ Trade shows Technical literature is clearly important in specifying the product. Complicated equipment can be captured on video and applications shown. Trade shows and exhibitions continue to grow in importance. Discounting and special price promotions are used extensively in industrial markets. Business gifts continue to have their value if not used excessively.

Co-ordinated marketing communications

4.13 Finally, it should be stressed that the concept of co-ordinated marketing communications is equally, if not more, important in industrial marketing. This is because there is likely to be a more complex promotional mix and definitely a more complex audience. Consistent delivery of images on a limited budget is therefore important.

Summary of strategic implications

4.14 The **principles of industrial marketing communications are the same as for consumer marketing** but the strategies differ. The table below summarises some of the strategic implications.

Principles	Strategic implications
Purpose of industrial promotion	Builds up the company's image in the mind of the purchaser.
Communication objectives	Must be geared to specific business objectives.
Communication methods	Different balance than for consumer markets. Personal selling more important.
Choice of media	Important to determine the best media to reach the participants in a complex decision-making process.
Measuring effectiveness	Essential to measure the contribution of communications in achieving business objectives.

5 Marketing communications for service organisations

5.1 The promotion of goods and services have many similarities. We do not need to discriminate between the two when considering:

- The **role of promotion** in meeting marketing objectives
- The need to **design** effective promotions
- The **managerial challenge** of efficient implementation
- The broad **choice** of methods and media
- The **agencies** available to support promotion

5.2 **Promotional objectives** for services are related to those for products, as the following examples show.

(a) Build awareness and interest in the service and the service organisation.
(b) Communicate and portray the benefits of the services available.
(c) Build and maintain the overall image and reputation of the service organisation.
(d) Advise customers of new channels.
(e) Advise customers of special offers or modifications to the service.
(f) Persuade customers to use or buy the service.

5.3 In spite of these similarities there are significant differences caused by the special nature of services. Gronroos, a Swedish writer on service marketing, draws attention to some of the complexity in the diagram below demonstrating service relationships.

5.4 In service markets there are four **elements of the service** that need to be taken into account in planning.

- ■ The **core service concept** and any auxiliary service.
- ■ The **accessibility** of the service.
- ■ The **interactive communications** that take place in delivering the service.
- ■ The **influence of the consumer** and other consumers receiving the service.

5.5 Four promotional methods are then used to influence the customer.

- ■ Traditional selling
- ■ Advertising and direct marketing
- ■ Public relations and sales promotions
- ■ The communication aspects of pricing policy

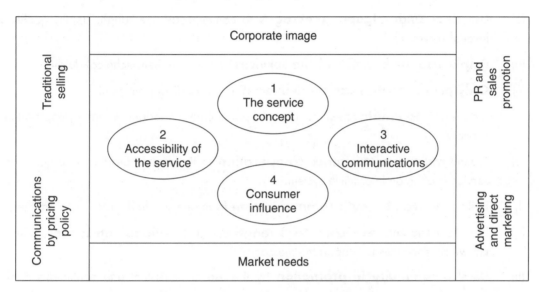

Model of service communications

5.6 There are differences in promotion necessitated by the characteristics of service industries and services companies.

Characteristics	Consequences
Lack of market orientation	Managers are untrained, unskilled and unaware of the role of promotion.
Professional and ethical constraints	Places limitations on certain promotion methods. Sometimes legal restrictions.
Small scale of many service organisations	Limits size of promotion budgets.
Nature of capacity available	Capacity for delivering the service may be limited. Promotion may produce too much demand.
Attitude to promotion methods	Limited knowledge of and attitude to wide range of promotion methods.

Characteristics	Consequences
Nature of the service	Services may be very specific, which excludes mass advertising.
Consumer attitudes	Consumers may rely on subjective judgements made at the point of service delivery.
Buying process	The need to develop a professional relationship with the service provider makes customer care important.

Source: D Cowell, *The Marketing of Services*, 1989

5.7 These differences lead to a number of guidelines that must be considered when designing communication campaigns for service markets.

(a) Use **clear unambiguous messages** to communicate the range, depth, quality and level of services.

(b) **Emphasise the benefits of the services** rather than their technical details.

(c) **Only promise what can be delivered**, to avoid disappointment.

(d) **Advertise to employees,** as they are particularly important in many people-intensive services.

(e) Obtain **maximum customer co-operation** in the service production process as the service is often an interactive system.

(f) Build on **word of mouth communication** from one satisfied customer to another.

(g) Provide **tangible evidence to strengthen promotional messages**. Use well known personalities to support the messages.

(h) Develop **continuity in promotion** by the use of consistent and continuous symbols, themes, formats or images.

(i) **Remove post purchase anxiety** by reassuring the buyer of the soundness of choice, especially where there is no tangible product.

(j) **Personal selling** becomes more important in the promotion of services as the following table shows.

5.8 **Differences between selling goods and services** are shown below.

Issue	Comment
Customer's purchase perception of services	■ Customers view service as having less consistent quality ■ Service purchasers have higher risks ■ Service purchasing is less pleasant ■ When services are bought greater consideration is given to the particular salesperson ■ Perception of the service company is an important factor when deciding to buy a service

Issue	Comment
Customer's purchase behaviour with services	■ Customers may do fewer price comparisons with services ■ Customers give greater consideration to the particular seller of services ■ Customers are less likely to be influenced by advertising and more by personal recommendations
Personal selling of services	■ Customer involvement is greater ■ Customer satisfaction is influenced by the salesperson's personality and attitude ■ Salespeople may have to spend more time reducing customer uncertainty

6 Marketing communications for non profit organisations

6.1 The major principles of marketing communications for non profit organisations are the same as for consumer and industrial marketing. There are, however, considerable differences of emphasis. The sum of money available for organised communication may be less. Public scrutiny of policies may be higher.

Marketing at Work

In the face of a severe shortfall in revenue (due to wildly optimistic forecast visitor numbers) the amount of grant funding to the New Millennium Experience Company rocketed to £628 million. Sir John Bourne of the National Audit Office said in a report:

> "Building and opening the Millennium Dome on the very short timescale required was a tremendous achievement. But the New Millennium Experience Company has experienced severe financial difficulties this year and has required considerable additional lottery funding.
>
> The main cause of these difficulties is the failure to achieve the visitor numbers and income required. The targets were highly ambitious and inherently risky leading to a significant degree of financial exposure on the project. In addition, the task of managing the project has been complicated by the complex organisational arrangements put in place from the outset, and by the failure to establish sufficiently robust financial management."

What went wrong? The whole issue illustrated the need for proper marketing communications planning. Strong negative word-of-mouth also had an impact. The following general points should have been considered.

■ Promotional strategies to attract visitors (pull strategy), communicate with those issuing tickets (push strategy), and promote the image of the 'Dome' and that of the Millennium Experience Company (Profile Strategy), should have been fully co-ordinated.

■ Messages should have been adapted to the various audiences.

■ Promotional strategies should have taken into account financial constraints imposed by the fact that this was funded in the main through public money. Sales were likely to fall short of targets if insufficient money and time was invested in marketing.

Adapted from CIM material

6.2 Almost certainly there will be a different set of **communication objectives**.

■ Making target customers **aware** of a product, service or social behaviour
■ **Educating** consumers about the offer or changes in the offer
■ **Changing beliefs** about negative and positive consequences of taking a particular action
■ **Changing the relative importance** of particular consequences
■ Enlisting the **support** of a variety of individuals
■ Recruiting, motivating or rewarding **employees or volunteers**
■ Changing **perceptions** about the sponsoring organisation
■ Influencing **government bodies**
■ Preventing the **discontinuity** of support
■ **Proving benefits** over 'competitors'
■ **Combating** injurious rumours
■ **Influencing** funding agencies

6.3 Once the non profit marketer has developed the broad objectives for the communications plan the next step is to decide specific messages. These messages may be developed within one of the three frameworks.

(a) **Rational, emotional and moral framework**

(i) Rational messages pass on information and serve the audience's self interest. For example messages about value, economy or benefits.

(ii) Emotional messages are designed to develop emotion to shape the desired behaviour. For example with fear, guilt, shame appeals to stop doing things like smoking, drinking, taking drugs or overeating.

(iii) Moral messages directed at the audience's sense of right or wrong. For example, to support a cleaner environment or equal rights or help the under-privileged.

 Marketing at Work

EShopAfrica.com is a website dedicated to selling the wares of African craftsmen. As well as the products themselves, the site features information about tribal traditions and personal stories about the craftsmen themselves.

Difficulties with credit card payments to Africa (the financial infrastructure is relatively underdeveloped) and the fact that the products can be obtained far more cheaply from bulk import/export businesses has meant that the site has struggled to break even. According to the site's founder, this misses the point of the venture.

The site is aimed at improving the lot of the craftsmen, and its avowed primary goal is to create sustainable businesses for five artisans a year. It aims to tap the snobbery market, and specifically that customer segment that is social/ego oriented and which seeks out the original and unusual at a premium price. This premium price can be seen by the customer to directly benefit an African craftsman and so the customer can feel good about him or herself.

Action Programme 3

Can you foresee any problems with the eShopAfrica promotional strategy? Is it sustainable in the long term, even if it is effective now?

(b) **Reward and situation framework**

   (i)   There may be four types of reward: rational, sensory, social or ego satisfaction rewards.

   (ii)   Rewards may result directly from use, or indirectly from the products in use, or be incidental to use. For example, think about the various rewards offered by cars with catalytic converters.

(c) **Attitude change framework**

   (i)   Changes in the importance of one or more outcomes
   (ii)   Changes in the beliefs about one or more outcomes
   (iii)   Adding new positive outcomes

6.4   Having decided what messages to transmit it is then necessary to decide the style of promotional execution. The following styles are appropriate for consumer goods advertising but can easily be adopted for non profit organisations.

6.5   **EXAMPLE: HEALTH EDUCATION**

Styles	Execution
Slice of life	Family doing healthy activities throughout the day
Life-style	Father and daughter off jogging early in morning
Fantasy	Dream of winning a marathon
Mood	Exercises in a field of wild flowers
Musical	Exercises to modern music
Personalities	Using a well known successful sports personality
Technical expertise	Quoting performance capability in exercises
Scientific evidence	Showing the benefits of less illness and greater longevity
Testimonial evidence	Members of the public give views on benefits

6.6 How marketers of non profit organisations can reach target audiences

Method	Comment
Paid advertising	Non profit organisations may have limited funds but this can still be an effective route even on low budgets, as the Save the Children Fund campaign showed. Alternatively the budget may be boosted by obtaining commercial sponsorship.
Unpaid (public service) advertising	Media owners may provide airtime or press space on a free of charge basis as a public service. However, there is little control over this and the times or spaces may occur at unpopular times or places.
Sales promotions	Short term incentives to encourage purchases or donations. Market control is strong and promotions are often newsworthy (for example Red Nose day or Poppy day promotions).
Public relations	Many of the stories of non profit organisations are of considerable interest. They may feature in the press or the broadcast media. Control over the message is good and feedback is possible.
Personal selling and communications	Staff at all levels of the non profit organisations should be trained in personal communications. They will often have the opportunity to 'sell' to their supporters and possible benefactors.

6.7 **Categories of non profit communications** include the following.

- Political party communications
- Social cause communications
- Charitable communications
- Government communications
- Religious communications
- Professional body communications
- Other private non profit communications (hospitals, universities, museums and so on)

Direct marketing

6.8 This is a medium increasingly being used by non profit organisations, particularly arts foundations and charities. It has seven important **advantages for non profit marketers**.

(a) It can be very focused for maximum effect on the target market.

(b) It can be private and confidential. This is especially important when dealing with sensitive issues.

(c) There is less direct regulation on direct mail promotions. In the past charitable advertising in the broadcast media has been limited.

(d) Cost per contact and cost per response is low and controllable, which is important where funds have to be used wisely.

(e) Results are clearly measurable and can make the programmers more accountable.

(f)   Small scale tests of proposed strategies are feasible.

(g)   The effectiveness of direct marketing can be assessed in terms of behaviour (ie orders, donations, requests for membership).

Behaviour channels

6.9   Non profit campaigns often call for behavioural changes on the part of the target audience. It is for this reason that it is valuable to monitor the effectiveness of such a campaign using a modification of the hierarchy of effects model. The model shown below has been adapted for a campaign to encourage the use of contraceptives to aid family planning.

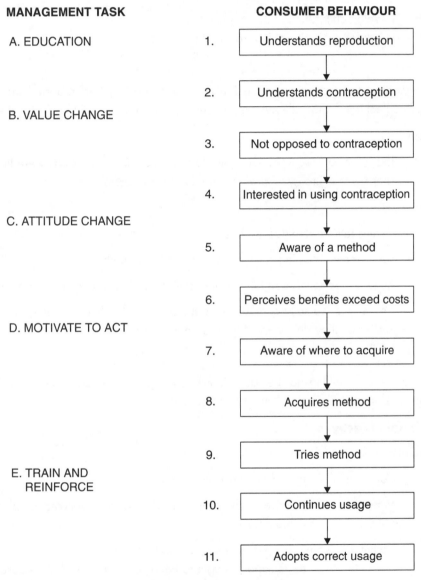

Contraceptive campaign
social behaviour change model

Source: Kotler and Anderson
Strategic Marketing for Non profit Organisations (Prentice Hall, 1987)

Marketing at Work

Campaign Title: NSPCC - Full Stop

Context

Business

1   The NSPCC set up a five vision programme to tackle the problem of child abuse, head on. This programme sought to:

- Set up an investigative service to run in parallel with the police
- Promote quality parenting
- Work with schools and teacher training colleges
- Develop children-friendly communities
- Work for cultural and legislative change

External

An independent national commission of enquiry (1995) had reported that 'child abuse and neglect can almost always be prevented, provided the will to do so is there'.

Organisational

- The financial resources necessary to implement the five visions were limited.
- There was a strong culture and drive to be successful

Customer

- Giving fatigue, NSPCC fatigue

- Suspicion concerning raising the standard of parenting

- Attitudes - scepticism at the charity's ambition to abolish child abuse/cruelty

- Abuse is universally condemned but people feel helpless ... they don't know what to do and they don't think it goes on near them

Stakeholder

Organisations willing to be associated with cause related issues which equate to sponsorship and assistance with fund raising.

Promotional objectives

The aim was to hit every household in the UK.

- Corporate: to end child abuse
- Marketing: to raise £250 million in 12 months - donated or pledged (normal amount £50m)
- Communication: to raise awareness of child cruelty
                 to persuade people to become involved with the cause

Promotional strategy

(a)   Strong pull campaign designed to raise awareness of child cruelty. Campaign to be delivered in two main steps. The first to develop awareness and the second step to be action orientated.

(b)   In parallel there should be a strategy designed to communicate with businesses in order to generate funds, goodwill and support.

(c)   The overall profile of the organisation (NSPCC) shall be raised and communications need to ensure that the integrity of the organisation and those associated with it are maintained. In addition, all communications need to be consistent.

Promotional mix used to create a dialogue with the public

- Public Relations
- TV, Posters
- Field Marketing
- Direct Marketing: Direct Mail, Telemarketing
- Website

First phase

Public relations were used at the initial stages of the campaign to help create awareness. Public address systems at railway stations and airports were used as a reminder mechanism.

A national TV campaign, supported by posters, broke soon after the public relations in order to raise awareness and provoke the question within each individual, 'what can I do?'. The message strategy was very emotional and used strong imagery to create shock and attention.

The heavy TV campaign looked to generate 600 TVRs, 85% coverage at 7.1 OTSs.

The supporting poster campaign used 48 sheets on 3,500 sites designed to deliver 55% coverage with 21 OTSs.

Initial enquiries to this wave of communications were heralded by an automated telemarketing bureau.

Second phase

This initial approach was followed up by a 23 million nationwide doordrop campaign. The aim was to provide the public with an answer to the question that the advertising had provoked, namely, to sign the pledge and/or volunteer as a donor or fundraiser.

The envelope picked up the TV creative treatment, repeating as a subdued background motif the image of nursery wallpaper with a teddy bear covering its eyes with its paws. 'Don't close your eyes to cruelty to children'.

It was thought that the doordrop letter addressed as 'Dear Householder' might offend established donors. To avoid this, 160,000 best donors were sent an early warning letter in advance of the campaign breaking in order to get their support. Another million received personal letters just ahead of the doordrop.

It was anticipated that the bulk of enquiries would come from the doordrop action and these were to be handled through personal telemarketing responses (inbound). The website was also adapted in order that it would be able to accept pledges.

In addition to this the campaign utilised a call-to-action weekend with volunteers staffing 2,000 sites around the country, including most city centres, to remind and raise cash donations.

Promotional mix used to communicate with businesses

- Sponsorship
- Direct Mail/Information Pack
- Internet

Sponsorship deals were made available enabling businesses to align themselves more closely with the campaign. Microsoft have been closely involved with NSPCC for a number of years and they acted as prime movers encouraging other businesses to pledge their support. The advertising for the campaign was sponsored by Microsoft.

Other sponsorship and cause related marketing packages were detailed in a Toolkit distributed to other major organisations.

Direct mail was also used to encourage businesses to make donations and electronic communications were used to promote pledges online.

(Source: Adapted from Goften K (1999) NSPCC aims to convert abuse anger into cash, *Marketing*)

This campaign sought to deal with an issue that most people choose to ignore. The ambitious targets needed an extraordinary marketing communications campaign if it was to be successful. The co-ordinated promotional plan enabled a simple yet hard hitting message to be conveyed to a substantial part of the nation.

It should be remembered that without knowing the budgets made available to fund the campaign and the extent of the contribution made by the business-to-business sector, it is doubtful whether a return on the investment will be made known outside of the charity. However, this should not detract from what is a major contribution to the social and moral welfare of the nation, made possible through astute use of an co-ordinated marketing communications campaign.

7 Marketing communications for small businesses

 Action Programme 4

Devise a marketing communications strategy and programme for a small business of your choice. Describe the advantages and disadvantages of such a low budget campaign.

7.1 A glance through the many books on small business management and especially those claiming to reveal the secrets of successful low budget advertising will show that readers are given watered down versions of the conventional promotional principles. This again demonstrates that these principles are of uniform application and this is reassuring.

7.2 However, there must be differences between small companies and large companies besides the sizes of the campaign budgets. The overriding differences are of course the limited resources in designing and implementing a communications programme and also the matching limitations in the target audience. The implications of these limitations and other aspects are discussed below.

Do-it-yourself

7.3 The key to saving money is to carry out many of the tasks yourself. This will mean learning about the principles and methods of marketing communications. This in itself is a valuable exercise.

You can use desk top publishing to design advertising material and local media owners will be only too happy to deal directly with you.

Small agencies

7.4 If you do need professional help there are many one person and small agencies able to offer a package of promotional help on a cost effective basis. Such agencies are keen to help small businesses grow because this is the best way of growing themselves.

Marketing research

7.5 To reduce risks, improve targeting and to get to know your customer's needs and competition better it is important to conduct marketing research yourself. Many small business people rely a great deal on intuition and may be reluctant to conduct research, but it will repay many times the effort devoted to it.

Personal selling

7.6 The owner manager of a small business will also usually be one of the company's main salesmen. This is another way of maintaining a low cost and cost effective marketing budget.

Public relations

7.7 This promotional method does not need substantial sums to get started. Simple press releases can be issued, opening events can be held and even a limited local sponsorship can be done for little expenditure. Again this will often mean doing it yourself or using a small local PR agency.

Direct marketing

7.8 Using direct marketing techniques, either telemarketing or direct mail, can be done cost effectively at local level. The volume of direct marketing activity can be regulated by the amount of time you have available and by the number of customers you are trying to reach.

Door drops

7.9 An alternative method of getting to households is to arrange for door to door leaflet distribution in your chosen target area. This can be considerably cheaper than incurring postal charges. It is also accurate in that particular districts and types of houses can be targeted.

Advertising

7.10 With the expansion of local media including free newspapers and local commercial radio stations, it is possible to tailor your campaign to particular locations. Designing advertising and buying media space or airtime, however, can become quite expensive, especially for frequently repeated advertisements.

Sales promotions

7.11 Using your imagination it is possible to devise a whole range of cost effective sales promotions, which will have the benefit of generating immediate sales and improving your cash flow.

Rapid feedback

7.12 All these methods then can be tried and evaluated at relatively low cost with the added value of a rapid feedback of results that will enable an improved campaign to be developed and implemented.

7.13 The characteristics specific to low budget campaigns are summarised below.

Feature	Comment
Do it yourself	Planning, implementation and control
Small agencies	Matching your size
Marketing research	Will reduce risk
Personal selling	Likely to be the main method
Public relations	Can be done at low cost
Direct marketing	Cost effective by telephone and mail
Drop drops	Very low cost targeting
Advertising	Likely to be more expensive
Sales promotion	Immediate benefits to cash flow
Rapid feedback	Allowing for improvements to be made

Chapter Roundup

■ This chapter includes **case studies** of successful campaigns.

■ **Industrial marketing communications strategies** can be very different from consumer campaigns. There are differences in such areas as purchase motivation, customer needs, product specifications, level of customer service needed and so on. This calls for different approaches in employing the various promotional tools.

■ The marketing of **services** is similar to the marketing of products in many ways, but there can be differences because of such factors as professional and legal constraints, the nature of capacity available, and the buying process itself. Personal selling is more important.

■ In **non profit marketing communications** there is likely to be less money available, messages are likely to be subjected to greater scrutiny and the objectives of the communication will be quite different from those applying in consumer marketing. The major categories of non profit communicators are political parties, social causes, the government, religious bodies and professional bodies.

■ The main feature of marketing communications for **small businesses** is that resources are limited. This will mean that more is done in-house and at a local level, though all the usual promotional tools can still be employed.

■ In attempting to understand the impact of communications it is important realise that every variable interacts with other variables and cause and effect cannot easily be distinguished. Effective communications are those that increase brand **awareness**, stimulate **trial purchase** and **reinforce** brand loyalty. The amount of communication to which people are now being subjected means that it is becoming increasingly difficult to communicate successfully.

Now try question 8 in the Question Bank

Quick Quiz

1 Ultimately communications are designed to meet three objectives.

    A..........   Increase brand .... and establish brand ....
    T..........   Stimulate trial ....
    R..........   Stimulate and .... brand ....

2 Fill in the gaps in the grid below:

Marketing communications methods	Examples of measurement
Personal selling	
Public relations	
Direct marketing	
Advertising	
Sales promotion	
Exhibitions	

3 When assessing the effectiveness of a communications campaign, why is simplification important?

A It is more cost-effective

B It is necessary in view of the avalanche of information faced by customers

C Less educated customers will pay more attention

D The message needs to be the same for everybody

4 A recall test is an example of

(a) Pre testing

(b) Post testing

5 Why is direct marketing particularly effective for non-profit organisations?

A The effectiveness of direct marketing can be assessed in terms of behaviour

B Results are clearly measurable

C It can be cheap and targeted

D All of the above

6 How can public relations be undertaken in a low budget campaign?

7 The amount of communication to which people are now being subjected means that it is becoming increasingly difficult to communicate successfully.

True ☐

False ☐

8 In non profit marketing communications there is likely to be less money available. What is a possible consequence of this?

Action Programme Review

1 (a) Size of business, market sector, fmcg/business-to-business/service/not for profit.

(b) These factors and issues should be based on result of context analysis – business, customer, stakeholder, internal and external.

(c) Communications objectives should focus on changes in awareness, attitudes and behaviour. These should relate to marketing and business objectives.

(d) Pull, push and profile are the main communications strategies available – what communications tools have you identified for each strategy?

(e) If you have identified sales or market share, remember the difficulty of direct association with communications due to other marketing factor effects. You should be measuring the effectiveness against the objectives set.

2 You should have identified integrating factors relating to different levels of strategy – business, marketing and communication – all linked via the objectives set. It is not just a question of using the same strapline or visual image on all of the communication, but also as to how the overall communications activities relate to what the business as a whole is attempting to achieve. Remember that internal communications play an important role in achieving integration and the relevance of push and profile strategies.

3　In theory, as more and more people buy the products and as the website becomes more and more successful, its 'snobbery' appeal will become tarnished by its own popularity. The targeted type of customer is only likely to buy from it once. Someone who is a 'snob' and who doesn't mind what they pay for an item, so long as it comes from the 'right' place, is unlikely to be loyal when the next 'in' thing comes along. The company will have to find new ways to differentiate itself from the competition. Given its product range and the fact that it is much more expensive than other distributors, this could prove extremely difficult.

4　Your answer should have looked at the advantages and disadvantages of different strategic options viz. push, pull and profile. The communications tools should be specific to the strategy or strategies selected. You can identify some of the advantages and disadvantages of a low budget campaign from the table at paragraph 7.13.

Answers to Quick Quiz

1

Awareness	Increase brand awareness and establish brand recognition
Trial	Stimulate trial purchase
Reinforcement	Stimulate and reinforce brand loyalty

2

Marketing communications methods	Examples of measurement
Personal selling	Sales targets
Public relations	Editorial coverage
Direct marketing	Enquiries generated
Advertising	Brand awareness
Sales promotion	Coupons redeemed
Exhibitions	Contacts made

3　B

4　Post testing

5　D

6　Simple press releases can be issued, opening events can be held and even a limited local sponsorship can be done for little expenditure. This will often mean 'doing it yourself' or using a small local PR agency.

7　True

8　Proposed media and messages are likely to be subjected to greater scrutiny, as resources are tighter

Part C

Marketing channels

BPP)))
PROFESSIONAL EDUCATION

Developing and maintaining marketing channels

Learning Outcomes

☑ Develop marketing communication and brand support activities based on an understanding of the salient characteristics of the target audience

☑ Explain how the tools of the promotional mix can be co-ordinated in order to communicate effectively with customers and a range of stakeholders

☑ Explain the importance of developing long-term relationships with customers, channel members, agencies and other stakeholders and transfer such knowledge to the development of marketing communication activities

☑ Suggest suitable methods to influence the relationships an organisation has with its customers, any marketing channel partners and other stakeholders, using marketing communications

Syllabus References

☑ Identify and explain how the promotional mix can be suitably configured for use in a range of marketing channels and business-to-business situations

☑ Explain, in terms of the impact on marketing communications within a relationship context, the structural concepts: interdependence, independence, disintermediation and reintermediation

☑ Explain the role of trust, commitment and satisfaction when developing marketing communication activities for use in the marketing channel and business-to-business contexts

☑ Identify the causes of conflict in trade channels and explain how marketing communications can be used to resolve such disagreements

Key Concepts Introduced

- Supply chain management
- Independence
- Interdependence
- Stakeholders

- Conflict
- Trust
- Commitment
- Disintermediation

1 Setting the scene

1.1 Business-to-business relationships include **marketing channel relationships** and **supply chain networks**. This chapter looks at the nature of various distribution structures and discusses some of the influences which affect the choice and configuration of the marketing channel.

1.2 For many manufacturers, distribution is the 'Cinderella' of the marketing mix, less glamorous and 'creative' than promotion, and less involved in the heart of the company than the product. However some firms use distribution as a means of competitive advantage and retailers, of course, take distribution very seriously. Marketing communicators also need to take account of its importance. Distribution has two aspects, expanded upon in the next paragraph.

- **Tangible** – the physical movement and delivery of goods

- **Intangible** – aspects of channel (or supply chain) management, control and communication. This forms the focus for this chapter.

1.3 A firm's **marketing communications** will be strongly influenced by the extent to which the firm is able to obtain wide distribution. Key issues in distribution are these.

(a) **Coverage and density**, in other words the number of sales outlets.

　　(i) Countries like the UK and US allow large stores.

　　(ii) In Japan, there have been restrictions on store size, to protect the livelihoods of small retailers.

(b) **Channel length** - the number of intermediaries between producer and consumer.

(c) **Power and alignment.** The marketer has to realise that distribution channel power is not equal. Different roles are played by retailers, wholesalers and agents. For example, wholesalers are most important where retailing is fragmented. In the UK, where, in groceries, concentration of retail power has gone furthest, the major supermarket chains are powerful.

(d) **Logistics and physical distribution**

Logistics systems are expensive and can be very damaging to corporate profitability if badly handled. There are several areas which are crucial.

- Transport and transport management (delivery time and costs)
- Inventory control (minimum stock without effective service)
- Order processing
- Materials handling and warehouse
- Fixed facilities location management

Marketing at Work

Downstream drift

Companies are drifting downstream. That is, they are gradually losing interest in how they make their products, and focusing more on how those goods and services reach their ultimate customer.

The car industry's new obsession with what happens to its products once they leave the factory arises in part because it has already cut the costs of production substantially. So it is planning to take an axe to distribution costs, too. Ford is the company that is reshaping itself most radically. It is handing over more of the responsibility for manufacturing to sub-contractors. But at the same time it is acquiring automotive servicing companies, such as the UK's Kwik-Fit and a Florida-based car recycling business.

The trend is visible in other industries, too. Personal computer manufacturers have delegated most of the important technical decisions that shape their products to component suppliers such as Intel and Microsoft. They increasingly delegate the mundane task of making their products to third-party manufacturers.

But they are following Dell Computer in seizing back customer relationships from distributors and dealers. Indeed, by offering customers free Internet access or free online training, they seek to infiltrate themselves into the customer's life.

Peter Martin, *Financial Times*, 14 September 1999

2 The chain of distribution

2.1 In order for a product to be distributed a number of basic functions usually need to be fulfilled.

Transport	This function may be provided by the supplier, the distributor or may be sub-contracted to a specialist. For some products, such as perishable goods, transport planning is vital.
Stock holding and storage	For production planning purposes, an uninterrupted flow of production is often essential, so stocks of finished goods accumulate and need to be stored, incurring significant costs and risks. For consumer goods, holding stock at the point of sale is very costly; the overheads for city centre retail locations are prohibitive. A good stock control system is essential, designed to avoid stockouts whilst keeping stockholding costs low.

Local knowledge	As production has tended to become centralised in pursuit of economies of scale, the need to understand local markets has grown, particularly when international marketing takes place. The intricacies and idiosyncrasies of local markets are key marketing information.
Promotion	Major promotional campaigns for national products are likely to be carried out by the supplier.
Display	Presentation of the product is often a function of the local distributor. Specialist help from merchandisers can be bought in.

Action Programme 1

For many goods, producers use retailers as middlemen in getting the product to the customer. Try to think of some of the disadvantages of doing this, from the producer's point of view

Points in the chain of distribution

2.2 An intermediary is someone who 'mediates' or brings about a settlement between two persons: in this case between the original supplier and the ultimate buyer. There are a variety of types of intermediary and several may intervene before a product gets from the original provider and the final buyer.

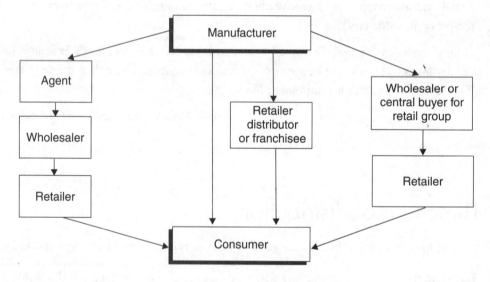

2.3 (a) **Retailers**. These are traders operating outlets which sell directly to households. They may be classified in a number of ways.

  (i)   Type of goods sold (eg hardware, furniture)

  (ii) Type of service (self-service, counter service)

  (iii) Size

  (iv) Location (rural, city-centre, suburban shopping mall, out-of-town shopping centre)

(v) **Independent retailers** (including the local corner shop, although independents are not always as small as this)

(vi) **Multiple chains**, some of which are associated with one class of product while others are 'variety' chains, holding a wide range of different stocks

(vii) Still others are **voluntary groups** of independents, usually grocers.

(b) **Wholesalers**. These are intermediaries who stock a range of products from competing manufacturers to sell on to other organisations such as retailers. Many wholesalers specialise in particular products. Most deal in consumer goods, but some specialise in industrial goods, such as steel stockholders and builders' merchants.

(c) **Distributors and dealers**. These are organisations which contract to buy a manufacturer's goods and sell them to customers. Their function is similar to that of wholesalers, but they usually offer a narrower product range, sometimes (as in the case of most car dealers) the products of a single manufacturer. In addition to selling on the manufacturer's product, distributors often promote the products and provide after-sales service.

(d) **Agents**. Agents differ from distributors.

(i) Distributors **buy** the manufacturer's goods and **re-sell** them at a profit.

(ii) Agents do not purchase the manufacturer's goods, but earn a commission on whatever sales they make.

(e) **Franchisees**. These are independent organisations which, in exchange for an initial fee and (usually) a share of sales revenue, are allowed to trade under the name of a parent organisation. Most fast food outlets are franchises.

(f) **Multiple stores** (eg **supermarkets**) buy goods for retailing direct from the producer, many of them under their 'own label' brand name.

2.4 Do not forget that **direct selling** also occurs.

- Mail order
- Telephone selling
- Door-to-door selling
- Personal selling in the sale of industrial goods
- An organisation which includes both manufacturing and retail outlets
- TV shopping
- E-commerce

Factors in relationships with distribution channels

2.5 In working with **distributors**, the marketer needs to bear in mind the following points.

(a) **The independent commercial objectives of the distributor**. Distributors are business organisations with their own requirements for efficiency and profitability. They do not stock products or run promotions as a 'favour' to the supplier!

(i) You need to negotiate and contract terms.

(ii) You need to promote the benefits of the product or collaboration to the distributor.

(b) **The distributor's relationship with competitors**. Bear in mind that a retailer or wholesaler may well be stocking and promoting competing products. You will need to be discreet to differentiate your product and promotions, and to be aware of opportunities to gain useful market intelligence.

(c) **The distributor's knowledge of the consumer.** Distributors are in the front line of contact with consumers. Be prepared to seek and respect their research or sense of what will work in terms of product and promotion.

(d) **The distributor's power in the market.** Major distributors have considerable buying power over suppliers, and good working relationships must be preserved with them, usually at the expense of autonomy and control over promotions. A major distributor may ask for exclusive rights to sell a product, or ask to sell it under an 'own brand' label. It may control all point-of-sale and media promotions regarding its sale of the product, charging a fee for promotional space and collaboration.

(e) **The mutual benefit of promotional collaboration**

    (i) If the supplier promotes the product to consumers through PR, advertising and consumer incentives, the distributor selling the product to consumers will benefit.

    (ii) If the distributor promotes the product to consumers - through advertising its availability through the distributor, or through in-store display and incentives - the supplier will benefit.

2.6 Choosing distribution channels is important for any organisation, because once a set of channels has been established, subsequent changes are likely to be costly and slow to implement. Distribution channels fall into one of two categories: **direct** and **indirect channels**.

2.7 **Direct distribution** means the product going directly from producer to consumer without the use of a specific intermediary. These methods are often described as **active** since they typically involve the **supplier** making the first approach to a potential customer. Direct distribution methods generally fall into two categories: those using **media** such as the press, leaflets and telephones to invite response and purchase by the consumer and those using a **sales force** to contact consumers face to face.

2.8 **Indirect distribution** is a system of distribution, common among manufactured goods, which makes use of intermediaries; wholesalers, retailers or perhaps both. In contrast to direct distribution, these methods are often thought of as being **passive** in the sense that they rely on consumers to make the first approach by entering the relevant retail outlet.

Exam Tip

Direct and indirect methods of distribution are used by the subject of the case study on the Specimen Paper, Country Style Kitchens.

2.9 In building up efficient channels of distribution, a manufacturer must consider several factors.

(a) How many **intermediate stages** should be used and how many dealers at each stage?

(b) What **support** should the manufacturer give to the dealers? It may be necessary to provide an after-sales and repair service, and regular visits to retailers' stores. The manufacturer might need to consider advertising or sales promotion support, including merchandising.

(c) To what extent does the manufacturer wish to **dominate a channel of distribution**? A market leader might wish to ensure that its market share is maintained, so that it could, for example, offer **exclusive distribution contracts** to major retailers.

(d) To what extent does the manufacturer wish to **integrate its marketing effort** up to the point of sale with the consumer? Combined promotions with retailers, for example, would only be possible if the manufacturer dealt directly with the retailer (rather than through a wholesaler).

3 Supply chain management

3.1 Many enterprises have been getting larger. Some writers are arguing that the trend will continue - so that for many sectors there will be fewer players of world class dominating the field. We have seen this in the automobile industry for example, with many European companies merging to be able to compete effectively with US giants and the Japanese.

3.2 There have been, at the same time, much **closer links** with companies in the supply chain in order to extract best value for money and reduce stockholdings. This has had major consequences on the distribution methods of companies in these supply chains, delivering to their customers on a **just in time** (JIT) basis.

3.3 Historically, businesses in the supply chain have operated relatively **independently** of one another to create value for an ultimate customer. **Independence was maintained** through holding buffer stocks, managing capacity and lead-times. This is represented in the 'Traditional' model shown below. There was very little control over other channel members, and no wider perspective on the system as a whole.

3.4 Market and competitive demands are now, however, **compressing lead times** and businesses are reducing inventories and excess capacity. This new condition is shown in the **'Integrated supply chain'** model.

3.5 There seems to be increasing recognition that, in the future, it will be **whole supply chains** which will compete and not just individual firms. This will continue to have a great impact upon distribution methods.

Supply chain model

 Key Concept

Supply chain management is about optimising the activities of companies working together to produce goods and services.

3.6 The aim is to co-ordinate the whole chain, from raw material suppliers to end customers. The chain should be considered as a **network** rather than a **pipeline** - a network of vendors support a network of customers, with third parties such as transport firms helping to link the companies. In marketing channels, organisations have to manage the trade-off between the desire to remain **independent and autonomous**, and the need to be **interdependent and cooperative**.

 Key Concepts

Independence: each channel member operates in isolation and is not affected by others, so maintaining a greater degree of control.

Interdependence: each channel member can affect the performance of others in the channel.

 Marketing at Work

The Hong Kong based export trading company, Li and Fung, takes the following approach to its manufacturing supply chain.

'Say we get an order from a European retailer to produce 10,000 garments. It's not a simple matter of our Korean office sourcing Korean products or our Indonesian office sourcing Indonesian products. For the customer we might decide to buy yarn from a Korean producer but have it woven and dyed in Taiwan. So we pick the yarn and ship it to Taiwan. The Japanese have the best zippers and buttons, but they manufacture them mostly in China. Okay, so we go to YKK, a big Japanese zipper manufacturer and we order the right zippers from their Chinese plants. Then we determine that, because of quotas and labour conditions, the best place to make the garments is Thailand. So we ship everything there. And because the customer needs quick delivery, we may divide the order across five factories in Thailand. Effectively, we are customising the value chain to best meet the customer's needs.

Five weeks after we have received the order, 10,000 garments arrive on the shelves in Europe, all looking like they came from one factory with colours, for example, perfectly matched. Just think about the logistics and the co-ordination.

This is a new type of value added, a truly global product that has never been seen before. The label may say "Made in Thailand", but it's not a Thai product. We dissect the manufacturing process and look for the best solution to each step. We're not asking which country can do the best job overall. Instead, we're pulling apart the value chain and optimising each step - and we're doing it globally... . The classic supply-chain manager in retailing is Marks & Spencer. They don't own any factories, but they have a huge team that goes into the factories and works with the management.'
(*Harvard Business Review*, 1998)

3.7 If the supplier 'knows' what his customers want, it does not necessarily have to guess, or wait until the customer places an order. It will be able to better plan its own delivery systems. The potential for using the **Internet** (see section 7) to allow customers and suppliers to acquire up-to-date information about forecast needs and delivery schedules is a recent development, but one which is being used by an increasing number of companies.

4 Stakeholders

4.1 Linked to the idea of networks is the **stakeholder concept**. To quote Fill (2002):

> 'The concept of different groups influencing an organisation and in turn being influenced is an important element in the development of integrated marketing communications. The concept enables an organisation to identify all those other organisations and individuals who can be or are influenced by [its] strategies and policies.'

Key Concept

Stakeholders are groups or individuals having a legitimate interest in the activities of an organisation, generally comprising customers, employees, the community, shareholders, suppliers and lenders. The organisation will generally seek to add value for stakeholders, in accordance with their varying objectives.

4.2 There are three broad types of stakeholder in an organisation, as follows.

- **Internal** stakeholders (employees, management)
- **Connected** stakeholders (shareholders, customers, suppliers, financiers)
- **External** stakeholders (the community, government, pressure groups)

Internal stakeholders: employees and management

4.3 Because **employees and management** are so intimately connected with the company, their objectives are likely to have a strong influence on how it is run. They are interested in the following issues.

(a) The **organisation's continuation and growth**. Management and employees have a special interest in the organisation's continued existence.

(b) Managers and employees have **individual interests** and goals which can be harnessed to the goals of the organisation.

Connected stakeholders

4.4 Increasing shareholder value usually assumes the core role in the strategic management of an international business. If management performance is measured and rewarded by reference to changes in **shareholder value** then shareholders will be happy, because managers are likely to encourage long-term share price growth.

4.5 Customers, suppliers and consumers can increasingly be thought of as 'investing in the company' whenever they buy or sell a particular product or service. They judge the **total value** that the company can offer. This can include:

- **Expertise** (eg support/training offered by manufacturers to retailers)
- **Information** (as offered by retailers to suppliers on market trends)
- **Influence**
- **Infrastructure** } (use of buying power to source raw materials)
- **Resources**
- **Responsive attitude** (such as alignment of ordering and payment processes between supply chain partners)
- **Social responsibility**

External stakeholders

4.6 External stakeholder groups - the government, local authorities, pressure groups, the community at large, professional bodies - are likely to have quite diverse objectives.

Exam Tip

In an exam question, you may have to:

- Identify the stakeholders in the marketing channel
- Identify what their particular interests are

Stakeholder networks and the marketing channel

4.7 Stakeholder 'maps' indicate the primary relationships and patterns of interdependence within the marketing channel. These networks 'not only constitute those organisations that make up the marketing channel but also seek to integrate all those other organisations that assist the channel members to achieve their objectives of satisfying customer needs'. (Fill, 2002)

4.8 Within the marketing channel, there are two primary stakeholder roles, connected to the idea of internal, connected and external stakeholders described above.

(a) **Performance** – directly involved with adding value in the marketing channel (manufacturer, wholesaler, retailer). These are interdependent.

(b) **Support** – banks, consultancies, government and so on, supporting the 'performing' members. These have no such interdependence.

Action Programme 2

Identify the 'performance' and 'support' organisations that make up the network in the marketing channel used by your company, or one with which you are familiar.

5 Channel design decisions

5.1 In setting up a channel of distribution, the supplier must consider five things.

- Customers
- Product characteristics
- Distributor characteristics
- The channel chosen by competitors
- The supplier's own characteristics

Customers

5.2 The **number** of potential customers, their **buying habits** and their **geographical locations** are key influences. The use of mail order for those with limited mobility (rural location, illness) is an example of the influence of customers on channel design. Marketing industrial components to the car industry needs to take account of the geographic distribution of the car industry in the UK. The growth of Internet trading, both in consumer and business-to-business markets, has been built on the rapid spread of fast Internet access.

BPP)))
PROFESSIONAL EDUCATION

Product characteristics

5.3   Some product characteristics have an important effect on the design of the channel of distribution.

(a)   **Perishability**

Fresh fruit and newspapers must be distributed very quickly or they become worthless. Speed of delivery is therefore a key factor.

(b)   **Customisation**

Customised products tend to be distributed direct. When a wide range of options is available, sales may be made using demonstration units, with customised delivery to follow.

(c)   **After-sales service/technical advice**

Extent and cost must be carefully considered, staff training given and quality control systems set up. Training programmes are often provided for distributors by suppliers.

(d)   **Franchising**

Franchising has become a popular means of growth both for suppliers and for franchisees who carry the set-up costs and licence fees. The supplier gains additional outlets quickly and exerts more control than is usual in distribution.

Distributor characteristics

5.4   The capability of the distributor to take on the distributive functions already discussed above is obviously an important influence on the supplier's choice.

Competitors' channel choice

5.5   For many consumer goods, a supplier's brand will sit alongside its competitors' products and there is little the supplier can do about it. For other products, distributors may stock one name brand only (for example, in car distribution) and in return be given an exclusive area. In this case, new suppliers may face difficulties in breaking into a market if all the best distribution outlets have been taken up.

Supplier characteristics

5.6   A strong financial base gives the supplier the option of buying and operating their own distribution channel. Boots the Chemist is a prime example. The market position of the supplier is also important: distributors are keen to be associated with the market leader but the third, fourth or fifth brand in a market is likely to find more distribution problems.

5.7   **Factors favouring the use of direct selling**

(a)   An expert sales force will be needed to demonstrate products, explain product characteristics and provide after-sales service.

(b)   Intermediaries may be unwilling or unable to sell the product. For example, the ill-fated Sinclair C5 eventually had to be sold by direct mail.

(c)   Existing channels may be linked to other producers or reluctant to carry new product lines.

(d)   The intermediaries willing to sell the product may be too costly, or they may not be maximising potential sales.

(e)   If specialised transport requirements are involved, intermediaries may not be able to deliver goods to the final customer.

(f)   Where potential buyers are geographically concentrated the supplier's own sales force can easily reach them (typically an industrial market). One example is the financial services market centred on the City of London.

5.8   Factors favouring the use of intermediaries

(a)   There may be insufficient resources to finance a large sales force.

(b)   A policy decision to invest in increased productive capacity rather than extra marketing effort may be taken.

(c)   The supplier may have insufficient in-house marketing 'know-how' in selling to retail stores.

(d)   The assortment of products may be insufficient for a sales force to carry. A wholesaler can complement a limited range and make more efficient use of his sales force.

(e)   Intermediaries can market small lots as part of a range of goods. The supplier would incur a heavy sales overhead if its own sales force took small individual orders.

(f)   The existence of large numbers of potential buyers spread over a wide geographical area. This is typical of consumer markets.

Making the channel decision

5.9   Producers have a number of decisions to make.

(a)   What types of distributor are to be used (wholesalers, retailers, agents)?

(b)   How many of each type will be used? The answer to this depends on what degree of market exposure will be sought.

- **Intensive** - blanket coverage
- **Exclusive** - appointed agents for exclusive areas
- **Selective** - some but not all in each area

(c)   Who will carry out specific marketing tasks?

- Credit provision
- Delivery
- After-sales service
- Sales and product training
- Display

Action Programme 3

How might the performance of distributors be evaluated?

5.10 To develop a co-ordinated system of distribution, the supplier must consider all the factors influencing distribution combined with a knowledge of the relative merits of the different types of channel available.

Multi-channel decisions

5.11 The distribution channels appropriate for industrial markets may not be suitable for consumer markets. A producer serving both industrial and consumer markets may decide to use the following.

(a) Intermediaries for his consumer division

(b) Direct selling for his industrial division. For example, a detergent manufacturer might employ salesmen to sell to wholesalers and large retail groups in their consumer division. It would not be efficient for the sales force to approach small retailers directly.

Industrial and consumer distribution channels

5.12 **Industrial markets** may be characterised as having fewer, larger customers purchasing expensive products which may be custom built. It is due to these characteristics that **industrial distribution channels tend to be more direct and shorter than for consumer markets**. It has to be remembered, however, that the most appropriate distribution channels will depend specifically on the objectives of the company regarding market exposure. There are specialist distributors in the industrial sector, which may be used as well as, or instead of, selling directly to the companies within this sector.

5.13 There are fewer direct distribution channels, from the manufacturer to the consumer in the **consumer market**. Examples may be found in small 'cottage' industries or mail order companies. It is more usual for companies in consumer markets to use wholesalers and retailers to move their product to the final consumer.

(a) **Wholesalers** break down the bulk from manufacturers and pass products on to retailers. They take on some of the supplier's risks by funding stock. Recently in the UK there has been a reduction in importance of this type of intermediary.

(b) **Retailers** sell to the final consumers. They may give consumers added benefits by providing services such as credit, delivery and a wide variety of goods. In the UK, retailers have increased in power whilst wholesalers have declined. Retailing has also become more concentrated with increased dominance of large multiples.

Exam Tip

Marketing channels in the car industry form the topic of a question in Section B of the Specimen Paper. This is a key example of an industry where distribution patterns are changing away from traditional dealer networks because of:

Increased price awareness by consumers – driven largely by the Internet

Regulations controlling 'price fixing'

Direct sales opportunities afforded by the Internet

6 Marketing channel strategy

6.1 There are three main strategies.

(a) **Intensive distribution** involves concentrating on a segment of the total market, such as choosing limited geographical distribution rather than national distribution.

(b) Using **selective distribution**, the producer selects a group of retail outlets from amongst all retail outlets on grounds of the brand image, or related to the retailers' capacity to provide after-sales service.

(c) **Exclusive distribution** is an extension of selective distribution. Particular outlets are granted exclusive handling rights within a prescribed geographical area. Sometimes exclusive distribution, or franchise rights, are coupled with making special financial arrangements for land, buildings or equipment, such as petrol station agreements.

Channel dynamics

6.2 Organisations group together when they cannot achieve their objectives independently. If a marketing channel is to function effectively, cooperation is paramount.

(a) A distribution system with a central core organising and planning marketing throughout the channel is termed a **vertical marketing system (VMS)**. Vertical marketing systems provide channel role specification and co-ordination between members. There is much more **interdependence** than is featured in a conventional system.

(b) In **corporate marketing systems** the stages in production and distribution are owned by a single corporation in a fairly rigid structure. This common ownership permits close integration and therefore the corporation controls activities along the distribution chain. For example, Laura Ashley shops sell goods produced in Laura Ashley factories.

(c) **Contractual marketing systems** involve agreement over aspects of distribution marketing. One example of a contractual marketing system that has become popular over the last decade is franchising.

(d) If a plan is drawn up between channel members to help reduce conflict this is often termed an **administered marketing system**.

Channel conflict

6.3 Channels are subject to **conflicts** between members. This need not be destructive as long as it remains manageable. Manufacturers may have little influence on how their product is presented to the public.

Key Concept

Conflict is the breakdown in cooperation between channel partners.

6.4 The causes of conflict need to be identified, so that strategies can be formulated to repair any damage. Conflict stems from four main problems (Fill, 2002).

- **Failure to do the job** as understood by the rest of the channel
- Disagreement over a **policy issue**, such as territory or margin
- Differing perceptions on **how to get the job done**
- Inadequate **communications**

Interorganisational communication

6.5 Communication is key to conflict resolution. The **management of communication** is usually undertaken by a dominant member – the channel 'leader' or 'captain' who holds most of the power in the channel. In industrial markets where channel lengths are generally short, power often lies with manufacturers of products rather than 'middlemen'.

6.6 **Communication within networks** travels not only between levels of dependence (up and down the network) but also across, such as from retailer to retailer. Reflecting its role in the **push** strategy, it has the following roles.

- Provide persuasive **information**
- Foster **participative decision making**
- Provide for co-or**dination**
- Allows the exercise of **power**
- Encourages **loyalty and commitment**
- Reduces the likelihood of **tension and conflict**

6.7 Trust in and commitment to the network is crucial for success.

Key Concepts

Trust: the degree to which partners are confident that each will act in the best interests of the relationship.

Commitment: the desire to maintain a valuable relationship.

Marketing at Work

The use of **trade promotions** and **trade advertising** by a company will be designed to keep the channel loyal. Techniques such as offering discounts to wholesalers, in return for extra promotion of the product, or extra shelf space, will help to increase sales as well (if the discount is passed on to the end consumer). Trade advertising in the form of brochures, leaflets and samples should focus on aspects such as margins, turnover, shelf space profitability and the level of manufacturer support.

Exam Tip

Distribution is often not represented and easy to ignore, but is key to issues of communication and profitability, and the new syllabus is keen to address it. Each channel has different needs and requirements.

Action Programme 4

One of the fastest growing forms of selling in the US over the past decade has been via factory outlet centres. Discount factory shops, often situated on factory premises, from which manufacturers sell off overmakes, slight seconds, or retailers' returns are already well-established in the UK, but in the US developers have grouped such outlets together in purpose-built malls.

What would you suggest are the advantages of this method of distribution for customers and manufacturers?

Marketing at Work

OTC Medicines

The supply chain is often a crucial element in the success or failure of a product. In the case of over-the-counter (OTC) medicines, because of the unique features of the product, the situation and the constraints on marketers, the supply chain plays a key role in consumer choice making.

Medicines satisfy a powerful and basic need - relief from pain. As a consequence, products tend to be evaluated in terms of their strict efficacy, and the functions of branding or advertising are far less prominent than usual. According to Mellors Reay and Partners, who work on the marketing of OTC medicines, this is compounded by regulations and restrictions on the advertising and retail promotion of products. These include:

(a)   strict regulation of claims and impact of advertising;

(b)   non-display of items on retailers shelves;

(c)   restrictions on merchandising, discounting, the use of personality endorsement, loyalty schemes, cross promotions and free trials;

(d)   huge price rises when products transfer from prescription to OTC;

(e)   similarity between brand names because of reference to ingredients (for instance, paracetamol based analgesics include Panadeine, Panadol, Panaleve, Panerel, Paracets, and so on); and

(f)   the influence of the pharmacist who can overcome or counter any promotional effect.

The role of the pharmacist is crucial, and is becoming more ambivalent, as the old semi-medical professional role is combined with one as an employee of commercial and market oriented enterprises. The increasing availability of OTC medicines previously only available on prescription only increases this power. Marketing OTC medicines directly to consumers must involve, to some extent, countering the respect and trust of consumers for pharmacists.

Yet brands can become established in spite of these problems. Nurofen, for example, an ibuprofen based analgesic, has established a powerful presence by building a brand which is distinctive by using advertising which suggests both power and empathy, and also by visualising and emphasising in an imaginative way the experience and relief of pain.

Admap

International channels

6.8 As markets open to international trade, channel decisions become more complex. A company can export using host country middlemen or domestic middlemen. These may or may not take title to the goods. Implications of channel management in the case of exporters include a loss of control over product policies like price, image, packaging and service. A producer may undertake a joint venture or licensing agreement or even manufacture abroad. All will have implications for the power structure and control over the product.

7 Marketing channels and information technology

Exam Tip

Relationships with other members of the marketing channel are increasingly being influenced and developed by the Internet. This formed part of the scenario question on the Specimen Paper.

7.1 In recent years new technologies have emerged that have changed, and are continuing to change, the way business is conducted. Among the most significant changes are changes relating to the following.

- Mobile communications
- Electronic communications and commerce (e.g. Electronic Data Interchange (EDI))
- Satellite and cable digital television
- The Internet

7.2 The full impact of new technology has only just begun, but already significant changes have occurred in some organisations distribution channels.

Marketing at Work

BSkyB is to launch a retail marketing channel called 'TV High Street' that will provide companies with half-hour direct-response infomercials to promote their products.

The channel will broadcast from September 2, offering a 'walled garden' of 12 companies including Argos and Kays, the UK's largest mail-order company.

Consumers will be able to choose which infomercials to view. As well as encouraging people to go out and shop, mail-order firms can publicise phone order numbers and websites. It is thought retailers will devise exclusive offers for TV High Street.

As well as appearing on the BSkyB channel, Argos will broadcast its output in-store at its bigger branches.

Unlike BSkyB's interactive TV service, Sky Active, the channel will not offer e-commerce, but will act purely as a product and brand marketing vehicle. It will reach the 5.7 million UK households that subscribe to BSkyB. Further retailers will be invited to join, although it is understood BSkyB is keen to limit partners to around 20.

Marketing, 11 July 2002

Internet distribution

Display

7.3 **Information gathering** is still the most common Internet activity, whether it be information about a historical fact, a medical problem or, hopefully, **about your product**. At present the five most common online **purchase** categories are books, CDs, clothing, toys and games, and computer software, but many buyers for other types of product do their initial **'window shopping'** online and then go to a more conventional distribution outlet to actually make their purchase.

7.4 The Internet is perfect for the display of many types of product – anything, in fact, that customers don't need to be able handle physically, but which can be adequately shown off in words, still and moving pictures and sound.

7.5 A website offers an effortless and impersonal way for customers to find out the details of the products and services that a company provides, and **spend as long as they like** doing so: much longer than they might feel comfortable with if they had a sales person hanging over them.

7.6 For businesses the advantage is that it is much cheaper to provide the information in electronic form than it would be to employ staff to man the phones on an enquiry desk or walk the shop floor, and much more effective than sending out mailshots that people would either throw away or forget about.

Exam Tip

This is a key point to think about when reading the case study on the Specimen Paper about 'Country Style Kitchens'.

Transport

7.7 The Internet can be used to get certain products **directly** into people's homes. Anything that can be converted into **digital form** can simply be uploaded onto the seller's site and then downloaded onto the customer's PC. The Internet offers huge opportunities to producers of text, graphics/video, and sound-based products. Much computer software is now distributed in this way.

Marketing at Work

The online grocery war continues. Tesco.com's pick-from-store business model took an early lead and is already profitable. Its pick-from-warehouse rivals lag way behind. Competitor Sainsbury's to You, whose costs for last year increased by a quarter to £50 million, does not foresee a profit for at least a year.

Despite this, Waitrose, John Lewis and European investment bank UBS have invested more than £60m into Ocado, a pick-from-warehouse online grocer that is opening a 111,484 square metre warehouse in Hatfield, north of London.

Picking in-store is fine in the short term, but warehouse fulfilment makes sense as online grocery orders increase, because warehouse space is cheaper than retail space, and offers more reliability and efficiency.

Successful online ventures require a lot of scaleable storage space, but walk-in supermarkets are geared to keeping smaller stocks of a wide variety of items. The warehouse fulfilment model will get more cost-effective as order volumes grow, but the pick-from-store model will not.

One of the main gripes of online shoppers is substitution. If an item in their order is not available, something similar (which they may or may not like) is put in to replace it. An online venture needs enough stock to keep substitutions to a minimum, and warehouse fulfilment can do this more reliably because the website is kept updated about exactly what it has to offer.

Picking in-store is not ideal for online selling because it is unpredictable. Operators can't promise to deliver a certain item because an in-store shopper may have just taken the last one.

Picking items for online order delivery is more efficient in warehouses, which are designed purely for picking speed, and not for luring customers or helping them navigate a store. And warehouse pickers aren't hampered by store customers, who could slow down in-store pickers.

These advantages for warehouse fulfilment increase as order volumes grow.

The cost of retail space in city centres is high, so expanding home-delivery capacity using picking in-store will be much more expensive than using out-of-town warehouses. Similarly, efficiency will increase greatly in pick-from-warehouse systems specially designed for high throughput, as opposed to stores that have been adapted for home delivery.

But capital cost and distance can hamper warehouse fulfilment. It is much cheaper to base online operations on existing infrastructure, such as premises and stock. This has given Tesco a head start, allowing it to bolt on an Internet arm at a much lower capital cost than the dedicated new facilities of rivals.

Revolution, 31 July 2002

Disintermediation

Key Concept

Disintermediation: the term referring to the process of 'removing the middleman', giving the consumer direct access to information that would otherwise require an intermediary, such as a salesperson or a retail channel.

7.8 The new technology of the **Internet** and **e-commerce** gives consumers the power to find product information directly, either removing the need for the salesperson altogether, or at least changing the relationship between buyer and seller.

Marketing at Work

(a)   **Online travel** sites are a manifestation of disintermediation. Internet-based search agents can now locate flights and fares and book them online. The Internet service may even generate the tickets themselves. Many customers 'surf' these sites without actually making a booking. (Nevertheless, airlines have been moved to lower the fees that they pay to travel agencies, in part because customers can now make purchases without using local agents.) Travellers often do their price research online and then call an agent to make their purchase.

(b)   In an article in *The Financial Times* (Value Chain: Exposed links in the established chain', 14 October 1998), Peter Martin discusses the specific case of **electricity supply**. Until recently, electricity was generated, transmitted and distributed by vertically integrated monopolies. Changes in regulation have meant that these monopolies are now split into separate generation, transmission and distribution companies. The next change - which, significantly, could not have occurred without the possibilities implied through electronic commerce - is the further split between distribution and supply. This means that one company may own the cables over which electricity travels, whilst another supplies the electricity to customers, having bought it in the first place from the generators.

As Martin points out, in this sort of operation, 'the **traditional strengths** of an electricity utility - reliability, technological depth, physical presence - may be **less important than skill in managing customer relationships and spot-marketing trading**.'

(c)   The electricity market is only one example of a development which is **crucially dependent on the presence of highly sophisticated electronic communication and data-management systems**, but what it also shows is the degree to which traditional value chains are being modified or even turned upside down. What could happen, in the final analysis, is that the competitive advantage will ultimately migrate to companies that have particularly strong customer relationships. Already, trusted retailers like Tesco, Marks & Spencer and Sainsbury in the UK are extending their brands into other industries, like energy supply or financial services.

BPP
PROFESSIONAL EDUCATION

The impact of the Internet on channel decisions

7.9 Strategic ('board level')

Improve corporate image
Increase visibility in the market
Create market growth opportunities
Lower costs
Appeal to customers
Access to the full competitive arena

7.10 Operational ('day-to-day' on the factory floor)

Speed of transactions increased
Management of information improved
Increased service levels
Removal of time and distance constraints
Complete transactions electronically
Opportunity for new revenues
Cost effectiveness
Closer relationships with business partners
Improved understanding of customer requirements

Exam Tip

Some of the most important topic areas from this chapter include:

- Identification of different channels of distribution
- Logistical issues
- Exclusive, intensive and selective distribution policies
- Criteria for channel selection
- The increase in direct marketing channels and technology
- The impact of the Internet on channel relationships

Chapter Roundup

- Distribution has two aspects – **tangible** (physical delivery) and **intangible** (control and management).

- Distribution channels provide **transport, stockholding** and **storage, local knowledge, promotion** and **display**.

- **Direct distribution** occurs when the product goes direct from producer to consumer. **Indirect distribution** happens via an intermediary.

- Companies may distribute direct to customers (by post; door-to-door etc.) or choose from a wide range of **intermediaries**: retailers, wholesalers, dealers, agents, franchisees and multiple stores are the main examples.

- When **deciding on a distribution channel** many factors come into play. How much support should be given to dealers? How far should marketing efforts be integrated up to the point of sale? What are the characteristics of the product or service? What do competitors do?

- In marketing channels, organisations have to manage the trade-off between the desire to remain **independent and autonomous**, and the need to be **interdependent and co-operative**.

- **Stakeholders** are groups or individuals having a legitimate interest in the activities of an organisation, generally comprising customers, employees, the community, shareholders, suppliers and lenders.

- Within the marketing channel, there are two primary stakeholder roles: **primary** and **support**.

- Different distribution strategies may be adopted for **consumer** and **industrial markets**. Industrial channels tend to be more direct and shorter.

- Different types of market exposure:

  - **Intensive** - blanket coverage
  - **Exclusive** - appointed agents for exclusive areas
  - **Selective** - some but not all in each area

- Ever-increasing customer demands, together with developments in technology have made **supply chain management** ever-more important. This looks at the whole picture, including the problems of ensuring smooth inflow of raw materials from suppliers so that end products can be available when customers want them.

- **Conflicts** can arise in marketing channels, and the key to managing them is to have good communications.

- **Technology** has brought new methods of displaying wares, new methods of paying for them, and for some goods, new methods of delivering them. The Internet and digital TV will become ever more important as distribution channels.

- The Internet has **strategic** and **operational** implications, and has contributed towards **disintermediation** in some markets.

Now try Question 9 in the Question Bank

Quick Quiz

1 Business-to-business relationships include (1).......... relationships and (2).......... networks.

2 What are the two aspects of distribution?

3 An intermediary is:

A Someone who 'mediates' or brings about a settlement between two persons
B The buyer in the distribution chain
C The supplier in the distribution chain
D None of the above

4 Why is a distributor's knowledge of customers important?

5 Fill in the gaps using the words from the grid below:

Direct distribution means the product going directly from producer to consumer without the use of a specific (1)............ Direct distribution methods generally fall into two categories: those using (2).......... such as the press, leaflets and telephones to invite (3).......... by the consumer, and those using a (4).......... to contact consumers face to face.

Sales force	Testing	Media
Interview	Intermediary	Response

6 Supply chain management is about

A Getting the goods to the customer in the shortest possible time
B Each channel member operating in isolation, so maintaining a greater degree of control
C Each channel member affecting the performance of others in the channel
D Optimising the activities of companies working together to produce goods and services

7 What are the two primary stakeholder roles in the marketing channel?

8 Why might there be conflict in the marketing channel?

9 What is 'removing the middle man' also known as?

10 A definition of 'trust' says that it is the degree to which (1)..........are confident that each will act in the (2).......... of the relationship.

Action Programme Review

1 Your answers might include some of the following points.

(a) The middleman's margin reduces the revenue available to the producer.

(b) The producer needs an infrastructure for looking after the retailers - keeping them informed, keeping them well stocked - which might not be necessary in, say, a mail order business.

(c) The producer loses some control over the marketing of the product. The power of some retailers (for example, W H Smith in the world of book publishing) is so great that they are able to dictate marketing policy to their suppliers.

2 Your own research

3   Some suggestions:

■ In terms of cost
■ In terms of sales levels
■ According to the degree of control achieved
■ By the amount of conflict that arises

4   Prices are up to 50% below conventional retail outlets and shoppers can choose from a wide range of branded goods, that they otherwise might not be able to afford. They can also turn a shopping trip into a day out, as factory outlet centres are designed as 'destination' shopping venues, offering facilities such as playgrounds and restaurants.

Manufacturers enjoy the ability to sell surplus stock at a profit in a controlled way that does not damage the brand image. They have also turned the shops into a powerful marketing tool for test-marketing products before their high street launch, and selling avant-garde designs that have not caught on in the main retail market.

Answers to Quick Quiz

1   (1) Marketing channel (2) Supply chain

2   Tangible – the physical movement and delivery of goods

Intangible – aspects of supply chain management, control and communication

3   A

4   Distributors are in the front line of contact with consumers. They are likely to have a strong sense of what will work in terms of product and promotion.

5   (1) Intermediary; (2) Media; (3) Response; (4) Sales force

6   D

7   Performance – directly involved with adding value in the marketing channel (manufacturer, wholesaler, retailer).

Support – banks, consultancies, government and so on, supporting the 'performing' members.

8   Failure to do the job as understood by the rest of the channel

■ Disagreement over a policy issue, such as territory or margin
■ Differing perceptions on how to get the job done
■ Inadequate communications

9   Disintermediation

10   (1) Partners (2) Best interests

The use of technology

10

Learning Outcomes

☑ Devise a basic media plan based on specific campaign requirements using both offline and online media

☑ Develop marketing communication and brand support activities based on an understanding of the salient characteristics of the target audience

☑ Explain the main elements, activities and linkages associated with the formulation and implementation of a marketing communications plan

☑ Suggest suitable methods to influence the relationships an organisation has with its customers, any marketing channel partners and other stakeholders, using marketing communications

Syllabus Reference

☑ Explain how Internet- and digital-based technologies can be used to enhance marketing communication and relationships within channels and between business-to-business partners

1 Setting the scene

1.1 The collapse in the share prices of many 'dot-com' enterprises has led some to question the expected impact of the Internet, but, in business-to-business markets especially, the Internet is radically affecting business life. According to Pelsmacker *et al* (*Marketing Communications*, 2001) the following communications objectives can be pursued on the Internet.

■ Creating **attitudes** and building brand/product **awareness**
■ Delivering detailed **information**
■ Stimulation of **customer response**, from information request to final purchase
■ Facilitation of **transactions**
■ **Retention** of customers

Exam Tip

The examiner will be very interested in the Internet when setting exams. Possible areas could include:

General impact of e-commerce

Does e-commerce turn products into mere commodities? (ie undoing all the carefully designed strategies to target, segment and position?)

Does the Internet destroy customer loyalty?

Comparing e-commerce opportunities across different businesses

This topic, therefore, could well arise in almost every exam.

1.2 At the time of writing, the uses of the Internet already embrace the following:

■ **Dissemination of information** - generally free of charge

■ **Product/service development** - through almost instantaneous test marketing

■ **Transaction processing** - both business-to-business and business-to-consumer

■ **Relationship enhancement** - between various groups of stakeholders, but principally (for our purposes) between consumers and product/service suppliers

■ **Recruitment** and job search - involving organisations worldwide

■ **Entertainment** - including music, humour, art and games

1.3 There is agreement on at least one thing, namely, that the Internet is **the greatest force for commoditisation the world has ever seen**. This is because it enables goods (and some services) to be sourced worldwide, easily and cheaply; it also enables them to be promoted worldwide, at relatively low cost. The Internet therefore drives prices downwards, with implications for marketing, margins, infrastructure costs, and customer dynamics.

Marketing at Work

Merlin Stone of IBM, in an article entitled *Marketing Management – has it changed that much?* asks how information technology has affected the marketer. He believes that it has affected the entire cycle:

- Objective setting
- Environmental analysis
- Strategy definition
- Planning
- Implementation
- Measurement
- Control
- Feedback

He identifies what he sees as key features of the marketing environment in the technological age.

(a) Other functions in the organisation such as **logistics** and **human resources** have changed to meet growing **customer expectations** of service, as technology shortens elements of the cycle such as delivery times. Such functions continue to support the marketer's role, but are growing in importance as companies realise that recruiting good staff, for example, is key to maintaining **quality**. The increased focus on corporate **governance** and **business ethics** is also relevant here.

(b) Innovations do not last - the design to delivery cycle is now shorter, as mentioned above. Companies are increasingly willing to **outsource** some of their functions, including IT departments. With outsourcing, **information flows** are quicker, so new **marketing** initiatives can be deployed almost instantly rather than having to wait for an in-house IT department to put new systems in place.

(c) **Interactive** and **direct marketing** is now far more common. Customer loyalty schemes provide an example. These are not universal, however – the low cost airlines, for example, have dispensed with relationship marketing in favour of concentrating on what improves their yield.

(d) All the aspects of dealing with the customer (from initial order to post-sales service and follow-up) have become integrated into **CRM schemes** aided by powerful **databases**, rather than being regarded as a set of distinct functional activities.

(e) The customer relationship cycle of **recruit / retain / develop** is much less firm now. Customers can switch between different companies very easily and are much more able to **compare offers**. Just by looking at Internet, they can become their own 'expert' on a range of matters from medical queries to cheap flights to better deals on international phone calls. They can even customise the exact product that they want – luxury cars being an often-quoted example.

(f) The new technology has made massive **data sets** available, although companies **often** struggle with how best to analyse and manage the mountains of customer data that often threatens to overwhelm rather than inform.

(g) Customers are able to influence each other very readily, through **e-mail** and **websites**.

(h) New communication channels such as **texting** via mobile phones, especially amongst younger consumers, have opened up new avenues for marketing communicators. Younger customers have their own access to marketing information and are choosing for themselves rather than leaving it to their parents.

(i) Thanks to the ease of access to information, the **decision cycle** for customers (both consumers and organisations) has become much quicker. Offers can be compared on the Internet on a Saturday morning and the purchase made in the afternoon, rather than spending several weekends searching the shops.

(j) **Feedback** arrives much more quickly for the same reason – companies may find themselves having to change their policies much more rapidly. The **cost effectiveness** of marketing initiatives is becoming more important, and the knowledge of costs is more complete.

(k) It is true that new sets of strategies are possible, focusing on **individual customers**. However, it is also true that it is **quality implementation** of those strategies that differentiates, because plans have become far more detailed and focused and need close control.

'Companies that are delivering what they planned are doing it because their planning is now classic marketing planning modified by the detailed, shorter time cycles (from conception to delivery and measurement) of direct marketing, further modified by the extremely short time-cycles and the experimental mindset of e-business.'

Adapted from *What's New in Marketing*, 2003

1.4 We have looked at the Internet and digital technologies in Chapters 4 and 6 in the contexts of their specific use in advertising and promoting. This chapter looks more at how the Internet is being used to **enhance communications and relationships**.

2 What is different about the Internet?

2.1 There are several features of the Internet which make it radically different from what has gone before.

(a) It **challenges traditional business models** - because, for example, it enables product/service suppliers to interact directly with their customers, instead of using intermediaries (like retail shops, travel agents, insurance brokers, and conventional banks).

(b) Although the Internet is global in its operation, its benefits are not confined to large (or global) organisations. **Small companies** can move instantly into a global marketplace.

(c) It offers a **new economics of information** - because, with the Internet, most information is free. Those with Internet access can view all the world's major newspapers and periodicals without charge.

(d) It supplies an almost incredible **level of velocity** - virtually instant access to organisations, plus the capacity (at least theoretically) to complete purchasing transactions within seconds. This is only truly impressive if it is accompanied by equal speed so far as the delivery of tangible goods is concerned.

(e) It has created **new networks of communication** - between organisations and their customers (either individually or collectively), between customers themselves (through mutual support groups), and between organisations and their suppliers.

(f)   It has led to **affiliate programmes** - involving the creation of 'portals' through which small enterprises can gain access to customers on a scale which would have been viewed as impossible a few years ago.

(g)   It **promotes transparent pricing** - because potential customers can readily compare prices not only from suppliers within any given country, but also from suppliers across the world.

Marketing at Work

Many organisations and businesses have flourished in the past precisely because their pricing has been opaque and they have deployed what has become known as 'confusion marketing', preventing consumers effectively from understanding precisely what they are getting for their money or, indeed, precisely how much money they are committed to pay in the first place. The Internet vastly reduces the potential for 'confusion marketing': once prices are transparent, buyers have power. They can compare one supplier with another; they can investigate alternative product/service options (so that, in effect, the order form becomes a 'what if' spreadsheet); average prices go down.

Both IBM and Oracle have put their product catalogues on to the web, thus (if nothing else) creating some uncertainty among their sales forces – 30,000 and 10,000 strong, respectively. The President of Oracle has said, 'We're betting that the increase in volume will more than compensate for the fall in prices', but this prediction is by no means guaranteed. There are some vague noises about the possibility that sales people may become 'consultants' and begin to charge for their customer visits, but this appears to reflect some wishful thinking rather than a genuine grip on the competitive realities.

(h)   It facilitates opportunities for very **high levels of (apparent) customer intimacy** between service suppliers and their clients because each client can believe that he or she is receiving personalised attention - even if such attention is actually administered through impersonal, yet highly sophisticated IT systems and customer database manipulation.

(i)   With **e-commerce**, customer intimacy can be secured without significant cost penalties.

(j)   It makes possible **sophisticated market segmentation opportunities**. Visualising and approaching such segments may be one of the few ways in which e-commerce entrepreneurs can truly create competitive advantage. As *Management Today* (March 2000) puts it:

> 'The starting point must be a neat niche, a funky few, a global tribe. You need to understand your particular tribe better than anyone else. You must know what makes them tick, what scares them, what gets them out of bed in the morning, what turns them on. The tribe is the basic unit of business... The good news is that there are lot of tribes out there - and some are enormous. It's just a question of identifying them, understanding them and meeting their needs better than anyone else.'

(k)   The web can either be a **separate** or a **complementary** channel. Although much prominence is being given to web-only businesses, in many cases organisations can use the web merely as an additional channel.

(l)   A new phenomenon is emerging in the form of **dynamic pricing**, whereby companies can rapidly change their prices to reflect the current state of demand and supply.

Marketing at Work

Amazon.com, one of the most celebrated website enterprises, aims to become the Internet's first one-step store, and has already diversified from its original bookshop business into such fields as electronic consumer products, mobile telephones, cars, leisure, gardening equipment, holidays, travel and toys. Its diversification programme has undoubtedly given it substantial breadth, helping to reduce the likelihood that its customers will feel the necessity to go elsewhere for some of their needs.

On the other hand, there are considerable cost burdens involved, not least in delivery. If customers order a variety of product items, it is likely that they will be delivered separately, from separate locations, with shipping expenses that vastly exceed the cost when goods are sent all at once. It is also relevant to note that, in Amazon's experience, it takes an average of 3.67 attempts before customer orders can be successfully delivered, because customers are themselves out during conventional delivery hours, and so forth. The necessity for repeat visits is a further cost-creating scenario.

Note, too, that Amazon, unlike many other 'dot.com' enterprises, does not subcontract its delivery activities, but undertakes them all through its own employees. This is cited as one of the explanations for its exceptional performance record.

Among Amazon's major assets is a massive customer database (29 million people) and an almost unparalleled level of information and insight into customer preferences and behaviour patterns. Cross-selling opportunities are accordingly impressive, and the company has embarked upon a number of co-branding arrangements with complementary retailers.

2.2 Overall these new trends are creating **pressure** for companies. As Gary Hamel has said, 'The main threat facing companies is that prices will be driven down by consumers' ability to shop around using the Internet'. This phenomenon, dubbed 'frictionless capitalism' by Bill Gates, will make it harder for companies to make money using traditional business models.

Marketing at Work

If you need a bullet-point summary of the differences which the Internet and e-commerce bring to the world of business (and let's not forget, the public sector as well), then it would be useful to memorise the following.

1 **Customers**

- ■ Can buy from any company, anywhere
- ■ Can find best prices and act accordingly
- ■ Can shop when they want

2 **Companies**

- ■ Can compete globally
- ■ Can procure globally
- ■ Can enter new co-operative alliances
- ■ Can achieve immediate access to revenue from sales

3 **Challenges**

- ■ Doubts over the future for retailing

- The achievement of reputations for reliability
- Creation of confidence about security among consumers
- Development of appropriate, cost-effective infrastructures
- Problems with fulfilment (delivery)

Growth of the Internet

2.3 This will be fuelled by:

(a) Many households have **multiple Internet access points,** through both parents and children.

(b) Changes in the **telecoms market** are likely to mean that Internet connection time will become much cheaper, if not free.

(c) **Digital TV** will permit the Internet to be accessed without the necessity for purchase of a personal computer. This in turn will widen the market place for the Internet to encompass those in the lower socio-economic categories who are more likely to subscribe to cable or satellite TV companies.

(d) **Web-enabled mobile phones** are already on the market. The emergence of **WAP** (Wireless Application Protocol) is allowing the use of mobile phones for a wide range of interactions with the web.

(e) For many, the preferred Internet interface is not the PC but the **PDA** (Personal Digital Assistant). In the USA and more recently in the UK, there are already several wireless-based PDAs being used to link investors to stock market information.

2.4 A critical factor in the long-run expansion of the Internet is its **use today by children**, the adult consumers of tomorrow.

2.5 As access to the Internet accelerates, so does the **provision of websites**. In May 2000 there were 15.7 million domain names. Of course, many of these websites are not commercial, have no transaction facilities, and are not truly significant from any marketing viewpoint, yet nonetheless the scale of Internet activity continues to grow at a rate which most observers describe as impressive.

2.6 At the same time, the Internet is not expanding at the same rate in every area of business. In reality its growth is very context-dependent, with the significant influencing factors being as follows.

(a) **The degree to which the customer can be persuaded to believe that using the Internet will deliver some added-value** - in terms of quickness, simplicity, price, and so forth.

(b) **Whether there are 'costs' which the customer has to bear** - not exclusively 'costs' in the financial sense, but also such psychological 'costs' as the loneliness of single-person shopping.

(c) **The market segment to which the individual belongs** - since the Internet is largely the preserve of younger, more affluent, more technologically competent individuals with above-average amounts of disposable income.

(d)   **The frequency of supplier/customer contact required**.

(e)   **The availability of incentives which might stimulate Internet acceptance** - for example, interest rates on bank accounts which are higher than those available through conventional banks (Egg), the absence of any charges (Freeserve), the creation of penalties for over-the-counter transactions (Abbey National), and the expectations of important customers (IBM's relationships with its suppliers).

2.7   The major growth so far in the field of e-commerce has concentrated on the **business-to-business (B2B) sector**. Intel claims to be doing more than $1 billion of e-commerce per month. Here are some examples to show the growing significance of the Internet in many business-to-business sectors.

(a)   **Major companies** are setting themselves up as e-businesses. In November 1999, both Ford and General Motors announced that they were switching a major portion of their procurement and supply chain management to the web.

(b)   IBM now requires all its suppliers to **quote and invoice electronically** - no paper documentation is permitted.

(c)   Many firms are using the Internet to **exploit the transparency of supplier prices**, and to maximise their purchasing benefits from the availability of world-wide sourcing. Robert Bosch, the German kitchen appliance manufacturer, requires all its suppliers to have web-based catalogues and prices.

(d)   Companies are also **increasing their customer service** through the web. Dell, the computer company, has created extranets for its major business customers, enabling them to receive personalised customer support, their own price lists, and some free value-added services.

2.8   In its survey, 'Business and the Internet' (26 June 1999), *The Economist* concluded:

'The Internet is turning business upside down and inside out. It is fundamentally changing the way companies operate, whether in high-tech or metal-bashing. This goes far beyond buying and selling over the Internet, or e-commerce, and deep into the **processes and culture** of an enterprise.'

'Some companies are using the Internet to make direct **connections with their customers** for the first time. Others are using secure Internet connections to **intensify relations with trading partners**, and using the Internet's reach to request quotes or sell off perishable stocks of goods or services by auction.'

'The Internet is helping companies to **lower costs** dramatically across their supply and demand chains, take their **customer service** into a different league, enter **new markets**, create additional revenue streams and **redefine business relationships**.'

2.9   What constitutes effective and efficient **customer service on the web**? To answer this question we must first disentangle and deconstruct the various elements of customer service from the customer's standpoint. As Kano has demonstrated, effective customer service (in any arena of activity, whether Internet-based or not) comprises three levels of perception.

(a)   **The foundation of service: what the customer expects**. Customers now expect that at least minimal levels of functionality will be met by any product or service they purchase; they expect that goods ordered will be delivered within an acceptable time-frame; they expect opportunities for redress if post-purchase problems are experienced. Merely to remain in business, companies must meet these basic customer requirements.

(b) **Customer-centred service: what differentiates one organisation from another**. This is the point at which customers begin consciously to choose one product/service supplier rather than another, because of perceptions about trust, value and customer focus.

(c) **Value-added service: what excites the customer**. What Tom Peters calls the "Wow!" sensation happens when the customer receives a level of service which is well beyond the conventional: when response times are almost immediate, when the degree of personal attention if exceptional, when service is proactively connected to customer needs.

Action Programme 1

Select a sample of five websites of customer service organisations and grade them according to how you feel they satisfy these criteria.

3 Creating a strategy for e-commerce

3.1 What follows is a set of **guidelines** for organisations which are considering **the addition of an Internet capability** to their sales/marketing repertoire. At the outset, this capability may solely dispense information (operating like a product catalogue), but it may eventually become transactional (so that individuals can place orders) and/or interactive (dealing with queries, complaints and other kinds of customer communications).

Marketing at Work

An immediately cautionary note is needed here. The Institute of Customer Service study, *Trusting the Internet* (ICS, 2000), addressed some of the major difficulties in stimulating directors and senior executives to take the Internet seriously, especially in more traditional enterprises. One respondent had plaintively said, for example: 'How do I justify investment in e-commerce to a group of senior executives and directors who get their secretaries to print out and type in all their e-mails?'

3.2 The typical questions which have to be asked by entrepreneurs, executives and managers responsible for existing organisations are these:

(a) **How will the Internet impact my industry?** Will it operate only at the periphery, perhaps opening up new market opportunities (for ourselves and our competitors), but no more, or will it fundamentally change our activities?

(b) **Will the Internet imply significant changes to our current business model?** If at present we communicate to our customers through conventional retail outlets, will we be able to approach them directly via a transactional website, thus cutting our costs but imperilling the future for our retailing 'partners'?

(c) **Will the Internet create new channels of distribution, customer contact, supplier relationships, and customer feedback?** If this happens, will these new channels eventually replace the existing ones, or will they remain purely supplementary?

(d) **What new roles will develop?** Will we ourselves become more dependent on IT and our software suppliers?

(e) **What about pricing transparency and the open access to information by customers?** The availability of pricing information, in detail, will undoubtedly facilitate product/service price comparisons – is that a problem for us? How will we (or can we) manage the opportunity created to our customers to contact us 24 hours a day, seven days a week?

(f) **What new markets and customer segment opportunities are now presented to us?** If, at least in theory, we can now gain access to worldwide purchasers, does that make it worthwhile to generate further product/service variations to cater for segments which were hitherto too small to be worthwhile?

(g) **Who will (or could) attack us?** Looking at the situation in other sectors like financial services, competitors can emerge from anywhere: if they did, where would they come from and (more importantly) what might they do in order to take away our customers? How can we pre-empt their activities?

3.3 Most observers and experts agree that a successful strategy for e-commerce cannot simply be bolted on to existing processes, systems, delivery routes and business models. Instead, management groups have, in effect, to start again, by asking themselves such **fundamental questions** as:

- What do customers want to buy from us?
- What business should we be in?
- What kind of partners might we need?
- What categories of customer do we want to attract and retain?

Ten key steps to constructing an effective strategy for e-commerce

Step 1: Upgrade customer interaction

3.4 The first thing for the organisation to do is to **upgrade the interaction with its existing customers**.

(a) Create **automated responses** for the FAQs (Frequently Asked Questions) posed by customers, so that customers become conditioned to electronic communication. Automated responses, perhaps surprisingly in view of their impersonal nature, can help to improve customer confidence and trust.

(b) Set **fast response standards**, at least to match anything offered by the competition.

(c) Use **e-mail** in order to confirm actions, check understanding, and reassure the customer that their business is being taken forward.

(d) Establish **ease of navigation** around your website and enhance the site's 'stickiness' so that there is a measurably reduced likelihood that actual or potential customers will migrate elsewhere.

Marketing at Work

Blackstar, a Belfast-based retailer, specialises in pre-recorded videos and DVDs (**www.blackstar.co.uk**). When sent an email enquiring about product availability, prices and so forth, they normally respond within five minutes with an e-mail which reads as follows:

Thanks for e-mailing blackstar.co.uk.

There are currently 181 e-mails in the queue in front of yours, and our average response time at the minute is 13.2 hours, so hopefully we'll get back to you within that time (if not faster!).

If your request is particularly urgent you can always ring us free on 0800 0529050 (outside the UK you'll need to ring +44 1232 225555, but we're afraid you'll have to pay for that call yourself!) between 8am and 8pm weekdays (10am - 4pm weekends).

Don't forget that you can track your order status online at:

http://www.blackstar.co.uk/circle/order_status

Many other common questions are also answered in our help section - click on the big question mark in the header bar or go direct to http://blackstar.co.uk/help/

This shows many elements of very good customer service:

- Fast response
- Automatic response
- Customer communication - length of queue, time to wait before a response
- Choice of phone follow up
- Ability to check status
- Links to Frequently Asked Questions (FAQs)

Step 2: Understand customer segments

3.5 Secondly, the organisation preparing its e-commerce strategy should **understand its customer segments** and classify each segment against the likelihood that it will be receptive to an Internet business route.

(a) Some will be eager to transfer to the new technology, others will do so if persuaded (or incentivised), and residual groups will prefer to remain as they are.

(b) Once the degree of profitability-per-customer has been established, efforts should be made to **automate the provision of customer service** and **transaction capability** so far as low-value customers are concerned.

(c) By contrast, the organisation may establish **personalised service relationships** with key (ie high profit-generating) customers, with privileged access to named personnel.

Step 3: Understand service processes

3.6 Thirdly, the organisation must **understand its customer service processes** in order to disentangle those processes which can safely be put on to the web and those which have to be delivered in other ways.

(a)   Typically, organisations serving customers may find that there are between five and ten **generic transaction types** which describe their relationships with these customers (eg information query, complaint, and so forth).

(b)   This analysis is essential for addressing such questions as: Which of these processes is appropriate for low-touch automation? Which of these processes will work better, from the customer's standpoint, if put on the web?

(c)   **Transaction costs** also need to be investigated, again from the perspective of the organisation and its overheads, and also taking into account the transaction costs incurred by the customer. These may involve money, but customers are often more conscious about time and timeliness.

(d)   A **short simple transaction** is often better conducted over the telephone.

Step 4: Define the role

3.7   Fourth, the organisation needs to **define the role for live interaction with its customers**.

(a)   Live interaction may be very useful if there is scope for cross-selling and the conversion of enquiries into sales.

(b)   The availability of service supplied by **human intervention** can also be appropriate if the organisation needs to build trust (eg it is a new brand which must work hard to establish confidence) and secure diagnostic information from the customer before any product or service can be delivered.

(c)   E-mail may not be sufficient as a communications route, especially if it involves a delay before replies or acknowledgements are forthcoming.

(d)   Live interaction can be essential for customers who have a strong preference for human contact.

Marketing at Work

Proactive Behaviour Analysis

One of the problems of conventional **Customer Relationship Management** is that it has limited power to enable the customer's overall relationship with the product/service supplier to be evaluated quickly (whilst the customer is online or conversing over the telephone, for example), and so valuable cross-selling opportunities may be missed. By the time a sales idea is generated, the customer has disappeared, clicked on to another website, or has put down the telephone. The trick, if it can be accomplished, is to analyse customer behaviour in advance.

Using very complex algorithms, a software company called Data Distilleries (affiliated to Accenture, the consulting firm) can enable sales ideas to be flashed up on a customer/service person's computer screen within two seconds: in fact the analytical processing begins as soon as the customer's call is received and before the service person actually responds.

The system has been tested with a financial services and insurance company in the Netherlands, Spaarbeleg (part of the Aegon group). This company normally receive two million customer phone calls each year; before the new software was installed, it was making only one sale per 4000 calls, largely because many of the apparent cross-selling 'opportunities' were actually unrelated to the customer's needs at that precise moment. After the new software became operational, however, the company has achieved a track record of more than one sale for every two calls where a product/service offer was made (during some conversations, of course, no offers are made because it rapidly becomes apparent not only that such offers would be inappropriate but also that they could stimulate customer defection). Almost incidentally, too, Spaarbeleg is now capable of more effective direct mailings, targeted precisely to the customers who are likely to respond positively.

Step 5: Decide technology

3.8 **Making the key technology decisions**, the fifth step, involves some tough choices. Given the pace of change and innovation in this arena, it is difficult to know whether to initiate a pilot programme immediately, with the full IT and people investment scheduled for later, or whether to go for full integration at once. The risk with a pilot programme is that the organisation can be overtaken by pioneering competitors; the risk with full integration is that new systems can be inadequate or may even collapse completely, causing irretrievable havoc with customers.

Step 6: Deal with the tidal wave

3.9 There is much evidence that offering an Internet-based service can lead to a major **increase in customer interaction**. This might involve:

- Ensuring **sufficient capacity** is available for worst-case scenarios.
- Using **low-touch technologies** and system design.
- Setting targets for **low-touch interaction**.
- Ensuring facilities are **scaleable** if demand rapidly outstrips supply.

Step 7: Create incentives

3.10 Seventh, especially if confronted by customer resistance, the organisation may have to **create incentives for use of the lowest-cost channels**, with savings passed on the customer through discounts, higher interest rates (in the case of bank accounts) or lower interest rates (in the case of credit cards). In the UK, banks have faced this by getting people to use automatic teller machines, utilities have encouraged customers to use direct debits. In essence, the alternatives are:

(a)   To **create incentives to switch** to the lowest-cost channels, through financial inducements, training, additional benefits, and so forth.

(b)   To **introduce disincentives for continuing to use existing channels**. Thus Abbey National has implemented a £5 charge for customers who pursue over-the-counter cash transactions in their branches. Such tactics almost invariably generate very hostile reactions from customers themselves and from consumer groups.

Step 8: Decide on channel choices

3.11 The eighth consideration involves the decision about **which channel choices to offer**, and whether, for instance, to confine operations to the 'click' route or whether to simultaneously maintain the 'brick' presence through a branch network. There are two crucial questions:

(a) **Whether to offer the customer a choice of channels**, eg face-to-face, post, phone and Internet. Many banks offer all four; some have single-channel accounts (phone or Internet only), whilst others (like egg) allow constrained choice: egg (the Internet and telephone banking arm of the Prudential Assurance Company) will allow telephone and Internet customer interaction, but only permits new customers to enrol via the web.

(b) **How to balance the costs of different channels whilst managing the Customer Relationship Management (CRM) database**. In most customer service environments, the quality and scope of the CRM database is central to the successful delivery of service, so it becomes desirable not to operate each customer/communication channel separately, but to integrate existing channels around a single CRM database.

Step 9: Exploit the Internet

3.12 The organisation should exploit the Internet in order to **create new relationships** and an experience.

(a) It is desirable to create **tailor-made service sites** for significant customers.

(b) **Proactive** product/service offerings should be regularly incorporated into the website architecture.

(c) **Communities** of users and/or customers (depending on whichever is appropriate) should be facilitated, since these generate additional business through referral and may well undertake a large proportion of the customer-service activity among themselves. Such communities may also stimulate product/service innovation, new uses for existing products and services, and product/service extensions.

(d) Deliberate mechanisms need to be developed in order **to turn browsers into buyers**, and transform one-off customers into repeat purchasers.

(e) Any successful e-commerce strategy presupposes the likelihood that the product/service supplier can engage the potential customer **emotionally** despite the technology which surrounds Internet availability.

Step 10: Implement

3.13 The concluding and tenth issue concerns the need to **implement the strategy**. No strategy is worth the paper is written on if it simply remains a document, gathering dust: as Peter Drucker once pointed out, 'Strategy is nothing until it degenerates into work.'

Action Programme 2

Does your employer have a strategy for e-commerce? If so, how do you rate it?

4   Customer dynamics and the Internet

A study by Jones Lang LaSalle (reported in the *Financial Times*, 30 November 2000) points out that the gap between trying out the Internet and using it for shopping is now a mere four months. This has to be coupled with the fact that, at the time of the survey, some 147.8 million people were online in the USA, plus a further 92 million in Europe.

4.1   It was once believed that potential customers for Internet businesses were relatively relaxed in their expectations about service, but even if this were the case in the first few years of Internet action, it is far from being the reality today. Internet customers are **just as demanding as customers everywhere**.

4.2   Effective, competent and acceptable customer service through the Internet is a combination of the following factors.

Factor	Comment
Rapid response time	If the website is not fast, the transient potential shopper will simply click on to another. These 'fickle' visitors to a website will only allow around five to eight seconds: if the site has not captured their attention in that time-frame, they will move elsewhere.
Response quality	The website must be legible, with appropriate graphics and meaningful, relevant information supplied. Generally speaking, website visitors are not interested in the company's history and size: they are much more concerned about what the company can offer them.
Navigability	It is important to create a website which caters for every conceivable customer interest and question. Headings and category-titles should be straightforward and meaningful, not obscure and ambiguous.
Download times	Again, these need to be rapid, given that many Internet shoppers regard themselves (rightly or otherwise) as cash-rich and time-poor.
Security/Trust	One of the biggest barriers to the willingness of potential Internet customers actually to finalise a transaction is their fear that information they provide about themselves (such as credit card details) can be 'stolen' or used as the basis for fraud.

Factor	Comment
Fulfilment	Customers must believe that if they order goods and services, the items in question will arrive, and will do so within acceptable time limits (which will generally be much faster than the time limits normally associated with conventional mail order). Equally, customers need to be convinced that if there is a subsequent need for service recovery, then speedy and efficient responses can be secured either to rectify the matter or to enable unsatisfactory goods to be returned without penalty.
Up-to-date	Just as window displays need to be constantly refreshed, so do websites require frequent repackaging and redesign.
Availability	Can the user reach the site 24 hours a day, seven days a week? Is the down-time minimal? Can the site always be accessed?
Site effectiveness and functionality	Is the website intuitive and easy to use? Is the content written in a language which will be meaningful even to the first-time browser (ie the potential customer)?

Marketing at Work

When asked, 'What is the core competency for Dell Computers?', Michael Dell replied with a single word: **Relationships**.

4.3 We have already seen that Internet customers display little loyalty. Many organisations are busily engaged in mechanisms which will promote **emotional connectivity** (and thus, it is believed, customer retention for reasons which go beyond the purely mechanistic and instrumental arguments of price). Some of these mechanisms involve 'real' people, whilst others call for simulations and 'virtual' people.

Marketing at Work

lastminute.com

1 The importance of correctly defining such terms as 'customer', 'user', 'payer' and 'subscriber' is impressively highlighted in the case of lastminute.com. This is a company whose website enables people to purchase gifts, make various forms of booking (for theatres, holidays and so forth), and generally to organise properly for the celebration of anniversaries, birthdays, Christmas, and the like, if they cannot do so under their own volition. There can be no doubt about the attractiveness of a service such as that which lastminute.com supplies, particularly in a world where people are naturally forgetful or lack the necessary time to engage in gift-buying themselves.

Lastminute.com will not only help in the identification of suitable and imaginative gifts, but it will remind the customer of what was purchased last time (once a track record has been established) in order to avoid embarrassing repetition or, indeed, the transmission of presents which are inappropriate. In March 2000 the financial columnists were claiming that lastminute.com was worth at least £400 million.

2   Lastminute.com claims to have 800,000 'subscribers' who are also its 'customers'. It is wrong on both counts. The 'customers' for lastminute.com are the businesses which pay for the sales and bookings which it brings them - and, as always, it is customer satisfaction which will determine the company's viability. As for the people which lastminute.com calls 'subscribers', they are nothing of the kind. Subscribers make regular payments and are thus a source of revenue; but those who log on to lastminute.com's website are more properly defined as '**users**', with none of the loyalty of real subscribers: they can move on at a click.

3   The 'customer offering' from lastminute.com is that it will sell unused capacity for a commission. Obviously, unsold 'perishables', like seats on aircraft and hotel bedrooms, suddenly become worthless, but successful businesses will try to get rid of them before this happens, even if the price is well below that customarily charged. One immediate issue for some of lastminute.com's 'customers' (ie the businesses whose spare capacity is offered through the lastminute.com route) is that they cannot know in advance who lastminute.com's 'users' (subscribers) are. This may not be a problem for, say, an airline, but it could become one for a restaurant which may find itself taking late reservations from people who could be quite inappropriate to the restaurant's image and market position, thereby jeopardising the restaurant's reputation with its current clientele.

4   Within a short while, it should become possible for many of lastminute.com's 'customers' to bypass lastminute.com altogether, in order to avoid payment of unnecessary commission fees. Equally, the company's 'users' are notoriously fickle and will have no enduring value to lastminute.com unless they buy frequently - which is itself improbable.

5   A key point concerning the future of lastminute.com (and many other Internet businesses) is that the very simplicity of the concept allows others to copy it. In the words of the UK Foresight Programme (www.foresight.gov.uk): 'the rapid development of electronic commerce (means that) you can now sell just about everything to anyone, anywhere - 24 hours a day. **So can everybody else**...' Organisations enjoying closer relationships with their customers - banks, holiday tour operators, airlines or supermarkets, for instance - could find it easy to launch 'lookalikes', especially if they find they are doing significant business via lastminute.com.

6   So, in summary, these are the factors which have to be in place in order to guarantee any long-term viability for lastminute.com and many other Internet businesses:

   ■   Extremely efficient systems to link with customers, to track that deals are consummated and payment received.

   ■   A 'customer' base which is sufficiently large, fresh and fashionable to interest and keep 'users'. (Don't forget that for lastminute.com, 'customers' are the businesses which supply lastminute.com with spare capacity, and 'users' are those who purchase the spare capacity.) Some 'customers' may be deterred from appearing on the lastminute.com website because of their fear that such listings are a tacit admission of failure.

   ■   The capacity of 'customers' to provide enough last minute bookings to meet demand. If they don't, then 'users' will migrate elsewhere.

   ■   Highly sophisticated IT systems in order to support lastminute.com's infrastructure.

So in conclusion, this is the situation faced by lastminute.com.

■ From a share 'value' of £830 million in March 2000, the company's worth had fallen to less than £90 million in April 2001. Admittedly, some of this decline was attributable to general disillusionment in world stock markets with 'dot.com' enterprises, following some spectacular collapses, the end of a 'honeymoon' period for this sector, and recognition that successful Internet companies must still adhere to the same basic business disciplines as companies elsewhere.

■ Lastminute.com has no proprietorial technology - and so its activities can be readily imitated.

■ There are no barriers to entry for would-be competitors (though Lastminute.com has been quite successful in establishing its name as a brand identity: any new entrants would have to undertake similarly vigorous marketing in order to establish themselves).

■ Lastminute.com's users are promiscuous - there is little - if any - loyalty among them.

■ Lastminute.com's *customers* (ie, its advertisers) are equally promiscuous - they will use Lastminute.com if they have to (ie if they have spare capacity), but it is a distress purchase rather than one undertaken enthusiastically.

■ The company's margins are no thicker than the shavings from commissions earned from its customers.

5 Digital TV

5.1 In the past, television was 'analogue'. The development of digital technologies can be applied to television. Digital TV takes a number of forms.

■ Digital terrestrial television delivered via the old 'analogue' arial

■ Digital satellite televisions, in which digital signals are sent via an existing satellite dish (eg Sky digital)

■ Digital cable television, in which digital TV is delivered via the cable network.

5.2 In outline, transmitting programmes by digital signal rather than by conventional means **dramatically increases the number of services which can be delivered to audiences**: as many as ten digital services will be able to occupy the frequency previously occupied by one conventional 'analogue' service. In addition, digital broadcasting allows viewers greater choice over how and when they watch, eventually allowing them to interact with programmes and select their own programme content. More immediately, the new technology offers many viewers the prospect of improved reception.

5.3 The impact was described in depth in a BBC document, *Extending Choice in the Digital Age*, from which much of the following is derived.

5.4 **Digital technology removes the constraints** imposed by conflicting demands within the confines of a few television and radio networks. Viewers and listeners often miss programmes, and it is hard to schedule a range of programmes which suit everyone all the time. At present, programmes can only be scheduled in sequence, with the viewer having to make an appointment with the television to watch a specific programme at a set time. In the digital world, a spectrum can be used to allow networks to have many layers and branches: there is much more flexibility to match services to the viewer's personal timetable.

5.5 Using digital flexibility and extra capacity, broadcasters are able to offer additional programmes, information, sound and graphics, to complement what is being shown on the main channel, and to allow viewers to catch up on programmes they have missed. These extra services can be offered alongside (and do not interrupt) the continuing programme schedule. They are there for viewers to activate and explore as they choose.

5.6 At the touch of a button, viewers are able to get **supplementary information** on the programmes they are watching. The BBC, for instance, envisaged that viewers could have instant access to the following.

- The musical scores for Young Musician of the Year
- A 'guess the value' game to accompany The Antiques Roadshow
- A summary of the story so far for viewers late to join a film or play

5.7 Broadcasters are also able to make use of the improved sound quality available on digital television to offer alternative soundtracks, for example the original language version of foreign films.

5.8 A key feature of the technology is the way it allows users to respond to, or interact with, the material they are receiving. Interactive programmes that can be used on computers, or eventually on-demand from the television, will transform on-screen education.

Action Programme 3

If programmers can do this, then so too, of course can advertisers.

See how may applications you can think of for extra information at the touch of a button, alternative soundtracks and matter you can respond to if the viewer is watching advertisements.

6 Impact of interactive systems

6.1 The **ability to shop from home** and choose items directly with the use of scanners can be co-ordinated with direct advertising. **Infomercials** (which combine information with a commercial) which the consumer has chosen from a databank will be relayed directly to the home down cable links. These may take the form of recipes, DIY hints, car repairs and so on. Consumers will also be able to purchase the necessary ingredients or parts simultaneously, simply by pointing a mouse on a computer screen at the desired goods and clicking its buttons.

6.2 It is, however, difficult to predict how successful and how big the market for home shopping will become in the UK.

(a) **Geography**. In the UK and other European countries, distances to retail shopping centres are small. (On the other hand, traffic congestion continues to be an issue.)

(b)   However, people are often **'time poor'** and Internet shopping with convenient delivery times is becoming popular for some consumers, for example books, CDs and now groceries.

(c)   Success depends on consumers' acceptance of technology and the reliability of that technology. Technology that is hard to use or unreliable will discourage sales.

6.3 Advantages of interactive systems

- Saving time spent in shopping visits
- Saving use of cars and car parking
- Reduction in congestion and pollution
- Greater variety of products to choose from
- Ability to watch demonstrations from the comfort of one's home
- Ability to browse
- Ability to interrogate, get technical advice
- Getting bank balances immediately
- Transferring funds between accounts
- Paying bankers orders
- Access to directories of suppliers
- It may be possible to closely segment markets
- The specific needs of individual customers could be met
- The costs of stockholding could be reduced

Marketing at Work

'Woolwich customers can pay bills as they watch Sky'

The Woolwich is expanding its interactive offering on Sky Digital. Viewers will be able to access their Openplan accounts at any time of day or night to view their mortgage balance, pay bills and transfer money via Sky Active. They will be able to continue to watch their Sky programme on a quarter of the screen.

Woolwich and Sky Active are promoting the service by offering a free Sky Keypad if customers register. More than 6 million households in the UK now have Sky Digital, with more than 63% having pressed the red button to try out one of the services offered.

Brand Republic, Revolution UK online, March 25th 2003

6.4   Home shopping in America is a £1 billion business and is growing at the rate of 20% per annum. These shopping channels are increasingly being used by professionals without time to wander around department stores. The amount of broad band multimedia will accelerate the process, first, by increasing the number of channels available, and secondly, by increasing the interactivity. Instead of having to ring up to order, viewers will be able to punch in a code on their handset and pay by swiping their credit card through a slot in the set top box.

Action Programme 4

What might be some of the limitations of interactive systems? Why do you think such limitations exist?

There are limitations to such interactive systems, which may be related to the state of the technology or to ingrained social and cultural habits.

- There are inevitably high set up costs.
- There is a lack of knowledge of the system.
- Some people suffer from technophobia.
- There is a lack of personal contact.
- Expectations of quality may not be realised.
- It is necessary to touch, feel, smell or taste some products.
- Shopping for some people has social benefits.
- Existing shopping centres may be destabilised.

7 Measuring the effectiveness of online marketing

7.1 We first looked at this briefly in Chapter 6. Many e-commerce enterprises are equipped with little more than guesswork when designing their initiatives and assessing their commercial value. As the e-commerce environment matures, so the necessity for objective and dispassionate measurement of performance accelerates. Here are some of the key issues.

7.2 First, the success of a commercial website has to be evaluated against the overall product/service offer from the company.

(a) In the words of www.emystery.shopper.com 'An e-commerce site has to be a complete customer service fulfilment picture; it can't just be one bit working online that is not supported offline'.

(b) Thus website usability + e-mail + telephone contact + product fulfilment + customer interaction = the customer experience; it is not website usability on its own.

7.3 **Channel satisfaction** is typically scored through online focus groups or online questionnaires, or both.

(a) Online focus groups are cheap but hard to moderate dispassionately.

(b) Online questionnaires are also cheap, but present problems with sample bias, since those most likely to respond are either committed advocates or deeply-hostile aliens (ie customers and ex-customers who are too alienated to be objective or constructive).

(c) For samples of online questionnaires, see www.epson.lco.uk.

7.4 **Channel buyer behaviour** is measured by the extent to which the customer interacts with on-site marketing communications. Website registration usually provides information about the prospective purchaser's lifestyle and can therefore contribute to segmented behaviour profiles. Techniques for quantifying customer reactions include log file analysis (see www.webtrends.com) and key ratios (eg page impressions per website visit).

7.5 **Channel promotion**. Significant criteria in this arena include volume (number of 'hits' or views of the website's home page) and quality (the degree to which visitors are appropriate to the target market and whether they have a propensity to purchase the products or services being offered). Log files can produce basic data about 'hits' but no more, so there are important data gaps here.

7.6 **Channel outcomes**. The traditional marketing objectives apply: sales, leads, conversion rates, repeat purchases, and so forth. Problems can occur (so far as website effectiveness is concerned) if customers obtain product information from the Internet, and then make their purchases through conventional retailing outlets.

Marketing at Work

As an example of an attempt at least partially to overcome this, Dell records on-site sales plus telephone orders received after web visits (the website supplies a special telephone number not accessible elsewhere, thus enabling close correlations to be established).

7.7 **Channel profitability**. The key index here is achievement of a targeted proportion of sales via the Internet channel. In 1998, EasyJet (the low-cost airline based in the UK) set out to achieve a contribution target of 30% of ticket sales via the Internet by the year 2000 – and this was achieved within twelve months.

Chapter Roundup

- The **Internet** is a worldwide computer network. **Websites** are points which it uses for dissemination of information, product/service development, transaction processing and so on.

- The Internet challenges business as it **avoids intermediaries** - small companies can also benefit through 'affiliated programmes'. The Internet is widely used by children, tomorrow's consumers.

- The Internet reduces transactions costs and switches **power to sellers**.

- **Customer service** on the web includes website responsiveness, case of navigation, website effectiveness, fulfilment, trust, service level transparency, configuration and customisation, proactive service, and value added service.

- Creating a strategy for **e-commerce** requires ten steps.

    - Upgrade interaction with customers
    - Understand customer segments
    - Understand service processes
    - Define the role for live interaction
    - Decide the technology
    - Deal with the 'tidal wave' of new business
    - Create incentives to use the cheapest channel
    - Decide on channel options
    - Exploit the Internet
    - Implement the strategy

- Effective, competent and acceptable customer service through the Internet is a combination of several factors, but it boils down to having a **quick response** to all requests/orders, and **quality delivery**.

- **Digital broadcasting** allows viewers greater choice over how and when they watch, eventually allowing them to interact with programmes and select their own programme content.

- The ability to shop and perform other tasks (such as banking) from home and choose items directly with the use of scanners, can be co-ordinated with direct advertising in interactive systems.

- Key **measures of online advertising success** can be grouped under the following headings:

    - Channel satisfaction
    - Channel buyer behaviour
    - Channel promotion
    - Channel outcomes
    - Channel profitability

Now try Question 10 in the Question Bank

Quick Quiz

1   What are the communication objectives that can be fulfilled by the Internet?

C...

R...

A...

I..

T...

2   Which is the following is true of the Internet?

A   It is currently most significant in the business-to-consumer market

B   It can enhance communications and relationships

C   For an SME with limited resources, the Internet is not appropriate

D   Enhanced customer service via the Internet is unlikely to occur

3   What is the 'tidal wave' referred to in section 3 of this chapter?

4   Why should download times be as quick as possible?

A   All customers who use the Internet are inherently impatient

B   It saves money for the company

C   Customers in the modern age regard themselves as increasingly 'time-poor', and expect to be able to view website contents quickly

D   The quicker the download time, the clearer the pictures on the website

5   Fill in the gaps using the words in the grid below:

(1)   .... takes a number of forms.

■   Digital (2).......... television delivered via the old 'analogue' arial

■   Digital (3).......... television, in which digital signals are sent via an existing (4)...........

■   Digital (5)........... television, in which digital TV is delivered via the (6)...........

Cable network	Digital TV	Terrestrial
Satellite dish	Cable	Satellite

6   Digital television technology allows users to respond to, or interact with, the material they are receiving

True   ☐

False   ☐

7   Give some advantages of interactive systems.

8   From the following grid, how can buyer behaviour on the Internet be measured?

Examining the extent to which the customer interacts with online communications	Log file analysis and key ratios (such as page impressions per website visit)
Examining conversion rates and repeat purchases	The use of online focus groups and questionnaires

Action Programme Review

1   Do try to gain access to the Internet and complete this activity. Refer to the 'website links' section at the front of this Text if you require further ideas.

2   If your employer doesn't have a strategy for e-commerce (or at lest a website), they probably soon will have!

3   The following extract from an American article on Interactive TV (ITV) may give you some ideas.

'When it comes to peddling high-ticket items, Paula George Tompkins, CEO of The SoftAd Group, a Mill Valley (Calif.) creator of interactive marketing materials, says the most effective efforts aren't 'full-motion video and razzle-dazzle ads.' They're the information-laden programs that help buyers make complex decisions such as choosing a car or an industrial-products supplier.

Consider the flow chart for a typical car purchase: talk to friends, buy (and read) consumer reports, spend weekends checking out local dealerships and weekdays checking out other cars on the freeway, test drive a few cars, decide on a model, make arrangements with a lender, and - whew! - buy the car.

Now, eliminate a significant portion of that legwork. Using a mouse and TV screen, the consumer would be able to flip through manufacturers' catalogues - complete with backup data related to performance and pricing - 'trying on' the various models in terms of size and color. The shopper could then request a test drive via his or her TV. Later, the dealer brings a car over and, if the buyer is ready, goes online with a laptop to check inventory, leasing vs. financing options, and even fill out the paperwork. Voila!'

4   ■   There are high set up costs
     ■   There is a lack of knowledge of the system
     ■   Some people suffer from technophobia
     ■   There is a lack of personal contact
     ■   Expectations of quality may not be realised
     ■   It is necessary to touch, feel, smell or taste some products
     ■   Shopping for some people has social benefits

Such limitations may be related to the current state of the technology, and also to ingrained social and cultural habits.

Quick Quiz

1   Customer response stimulation
    Retention of customers
    Attitude and awareness building
    Information delivery
    Transactions facilitated

2   B

3   A dramatic increase in the level of customer interaction

4   C

5   (1) Digital TV; (2) Terrestrial; (3) Satellite; (4) Satellite dish; (5) Cable; (6) Cable network

6   True

7   Check your answer against the list in paragraph 6.3

8   All of these could be used!

Part D

Relationship management

Developing relationship marketing

11

Chapter Topic List	
1	Setting the scene
2	The nature of the customer
3	Internal marketing
4	Types of outside resources
5	Management of external suppliers

Learning Outcomes

☑ Explain the importance of developing long-term relationships with customers, channel members, agencies and other stakeholders and transfer such knowledge to the development of marketing communication activities

☑ Suggest suitable methods to influence the relationships an organisation has with its customers, any marketing channel partners and other stakeholders, using marketing communications

Syllabus References

☑ Compare the principles of transaction and relationship marketing

☑ Explain the characteristics of relationship marketing including the features, types, levels, development and implementation steps and communication issues

☑ Describe how marketing communications can be used to develop relationships with a range of stakeholders, based on an understanding of source credibility, trust and commitment

☑ Explain how marketing communications can be used to launch new products, support brands, maintain market share, develop retention levels, encourage customer loyalty, and support internal marketing within the organisation

BPP PROFESSIONAL EDUCATION

☑   Describe the main characteristics of key accounts and explain the stages and issues associated with key account management

☑   Describe how co-ordinated marketing communications can be used to develop key account relationships

Key Concept Introduced

■   Relationship marketing

1 Setting the scene

1.1 The syllabus emphasises the **wider relationships marketers must nurture** if they are to succeed. This chapter deals with the management of some of those relationships. Section 2 considers the nature of the customer, emphasises the advantages to be gained from customer retention and discusses the concept of relationship marketing. Section 3 deals with internal marketing, a phrase which has a range of meanings.

1.2 The remainder of the chapter is concerned with the organisation's **use of outside resources**. Section 4 illustrates the wide range available and Section 5 offers some ideas on their applicability, including the possibility of establishing a 'virtual company'. Where external services are used, it is important that control is not abdicated; the client organisation must ensure that the contractor performs properly. Section 6 is about the management of external suppliers.

2 The nature of the customer

2.1 As you must be aware from earlier in this text, customers make up one of the groups of **stakeholders** whose interests marketing management should address. **The stakeholder concept** suggests a **wider concern** than the traditional marketing approach of supplying **goods and services which satisfy immediate needs**.

2.2 The stakeholder approach demands that the supplier-customer relationship extends **beyond the basic transaction**. The customer needs to **remain** satisfied with his purchase and positive about his supplier, long after the transaction has taken place. If his satisfaction is muted or grudging, future purchases may be reluctant or non-existent and, most importantly, he may advise others of his discontent. We have already discussed the power of **word of mouth communication**.

Action Programme 1

'Not all customers are the same'.

Do you agree with this statement? How might they differ?

2.3 Customer variation will exist to a greater or lesser extent in all industries. However, even within a single business, customers will vary significantly in the following areas.

- The **frequency** and **volume** of their purchases
- Their **reasons** for buying
- Their **sensitivity to price** changes
- Their **reaction to promotion**
- Their **overall attitude** to the supplier and the product

2.4 Many businesses sell to intermediaries rather than to the end consumer. Some sell to both categories. You must recognise that **the intermediary is just as much a customer as the eventual consumer**.

Marketing at Work

An example can be found in manufacturers who maintain their own sales organisation but appoint agents in geographically remote areas, and companies who combine autonomous operations with franchising. While it is reasonable to give the highest priority to the needs of the ultimate consumer and insist on some control over the activities of the intermediary, it must be recognised that he will only perform well if his own needs are addressed. For instance, a selling agent who has invested heavily in stock after being given exclusive rights in an area should be consulted before further demands are made on his cash flow by the launch of a new product.

Customer retention

2.5 Variation in customer behaviour was mentioned above. The most important aspect of this variation is whether or not the customer comes back for more. Customers should be seen as potentially providing a lifetime of purchases so that **the turnover from a single individual over time might be very large indeed**.

2.6 It is widely accepted that there is a non-linear relationship between customer retention and profitability in that **a fairly small amount of repeat purchasing generates significant profit**. This is because it is far more expensive in promotion and overhead costs to convert a non-buyer into an occasional buyer than to turn an occasional buyer into a frequent buyer. The repeat buyer:

- does not have to be persuaded to give the product a try
- does not need to be tempted by special deals
- needs less attention from sales staff
- already has his credit account set up

2.7 Today's highly competitive business environment means that customers are only retained if they are **very satisfied** with their purchasing experience. **Any lesser degree of satisfaction is likely to result in the loss of the customer**. Companies must be active in monitoring customer satisfaction because very few will actually complain. They will simply depart. Businesses which use intermediaries must be particularly active, since research shows that even when complaints are made, the principals hear about only a very small proportion of them.

Marketing at Work

Customer care

In the increasingly competitive service sector, it is no longer enough to promise customer satisfaction. Today, customer 'delight' is the stated aim for companies battling to retain and increase market share.

British Airways, which lists delighting customers among its goals, says ensuring the safety of passengers and meeting all their needs drives everything it does. 'Other airlines fly the same routes using similar aircraft. What BA must do is provide a superior standard of efficiency, comfort and general service which persuades passengers to fly with us again and again.'

Kwik-Fit, the car repair group, is another company that has included customer delight in its mission statement. Its forecourt promises to deliver '100 per cent customer delight' in the supply and fitting of vehicle brakes, tyres and exhausts leaves little margin for mistakes - and none at all for making any customer unhappy. Staff attend courses at company-run centres covering 'all practical aspects of their work, customer care and general management techniques'. Commitment is encouraged by 'job security', opportunities for promotion and a reward package that includes profit-related pay and shares in the company.

Customer satisfaction is monitored via reply-paid questionnaires distributed after work is carried out and through a freephone helpline that is open 24 hours a day. Kwik-Fit also says its customer survey unit 'allows us to make contact with 5,000 customers a day, within 72 hours of their visit to a Kwik-Fit Centre.'

Financial Times

2.8 The most satisfactory way to retain customers is to offer them products which they perceive as providing superior benefits at any given price point. There are specific techniques to increase customer retention. **Loyalty schemes** such as frequent flyer programmes augment the product in the customer's eyes. The club concept, as used by Sainsbury and Tesco, offers small discounts on repeated purchases.

2.9 The principal benefit of both these types of scheme is the **enhanced knowledge of the customer** which they provide. Initial registration provides name, address and postcode. Subsequent use of the loyalty card allows a detailed **purchasing profile** to be built up for individual customers. This enables **highly targeted** promotion and cross-selling later.

2.10 Research indicates that **the single largest reason why customers abandon a supplier is poor performance by front-line staff**. Any scheme for customer retention must address the need for careful selection and training of these staff. It is also a vital factor in **relationship marketing**.

Marketing at Work

Complaints

Complaints are among the best things that can happen to a company. They give managers

- the chance to rectify the situation over and above customer expectations
- low cost feedback on how products and services are perceived

Handled properly, they create 'goodwill ambassadors' for your brand. TMI, along with the Institute of Customer Service, the trade body, recently published research into how and why people in the UK complain and how they are dealt with. Among other findings, it confirmed the old management cliché that people tend not to complain - they simply walk away. It is the expense of replacing customers that makes handling complaints well so cost-effective.

Julie Robinson, director of service delivery at Virgin Atlantic, the airline, said: 'As part of our staff training we need to show people that giving compensation when something goes wrong is not giving away the company's profits. Quite the opposite.' So what is the 'right' way to handle a complaint? Almost everyone agrees on step one: listen. 'You must listen to the customer,' says Ms Robinson, 'and not interrupt until you have under stood the problem.' But what then?

An eight-step process has been advocated. After saying 'thank you' comes:

- Explaining why you appreciate the complaint
- Apologising
- Promising you will do something about it straight away
- Asking for more information
- Correcting the mistake
- Checking customer satisfaction
- Finally, preventing future mistakes

Marks and Spencer, the retailer, a UK company that is almost synonymous with handling complaints effectively, also welcomes complaints. 'The information people give you when they complain is invaluable to the organisation. We run a central database where complaints are logged, from which we can feed information back to the relevant buyer and suppliers, often on the same day. Customers are looking for a quick resolution of the problem and an assurance that we will do what we can to ensure it doesn't happen again.'

Managers of big companies can also use complaints to develop one-to-one relationships with customers. 'Complaints offer an excellent chance to deal with customers face-to-face. If you take a complaint seriously, and deal with it in a generous way, you can buy them for life.'

David Baker, *Financial Times*

Relationship marketing

Relationship marketing is defined very simply as the management of a firm's market relationships.

2.11 Much has been written in recent years on **relationship marketing**. It can only really exist when the marketing function fosters a customer-oriented **service culture**, which supports the **network of activities** that deliver value to the customer. The metaphor of **marriage** has been used to describe relationship marketing, emphasising the nature of the necessary long-term commitment and mutual respect.

2.12 It must be remembered, however, that the effort involved in long-term relationship building is more appropriate in some markets than in others. Where customers are purchasing intermittently and **switching costs are low**, there is always a chance of business. This tends to be the pattern in commodity markets. Here, it is reasonable to take a **transaction approach** to marketing and treat each sale as unique.

2.13 A **relationship marketing approach** is more appropriate where **switching costs are high**, and a lost customer is thus probably lost for a long time. Switching costs are raised by such factors as the need for training on systems and high capital costs.

2.14 The conceptual or philosophic nature of relationship marketing leads to a simple principle, that of **enhancing satisfaction by precisely meeting the needs of individual customers**. This depends on extensive **two-way communication** to establish and record the customer's characteristics and to build a long-term relationship. Three important practical methods contribute to this end.

- Building a **customer database**
- Developing **customer-oriented** service systems
- Extra **direct contact** with customers

2.15 Modern **computer database systems** have enabled the rapid acquisition and retrieval of the individual customer's details, needs and preferences. Using this technology, relationship marketing enables telephone sales staff to greet the customer by name, know what he purchased last time, avoid taking his full delivery address, know what his credit status is and what he is likely to want. It enables new products to be developed that are precisely tailored to the customer's needs and new procedures to be established which enhance his satisfaction. It is the successor to **mass marketing**, which attempted to be customer-led but which could only supply a one-size-fits-all product.

2.16 Relationship marketing extends the principles of **customer care**. Customer care is about providing a product which is augmented by high quality of service, so that the customer is impressed during his transaction with the company. The customer is anonymous. **Relationship marketing is about having the customer come back for further transactions by ending the anonymity**. The culture must be right; the right people must be recruited and trained; the structure, technology and processes must all be right.

2.17 It is inevitable that **problems** will arise. A positive way of dealing with errors must be designed into the customer relationship. Front line sales people cannot usually deal with the causes of mistakes as they **are built into the products, systems and organisation structure**. It is therefore necessary for management to promote vertical and horizontal interaction in order to eliminate the **sources** of mistakes.

Marketing at Work

Customer Loyalty

The problem with profitable customers is retaining them, because they will attract the attention of your competitors. Building customer relationships may be the answer to both types of problem.

Relationship marketing is grounded in the idea of establishing a learning relationship with customers. At the lower end, building a relationship can create cross-selling opportunities that may make the overall relationship profitable. For example, some retail banks have tried selling credit cards to less profitable customers. With valuable customers, customer relationship management may make them more loyal and willing to invest additional funds. In banking, these high-end relationships are often managed through private bankers, whose goals are not only to increase customer satisfaction and retention, but also to cross-sell and bring in investment.

In determining which customers are worth the cost of long-term relationships, it is useful to consider their lifetime value. This depends on:

- Current profitability computed at the customer level
- The propensity of those customers to stay loyal
- Expected revenues and costs of servicing such customers over the lifetime of the relationship

Building relationships makes most sense for customers whose lifetime value to the company is the highest. Thus, building relationships should focus on customers who are currently the most profitable, likely to be the most profitable in the future, or likely to remain with the company for the foreseeable future and have acceptable levels of profitability.

The goal of relationship management is to increase customer satisfaction and to minimise any problems. By engaging in 'smarter' relationships, a company can learn customers' preferences and develop trust. Every contact point with the customer can be seen as a chance to record information and learn preferences. Complaints and errors must be recorded, not just fixed and forgotten. Contact with customers in every medium, whether over the Internet, through a call centre, or through personal contact, is recorded and centralised.

Many companies are beginning to achieve this goal by using customer relationship management (CRM) software. Data, once collected an centralised, can be used to customise service. In addition, the database can be analysed to detect patterns that can suggest better ways to serve customers in general. A key aspect of this dialogue is to learn and record preferences. There are two ways to determine customers' preferences: transparently and collaboratively.

Discovering preferences transparently means that the marketer learns the customers' needs without actually involving them. For example, the Ritz Carlton Hotel makes a point of observing the choices that guests make and recording them. If a guest requests extra pillows, then extra pillows will be provided every time that person visits. At upmarket retailers, personal shoppers will record customers' preferences in sizes, styles, brands, colours and price ranges and notify them when new merchandise appears or help them choose accessories.

Barbara Kahn, *Financial Time*

2.18 **Differences between transactional and relationship marketing**

Transactional	Relationship
Importance of single sale	Importance of customer relation
Importance of product features	Importance of customer benefits
Short time scale	Longer time scale
Less emphasis on service	High customer service
Quality is concern of production	Quality is concern of all
Competitive commitment	High customer commitment
Persuasive communication	Regular communication

The most important issue in customer retention is focussing marketing effort on activities that promote a strong relationship rather than a single transaction.

Key accounts

2.19   We have already looked briefly at this topic in Chapter 5 in the context of marketing communications strategy. So far in this chapter we have considered the retention of customers as an unquestionably desirable objective. **However, for many businesses a degree of discretion will be advisable**. 'Key' does not mean large.

Action Programme 2

If not 'large', what *does* 'key' mean in this context?

2.20   Customer analysis will almost certainly conform to a Pareto distribution and show, for instance, that 80% of profit comes from 20% of the customers, while a different 20% generate most of the credit control or administrative problems. Some businesses will be very aggressive about getting rid of their problem customers, but a more positive technique would be to concentrate effort on the most desirable ones. These are the **key accounts** and the company's relationship with them can be built up by appointing **key account managers**.

2.21   **Key account management** is often seen as a high level selling task, but should in fact be a business wide team effort about relationships and customer retention. It can be seen as a form of co-operation with the customer's supply chain management function.

2.22   The key account manager's role is to

- **Integrate** the efforts of the organisation in order to deliver an enhanced service
- **Maintain communication** with the customer
- Note any **developments in his circumstances**
- Deal with any **problems** arising in the relationship
- Develop the **long-term** business relationship

(a)   The key account relationship may progress through several stages, leading ultimately to **trust and commitment**.

(b)   At first, there may be a typical **adversarial** sales-purchasing relationship with emphasis on price, delivery and so on. Attempts to widen contact with the customer organisation will be seen as a **threat** by its purchasing staff.

(c)   Later, the sales staff may be able to foster a mutual desire to increase understanding by wider contacts. **Trust** may increase.

(d)   A mature **partnership** stage may be reached in which there are contacts at all levels and information is shared. The key account manager becomes responsible for integrating the partnership business processes and contributing to the customer's supply chain management. High 'vendor ratings', stable quality, continuous improvement and fair pricing are taken for granted.

Exam Tip

Relationship marketing in the context of the relationship between advertising agency and client is examined on the Specimen Paper.

3   Internal marketing

3.1   The term **internal marketing** has been used in a variety of ways. It has, for instance, been adopted in the field of **quality management** where the concept of the internal customer is used to motivate staff towards achieving quality objectives. In its most common usage, internal marketing means the **promotion of a marketing orientation throughout the organisation** and, in particular, creating customer awareness among staff who are not primarily concerned with selling. Hotel housekeeping staff, for instance, may rarely be seen by the guests, but their work makes a major contribution to the guests' perception.

3.2   The achievement of such a widespread marketing orientation may involve **major changes in working practices and organisational culture**. The successful management of organisational change depends to a great extent upon successful communication and communication is a major marketing activity. 'Internal marketing' has therefore also come to mean the communication aspect of any programme of change and, even more simply, **the presentation by management to staff of any information at all**.

Internal marketing as part of marketing management

3.3   If we concentrate on the use of the term to mean the use of marketing approaches and techniques to gain the support and co-operation of other departments and managers for the marketing plan, we will see that a number of challenges may exist. The first is that we may well be looking at a **major cultural shift**. Even in businesses which have highly skilled and motivated sales teams, **there may be areas of the organisation whose culture, aims and practices have nothing to do with customer satisfaction**.

Marketing at Work

The old nationalised industries like British Railways and Post Office Telecommunications saw engineering effectiveness as their major goal, with customer service nowhere. A business which takes this view is unlikely to succeed, but achieving a change of orientation can be a long, difficult and painful process. It will involve a major change in culture and probably entail significant changes to the shape of the organisation, as departments which contribute little to customer service lose influence and shrink or even disappear as the cost base is cut.

3.4 Organisational change

(a) Measuring activities against contribution to customer satisfaction means that some areas of the organisation are likely to shrink. The process of **delayering** may be necessary. This utilises modern information technology systems to replace the chiefly 'communications' role of middle management. The result is a much reduced requirement for general managers and an increased span of control.

(b) At the same time as these changes are being made, front line sales and marketing capability will probably have to be enhanced. This is likely to involve more than just an increase in numbers. New methods of working will be introduced, including working in cross-functional teams. In particular, the natural partner of delayering is **empowerment**. Front line staff will take greater responsibility for delivering customer satisfaction and will be given the necessary authority to do so. Relationship marketing databases and staff will be installed and key account managers appointed.

3.5 Such restructuring of the organisation has important **human resources (HR)** implications.

(a) There are likely to be **redundancies**. Staff who cannot adjust to the new methods must be released, with proper attention to both the legal requirements relating to redundancy and the organisation's policies on social responsibility.

(b) **Recruitment** will continue, because of natural wastage, but it will probably be necessary to adjust recruitment policy and practice to reflect the new requirements. Recruits must be selected who will be able to absorb the new approach and respond to the necessary training.

(c) **Training** will become a major feature of the change management programme. As well as new recruits, existing staff must be educated in the new methods and approach. The marketing department may have an input here, or the task of inculcating the marketing orientation and ideal of customer service may be contracted out to consultants.

3.6 Research suggests that although the principles involved may be acknowledged by a large number of companies, **formalised internal marketing programmes in the UK are still fairly uncommon**. Initial findings make several other suggestions.

(a) Internal marketing is **implicit in other strategies** such as quality programmes and customer care initiatives, rather than standing alone as an explicit policy in its own right.

(b) Where it is practised, internal marketing tends to involve a **core of structured activities** surrounded by less rigorously defined *ad hoc* practices.

(c) To operate successfully, internal marketing relies heavily on **good communication** networks.

(d)   Internal marketing is a key factor in **competitive differentiation**.

(e)   **Conflicts** between functional areas are significantly **reduced** by internal marketing.

(f)   Internal marketing depends heavily on **commitment at the highest level of management, co-operation,** and on the presence of **an open management style**.

Marketing at Work

Scandinavian Airlines Systems

Companies using this approach to great effect include SAS (Scandinavian Airline Systems), who have increased the involvement of employees in the decision-making process to achieve the highest levels of satisfaction, empowered them to make decisions appropriate to the requirements of particular customers, and trained them to feel a responsibility towards customers of all kinds. As a consequence, the company culture fosters a caring relationship internally and externally.

The marketing mix for internal marketing

3.7   **Product** under the internal marketing concept is the changing nature of the job. **Price** is the balance of psychological costs and benefits involved in adopting the new orientation, plus those things which have to be given up in order to carry out the new tasks. Difficulties here relate to the problem of arriving at an accurate and adequate evaluation of psychological costs.

3.8   Many of the methods used for communication and **promotion** in external marketing may be employed to motivate employees and influence attitudes and behaviour. HRM practice is beginning to employ techniques, such as multi-media presentations and in-house publications. Presentational skills are borrowed from personal selling techniques, while incentive schemes are being employed to generate changes in employee behaviour.

3.9   **Advertising** is increasingly used to generate a favourable corporate image amongst employees as well as external customers. Federal Express has the largest corporate television network in the world, with 1,200 sites.

3.10 Distribution for internal marketing means e-mails, meetings, conferences and physical means like noticeboards which can be used to announce policies and deliver policies and training programmes.

3.11 Physical evidence refers to tangible items which facilitate delivery or communication of the product. Quality standards such as BS 5750/ISO 9000, for instance, place great emphasis on documentation. Other tangible elements might involve training sessions, which would constitute a manifestation of commitment to standards or policies.

3.12 Process, which refers to how a 'customer' actually receives a product, is linked to communication and the medium of training which may be used to promote customer consciousness.

3.13 Participants are the people involved in producing and delivering the product, and those receiving the product, who may influence the customer's perceptions, are clearly important within the internal marketing process. Communications must be delivered by someone of the right level of authority in order to achieve their aims. The way in which employees act is strongly influenced by fellow employees, particularly their immediate superiors. Inter-departmental or interfunctional communications are likely to be least effective, because they have equal status or lack the authority to ensure compliance.

3.14 Segmentation and marketing research can also be used in internal marketing. Employees may be grouped according to their service characteristics, needs, wants or tasks in order to organise the dissemination of a service orientation. Research will monitor the needs and wants of employees, and identify the impact of corporate policies.

3.15 Problems with the internal marketing concept

Even effective use of inwardly directed marketing techniques cannot solve all employee related quality and customer satisfaction problems. **Research clearly shows that actions by the personnel department, or effective programmes of personnel selection and training, are likely to be more effective than marketing based activities.**

Marketing at Work

In the UK retail sector, for example, while many large scale operations now operate Sunday trading, there has been significant resistance from employee organisations. Internal marketing would argue that employees should be persuaded by means of a well-executed communications campaign and by the offer of proper incentives. Although these strategies have been tried, they have met with little success, or, in the case of incentives, have been too expensive. Employers have solved the problem by specifically recruiting employees who are required to work on Sunday, and who may be paid slightly higher wage rates for the time in question. Rather than internal marketing, external recruitment proved to be the solution.

3.16 Claims that marketing can replace or fulfil the objectives of some other functions are clearly overstated. However, the internal marketing concept has a major role to play in making employees customer conscious.

Exam Tip

Do not marginalise this topic. Internal marketing is mentioned specifically in the syllabus. It came up in an exam in June 2002 under the old *Integrated Marketing Communications* syllabus when candidates were asked why internal marketing communications could be an important aspect of a low cost airline's marketing communications.

4 Types of outside resources

4.1 In the modern world, it is possible to outsource everything. There are a great many management and marketing consultants in the UK. The CIM, for example, provides a comprehensive service. Some consultants specialise in design, research or promotion.

Marketing research agencies

4.2 Not many organisations have all the in-house facilities needed to cater for their total information requirements. Nearly all organisations find it necessary from time-to-time to outsource surveys to specialists.

Promotional agencies

4.3 There is a great variety of **promotional agencies** including advertising agencies and agencies specialising in sales promotion, in PR, in telesales/telemarketing. Within sales promotion there is a range of specialists in such areas as packaging design, POS display material, exhibition services, and mail-order.

Full-service agencies

4.4 **Full service agencies** supply the full range of marketing services.

4.5 In smaller companies, many of the functions associated with marketing may actually be sourced from outside the company. Obvious examples would be market research services, advertising, design of packaging, and specialist aspects of product testing (for example, sensory testing of new food products, or safety tests on new electrical goods). When promotional campaigns are being mounted, 'leafleting' is typically the province of small subcontractors as are teams who dispense free samples during in-store promotional exercises.

4.6 Employing **advertising agencies** not only gives access to their expertise but may also improve the finances of a media campaign because of the commission which the media pay to *bona fide* agents only.

4.7 **The use of outside resources can add a great deal of flexibility to an organisation**. It reduces the need for investment and offers the possibility of greater profits.

4.8 Outsourcing also reduces the strain on the organisation's **limited human resources** and frees marketing management to concentrate on the more important strategic rather than tactical aspects of its marketing plans.

Action Programme 3

What are the main advantages of outsourcing?

BPP
PROFESSIONAL EDUCATION

5 Management of external suppliers

Exam Tip

The CIM syllabus document for this module emphasises how trust and commitment can be developed. This applies to relationships with suppliers as well as customers. Services upon which organisations depend to function properly must be well managed, so that the outside suppliers who are called upon to carry out these tasks are a key aspect of the overall functioning of the organisation.

Briefing

5.1 **Good briefing ensures good working relationships**. Bad briefing will lead to misunderstandings between client and supplier to the detriment of the ultimate customer. In the event of a dispute, a full brief will leave less room for doubt as to the requirements of the contract. There must be basic ground rules for briefing outside suppliers.

- To what extent do we take outside suppliers into our confidence?
- What do they need to know?
- Who will draw up the briefs?
- How often should the brief be reviewed?

Management of externally sourced factors

Control and review

5.2 Direct supervision of externally sourced staff and equipment will normally be the responsibility of the contractor, but the hiring company must maintain its own management input into the relationship. Costs, benefits and risks must be considered during the life of the contract as well as before it is let. **The company must be clear about what it wants to achieve from outsourcing and set quantifiable standards against which the contractor's performance can be reviewed**.

5.3 One or more managers should be charged with oversight of every important aspect of every contract. These managers should also maintain communication with the contractors and promote good relations between the parties. If performance is unsatisfactory, the contractor must be informed directly rather than via the operational staff so that effective corrective action is taken.

5.4 **Costs, risks and performance should be reviewed regularly** and the results reported to the senior managers responsible for outsourcing policy. A framework for review is given below. The supervising manager should be particularly alert to developments which may affect the relationship, such as new legislation and changes in labour relations. For instance, minimum wage legislation will undoubtedly affect the profitability of many contractors, and some will be tempted to evade it. No company conscious of its image would wish to be associated with such evasion.

5.5 One of the main potential problems is lack of response to client input. There are some mechanisms, such as staged payments and incentive structure, which attempt to address this issue by making the outsourced function responsible for meeting particular targets, and holding back payment. There is a tendency for this to be seen as somewhat excessive in smaller contracts. Control rests, ultimately, upon the **market power of the client**, and on the **quality of the management control system** operated within the client organisation.

5.6 Control might be applied selectively. Should a supplier who involves small or spasmodic expenditure be subjected to the same degree of control as a supplier the organisation uses regularly or extensively? The answer cannot depend on expenditure alone. The organisation could, for example, be making a relatively small spend with an agency on concept testing a proposed new product. However, this proposed new product could be vital to the organisation's future and therefore the agency could require stricter control than a dependable supplier of raw materials.

5.7 The nature of the control should perhaps be different **according to the nature of the product or service being bought**. For raw material suppliers, an organisation might have scientific tests on quality and maintain records of deliveries late/on time/before time. However, for an advertising agency, control might be more informal and based on frequent personal meetings.

5.8 A framework for review

- Supplier's name, address, telephone number
- Names and positions of contacts
- Description of types of goods and services supplied
- Total annual spend for last three years
- Splits of annual spends by types of product/service where relevant
- Number of years we have been trading with this supplier
- Perceived strengths and weaknesses of supplier
- Record of improvements made by supplier during trading period
- Record of growth of supplier: turnover, staff, number of branches
- List of alternative suppliers
- Perceived strengths and weaknesses of top three alternative suppliers
- Date of last review of this supplier
- Name/position of person conducting this last review
- Recommended date of next review

Chapter Roundup

- **Customers are stakeholders**. This means that they should be valued and not taken for granted. They differ in their characteristics and can be analysed or segmented to increase profitability.

- **Intermediaries** such as agents and franchisees are also customers. They have their own different needs which must be considered.

- **Customer retention** is an important contribution to profitability since each customer can represent a lifetime's cash flow and creating a new customer requires far more promotional and administrative effort than retaining an existing one. The vital factor in customer retention is the skill and approach of the front line staff.

- **Relationship marketing** is more than customer retention. It is the fostering of a mutually beneficial relationship by precision in meeting the needs of individual customers. It uses powerful computer database systems.

- Customers can be analysed for their **value to the business**. **Key account management** allows the most valuable customers to be given an enhanced service.

- **Internal marketing** has a range of meanings but the most useful relates to the promotion of a high level of customer awareness throughout the organisation using marketing communication techniques to change culture and deliver training.

- Almost any activity can be **outsourced**. Typical areas for outsourcing activities are manufacture, distribution, finance and marketing. Marketing activities which can be outsourced include consultancy, marketing research, promotion and 'full service'.

- As a general rule, the use of **outside resources** can be considered whenever external suppliers can provide better services at the same cost or equivalent services at a lower cost.

- **Good briefing** provides a solid foundation for a successful working relationship.

Now try Question 11 in the Question Bank

Quick Quiz

1   Customers make up one of the groups of stakeholders whose interests marketing management should address.

   True ☐

   False ☐

2   Why is 'word of mouth' communication so powerful?

   A   People tend not to write things down these days
   B   It always happens when the customer is happy
   C   The company does not have to pay for it
   D   An unhappy customer may advise many others of his discontent

3 Even within a particular business, customers will vary. What are some of these variable factors influencing their purchasing decisions?

4 An intermediary is not a type of customer

True ☐

False ☐

5 Give a simple definition of 'relationship marketing'.

6 Classify these characteristics as features of either 'transactional' (T) or 'relationship' (R) marketing:

Importance of single sale	T/R	Importance of customer relationship	T/R
Importance of customer benefits	T/R	Competitive commitment	T/R
Short time scale	T/R	Less emphasis on service	T/R
Longer time scale	T/R	High customer service	T/R
Quality is concern of production	T/R	Quality is concern of all	T/R
High customer commitment	T/R	Importance of product features	T/R
Persuasive communication	T/R	Regular communication	T/R

7 Fill in the gaps using words from the grid below.

The key account relationship may progress through several stages. At first, there may be a typical (1).......... sales-purchasing relationship. Later, the sales staff may be able to foster a mutual desire to increase (2)...........A mature (3).......... stage may be reached in which there are contacts at all levels and (4).......... is shared.

Information	Trust	Management
Conflict	Adversarial	Partnership

8 Advertising can be used to generate a favourable corporate image amongst employees (internal marketing) as well as external customers.

True ☐

False ☐

Action Programme Review

1 Here are some ideas on how customers differ.

(a) Some appear for a **single cash transaction** and are never seen again.

(b) Others make **frequent, regular purchases in large volumes**, using credit facilities and building up a major relationship.

(c) Yet another type of customer **purchases infrequently but in transactions of high value**, as for instance in property markets.

2   The definition of a key account depends on the circumstances, but a customer's **potential** is very important. In addition, customers might be assessed for desirability according to the following criteria.

- **Profitability** of their accounts
- **Prestige** they confer
- Amount of **non-value adding administrative work** they generate
- **Cost of the selling effort** they absorb
- **Rate of growth** of their accounts
- **Turnover** of their own businesses
- Willingness to **adopt new products**
- **Credit history**

3   (a)   Cost savings

    (b)   Specialism of the company

    (c)   Accountability is tied to specific performance

    (d)   Introduction of desirable outside qualities such as imagination and fresh ideas into particular sorts of activities

Answers to Quick Quiz

1   True

2   D (although there is some merit in option C as well)

3   Check your answer against paragraph 2.3

4   False

5   The management of a firm's market relationships

6

Importance of single sale	T	Importance of customer relationship	R
Importance of customer benefits	R	Competitive commitment	T
Short time scale	T	Less emphasis on service	T
Longer time scale	R	High customer service	R
Quality is concern of production	T	Quality is concern of all	R
High customer commitment	R	Importance of product features	T
Persuasive communication	T	Regular communication	R

7   (1) Adversarial; (2) Trust; (3) Partnership; (4) Information

8   True

The marketing communications industry

12

Chapter Topic List	
1	Setting the scene
2	Research agencies
3	Other marketing communications agencies
4	Creative agencies
5	Agency selection
6	Briefing the agency
7	Managing the relationship
8	International agency selection and management
9	Controlling the marketing communications industry

Learning Outcome

☑ Use the vocabulary of the marketing communications industry and be able to communicate effectively with other marketing practitioners

Syllabus References

☑ Explain in broad terms the nature, structure, ownership and any key issues facing the marketing communications industry in any single country or region

☑ Describe how agencies manage their operations in order to meet client needs: pitching, briefing, structure, review, the role of account planners and managers, relationship management

☑ Explain how advertising agencies and marketing communication agencies use resources to meet the needs of clients with international and global requirements

 BPP PROFESSIONAL EDUCATION

☑ Describe in broad terms the regulatory and voluntary arrangements that are used to manage relationships between the public, customers, clients and agencies

Key Concepts Introduced

- 'Media only' service
- 'Full' service
- Brief

1 Setting the scene

1.1 External agencies exist to provide services that a client does not retain **in-house**. Indeed, the argument that communication activity should be kept in-house is discredited, as the **communications techniques available are now so varied** that it makes no commercial sense to retain in-house the entire range, when each specialism is only likely to be called upon infrequently. Agencies are generally dealing with a number of clients and will be more in touch with the latest techniques and developments. Competitive deals on **media buying**, for example, are far more likely to be achieved by a large agency than by a single staff member in a relatively small marketing department.

1.2 So, in the last few decades marketing techniques have increased dramatically in range and complexity. The marketing communications industry has had to evolve as technology and business realities contribute to both **audience** and **media fragmentation**.

1.3 Standard **'above-the-line'** marketing (where media space is paid for), handled by large advertising agencies, has been increasingly replaced by **'below-the-line'** (promotional) and **'through-the-line'** activities, as we saw in Chapter 4. Agencies specialising in sales promotion, direct marketing and PR have sprung up as independent operations and divisions of large advertising agencies. Many companies now use more than one agency to handle a **portfolio** of techniques above-, below- and through-the-line, or to cover **local and on-going** work as well as **national strategic** campaign. As a result, many larger, integrated agencies now have divisions specialising in various areas.

- Sales promotion
- Direct marketing
- Public relations
- 'New' media (Internet, CD-ROM)
- Design

1.4 According to Fill (2002), the marketing communications industry consists of four principal groups.

- **Media**
- **Clients**
- **Agencies**
- **Support organisations** (such as production companies and research agencies)

1.5 There is a certain level of **interdependence** between these organisations, so co-operative working relationships between them are required.

We will discuss relationships with advertising agencies in detail in section 6 below. The CIM syllabus document for this module discusses the importance of what it terms 'the agency dimension', and the relationships that develop between client and agency.

1.6 Broadly speaking there are only two types of agency that a marketing communicator will deal with: **creative advertising agencies** and **research agencies**.

1.7 Advertising agencies are still the most commonly used marketing service. Agencies come in a range of sizes and specialisms to reflect the increasingly fragmented and diverse range of media.

Key Concepts

(a) '**Media only**' service: the agency selects schedules and books advertising space at a discount, which is in part passed onto the client.

(b) '**Full service**': the agency creates the whole campaign from concept through production to press/air.

2 Research agencies

2.1 It is essential that a marketing communicator has a thorough understanding of the role, scope, and reliability of both **quantitative** and **qualitative** research. Thus equipped he can develop a healthy distrust of data that is presented in the form of research. Unless the research proves itself to be both relevant and valid for the intended purpose it should not be trusted.

The cost of research

2.2 Cost is a major problem in securing accurate **primary research**. Budget constraints sometimes reduce a sample size to a very low level and however impressively they may be presented, the results can be misleading. **Secondary sources**, such as syndicated surveys, tend to carry a high price, and value must therefore be the criteria of purchase.

Action Programme 1

Wait for the next publication of ABC audit figures and examine how each major newspaper presents the results. What conclusions can you draw from what you observe?

Research decision sequence

2.3 Prior to commissioning research the decision sequence should be this.

Step 1. Do we need research?
Step 2. If so, what for?
Step 3. By when is it needed?
Step 4. How much can we afford?
Step 5. Can we locate a quality researcher who is free at the time needed?
Step 6. Is our budget (cost and time) sufficient?
Step 7. Do we go ahead and commission the research?

2.4 When deciding on sources of research it is essential to consider what is really needed in terms of sample reliability rather then to choose on the basis of availability or cheapness. It is essential to check the credentials of any research organisation: can it deliver what you want at the time that you want it? Most will say they can, but what is their record?

2.5 **All advertising agencies have links with the other specialists that are needed**. Clients should therefore remember that the benefit of engaging specialists who are used to working together could be outweighed by the specialists' natural desire to continue working together whether or not it is appropriate to the client's needs to do so.

Retail audits (eg A C Nielsen)

2.6 (a) These measure stocks moving through retail outlets. However, Nielsen have been denied access to certain major stores such as Marks & Spencer so their data has to be adjusted. Their data shows sales in any two-month period, but does not show usage.

(b) Such research can be self-fulfilling, however. When Nielsen declare the market shares for each segment shops tend to adjust their shelf-space allocation so that the market share percentage is given to each brand stocked.

2.7 **Consumer panels** comprise shoppers who complete diaries showing purchases in detail. Alternatively, researchers are sent into the home to carry out 'pantry checks' in similar fashion to retail audit. They have not made inroads into Nielsen's supremacy, but provide very useful data that helps in the marketing communications task.

2.8 **Omnibus surveys** are vehicles provided by a research organisation that carries out a regular survey on a syndicated basis.

(a) Client companies are invited to buy questions at a fixed price. Discounts are usually available for several questions and/or for repeating the questions in a series of surveys.

(b) The research is carried out at a far lower cost than could be achieved by individual commission. They are particularly suitable for those who want to ask a limited number of questions of a large, representative sample of the population. The largest is the ICD Survey.

(c) There are many general omnibus surveys available and each claims to offer unique benefits. Potential clients should consider not only the sample size, but also its quality in terms of structure and method of data collection.

(d) There are a wide variety of specialist omnibus surveys working to niche markets such as motorists or mothers with children under two.

The Target Group Index

2.9 The TGI is a national product and media survey which collects information from 24,000 adults each year. The TGI is a 'single source' measurement and all elements of the survey can be cross-referenced, for example media usage to product usage; brand usage to demographics.

Action Programme 2

Here are two small ads from a recent edition of *Marketing Week*. (The names have been omitted.) What sort of companies/products might use these services?

Market Research Limited **Trade Research Specialists** ■ Retail audits ■ Product availability surveys ■ Mystery shopping ■ Shop testing ■ Trade interviews ■ Tailor made studies ■ Overnight pricing checks ■ Customer interviews ■ Consumer research	**CHILDREN AND YOUTH** **BRITAIN AND CONTINENT** **GB** *Core Sample:* 1200 7 - 19 year olds with bi-monthly extensions to include ages 3 to 6 and 20-24. Any age range within these limits. *Field dates:* every 2 - 4 weeks. *Rates:* from £290 per question according to age range covered. **Continent:** Five country child and youth surveys

3 Other marketing communications agencies

3.1 Before we look at creative agencies in detail in the next section, here is an outline of some other agencies available for the marketing communicator.

Promotion agencies

3.2 **Promotional activities** – collaborations between brands, competitions and incentives – have been a huge growth area in marketing. Some agencies specialise in these areas.

■ Sourcing promotional incentive products and merchandise
■ Devising links and negotiating deals between brands
■ Organising competitions
■ Designing and producing promotional packaging and information material

3.3 **PR consultancies** handle several areas.

(a) **Media or press relations** (keeping the media informed, in order to manage the company's portrayal and secure 'free' coverage of product/service information)

(b) **Corporate relations** (promoting a corporate image to the public, market and business world, through a range of PR techniques)

(c) **Marketing support** (promoting specific products or services via publicity, events, press coverage and so on)

    (d)   **Government relations** (lobbying on behalf of the company's interests)

    (e)   **Community relations** (targeted at the general public or local residents, via communication and social programmes, community involvement, sponsorship etc)

    (f)   **Financial relations** (communicating with shareholders, financial media, the Stock Market)

    (g)   **Employee relations** (communicating with staff)

3.4   PR agencies are less easy to manage than advertising agencies, because their activity and output is often less tangible. The major cost is their time plus expenses. In order to make cost effective use of their services you need to consider the following.

- Set clear **objectives** for the on-going PR plan or specific project
- Set a project **fee** where possible
- **Brief** comprehensively
- **Monitor activity** perhaps via an independent cuttings or media monitoring agency
- **Monitor expenditure**

Direct marketing services

3.5   **Direct marketing agencies** (and separate specialists) offer a range of services from database and mailing list development, analysis and segmentation to telemarketing, direct mail package design, copy writing, mailing and fulfilment. This area of marketing has grown with Internet usage , as many of the 'dotcoms' have used direct mail to drive visitors to their websites.

Brand identity

3.6   There are specialist agencies which perform specific brand-related services.

- Design and produce product **packaging** and display
- Orchestrate the up-dating of **brand identity** and style
- Research, devise, market-test and register **brand names**

Sponsorship

3.7   Agencies undertake negotiations

- **Sponsorship agreements**
- **Product endorsements** by celebrities
- **Product placement** (the inclusion of branded products in films or TV programmes)

4 Creative agencies

4.1 Types of agency

Full service agency	This is an agency which provides a complete advertising service encompassing creative work, production, media planning and buying. The full service agency may also provide or sub-contract research services for a client. Some large advertising agencies will provide other communications services, for example direct marketing, public relations or sales promotion. There has been some concern that such large agencies may not always be able to provide a full quality service in all the areas that they cover. Some creative teams left large agencies to set up their own **creative shops** (or '**HotShops**') to provide an alternative.
Media independents	Media independents provide media services (such as planning and buying) only.
A la carte	A client may decide to share out his communication tasks, choosing to cherry pick services *à la carte* from the different providers available. Responsibility for controlling and co-ordinating the activities of these service providers rests with the client, usually in the form of the brand or marketing Manager.
New media	This area has grown hugely in recent years. The main area of work is the provision of Internet facilities. Agencies tend to fall along a spectrum of expertise and be either marketing orientated, or technology specialists.

5 Agency selection

5.1 The pages of the trade magazine *Campaign* regularly carry news of client accounts on the move from one agency to another. There are a number of reasons why clients may change agencies. The client may feel the agency is lacking in new ideas, or is overcharging. Alternatively, a new client won by the agency may result in a conflict of interests between new and old clients. Often, a change in personnel on either the client or the agency side can result in an account moving on.

Search

5.2 **Sources of information** include the following.

(a) Publications such as *Campaign Portfolio* provide a listing of agencies and the types of business they handle, alongside addresses and contact numbers.

(b) The Advertising Agency Register (AAR) is a specialist intermediary type service which clients can use to help them with their search. For a fee, AAR will provide a list of candidate agencies and a selection of their work.

(c) Many agencies engage in self promotion via advertising, direct mail or even cold calling.

(d) Personal recommendation may bring some agency names to light.

(e) Some agencies now produce CD-ROMs containing case studies, examples of work and background information about them and their offices.

Shortlist

5.3 From the initial search, a shortlist of perhaps six to eight agencies will be drawn up, usually on the basis of their current work and past track record. The prospective client will then visit those agencies for a series of what are known as credentials presentations. A preliminary evaluation of the agencies may be carried out using the criteria below.

(a) Previous work handled

(b) Experience in relevant fields of business (for example, do they handle other clients with similar target audiences to mine? Have they carried out work in the fmcg/industrial/business-to-business market before?)

(c) Agency costs/terms of business

(d) Resources in-house as opposed to bought in

(e) Staff expertise

(f) Personalities

Agency pitch

5.4 Following these initial visits, it is likely that a smaller number of agencies will be formally invited to **pitch** for the client's business. There is some controversy regarding whether an agency should be reimbursed for a pitch. Some agencies will only carry out pitches if they can claim some of the expense back again from the potential client. Other agencies will only carry out an ideas pitch as opposed to presenting creative work.

5.5 Normally, three or four agencies will be invited to compete for the client's business. All will receive a standard brief and will be given a set period in which to reply to the brief.

Detailed selection process

5.6 It is essential that each agency is judged by the same criteria. The criteria should be established by the client in advance, and they must be understood and agreed by all who will be part of the selection team.

5.7 **Criteria for assessing an agency**

Item	Comment
Present work	■ Is it exciting/interesting? ■ Is it effective? What proof is there? ■ It is allied to our marketplace?
Present clients	■ Are there any clashes that will worry us or the agency or the other client(s)? ■ Do previous clients come back for more or are agency/client relationships short-lived?

Item	Comment
Chemistry	■ Is the chemistry between us good? ■ Will we feel able to trust the agency all the way? ■ Will the trust be reciprocated?
Staffing	■ Will the people who worked on the pitch work on the account? ■ How stable will our account team be? ■ What depth of experience can the account team offer?
Evidence	■ Have we seen evidence of creativity, of production, of media planning, of management, of the particular skills we need?
The pitch	■ Is it a package or tailored specially? ■ Does it arouse us to buy?
The agency	■ Is its size, age and structure suitable? ■ Does it have to have international capacity? ■ Is it a full service agency or a specialist? ■ What is its workload? Does it have time for us? ■ Does it possess the necessary business skills? (For example, has it negotiated a fee for specialised work necessary to meet the requirements of our invitation to pitch for the account?)
Specialised knowledge	■ Has it demonstrated realistic and satisfactory understanding of our organisation and market?
Price	■ Does the asking fee represent value for money when the above points are taken into account? ■ Does the agency know its value to us?
Judgement	■ Is this the agency for us?

Final selection

5.8 The final selection will involve a judgement about how well the client believes the agency has responded to the brief in terms of the strategic thinking involved, the creative work (if presented) and the agency's all round understanding of the client's industry. Courtesy dictates that the client should inform both the successful agency and the unsuccessful ones in a prompt manner.

Criticism of the formal selection process

5.9 The formalised process is now being questioned, especially because with the arrival of new media and Internet technology, campaigns are having to be resolved in days rather than weeks. The **pitching process** can lead to tensions, especially on the part of unsuccessful agencies who may have invested a great amount of time and effort for no reward. Perhaps most significantly for them, they will have shared their ideas, over which they will have no subsequent control .

5.10 The pitching process also gives little insight into **subsequent working relationships**.

Marketing at Work

An example solution to this particular problem (cited by Fill, 2002) is that adopted by Iceland and Dyson. They invite agencies to discuss and work with client staff on 'mini-briefs' for a day. Such briefs are more like discussion topics for the agency to think about, as opposed to the traditional 'outline your proposed campaign for Product X and we'll tell you if we like it' approach. Most importantly, it gives senior management the chance to see agency and client staff working together on a task, and the agencies are spared weeks of costly preparation work.

Exam Tip

The Specimen Paper features a question on the ways in which trust between clients and agencies may be improved.

6 Briefing the agency   (Specimen paper)

6.1 The **agency brief** is the initial and most important stage of any project undertaken. The planning and creative teams of the agency need initially to get to know the client, its products, brands, market and customers, and its culture, style, self-image and designed image.

Key Concept

A **brief** (in advertising agency terms) is 'an interpretation of a given market in relation to the product, plus every usable detail about the features and benefits of that product.' (Quinn)

6.2 A comprehensive brief will include the following details.

(a) **The product**, including its design and marketing history, and current 'life cycle' stage, its technical specifications, pack sizes, shelf-life, packaging/distribution arrangements and associated after-sales services.

(b) **The market**: who uses the product, how, when and why, how it is distributed (via wholesale, retail or direct selling), the product's current and desired market share, pricing and discount/margin policies for the product, and sales strategies.

(c) **Previous advertising**: the previous advertising budget (if any), competitors' advertising spend, breakdown of spend above- and below-the-line.

(d) **Current advertising policy**: budget available, desired image for the product and company, objectives of advertising.

6.3 The brief may also contain the company's current ideas about the theme for advertising: what it believes is the key concept or **unique selling proposition (USP)** of the product or brand.

6.4 The brief is usually given to the agency account executive who relays it to the relevant agency personnel.

6.5 A **proforma for a creative brief** is set out below.

CREATIVE BRIEF

Agency

Briefing date

Company

Contact name

Project name

Project description

Budget

Key deadlines

Company background

Business objectives

Background to the brief

Communications objectives

Target audience

Proposition

Action Programme 3

Explain the significance of each of these elements of the creative brief.

Exam Tip

The nature and characteristics of the client brief features on the Specimen Paper.

7 Managing the relationship (Specimen paper)

7.1 The specialist agencies providing support services (advertising, public relations, sales promotion, research) usually all work to much the same principles. There will be an **account director** directly responsible for the client's account and working directly with the client **brand manager**. Thus all contact between client and agency is via the conduit established by these two individuals.

Who's who in the agency?

7.2 The simplest form of **agency structure** is as follows.

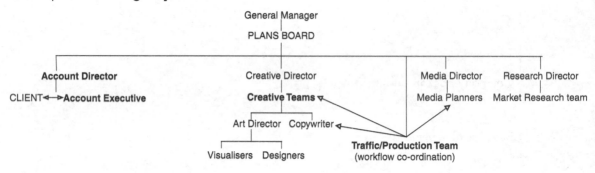

- The **account executives** service the clients on a day-to-day basis

- The **account director** monitors work on given accounts

- The **creative team** 'produces' the ad

- The **traffic/production team** plans and schedules agency workflow, monitors progress against deadlines and 'chases' work

7.3 **The account director/manager is vitally important because a full service agency will provide the services of not fewer than 20 departments**, and these need to be co-ordinated around a client focus. The departments commonly found in a full service agency are as follows.

- Creative
- Typography
- Presentation
- Studio
- Account management
- Economic forecasting
- Research

- TV and radio production
- Press production
- Press buying
- Print buying
- Art buying
- TV and radio buying
- Sales promotion

- Marketing
- Media planning
- Market intelligence
- Personnel
- Finance
- Administration
- Management

7.4 A large full service agency might look more like the organisation chart on the next page.

7.5 The flow of work through the agency can be depicted as follows.

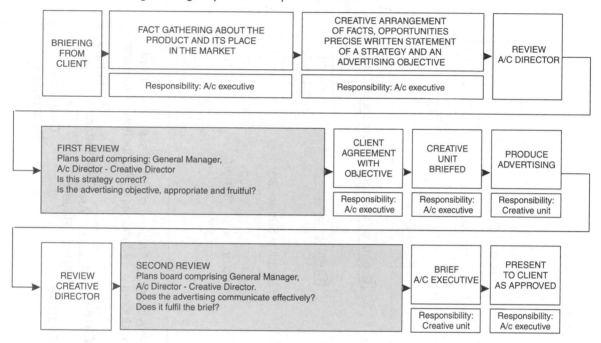

(*Source*: James Hearne, *Advertising Management*)

7.6 Note the **client's responsibilities** implied by the above flow-chart.

(a) The advertising co-ordinator (or marketing department head) briefs the agency.

(b) The marketing department head approves the agency's assessment of the advertising objective, strategy, schedule and cost estimates.

(c) The advertising co-ordinator provides the agency with all available materials and information to help the creative team to produce effective ads.

(d) The advertising co-ordinator is the first one to see work that comes back from the agency at each stage of production (copy, story boards, sketches), and will probably check, correct and recommend any necessary changes before the ad is finally approved by the marketing department head.

(e) The ad is returned to the agency for typesetting, final art, filming and sound production.

(f) The advertising co-ordinator carries out final checks, and gets final approval before giving the agency clearance to release the ad to the media.

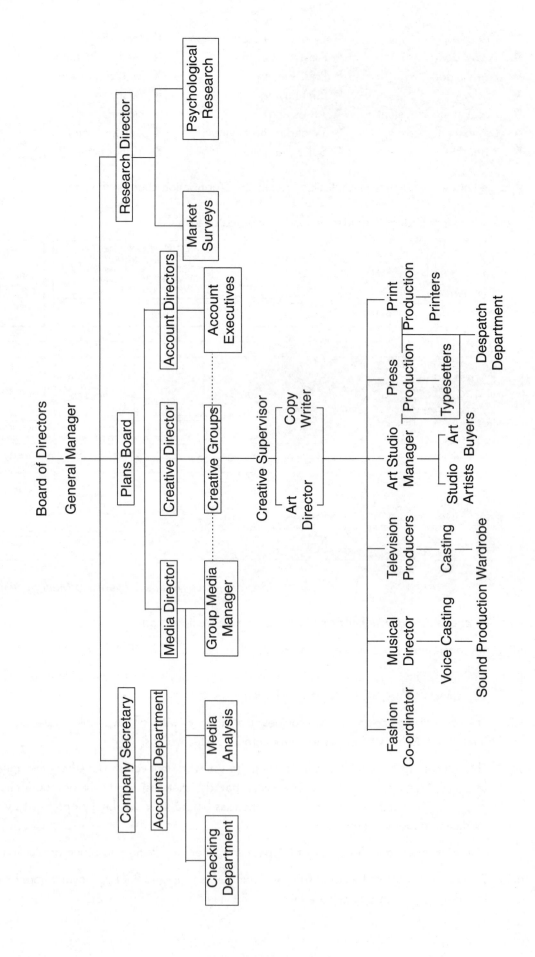

7.7 **Establishing a relationship with a creative agency takes time**. The end result has to be an on-going relationship based upon mutual understanding and respect. Therefore both the selection process and the day-to-day relationships have to receive very careful attention.

7.8 **A creative agency should be a full member of the client's marketing team**. As such, members of the agency have to be trusted with market information and, to some extent, with profit information as well. If they are not, then information will be withheld and the relationship will suffer. The creative work will suffer too, and sales and profitability will fall. If an agency understands the costing of a package it is less likely to spend time devising a promotion that the client will not be able to afford, and so keeping working data from an agency is counter-productive, morale sapping and expensive.

7.9 The only reason an agency is engaged is because it can do a job or provide a service better (and more quickly) than the client can do it for himself. It follows that the client should not meddle with their work. If the client does not like it, of course, he must say so, but **the test must be 'will it work with the target audience?'**.

7.10 Key principles for managing the relationship

1	Management is by the client.
2	The agency team must work closely within the client's marketing department.
3	Briefings must be specific and unambiguous.
4	All research data and management control information available to the brand manager must be provided to the agency.
5	The agency should sit in on the client's strategic planning meetings as an equal member, and of right.
6	Time and cost requirements must be reasonable and must be accepted by the agency.
7	The client should not meddle in the creative process and the agency should not interfere with the production of the package, although both may make an input, as appropriate, as part of the strategic planning process.
8	Full credit must be given when the agency is successful, and shared responsibility must be accepted as appropriate.
9	Fees and commissions should be agreed in advance and accounts should be paid promptly.
10	Copy should never be changed once it has been approved. It should be fully checked before it is signed off. Changes after that stage are not only expensive but, more importantly, they are damaging to the brand manager's personal credibility with the agency.

7.11 Given that the agency is accepted as part of the marketing communications team it should take full responsibility for the production of cost-effective work that meets the brief and hits time targets.

Payment of creative agencies

7.12 Historically, agencies have earned their money through commission on media space purchased for their clients. The practice arises from the time when the advertising agent was a media broker who also provided other services. This method of payment also highlights the agency's legal standing. The agency is liable for bills to the media if the client defaults on payment. Nearly 50% of agency income still comes from commission, according to a recent survey.

Agency commission

7.13 15% used to be the standard rate of agency commission. This is now no longer the case. Some large clients, have argued that they should pay the agency a discounted rate of commission, because of the volume of media throughput that the agency handles. Other clients, themselves under pressure to make advertising money work harder, have argued for commission rates of 10% or 13%.

Fee payment

7.14 Some advertisers and their agencies prefer to work on a project by project fee system. This ensures the agency earns money, whether or not the work is media based. About 40% of agency income is earned in this way.

Marketing at Work

David Ogilvy is on record as saying 'I pioneered the fee system but I no longer care how I get paid, providing I make a reasonable profit. With a fee system the advertiser pays only for the services he wants, no more and no less. Every fee account pays its own way. Large profitable accounts do not subsidise small, unprofitable ones. Cuts in client's budgets do not oblige you to cut staff. When you advise a client to increase his advertising he does not suspect your motive.'

7.15 It is essential for the agency to have an efficient system to capture accurately and promptly all data relating to the allocation of staff time, and the utilisation of other resources. It is reasonable for a client to expect to be shown the control method in use, but not to have access to the agency's detailed profitability. A typical fee calculation is shown below.

Advertising agency: typical fee calculation

	Actual hours	Amount £
Direct time cost*		
Account management	1,000	40,000
Creative	1,500	60,000
Media	300	12,000
Production	400	16,000
Research and planning	750	30,000
		158,000
Overheads at 110% (including secretarial, managerial, accounting and administration payroll; also establishment and general costs)	-	174,000
Direct expenses (including directly attributable travel and presentation costs)	-	14,000
Total hours/cost	3,950	346,000
Gross profit at 25%	-	86,500
Total (£109.50 per hour)	3,950	432,500

* Includes direct and indirect payroll costs of all staff who allocate their time.

7.16 The sums charged per hour will obviously vary from agency to agency and over time. The hours needed, however, should remain constant. It will be seen that a new product development can occupy many hours. Even more hours will be used within the client, but they are unlikely to be controlled as rigorously. There is therefore considerable unquantified investment in any new creative development. The only party able to account for its involvement accurately is the agency. (Unfortunately for the agency, its efficiency in this respect means that is likely to be the first target in any cost-cutting exercise!)

Payment by results

7.17 Payment by results schemes have been used mainly in the USA, although they are becoming more common in the UK. With performance-related payment, the agency is judged on the effect its advertising has on client company sales. Different rates of commission then come into force, depending on performance to target, over-achievement or under-achievement. The major drawback to this method of remuneration is that it pre-supposes a direct correlation between advertising effort and sales.

Marketing at Work

Every year *Campaign* conducts a survey on choosing an agency. The results shed some further light on the best approach to managing the relationship - or not managing it, as the case may be.

Marketing directors were asked a series of questions and given suggested answers. The questions and the percentages agreeing with the answers are as follows.

(a)   *Why do you change agency?*

(i)	It is not devoting enough time/resources to your account	87
(ii)	It has lost its enthusiasm for working on your product/service	85
(iii)	It is working on a conflicting account	61
(iv)	There is a personality clash	44
(v)	It lacks *co-ordinated* communication skills	32
(vi)	It lacks the technology to service your account	15
(vii)	You change agency regularly as a matter of course	2

(b)   *How do you go about drawing up a shortlist?*

(i)	You take into consideration advertising you admire	86
(ii)	You ask acquaintances for recommendations	77
(iii)	You read the marketing press	59
(iv)	You read *Campaign*	45
(v)	You take into consideration creative/effectiveness ad awards	44
(vi)	You use the Advertising Agency Register	38
(vii)	You use *Campaign Portfolio*	36
(viii)	You appoint a selection consultant	5

(c)   *What do you look for at the pitch?*

(i)	Evidence the agency understands and can enhance your brand	95
(ii)	Quality of thinking	94
(iii)	Good chemistry between both parties	90
(iv)	Presence of senior agency staff who will stay on your account	81

(v)	Evidence of sound business/management skills	75
(vi)	Strategy that offers value for money	73
(vii)	A powerful creative idea	68
(viii)	An agency culture which fits your own	64

(d) *What do you look for in a new agency?*

(i)	It is fundamentally committed to creative excellence	74
(ii)	It has previous experience working in your market sector	46
(iii)	It offers a remuneration system based on fees not commissions	41
(iv)	It has embraced new technology and uses it	38
(v)	It offers a fully *co-ordinated* service, including below-the-line	35
(vi)	It is able to advise you on the information superhighway	22
(vii)	It offers international resources	16

(e) *How could your agency improve its service to you?*

(i)	Unprompted original ideas	78
(ii)	Cut costs	66
(iii)	Not be afraid to challenge your viewpoint	56
(iv)	Devote more time/resources to your account	49
(v)	Embrace new technology and use it to your advantage	44
(vi)	Offer a more through-the-line approach	41
(vii)	Spend less time wining and dining and more time working	21

(f) *In which of the following areas could your agency improve its skills?*

(i)	Creativity	55
(ii)	Strategy	50
(iii)	Research	42
(iv)	Planning	36
(v)	Below-the-line	27
(vi)	Media	23

Perhaps not surprisingly *quality* seemed to be main issue in each case. Notable trends were the interest of a sizeable minority in *co-ordinated* communications and in the possibilities of information technology.

Agency structures

7.18 Within the agency, a variety of personnel will be involved in handling the client's business. The account executive or account manager is the lynchpin between the numerous agency personnel and their client. His role is to liaise with client staff and to brief, supervise and co-ordinate the appropriate agency staff at appropriate times.

Exam Tip

The role of the account manager is examined on the Specimen Paper.

7.19 The internal structure of an agency can best be explained by considering how the agency handles a piece of client work.

(a) **The client problem**

A client and agency who have been together for some time will have built up a good working relationship. The agency will understand the client's business, and the motivations and decision-making processes of end consumers. A new product or service, new situation or changing market conditions may provide the starting point for a new role to be performed by advertising. The client needs to brief the account executive on the task in hand.

(b) **The internal briefing**

The account executive will brief the members of the account team who work on the client's business. These members are:

(i) An **account planner**, responsible for using market research to develop advertising strategy for the clients.

(ii) A **creative team** or duo of art director and copywriter, responsible for conceiving a creative idea which meets the advertising brief and working that idea up into visual form and written copy.

(iii) A **media planner/buyer**, responsible for recommending an appropriate media strategy and ensuring media is bought cost effectively.

(c) **The client presentation**

The account executive will present back to the client. He will show examples of how the final advertising execution will look, using rough visuals or storyboards and will explain the rationale for the ideas presented. Depending on the client's reaction to the team's interpretation of the brief, the team will either be asked to go ahead in developing the work, or will be asked to rework their ideas.

The go-ahead stage may include a decision to test the advertising in research prior to full production of the advert.

(d) **Production of advert(s)**

Some simple advertising executions will be carried out almost entirely in-house by the advertising agency. For more complex executions, the agency will buy in specialist functions on behalf of the client.

Whilst production is ongoing, the media department will be involved in the actual commitment of the media budget. Dates, times and positions will be agreed with media owners.

During this stage, there will be continuous liaison between the account executive and the client. The client is likely to attend some of the key production stages such as filming or photography of the commercial.

If time allows, further research may take place to identify the need for any additional changes.

(e) **The campaign appears**

The time span between the briefing of the account executive by the client and the campaign appearing can be as little as six or eight weeks for a simple photographic newspaper execution, to 20 weeks plus for an animated TV commercial. Once the campaign has appeared, it is important that it is properly evaluated against the objectives initially set.

7.20 Members of the account team, who work directly on the client's business in creating a campaign, are those the client is most likely to come into contact with, although the main point of contact will of course be the account executive. There are other behind the scenes staff with whom the account executive must liaise but who will not have direct client contact.

(i) **Accounts department**, responsible for billing the client and paying agency invoices

(ii) **Vouchers department** checks that press adverts appear

(iii) **Traffic department** ensures that jobs are taken through their different stages on time

(iv) A large agency may additionally have an **information** or **library service**, and **legal department**.

Marketing at Work

An IPA (*Institute for Practitioners in Advertising*) booklet 'Getting the most out of the client – agency partnership' suggests the following checklist of questions.

1   Are the client's **corporate objectives**, and the **marketing objectives** that derive from them, entirely clear to both parties? Have the marketing and communications tasks been quantified, together with their financial and profit implications?

2   Are the marketing and communications planners fully informed about **relevant factors in the commercial environment**, particularly:

■ Actual and potential customers
■ Product advantages and limitations
■ Competitors
■ Current or predictable marketing problems
■ Product and marketing development plans?

3   Has sufficient **lead-time** been allowed for planning purposes?

4   Has the agency's **creative policy** been fully thought through and discussed in relation to the defined communications tasks?

5   Do the various creative manifestations (whether advertisements in paid media, explanatory literature, direct mail shots, audio-visual and other sales aids, exhibition stands or press publicity) **express the policy** effectively?

6   Have the **media plan and budget** been fully thought through and discussed? Are both agency and client convinced that they are as cost-effective as available information will permit?

7   If **results** in one area or another have not come up to expectations, has there been a serious effort to find out *why*, instead of shrugging it off or explaining it away?

8   Is there sufficient readiness not just to change for change's sake, but progressively to **improve performance** within an agreed long-term policy?

9   Is the level of **financial and administrative control** satisfactory on both sides?

10   Is the level of **client-agency communications** – in both directions – as good as it should be?

11   Is there **mutual understanding and respect** between the individuals working on the account, on the client and on the agency side?

8   International agency selection and management

International agencies

8.1   Over the last forty years, as companies have expanded their operations internationally, so too have advertising agencies. Many of the large agencies have developed internationally, either by setting up branch offices in foreign countries or by merging with or acquiring local agencies.

8.2   Some agencies expanding abroad prefer to establish international networks or alliances where local offices are not wholly controlled. The argument is that local partners with a stake in the agency will be motivated to produce superior work.

8.3   **Media independents** have mirrored the pattern of agency development and many belong to international media planning and buying groups.

8.4   The trend amongst clients is towards the centralisation of advertising. Many large companies believe **international brands** are best served by an agency operating internationally.

Selection

8.5   Selecting an international advertising agency will follow a series of well defined stages. Locating suitable agency candidates is the first step in the process.

(a)   **Initial search**. Prospective clients will probably be aware of the large multinational agencies based within their own country.

(b)   A **shortlist** of agencies will then be drawn up, usually on the basis of their current work and past track record.

(c)   The **client will then visit** the local offices of those agencies for a series of credentials presentations. These initial visits will help to form an opinion about which candidates should be requested to formally pitch for the client's business. All agencies involved in the pitch should be given the same written brief to follow.

(d)   The **agency's response to the brief** will usually involve a formal presentation backed by a written proposal document with several important features.

- The agency's interpretation of the client's advertising problem
- The creative and media strategy which will ensure objectives are met
- Control mechanisms to be used
- Timing schedules
- Allocation of responsibilities
- Costings
- Terms and conditions of business

(e)   The **final selection decision** will have to take into account many client side factors such as the client's organisational structure and management style, the number of brands to be advertised and the degree to which brands penetrate different markets.

8.6 Other criteria for selection would include the following.

(a) The **types of advertising** and other communications services offered

(b) Level of **expertise** in the client's field of work

(c) The agency's **international creative track record**

(d) The **balance** within the agency of campaigns handled for local clients and those handled for international ones

(e) Whether the agency has **strong local offices** in the client's home and other key markets

(f) The extent to which the agency's **culture and management** style fits with that of the prospective client

(g) The **potential conflict** with existing business handled within the agency network

(h) The **control and co-ordination** procedures in place

Action Programme 4

Your company is about to launch a group of new consumer toiletries products in the Middle East. What sorts of assurance would you want from an advertising agency pitching for this account?

8.7 The **advantages** of using an **international agency**

- Less duplication and dilution of effort on the part of agency and client
- Centralised control of all advertising effort
- Speedy response across markets
- Pooling of talent and ideas from the entire agency network
- Specialised resources available
- Standardised working methods by the agency
- Reduced costs due to economies of scale

8.8 Possible **criticisms of international agencies**

- They provide an uneven quality of service in their different branches
- They produce bland campaigns
- Quality control suffers due to handling hundreds of campaigns simultaneously
- Clients have to tailor their campaigns to suit the conventions of the agency
- Small or medium sized clients suffer a lack of attention from senior staff
- High staff turnover rates exist amongst creative employees

Local or international?

8.9 Despite the increasing presence and power of international advertising and media networks, **independent local agencies** exist in the markets of most countries. Some companies prefer to retain country by country agency arrangements, believing local agencies to be **creatively closer** to their own markets.

8.10 Cherry picking **local agencies** is an appropriate strategy for the client who has only a small portfolio of products to be advertised in a limited number of markets.

Management issues

8.11 **External factors**, such as **market diversity,** segmentation and competition affect the type of co-ordination chosen. **Internal factors,** unrelated to the market, can also dictate the management and co-ordination of international promotions.

(a) **Organisation structure**

    (i) **Local autonomy**. Each subsidiary of an international agency may act as a separate profit centre, attracting its own clients in the home market. Upon appointment, the subsidiary which has brought in the client takes the role of lead agency office, with overall supervision of the client's account.

    (ii) **Central control**. Alternatively, an agency may exert strong central control on regional offices from its headquarters base.

(b) **Organisation culture**. Managers may have different assumptions as to how advertising ought to be done, and it might be a basic hidden assumption that decisions are taken at the top or, on the other hand, by giving local managers their head.

(c) The need for **co-ordinated marketing communications**; firms with worldwide exposure may need central control of marketing communications to ensure they are, in fact, co-ordinated.

Control

The advertiser

8.12 A number of management and control problems need attention.

(a) **Budgets**. If advertising budgets will be split among the different units, the money might be spent less effectively than if control is centralised.

(b) **Timing**. The local advertising campaigns might need to be co-ordinated so that the production side can cope with demand. This is especially true if the firm is an exporter, with a number of local sales offices and warehouses. Local advertisers may generate demands which cannot be met.

(c) Some central review is necessary so that good ideas can be passed around within the group.

(d) **Expertise**. The person responsible for advertising in a 'small' subsidiary may not have a great deal of expertise and may rely too much on local advertising agencies for ideas, rather than controlling the output directly.

(e) Finally, all advertising campaigns need to be **evaluated** for effectiveness.

    (i) Local campaigns may have different objectives, and so appropriate effectiveness measures need to be outlined.

    (ii) It is easier to measure message recall and media buyer efficiency in advanced economies, and there may not be the facilities in less developed countries, even if these promise high growth.

Between client and agency

8.13 Relationships with agencies need to be managed. In many agencies, there will be an 'account manager' responsible for overall liaisons with client. It is in the agency's interests to establish a long-term relationship with the client.

8.14 The agency's account executive is a lynchpin, in communicating the client's needs to the creative team. The agency must also be able to liaise, where necessary, lower down the chain of command, and to communicate to the units of the business, in clear terms, the objectives of the promotion campaign.

Within the agency

8.15 Within the agency, there are the following issues of management and control.

(a) A general problem of **central direction vs local freedom**. This we have already discussed, in terms of tailoring local advertising campaigns or adopting a standard approach.

(b) **Conflicts of interest**: how free are local offices to tout for business, if this involves offending a major client?

(c) How do you co-ordinate the activities of **different creative teams**?

(d) There may exist problems of corporate culture, particularly if an agency grows up as the result of a takeover.

(e) **Performance appraisal** and culture.

(f) Many human resources issues are relevant (eg corporate culture, details of organisation structure).

Current client/agency issues

8.16 As markets expand, clients are likely to forsake traditional, vertical organisational structures where brands are managed on a country by country basis, in favour of a horizontal structure which cuts across country divides. This implies **brand and product management at a centralised level** and may result in a preference for centralised agencies. Consequences might be as follows.

(a) **Clients** are likely to become more demanding of their agencies, as clients strive to ensure that their advertising is accountable and effective. In America, the trend is already towards payment by results. Clients are also likely to demand a larger base of expertise in terms of communications and research services provided.

(b) **Agencies** will continue to expand internationally to meet the needs of their clients. This may lead to a concentration in advertising agency ownership as the large agencies seek to expand still further by way of acquisition and merger.

(c) Agency expansion will also mean that an increasing number of local agency offices will be established in new markets (eg Russia, Eastern Europe, China). Agencies may need to take a **long-term perspective** on emerging markets. Initial resource requirements will be high.

8.17 **Media buying and selling power continues to concentrate**. On the one hand, large international media independents hold consolidated buying power and have the ability to level volume or other discounts. On the other hand there is increasing concentration in global media ownership.

9 Controlling the marketing communications industry

9.1 There are two types of control in the marketing communications industry in the UK, and they are specifically mentioned in the syllabus.

- **Voluntary**. This provides self regulation to promote high standards of practice, often in areas that are difficult to judge in law.

- **Statutory** protection afforded to consumers by the legal framework

Self regulation

9.2 The self regulatory system of advertising control consists of the following bodies, between them covering non-broadcast and broadcast media.

(a) **The Advertising Standards Authority (ASA)**

　(i) This covers the **non-broadcast media** (press, posters, cinema, direct mail, sales promotion, lists and databases), and ensures that the **British Code of Advertising Practice** functions in the public interest. This is the body to which the public and industry complain about advertisements that are not '**legal, decent, honest and truthful**'.

　(ii) It **scrutinises advertisements** in order to anticipate potential complaints and problems

　(iii) It provides a **copywriting advice service** to advertisers

(b) The **Committee of Advertising Practice (CAP)** runs in parallel with the ASA and co-ordinates the trade and professional organisations that comprise the advertising business. Together, the ASA and the CAP ensure that the British Code of Advertising Practice (as put together by CAP) is followed.

(c) The **Independent Television Commission (ITC)** governs television advertising with its own code of Advertising Standards and Practice, which has the force of law.

(d) Radio advertising is regulated by the **Radio Authority (RA)**, which also has its own code with statutory force.

(e) Bodies representing particular sectors in the industry, such as the **Institute of Sales Promotion** and the **Direct Selling Association**, also have their own codes of practice.

Statutory regulation

9.3 This system of self regulation (which is not punishable by the courts) is designed to operate alongside the **legal protection** that is now afforded to the consumer by statute, via government departments including the Office of Fair Trading. Criminal and civil prosecution could be expected by those who break the laws contained within the following:

- Trade Descriptions Act 1968
- Fair Trading Act 1973

- Unfair Contract Terms Act 1977
- Food Act 1984
- Weights and Measures Act 1985
- Consumer Protection Act 1987

Chapter Roundup

- Marketing communicators need to be fully aware of the range of **qualitative and quantitative research data** that is available or obtainable and also of the limitations of research.

- Clients can choose to handle their advertising function in a number of ways. Very large advertisers may keep the function internal to the company. Alternatively, a client can buy in expertise from a **full service advertising agency**, or combine services from a **creative shop** and a **media independent**.

- A variety of agency staff will handle the **workflow** on a client's account. The account executive acts as the key intermediary between agency and client.

- It is the responsibility of the client to provide a **full campaign briefing** for any new piece of advertising work. An oral brief is usually backed up by a written document. The account executive in turn will provide a creative briefing for the specific use of the creative team.

- The **process of selecting a new agency** involves initial search; credentials presentation and shortlist; competitive pitch and final selection. The client will gauge competing agencies against set criteria such as expertise in the client's field of business, previous work handled, resources provided and costs. The final selection decision will involve a judgement about how well the agency has answered the client brief.

- Managing the relationship requires **trust**, a free flow of **information**, proper allocation of **responsibilities** and careful **control**.

- Clients and their **agencies** can choose to handle **international advertising campaigns** in a number of ways. Although a variety of factors will influence the management of any particular campaign, the organisational structure of the client company will play an important role.

- Some agencies have expanded abroad by setting up their own overseas subsidiaries. Others have established alliances with local agencies already in existence.

- There are arguments both for and against using the services of an **international advertising agency**. The current preference amongst large clients is to centralise advertising with an internationally based agency.

- The **standardisation versus adaptation** debate has implications for agency management. If campaigns are totally standardised across markets, the lead market agency office will take the major role in designing and implementing the global campaign.

- There are two types of **control in the marketing communications industry** in the UK.

  Voluntary. This provides self regulation to promote high standards of practice, often in areas that are difficult to judge in law.

  Statutory protection afforded to consumers by the legal framework

Now try questions 12 and 13 in the Question Bank

Quick Quiz

1   Most companies use one agency to handle a portfolio of techniques.

    True ☐

    False ☐

2   Why does it often make no commercial sense to retain in-house the full range of marketing expertise?

    A   Agencies deal with a number of clients and so have relevant up-to-date experience

    B   Each marketing specialism is likely to be only called upon infrequently

    C   Competitive deals on media buying are difficult to achieve for small marketing departments

    D   All of the above

3   The marketing communications industry consists of four principal groups.

    M..........

    A..........

    C..........

    S..........

4   What services can direct marketing agencies offer?

5   How does a full service agency differ from a media independent?

6   What influence has the development of the Internet had on the formal agency selection process?

7   List the elements in the creative brief.

    N..........   B..........

    D..........   B..........

    B..........   C..........

    K..........   T..........

    C..........   P..........

8   What role does the Advertising Standards Authority (ASA) play?

Action Programme Review

1   Each newspaper will have presented the aspects of the data which showed itself in the best light. The *Sunday Times* may have increased overall circulation, and increased the percentage of AB readers. The *Sunday Telegraph* may have lost circulation (you will know from the *Sunday Times*), but have increased its colour magazine readership. The *Guardian* may show a large *percentage* gain in readership, and an increasing number of ABC1 readers. Only by researching back to the original ABC report will you be able to ascertain the truth, but you can come close by cross-referencing the data provided by each, and filling in the gaps from the rivals and by inference. Beware the switch from real numbers to percentages!

2 Market Research Limited will provide retailers of different kinds of products with useful information as well as the product manufacturers, most likely consumer goods given this description. Children and Youth - companies producing goods and services aimed at the youth markets who want to conduct research but may not have the resources to undertake surveys independently.

3 (a) *Project name and description*

   The project needs a meaningful name to refer to. The specifics of the product along with the style are needed.

  (b) *Budget*

   Client and agency needs to be clear about what the budget covers. For example, how many new photographs need to be shot? This will have a bearing on the production costs. The budget for media will determine the choice for media selection. The agency can alter the resources according to the job.

  (c) *Key deadlines*

   Important key deadlines must be listed. The agency should draw up a timetable for presentation of design concepts, proofs, final proofs and so on.

  (d) *Company background*

   A brief description of the company will assist the agency in getting a 'feel' for an appropriate design.

  (e) *Business objectives*

   This will help the agency position the campaign (or whatever the project involves).

  (f) *Background to the brief*

   For example, is this a complete redesign, or just a freshen up?

  (g) *Communications objectives*

   The primary objective may be to increase sales. This can be incorporated in the design.

  (h) *Target audience*

   The agency needs a full description of the characteristics of the audience. This will enable them to design the campaign with them in mind.

  (i) *Proposition*

   Be clear what the USP is. For example, you cannot have high quality, cheap products, top brands and commodity goods all in the same catalogue. With a clear picture, the agency will be able to focus on producing what is required without constantly referring back to the client.

4 Ideally, the agency should be able to assure the client of experience in both consumer market generally and the toiletries market in particular. The agency should have local offices in a number of the Middle East states in which the client does business and be used to handling local and international campaigns in those countries.

The agency must demonstrate knowledge concerning cultural, legal, and media difficulties which may be encountered and be able to propose solutions for overcoming these problems. Proof of successful campaign outcomes for other British based clients advertising in related markets would also be reassuring.

Answers to Quick Quiz

1   False

2   D

3   Media
    Agencies
    Clients
    Support organisations

4   Check your answer against paragraph 3.5

5   A full service agency provides a complete advertising service encompassing creative work, production, media planning and buying. A media independent provides media services (such as planning and buying) only.

6   With the arrival of new media and Internet technology, campaigns are having to be resolved in days rather than weeks, so a long drawn out selection process is inappropriate.

7   Name   Business objectives
    Description   Background to the brief
    Budget   Communication objectives
    Key deadlines   Target market
    Company background   Proposition

8   It covers the non-broadcast media and ensures that the British Code of Advertising Practice functions in the public interest. This is the body which receives complaints about advertisements that are not 'legal, decent, honest and truthful'.

Question bank

BPP
PROFESSIONAL EDUCATION

1 Opinion leaders

Many marketing communication campaigns make use of opinion leaders and opinion formers. Using examples to illustrate your points, explain how and why these personal influencers might be used. **(25 marks)**

2 Different sectors

Using consumer and business-to-business marketing communication campaigns to illustrate your answer, explain the differences in the purpose and use of marketing communications in these two different sectors. **(25 marks)**

3 Marketing communications strategy

Prepare an outline of a talk you are to give to a group of Marketing Managers on the subject of Marketing Communications Strategy. Describe the key elements of the communications planning process, showing how marketing communications strategy is distinguishable from, though part of, overall marketing strategy. Plan to illustrate your talk with examples of strategy drawn from your experience. **(25 marks)**

4 Promotional mix

In your capacity as an entrepreneur who has established a successful regional marketing communications agency you have been asked to make a presentation to an audience of local business people.

Prepare notes for this presentation entitled 'The Strategic Significance of the Promotional Mix'. You aim to cover each of the main tools of the promotional mix and provide brief examples to illustrate each point. **(25 marks)**

5 Push and pull

An office furniture manufacturing company is about to launch a new range of products.

(a) Explain what is meant by a push communication strategy and contrast this with a pull communication strategy. **(13 marks)**

(b) Briefly outline the main characteristics of the marketing communications mix used to reach members of the marketing channel. **(12 marks)**

(25 marks)

6 Internet based communications

For many organisations, business-to-business marketing communications have been transformed by the development of the Internet and related digital technologies. Prepare notes for a meeting at which you are expected to argue the case for the development of Internet based marketing communications for a business or company of your choice. **(25 marks)**

7 Managing global communications

Determine and explain the key issues that an international advertising agency might advise a client about when discussing the development of an co-ordinated marketing communications strategy for consumer products across several countries. **(25 marks)**

8 Measuring success

As manager of a small/medium sized direct marketing business, producing and distributing toiletries for a number of niche markets, prepare a short report for your managing director evaluating the methods available to measure the success of your promotional strategy.

(25 marks)

9 Distribution channels

As the Marketing Operations Manager of a tour operations business that targets package holidays at the 55 and over age group, you have been asked by your Marketing Director to review your distribution strategy.

(a)   Outline the various channels of distribution available.   **(7 marks)**
(b)   Identify a set of criteria for their evaluation.   **(8 marks)**
(c)   Recommend an appropriate strategy for your target market.   **(10 marks)**

(25 marks)

10 Internet

Evaluate the ways in which the rapid growth of the Internet is changing the way businesses communicate with their customers, suppliers and within their own organisations.

(25 marks)

11 Managing outside suppliers

You have been asked to write an article for *Marketing Business* which describes the types of outside resources which various Marketing Directors use, that suggests how outside suppliers should be briefed, and indicates how the relationship with such suppliers might be managed and controlled. You should use examples throughout the article to illustrate the points you raise.

(25 marks)

12 Agency restructuring

It has been noted that many advertising agencies have failed to adapt and restructure themselves in order to keep pace with the increasing demands and international communications strategies of their clients. What are the reasons for this apparent incompatibility and suggest how agencies might adjust to better meet their client needs.

(25 marks)

13 AP Engineering

AP Engineering (AP) is a privately owned civil engineering company, employing approximately 4,200 people in the Asia Pacific region. The company designs and manages the building of major civil engineering projects in a variety of vertical market sectors.

The company wins contracts by bidding for client-specified projects and offering the best (perceived) value for money. The problem with this approach is that the appointed civil engineering company has limited input to the original requirements/specification and, as soon as the project is completed, its involvement is normally terminated. Perhaps even more importantly, the margins earned on such projects are notoriously slim, so in order to grow the business, higher margins need to be generated.

Following a review of the business, AP's new strategy is based upon a total engineering service, one which centres on client needs and their total project requirements, rather than the previous engineering/product focus. In other words, the company now adopts a relationship marketing approach. The emphasis is upon providing added value by shifting the offering both upstream and downstream. Therefore, AP Engineering now provides three connected offerings.

(a)   The front-end work, which involves undertaking the planning and risk analysis work for its clients

(b)   The core work, which is about the design and build aspect of the project

(c)   The tail-end work, which is essentially Facilities Management

Among the many advantages this strategic approach presents, there are two significant benefits. The first lies in the substantially higher margins that the front- and tail-end work attracts. The second concerns the reduced 'resource' wastage by being able to help accurately define the client problem at the earliest possible stage in the project life cycle.

In order to develop and implement this strategy, AP has had to evolve a new skills mix, namely Asset Management and Facilities Management skills. AP chose to purchase a number of small consultancies and formed alliances with other targeted companies specialising in these particular skill areas.

Whilst this might sound reasonably straightforward, AP has had to address further issues concerning the development of a suitable commercial culture for the established employees and those new to the enlarged organisation. The company now views each project as a commercial activity and all employees must adopt increased levels of commercial awareness (eg project risk assessment, the importance of working within budget and invoicing on time). In addition, the employees of the newly acquired organisations have to be incorporated into the values and corporate philosophy of the new company culture. A further issue concerns the way the company presents itself to clients and other key stakeholders.

The organisation is deliberately seeking to develop closer client relationships based upon trust and empathy. It has done this by improving understanding of its clients' business, by getting involved right from the start of a new project, by completing projects on time and within budget, and by a willingness to share sensitive information. It also helps that the AP Engineering brand is highly visible and has developed a credible reputation based upon clients' perceived value.

The level of communication frequency between client and AP Engineering varies across the life of a project. There is a great deal of communication at the outset of a project as the brief is determined by all parties. As the project moves to the design phase, the level of communication tends to fall. However, projects often run tight on their deadlines; hence interorganisational, and even intraorganisational communication levels intensify in an attempt to resolve on-site problems as quickly as possible.

The company realises that personal contact is the most significant communication tool used in the development and maintenance of client relationships but the company is undecided about its communication strategy, and has asked you, in your capacity as Marketing Communications Consultant, for your advice.

Required

As a Marketing Communications Consultant, advise AP with regard to the following questions:

(a)   Identify a communication strategy that AP should pursue in the next year.   **(8 marks)**

(b)   What is the justification for your strategy?   **(12 marks)**

(c)   Which tools of the promotional mix might best be used to implement this strategy? Why?
    (12 marks)

(d)   What might be the core message that needs to be delivered over the next year?
    (6 marks)

(e)   Make a list of the issues that AP might consider before implementing an co-ordinated marketing communications policy.   **(12 marks)**

    (50 marks)

Answer bank

BPP
PROFESSIONAL EDUCATION

1   Opinion leaders

Multi-step Flows of Communication

The flow of communication in a campaign was first considered to be linear, in that information flowed from a **source** through a **channel** to a **receiver**, who then provided **feedback**. This interpretation proved to be inaccurate in that it failed to account for the many variables that can impact on the communication process. One of the main variables is the **influence of other people** as they shape and redirect the **flow**, **content and intended meaning** of messages.

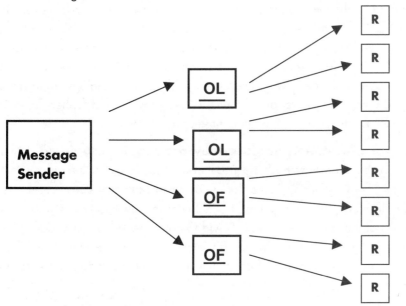

Figure 1
The Two-Step Model
of Communication

The **Two-Step Model** (see Figure 1) and multi-step flow models of communication reflect the potential impact that these individuals might have on communications.

Types of Influencers

There are two main types of influencer, **opinion leaders** and **opinion formers**. The first are usually members of a peer group who have a particular interest and knowledge about a product category or area of interest. They may be friends, family or work colleagues to whom others **(opinion followers)** turn for advice and reassurance when contemplating a particularly significant purchase. They believe the information they receive is both **credible and unbiased** when considered in the light of many commercial messages.

Opinion formers on the other hand are people who are designated as expert and knowledgeable about a particular topic or subject. Very often these people are public figures and it is the nature of their work that bestows the perceived expertise. Opinion formers therefore help shape the thoughts of others by providing information and advice that opinion followers value and believe is credible. Pharmacists, motoring journalists and qualified accountants for example, can provide **credible information** about medicines, cars and taxation issues respectively for those active in the decision making process. This information may be **communicated person to person**, or through broadcast or print **media**.

In a marketing context this is an important factor because if it is possible to identify and **direct marketing communication messages to those people who are capable of influencing** other people, then the implications for the efficiency and effectiveness of marketing communications activities is enormous. A popular advertising format is to use a 'slice of life' approach, where typical members of the target market are observed discussing issues, and one of the characters uses the sponsor's product to resolve the difficulty (eg soap powders and shampoo).

Opinion leaders provide information for a number of reasons. People like to talk about their product purchases because it can relieve post purchase tension, bestow status on them and provide a means of advising and showing care for others (in this case those considering a similar purchase).

Whilst it is difficult to isolate opinion leaders and target them directly, many are known to be **innovators** or part of the **early adopters** group within the **process of diffusion**. These people are actively interested in their topic/area and seek out information in advance of the general population. Identification therefore is helped because they are more likely to attend exhibitions, access specific websites and read the specialist press. For example, when Sony launched the mini disc they targeted specialist music equipment retailers and held premium prices. The hi-fi enthusiasts (opinion leaders) were keen to buy the latest technology (regardless of price) and they then told others (followers) about their discovery, which fed further demand and then allowed Sony to release the product through mainstream outlets.

Opinion formers provide information because they are required to do so, either because it is part of the job, because they have been contracted to do so, or because it is a means of maintaining their own position. Some forms of **sponsorship and celebrity endorsement** can be regarded as opinion forming, if only because they might be regarded as supporting the central object of the sponsorship itself. David Ginola may act as an endorser for L'Oreal haircare products, but he is not known as an expert in haircare. He is seen as supporting the brand in return for a specific reward (which may however induce cynicism in some of the target audience!).

Conclusion

Recognition of the role that opinion leaders and formers can play in assisting the marketing communication process is important if the potential of a brand, and especially new brands and product launches, is to be fulfilled.

2   Different sectors

> **Tutorial note.** This question requires you to explain how the purpose and use of marketing communications differs, not just explain what the differences are between the two sectors. A good answer discusses marketing communications by exploring what the tasks are in the two sectors, how the sector characteristics demand a different approach, and how strategy and tactics can be accommodated through different approaches and the deployment of marketing communication tools.

Introduction

This essay sets out to identify the main differences between **business-to-business** and **business-to-consumer** sectors, and highlights the **impact of these differences on the**

marketing communications strategies. It offers examples of each sector and concludes that the differences are perhaps becoming less pronounced, as companies from both sectors are using a variety of promotional tools and pay considerable attention to the role of **branding**.

	Consumer Markets	Business Markets	Impact on Marketing Communications
No of buyers	Many	Few	Personal selling more relevant in b-t-b markets. Mass communication methods like advertising more often used in consumer markets
Decision making unit	The family	Gatekeepers Influencers Deciders Buyers	Targeting is easier for the consumer markets. Many different types of media and message may be necessary to reach the different members of the DMUs in b-t-b markets
Buyer Behaviour	Influenced by intangible and tangible differences	Rational, based on benefits	Branding important in consumer markets. May also be important in business markets if the buyer is a risk avoider and where there are not many perceived functional differences
	Impulse purchase	Likely to be extended decision making	Sales promotion less relevant in b-t-b markets
	Price may be more important	Functional benefits more important	Impact on marketing communications messages

Main Differences

The main difference between business-to-business communications can be seen in the choice of marketing communications methods and messages. This becomes clear when we consider the communications strategies for the following companies.

Siebel - selling customer relationship management (CRM) systems

This company will rely largely on **personal selling**, with a sales team made up of a number of different experts. Each expert will communicate with his or her opposite number in the client company.

They may do some **trade advertising** but in different magazines - the marketing manager will hear about the benefits of data mining systems in a direct marketing magazine, whereas the IT manager will hear about the technicalities of the system in the IT trade press.

Public relations activity will concentrate on press releases, using a case study approach to reduce perceived risk.

Direct marketing methods will be used alongside **exhibitions and road shows**.

The buying of a full CRM system is extremely expensive, and so the amount spent prior to and post purchase will be high. As the **distribution chain** is likely to be short, the **push strategy** will concentrate on personal selling, allowing control of message and methods.

The message will vary, depending on the role in the decision-making unit, but is likely to be technical. **Profile strategies** are becoming increasingly important here since by having a good profile (and hence brand name) the initial approach to a new customer will be eased.

Thomson Holidays

Much **above-the-line** activity and **sales promotion** activity will be used, to stimulate interest and get a booking from the decision making unit. The whole family is involved and Thomson has recognised this by providing special videotapes for the youngsters showing them what the holiday will be like.

Branding is very important, and as this is a **service**, trust must be established at the beginning. **Membership of trade bodies** will help. Exhibitions are less likely to be used although they may attend lifestyle shows at relevant times. Communications with the marketing channel and a **push strategy** is important here, along with possibly some **direct marketing** activity.

It is important to note, especially in the context of the travel industry, that the adoption of new methods of promotion and booking via the **Internet** has removed some of the reliance on distributors and agents. Public relations is important, and sponsorship of popular television shows like 'Wish you were here?' develop the profile of the company and keeps it in the memory of the target audience.

Conclusion

It can be seen that there are differences between the two sectors, but these differences are becoming blurred as business-to-business markets realise the importance of branding and profiling and consumer markets start to adopt CRM techniques through the opportunities offered by new technologies, especially the Internet.

3   Marketing communications strategy

> **Tutorial note.** This challenging question requires a well structured answer. Students are required to have a thorough knowledge of:
>
> (a)   the business and marketing planning processes
>
> (b)   the marketing communications planning process
>
> (c)   how to co-ordinate the two processes
>
> (d)   examples of practical and successful communication strategies derived from such an co-ordinated process

REPORT

To: Marketing Managers
From: Marketing Communications Manager
Date: June 2003
Ref: Presentation on the subject of marketing communication strategy

1   Audience/objectives

The audience consists of marketing managers. We can assume therefore that they are reasonably well versed in the actual **marketing planning process**.

Although they will be knowledgeable about the planning process their involvement in the detail will vary from person to person. Some will have a close working knowledge; others will only have limited experience of planning directly themselves.

The objectives of the talk can therefore be defined as follows.

(a)   To show how **marketing communication planning is an integral part of the overall company planning process**.

(b)   To demonstrate that **without this link communications planning would be less effective**.

(c)   To illustrate the talk with **practical examples** of strategy.

2   The total planning process

It is vital that marketing managers understand the corporate planning process and the role of marketing planning within it. Furthermore, because marketing communications accounts for a significant share of the marketing mix, it is important also to understand the co-ordination of the marketing communications planning process.

Each level of the organisation has a **hierarchy** of:

- Objectives
- Strategy
- Tactics

The tactics of the upper level then become the objectives of the next level down in the organisation. The levels we can consider usually are:

- Corporate
- Functional (including marketing)
- Activity (including marketing communications)

Clearly the actual situation will vary from company to company according to size, nature of business, and experience of planning. In some predominantly marketing organisations, the link between corporate and marketing objectives will be a very close one. The following diagram shows **how marketing objectives will fit with overall company objectives**.

The strategic marketing and tactical communications planning process within the overall strategic marketing planning process

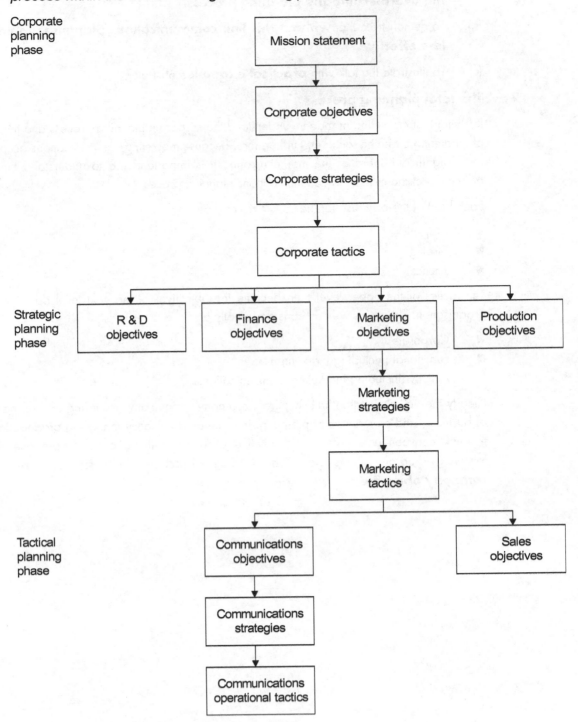

3 The details of the planning process itself

The **situation analysis**, which starts the process, can be seen as part of the overall corporate and marketing analysis and audit process. Four areas of analysis are carried out.

- Internal company analysis
- Analysis of the market and customers
- Analysis of competitors
- Analysis of the external environment

In the case of marketing communications planning in particular, note is made of any strengths, weaknesses, opportunities or threats which have a direct bearing on possible communication solutions. The stages of planning are then as follows.

Objectives

Objectives can be developed under the following headings, depending upon the goals of the campaign for the product in question.

- **Market penetration or**
- **Market development or**
- **Product development**

Each of these broad areas will require a different communications objective.

Strategy

Strategy in communication terms is then best developed by reference to particular target audiences. The most useful approach to this is to work through the steps of:

- **Segmentation**
- **Targeting**
- **Positioning**

Positioning is achieved by a judicious choice of the marketing mix, including promotions or marketing communications.

Tactics

To help to remember a systematic approach to the tactics of marketing communications we can use 3Ms.

- Which **methods**?
- Which **media**?
- Which **messages**?

Implementation

Before the plan can be implemented, the following elements need to be defined.

- **Responsibilities**
- **Timescales**
- **Budgets**

Control

Finally it is necessary to control the effectiveness of the marketing communications process by measuring the achievement of the objectives against the original planned measures and budget.

4   **Examples of strategies**

The most powerful examples of marketing communications strategies are those linked directly to the corporate and marketing strategies. A number of such examples are given below.

(a)   *Boddington's beer*

Whitbread's marketing objective was to launch the beer nationally in a controlled manner. The communication strategy was to promote the brand as an authentic regional beer brewed in Manchester using the slogan 'The Cream of Manchester'. This reflected the creamy full head obtained from this cask conditioned beer. The media strategy was to use the rear covers of colour magazines to promote the golden colour of the product. Television was not used initially in part because of limited brewing capacity.

(b)   *PPP Healthcare*

PPP were facing increasing competition in the health insurance market, especially from the commercial insurance companies such as Norwich Union. The PPP management decided to plan for an increase in market share, to distinguish themselves from their rivals and to rebrand. Marketing communications obviously had an important role to play in this. To increase the awareness of the new company name (PPP Healthcare) and to reposition itself as a healthcare rather than an insurance company, PPP chose to use a television and national press campaign which stressed the support it provides to customers.

(c)   *BMW cars*

BMW cars were exported to the UK mainly as performance cars. BMW (GB) was established in 1979 with the ambitious aim of tripling UK sales by 1990, whilst maintaining high profit-margins. The 'Ultimate Driving Machine' campaign was developed and is still running 17 years later. The marketing communications objectives were:

(i)   To enrich the image of the vehicle
(ii)   To build positive aspects of the image
(iii)   To raise the brand's image

These objectives have been met over a prolonged period in spite of the sales targets meaning that there would be more models on the road, making them ultimately less exclusive. An advertising strategy was developed partly through TV, but mainly through quality colour magazines.

5   Conclusions

These are examples of successful marketing communications strategies which have produced outstanding business results. This has only been possible because the management of those companies have had clear business and marketing objectives which in turn have provided the drive for clear marketing communications plans.

The marketing communications planning process has therefore to be a close and integrated component of the overall planning process. One way of achieving this is to use the SOSTAC planning framework which is memorable, easy to apply and powerful in its effect.

4   Promotional mix

'The Strategic Significance of the Promotional Mix'

by

CIM Student

Slide 1 – Introduction and Welcome

May I take this opportunity to thank you for inviting me to talk to you about marketing communications and in particular the strategic impact of the various elements of the promotional mix.

Slide 2 – Agenda

As you can see, my plan for this session is to first consider the elements of the promotional mix before examining the strategic significance and benefits of an co-ordinated approach to marketing communications practice.

The promotional plan
Strategic significance
Integration
Benefits and difficulties
Conclusions
Questions

I shall be using a few examples to illustrate my points and, of course, I welcome questions at any time, although there will be some time at the end to discuss points of interest.

Slide 3 – The Promotional Mix

Marketing communications is just a part of the total marketing plan or marketing mix. These two elements are often confused, but for clarity the marketing mix is composed of a number of different elements such as price, product, distribution, people and promotional activities. It is these elements in combination that provide the overall marketing plan.

One of these elements, promotion, provides a powerful means by which a marketing mix is presented to its target audience. **The successful communication of the marketing mix is paramount if target markets are to understand the offer being made to them**.

In order to effect this communication, there are a number of **promotional tools** that are used or 'mixed' together. These are:

- Advertising
- Sales promotion
- Public relations
- Personal selling
- Direct marketing

By mixing the tools together in different ways to meet the needs of the marketing plan, it is possible to achieve one of a number of **goals**. These are to:

Create awareness
To persuade
To remind/reassure
To differentiate

The first of these is to **make an audience aware of an offering**, existence or benefits. Before anyone can form an opinion or attitude, it is necessary to be informed of a product's existence.

Alternatively, awareness levels may already be adequate, so the task becomes that of **persuading an audience to try a product**, or to resist defecting to a competitive product offering.

A third requirement may be to **remind and/or reassure** an audience of a product or of the experiences associated with a previous purchase.

Finally, communications can be used to **differentiate a product offering** and set it aside from the competition.

Slide 4 – Strategic Significance

Plans are the articulation of strategy, a means of bringing together the various means by which a strategy is implemented and goals achieved.

Promotional strategy is about the overall direction and focus of communications. There are three main options: a pull strategy, a push strategy and a profile strategy.

A **pull strategy** is concerned with communications directed at end users or customers.

A **push strategy** concerns those channel partnerships formed to deliver products and services to end users, commonly referred to as the trade or distributors.

A **profile strategy** concerns the way an organisation is presented to a range of stakeholder audiences and is essentially about corporate image and reputation management.

These three strategies (3Ps) are not used independently of each other. They need to work together, and management need to make a judgement about the appropriate balance.

Please remember that this balance need not be static, but must be expected to shift as the context within which **each communication campaign changes and evolves**, as the environment inside and outside an organisation reshapes itself.

Slide 5 – Co-ordination

If this is to be achieved, then understanding and setting the strategic balance of an organisation's communications is very important.

For successful implementation of each of the 3Ps it is necessary to utilise a different promotional mix. The tools have different properties and enable different goals to be achieved.

For example, when launching a new consumer product such as Sunny Delight, it is first **necessary to create distribution (push)** through the major grocery multiples. This involves **personal selling and direct marketing**.

Once distribution is secured, **awareness needs to be established in the target audience**. This strategy (pull) may require the use of **mass communications**, which involves the use of television, poster and print advertising. This can be supported with **public relations activities** designed to create credible third party comment, and **endorsement** of the brand.

Procter & Gamble do not use a profile strategy to any greater degree partly because of their multi-brand policy. However, other companies, such as the AA or British Airways focus a great deal of their communications on raising and sustaining their corporate brands. The **corporate brand** can act as an umbrella, under which **product brands** can be infused with the corporate ideal and values, saving investment and human resources.

Slide 6 – Benefits and Difficulties

The promotional mix should be co-ordinated if a consistent message is to be conveyed to each of the various audiences with which a brand and its parent organisation interacts. By adopting a strategic approach, promotional activities can be targeted, streamlined, made efficient and effective.

If the goal is to **differentiate through positioning**, then by using the different tools of the promotional mix and by delivering clear messages positioning can be used as a form of sustainable competitive advantage and thus be difficult for a competitor to replicate.

Communications used by Procter & Gamble enabled Sunny Delight to be positioned as a distinct new refreshing drink for kids. The communications also informed people where to find it in supermarkets (chiller cabinets) and where it should be stored at home (in refrigerators).

Slide 7 – Conclusions

The promotional mix consists of different tools which are each capable of undertaking different tasks. By setting a communication strategy and then by using the right mix of tools in the right way, it is possible to create awareness, persuade, remind/reassure and differentiate a product brand or a corporate brand.

Slide 8 – Questions

Have you any questions?

5 Push and pull

> **Tutorial note.** A contrast between push and pull should be made in part (a), and part (b) should emphasise the importance of key account management and long-term support.

(a)   There are three strategies that can be used by this company when launching a new range. They can be used independently, or together, depending upon the resources available, the target audiences, the objectives set, the competition and the present reputation of the company.

  (i)   **Push**- to influence the distributor to stock the new range and develop our relationship. They, in turn, will encourage the end user to buy our range at point of sale.

  (ii)   **Pull**- Communications aimed at the end consumer so that they be aware of the range and wish to buy.

  (iii) **Profile**- aimed at all relevant stakeholders, including internal audiences, to build company reputation.

  Our company has an established reputation amongst office retailers, but the new range is also appropriate for home office use. Therefore a mix of push and pull strategies should be used.

  Firstly, distributors will be encouraged to take the full range and display it well, and include it in their catalogues and own promotions (push).

  Secondly, a pull strategy aimed at end users (both purchasing managers and home customers) will create awareness, generating demand and store traffic. This will in turn encourage distributors to support the launch.

(b)   **Suggested mix to reach channel members**

  (i)   **Personal selling** is important in business-to-business relationships since it builds trust. The sales force can demonstrate the product benefits and negotiate discounts and local promotional support. They will also advise on **merchandising** displays and give training.

  (ii)   **Point of purchase** material will be made available, stressing the quality of the product, along with literature that can be used by the distributor to mail out to their customers or distribute in store.

(iii) **Non personal direct marketing**. This might include a secure **extranet** site, so that distributors can get information on stock availability, order status and product specifications. **Direct mail** to launch the range may be used to pre-warn distributors, or initially to tell new retailers about the range, and the special benefits of stocking the range.

(iv) **CD ROMs** could be mailed out to distributors with room design software included, so that distributors can offer this benefit to their customers when selling the new range. The disk will carry the catalogue.

(v) **Sales promotions.** Special discounts for large orders or pre launch discounts will encourage sales into the distributor. Incentives and competitions for distributor sales teams will encourage their support at the point of sale.

(vi) **Exhibitions** supported by corporate hospitality will create interest in the new range and facilitate dialogue between the company and its distribution network.

(vii) **Advertising** in trade journals will create awareness and may encourage opportunities for PR support.

(viii) **Public relations** will feature the new range and tell of the support that will be offered to the distributors on taking the new range

Conclusion

Support from members of the supply chain is extremely important for a furniture manufacturer such as ours. **Push strategies must be undertaken to encourage dialogue with channel members**, and ensure that they have the right tools to sell on the products. The mix will be used to create awareness, persuade distributors to take stock, develop relationships and create sales. The push strategies must be integrated with pull techniques to ensure long-term success for the new range.

6 Internet based communications

> **Tutorial note.** This is a straightforward question with an easy format. Facts about the Internet need to be related to the context of the question. Better answers will recognise the development of relationships as an important factor, and address the strategic aspects.

In business-to-business (B2B) markets, organisational **buying behaviour** is more complex than that observed in consumer markets. This is because of the increased number of people involved in the **decision making process** and the nature of the relationships between organisations.

As a result of this and other factors, marketing communications in the **B2B** market is traditionally characterised by the predominance of **personal selling**, and relatively little use of advertising. In fact it is the complete reversal of business-to-consumer based promotional activity **(B2C)** where **mass media communications** have tended to be the most important route to the target audience.

The development of the **Internet and related digital technologies** has introduced new ways in which audiences in both sectors can be reached. There are many other ways in which organisations can benefit from these developments but these notes will concentrate on communications in the B2B sector.

Very briefly, the Internet and digital technologies can lead to

- Faster communication
- More information
- Lower costs
- More effective transactions
- A reduction in sales force personnel costs
- Improved relationships with intermediaries
- The development of new/revised types of intermediary
- Potential for improved levels of customer satisfaction
- Speedier problem resolution
- Greater accuracy and less noise in the communication system
- Provision of exit barriers for intermediaries
- Improved use of the communication mix

I will not go into these in detail but will highlight some of the points made.

In the B2B sector, the development and maintenance of **profitable relationships** is important. Part of marketing communications' role is to develop these relationships by **reducing perceived risk and uncertainty**. It also needs to provide **clarity** and provide fast, pertinent and timely **information** in order that decisions can be made.

Loyalty

Loyalty between organisations can be improved by **targeting information and customised messages** at the right people within the partner organisation. **Speed of response** to customer questions, and the **clarity of the information** provided, is important for the development of trust and loyalty.

Productivity

Productivity should be increased as electronic communication not only saves time, but also **shortens the time between order and delivery**.

Reputation

The reputation of our organisation should be enhanced considerably, not only through our website but also through the way we are perceived to meet the needs of our customers. Subject to the actions of our competitors in this area, we may also have a competitive advantage.

Costs

The costs of our communications can also be considerably reduced. Just as sales literature and demonstration packs take time to prepare, change and update, and are quite expensive with a great deal of wastage, **brochureware on the website** is fast, easily accessible and adaptable.

Further website development will enable us to collect names and addresses, respond to **e-mail** questions and provide **data** for our sales force. If we develop the website still further, then **e-commerce transactions** will enable routine orders to be completed quickly and at a lower cost.

This frees up the sales force to visit established customers more often, and gives them the opportunity to open new accounts and attentively manage those accounts that are strategically important. This is referred to as **key account management**.

Marketing communications mix

Digital technologies enable the **collection of data** for use through online and offline sources. So our **direct marketing** activities can be improved, and our **sales promotions** targeted to provide real and valued incentives. Even our **public relations** activities can benefit by placing suitable material on our web pages.

Effectiveness

Finally, digitally-based communications can improve the **accuracy of the information** we provide and also enable us to measure the **effectiveness** of our marketing communication activities. However, we must not forget that **offline communications** will still be important, and these new communication formats should be considered as an addition to rather than a substitution for our current marketing communications.

Now, whilst I have set out the advantages we must be aware of some of the drawbacks.

Traditional customers

Internet access for some of our smaller business partners may be restricted and they may prefer to continue having **face-to-face contact** with our sales force. This must be respected. We need to deploy our new marketing communications mix carefully and not impose it on unwilling organisations.

Investment/set up costs

The set-up costs will be expensive, and an **appropriate investment approach** needs to be adopted. Some parts of this technology can also lock us into relationships which might be difficult to get out of, should conditions change. In effect, these are barriers to exit for each party.

Legal and security

There will also be some legal and information **security issues** that we need to address in order to **reduce any risk** our partners might perceive.

End notes

To conclude and summarise, our marketing communications with business partners will improve through improved efficiency and effectiveness, which in turn will be reflected in the nature and **quality of the relationships** we hold. This will ultimately be reflected in our overall performance in meeting our corporate goals.

Improved trust, commitment and a higher propensity to share information must lead to increased business performance. The development of Internet based communications is a strategic decision that needs to be thought through in terms of the impact it will have on the way we and our partners do business.

7 Managing global communications

> **Tutorial note.** This question requires a detailed look at the effect on marketing communications strategy of the issues of globalisation. It is often tempting to repeat the typical International marketing theory without considering the impact of these on the management of the campaign. This answer takes the form of a presentation, although you may have chosen to do a standard essay. Either approach is fine, given the question wording.

Presentation to Client, 'Happy Foods'
By
'Global Advertising'
Going Global- the Pitfalls and Opportunities

Introduction

Our agency has been helping to develop the advertising for your UK business for several years. Now we would like you to consider us as you expand your operations further into international markets. Today we would like to present to you some of the issues that you might wish to consider when developing your international marketing communications strategies. Our presentation this morning will cover the following.

- Strategic issues in international marketing communications
- Pitfalls and opportunities
- How 'Global Advertising' can help

Strategic Issues

Branding

Although your brand is extremely well established in UK markets, it is relatively unknown in the new regions. A decision must be made on the **branding strategy** - should the brand be **positioned** in a different way in the new markets? As an imported brand there may be an opportunity to position the product as a luxury, which will command a much higher price than the cheaper home brands. This will affect the promotional **mix**, **media** (target markets will be exposed to a different media) and **message**.

Your **marketing communications objectives** will tend to focus on **creating awareness**, rather than developing brand values to maintain market share. This will require a potentially large **share of voice**.

Push or pull?

As a new entrant to the market, a **push strategy** will need to be considered, particularly in markets with **strong distribution networks**. However, shelf space is not necessarily the only challenge, and **local custom and legislation** must be considered. For example:

- Would **sampling** by door drop be allowed?
- Could **coupons** be offered to allow a trial of the product?
- What **merchandising** is possible?

Standardisation or adaptation?

The marketing communications debate needs to reflect whether a **standardised global strategy** is acceptable, or whether an **adapted campaign** is more suitable to reflect tastes, culture, and market trends.

A standardised approach offers benefits in terms of global **synergy** and **economies of scale**, and allows a corporate **branding** approach, but there is the danger that the brand message becomes bland, and irrelevant to local markets. The communications must take account of the **political, legal, economic, social and technological differences** in the new markets.

The following must be considered before a solution to this question is found.

Pitfalls and opportunities

1 Market differences
2 Internal organisation
3 Message
4 Media
5 Measurement and research

1 **Market differences**

(a) **Social and cultural aspects**

As you operate in the food industry, your products may be culturally bound, and so may not be eaten in the same context as in domestic markets. The **message** will therefore be affected, along with **packaging**.

(b) **Language**

Checks will be needed to ensure that your **brand names and labelling** do not offend local tastes, and to see if promotional material needs to be accurately **translated** in full. Messages using **music and non-verbal content** are often considered better if a global standardised approach is going to be taken.

(c) **Competition**

The level and nature of competition may well affect the best tactics to use in the promotional mix. If **sales promotion** is the norm for this type of product then some use of this may be necessary to enter distribution channels and consumer **awareness sets**.

(d) **Economic aspects**

This may affect the positioning of the brand - if a **premium position** is to be taken then the **message and media must be consistent** with this, even if the actual price is lower than may be expected in home markets.

(e) **Legal aspects**

As referred to above, we must ensure that no laws are broken. **Knocking copy** is not tolerated in some countries.

(f) **Technology**

The **use of and access to technology** does vary across the world. Although the website in the UK has been extremely effective at gaining involvement from children, this may not be the case in all countries. The address of the website needs to be considered to suit local conditions.

2 **Internal organisation**

Your company is not manufacturing overseas at the present time, but there will be **local sales and marketing** people on the ground. It is important that you use an **agency** which has local offices and contacts in the countries in which you operate. They will be able to advise on the above issues, and also **feedback** information on how the campaign is being received.

It will be important not to alienate the local managers, and so one way to **manage the campaign** would be to **circulate the strategy in advance** to gain approval and allow them an opportunity to **brief local agencies** on their own needs. There will be some aspects of the Happy Foods brand position that you will wish to keep constant, and the use of a **brand manual** showing what can and cannot be altered will be essential.

3   **Message**

This should be appropriate to the local market needs, method and media used, but reflect **consistent brand values**.

4   **Media**

Availability of media for advertising varies from country to country. Cinema advertising and the use of radio may be more appropriate in rural India, but the use of press advertising may be significant elsewhere.

The availability of **media research** to help with media selection is potentially less sophisticated. Local guidance about the best space to buy will be necessary. Although there are many more **global media** available (e.g. satellite stations like MTV) these may not be appropriate for all audiences. **Local advertising opportunities** might exist and should be used. **Set an objective in terms of share of voice expected**, and then allow local representatives to buy media, taking account of last minute opportunities, within pre-determined **budget constraints**.

5   **Measurement and research**

Access to relevant measurement methods and market research could be sketchy, and so decisions may need to be based on less scientific methods. It remains the case that progress towards the achievement of objectives must be measured appropriately.

How can we help?

Global Advertising has offices or associates in the first countries that you will be investigating, with skilled local personnel to handle your business. Although they will liaise with your own local staff, you will have access to what is going on through our own **account directors** who will be able to **consolidate all local activity** on your behalf.

We can advise on **local legal, economic and cultural differences** and we understand **local media buying** conditions. In addition, our **full service capabilities** extend to overseas markets, through our creative and other associates. This will save costs in the long term, since a single contact ensures that **communication is more direct** and less likely to be distorted.

Most importantly, because of our existing relationship with you we feel that we understand your brands and can ensure an integrated brand strategy, albeit with local differences.

8   Measuring success

Tutorial note. The key in this question is the term 'direct marketing'. Do not fall into the trap of discussing evaluation for any type of mass communication campaign.

> How successful is our direct Marketing?
>
> To: Managing Director
>
> From: Manager
> Bubbles Aromatherapy Ltd
>
> June 2001

> Contents
>
> 1 Introduction and background
> 2 Direct marketing methods
> 3 Evaluation methods
> 4 Appraisal of methods
> 5 Conclusions

Introduction

Since our launch last year it is now time to formalise the **effectiveness of our direct marketing techniques**. This will enable us to review our plans for the next few years and also provide a benchmark for measuring subsequent activity. The report will look at each method in turn, and **evaluate** each one to see if a better method could be used.

Background

Bubbles Aromatherapy is a relatively small company offering a range of up market aromatherapy toiletries. **Direct marketing** has been the main method of distribution and communication since the launch.

(a) The **target market** consists of a relatively small niche of prosperous buyers who are involved in alternative products, seeing aromatherapy as an important part of their **lifestyle**.

(b) Distribution via chemists and supermarkets would require heavy investment in **mainstream advertising**. This would negate our positioning as 'real' aromatherapy products.

(c) The launch has been supported by some fairly successful **public relations** activity.

Direct marketing methods

The following direct marketing methods have been utilised at various stages throughout the year. The method used to evaluate the campaign is stated in each section.

(a) **Direct response advertising**, offering a free catalogue, to stimulate interest and contribute towards a database, in a number of different publications including female titles, some specialist alternative therapy magazines and small classifieds in more mainstream titles like *The Guardian*.

These have been evaluated using the number of catalogue **enquiries**, and **subsequent sales**. Analysis has been undertaken on an ad-by-ad and title-by-title basis.

(b) **Direct mailing** of catalogue twice a year to British Association of Retail Therapists list, subscribers to *Alternative Today* and own list of previous buyers.

Evaluated through number of orders, value of orders and cost of order.

(c) **Internet banner advertising** on websites of similarly minded manufacturers. Orders not taken online, but number of 'hits' established and also 'click throughs' on the site monitored.

(d) **Telemarketing** - customer rings order through, and telemarketing team is charged with order administration and **customer satisfaction surveys**.

Evaluated through **sales conversions**, length of call, **survey results**.

(e) **Personal selling – product demonstrations** are held each year at Women's Institute meetings.

(F) **Evaluation methods**

Evaluated by **sales** per event and per number of attendees.

Method appraisal

It would appear that much of our direct marketing activity is wasted, since the evaluation suggests that much of our activity yields little in the way of sales. This may be due to a flaw in the evaluation methods used, which are largely **quantitative**. The following suggestions are made, which may complement our existing evaluation methods.

(a) **Customer lifetime value** might be a more strategic measurement method.

(b) **Conversion rates** and **cost per sale** would demonstrate where effort is wasted.

(c) **Measurement must be related to objectives**. Only direct methods have been used so far, based on sales, which is a fairly crude measure.

(d) Measurement on **qualitative issues** should be undertaken. This would give some understanding on why customers bought (or did not buy).

(e) **Methods should be tested** before they are rolled out. Testing of lists, media used, message, promotional offer and all elements of our direct marketing is possible as we now have some history of what has been successful in the past.

(f) Direct marketing is just one aspect of our **overall marketing communications strategy**. The other communications strategies that we use (such as public relations) must also be evaluated.

(g) More use could be made of our **online** presence, and it is also hoped that this method can be used to pre- and post-test our strategies through online surveys.

(h) Our **direct selling activity** is an ideal basis for **focus groups** to evaluate our own and competitors' marketing communications strategy.

Conclusions

Evaluation of direct marketing activity is crucial and many methods can be used to complement our existing methods of evaluation. However as a small company we should not be too sophisticated, and should ideally use evaluation to help identify the best possible future strategies and keep us from wasting money on the worst ones.

9 Distribution channels

Review to: The Marketing Director
From: The Marketing Operations Manager
Date: June 2003
Subject: DISTRIBUTION STRATEGY

Introduction and outline of the various channels available to our company

Distribution is increasingly important for effective marketing operations in the modern context. Innovative distribution can create competitive advantage, as evidenced by Amazon.com's use of the Internet. **Alternative distribution channels** today include the following.

- Manufacturer to agent/factor/broker to wholesaler to retailer to consumer/user
- Manufacturer to wholesaler to retailer to consumer/user
- Manufacturer to retailer to consumer/user
- Manufacturer to franchisor to consumer/user
- Manufacturer to consumer/user

In the latter case, manufacturers can use **mail order** or a **call centre**, perhaps **outsourced**. Companies increasingly use a multiplicity of channels to reach different target market segments.

In our company's case there are two alternative channels.

- Wholesaler (tour operator) to retailer (travel agent) to consumer/user

- Tour operator to consumer/user

The use of travel agents entails the payment of a **commission**, which raises the question of whether we should market **direct to consumers** via the **Internet, direct mail brochures, or telemarketing** (or all three). Another option would be to **vertically integrate** downwards, by setting up our own travel agencies. Furthermore, we could offer **exclusive distribution** to retail chains (Co-op Travel), perhaps in the form of own-brand or label. We have to recognise that distribution channels are changing and look for opportunities to increase business by seeking new outlets.

Criteria for the evaluation of alternative channels

Overall distribution strategy, whether **intensive, selective or exclusive**, needs to be **consistent with brand strategy**. If we want to develop an up-market brand image, then we should pursue an exclusive distribution strategy.

Equally, there should be **strategic fit** between distribution and company objectives. The right **channel mix** is also dependent on:

- Market size
- Market dispersion
- Buying behaviour and complexity
- Product characteristics
- Technology
- Competition
- Regulations

When **evaluating individual channel choices**, the following evaluation criteria apply.

- Access to and coverage of target market segments
- Cost of operation and margins
- Expected return

- Amount of control over brand
- Reputation/image
- Compatibility of culture
- Creditworthiness
- Degree of promotional support needed
- Staff knowledge/expertise
- Power-dependency relationships

The acid test when deciding whether to market direct to consumer is – can we do a better job than the travel agents at an equivalent cost, or can we do an equivalent job at a lower cost?

Recommendation of an appropriate strategy for our target market

Since we address **a number of target markets** with a **range of products**, a **multiplicity of channels** is appropriate.

For our exclusive **luxury** cruises, a **direct channel** is the most appropriate since this affords us maximum control over the quality of the service. Advertising the cruises can be targeted more accurately by choosing media used by people with particular characteristics, who would not appreciate having to consult a down-market travel agent catering for the mass market.

Equally, our new range of **special interest** tours is best suited to a direct channel using the **Internet**, which can be backed up by a dedicated chat-room and help-line.

For our **standard packages**, we should continue to use the travel agents who provide a service meeting the needs of our target customers for this product, and who have the necessary presence in the population conurbations.

10 Internet

> **Tutorial note.** To produce a good answer, you need to stick closely to the question asked - ways in which the Internet is being used (and will be used) by suppliers, customers and internally. Do not be tempted to reproduce general lists of advantages and disadvantages of the Internet.

What is the Internet?

The Internet is a worldwide network of computers. These are linked together so that users can search for and access data and information provided by others.

The World Wide Web is the element which provides facilities such as full-colour, graphics, sound and video. **websites** are points within the network created by members who wish to provide an information point for searchers to visit and benefit by the provision of **information** and/or by entering into a **transaction**.

Current uses and development issues

There are an increasing number of interactive uses that the Internet can be used for:

- Communication (information provision)
- Product development
- Facilitating transactions
- Fostering dialogue and relationships with different stakeholders

The attributes of the Internet that allow for these uses also need to be considered.

- High speed of interaction
- Low cost provision and maintenance
- Ability to provide mass customisation
- Global reach and wide search facilities
- Instant dialogue
- Multi-directional communications (eg: to suppliers, customers and regulators)
- High level of user control
- Customer (visitor) driven
- Moderate level of credibility

Use with customers

The use of the Internet by organisations with their customers has generally to date been focussed upon the **business-to-business sector** rather than consumer end users. Those customers that have used the Internet do so primarily in search of entertainment and information. Web sites have become increasingly sophisticated and are a useful means of meeting the needs of customers and organisations.

Businesses can communicate more **cost-effectively** with their customers and provide a wide range of facilities. The **volume of customer traffic** that can be handled is far larger and quicker than through traditional means. Sales literature, product designs and innovations, ideas, price lists, complaints, sales promotions such as competitions, and orders and sales can all be undertaken over the Internet.

The objectives are essentially two-fold. The first is to **generate the first steps of a relationship** (or maintain one already established). The second is the collection of **customer profile information** to be added to the database. Names, addresses and other demographic and psychographic data can be collected without any human intervention or the associated costs.

The execution of financial transactions over the Internet has been a stumbling block, due to the fear of fraud. More **secure systems** and protection devices are now becoming available and this will spur the growth of purchasing activities.

A further development is to **integrate the Internet with other elements of the marketing and promotional mix**. For example, the Tesco and Sainsbury's initiatives to develop home shopping have met with great success in influencing shopping patterns.

Use with suppliers

The use of the Internet with suppliers will provide a more **dynamic form of communication exchange** via

Problem identification

Formation of solutions, including tailored product modifications

Constant dialogue opportunities

These factors will enable suppliers to forge **closer relationships in the marketing channel**.

Marketing communications opportunities will arise where, for example, **new products** can be presented to suppliers much more quickly, **sales literature and product specification data can be relayed instantly** and advertising materials presented more effectively.

Use within organisations: intranets

Internally the greatest advance is the development of intranets. The provision of internal, password-protected communication networks allows for the **rapid dissemination of corporate and marketing information**. For global organisations this represents a tremendous step forward, as an intranet can overcome time barriers and allow for the transmission of materials to all parts of a company.

The development of and interest in **internal marketing** has been assisted by this new form of communication. The involvement of staff, and the motivational opportunities afforded by intranet technology, enable employees and management to work more closely together.

Future of the Internet

The future of the Internet is bounded only by imagination and technological advances. Essentially there will be greater **interactive opportunities**, which will enable a **range of stakeholders** to interact with organisations for information, education, entertainment, products, services and financial transactions quickly and efficiently.

11 Managing outside suppliers

Article (Marketing Business): 'Getting to grips with outsourcing'

From: A Marketing Director

1   **Introduction**

In this world of increasing globalisation and faster change, organisations need to continually **review their core competences** and to consider which marketing activities might be better **outsourced**.

Generally speaking, if an outside supplier can do a better job than your own company at an equivalent cost, or an equivalent job at a lower cost, then a switch should be made.

When reviewing the possibilities, the process should cover

- The types of outside marketing resources the company could use
- How contenders for these services should be briefed
- How the selected suppliers should be managed and controlled

2   **Types of outside marketing resources we could use**

2.1   **Consultants**

There are a great many management and marketing consultants in the UK. The CIM, for example, provides a comprehensive service. Some consultants specialise in design, research or promotion.

2.2   **Marketing research agencies**

Not many organisations have all the in-house facilities needed to cater for their total information requirements. Nearly all organisations find it necessary to outsource surveys to specialists.

2.3   **Promotional agencies**

There are a great variety of promotional agencies, ranging from advertising agencies to agencies specialising in sales promotion, PR and telesales/telemarketing. With sales promotion there is a range of specialists in packaging design, POS display material, exhibition services, mail order and so on.

The opportunities provided by the Internet have given rise to a number of agencies specialising in website design.

2.4 Marketing training organisations

Universities and professional bodies can be used to improve the skills of marketing departments and provide specialist courses.

2.5 Full-service agencies

These endeavour to supply the full range of marketing services from consultancy to marketing research and promotion and are particularly suitable for smaller organisations.

2.6 New product development

This is a controversial issue and covers a very wide field, but pharmaceutical companies, for example, will often subcontract at least part of their extremely costly and risky laboratory research to a number of selected specialists, such as biotechnology companies.

3 How outside suppliers should be briefed

3.1 The **briefing** of outside suppliers is of paramount importance, since an inadequate brief will lead to misunderstandings.

3.2 We need to adopt a position of mutual **trust** with our suppliers. Being able to trust them should be the most important criterion for doing business. We can then provide them with a full statement of our requirements.

3.3 Our detailed requirements should include a full **specification** of the services we are seeking, the standards we expect and any special conditions of contract such as penalty clauses.

3.4 We should make suppliers aware that competitive tenders will be sought.

3.5 Suppliers should be given the right to query the detail of our requirements, and to make suggestions for any amendments.

3.6 An indication of the **budget** and any other limitations should be provided where appropriate.

3.7 Suppliers should be made fully aware of the **timescales**.

3.8 Finally, all suppliers should be made aware that their performance will be **appraised**.

4 How suppliers might be controlled and measured

A decision has to be made whether to **apply controls selectively**. A supplier we use irregularly or for small amounts should not be subjected to the same degree of control as a supplier whose goods/services are a major item of expenditure.

However, the answer cannot depend on spend alone. We could, for example, be spending relatively little on an agency on concept testing for a proposed new product. However, this proposed new product could be vital to our future and therefore the agency could require stricter control than a supplier of high cost materials who has proved to be highly dependable for a number of years.

The nature of the control should perhaps be different according to the nature of the product/service being bought. For some materials suppliers we would, for example, have scientific tests on quality and maintain records of deliveries late/on time/before time.

However, for our advertising agency, control might be more informal and based on frequent personal meetings.

Bearing in mind the above difficulties in setting standards and the rating of performance, I would recommend the following controls.

- Suppliers' name
- Type of goods/services supplied
- Estimated annual expenditure
- Record of complaints made by us
- Record of actions taken by supplier

> *Performance standard*
>
> *Rating (scale 0 to 10)*
> *Notes*

- - Quality of product/service
- - Reliability
- - Prices relative to competitors
- - Working relationships
- - Overall
- Special terms and conditions relative to this supplier
- Recommended special controls, if any
- Recommended frequency of review
- Person responsible for review, position/department

There should, following the initial review, be a **rolling system of reviewing** outside suppliers, on the recommended frequencies and against the agreed standards. **Formal ratings are preferred to informal measures**. The frequency of the reviews and the nature of the standards set should be changed in accordance with circumstances.

All suppliers should be informed about our review system and invited to comment/co-operate.

5 **Conclusion**

There are of course a number of implications for other business functions in the decision to extend the number of subcontracted marketing activities. Not the least of these are the implications for staffing and finance. It will be necessary for me to meet with co-directors before taking any further action on this organisational issue.

12 Agency restructuring

Introduction

Advertising agencies have been subjected to a number of significant external pressures in the last ten to fifteen years. Their response to these pressures has been mixed and in many cases cautious, perhaps mindful of the need to monitor and avoid fashion swings and management fads.

Reasons for possible incompatibility

The reasons why some of these organisations have failed to keep pace with their clients' needs are as follows.

1   Hierarchical structures
2   Market complexity
3   Reliance on the commission payment scheme
4   Failure to implement integrated marketing communications
5   The plethora of new media and subsequent fragmentation
6   Audience fragmentation
7   The variable quality of overseas support
8   Poor positioning
9   Agency complacency

Many of these points are interrelated and the causality factor often hard to determine. Time does not permit a full examination of all these issues, so I shall select a few and consider some of the points in more detail.

The structure adopted by many advertising agencies is **hierarchical** and in many ways ill-suited to flexibility and the necessary **speed of reaction** required by many clients. These structures have strong historical roots, and in that sense are hard to change.

International operations demand consideration and preferably experience of **cross cultural issues**, **networking** and, in many cases, **delegation** to country agencies, some of whom may require more support and guidance than others. Hierarchies require authority and control in order that they function appropriately. Such conditions may not always exist overseas, may be incompatible with client structures and may hinder the decision making process.

Developing international and global brands is a complex activity which requires special skills, from both a client and agency perspective. These may be hard to secure. When looked at in terms of the level of investment associated with **international brand support**, the issue becomes increasingly more complex and difficult.

Management consultancies have taken a lot of strategic work away from many advertising agencies. This has had a knock-on effect in terms of international brand support. Poor positioning therefore has been a contributory factor to this problem of incompatibility.

The plethora of **new media and subsequent fragmentation** of both audiences and media have proved problematic. Some traditional full service agencies have developed central **media buying** units in order to provide added value for clients, but the issue of media planning and scheduling has become more complex. When an international dimension is superimposed, so the degree of complexity increases.

Complacency and a lack of drive to change is a contributory factor in many cases. A predilection to preserve the status quo regarding their relationships with clients suggests that some agencies lack strategic vision and may also not be fully aware of their **clients' goals**. The fault may, perhaps, lie with clients not communicating their marketing communication strategies effectively. Matters are certainly not helped by the willingness of many clients to change agencies mid term.

How might agencies adjust?

There are therefore, many potential gaps between the expectation of clients and their respective agencies. One of the choices agencies need to make is whether to anticipate client needs internationally or whether to remain orientated to the domestic arena and make ad hoc arrangements to support any client who develops an overseas requirement.

How integrated does the agency need to be?

Full integration for all agencies is obviously not practical or strategically viable. However, in terms of meeting client needs, restructuring and adaptation to the new environment with a view to establishing differing levels of integration, and in this case international support, may be useful. Agencies need to establish the right balance to suit their client needs.

At the heart of this problem about incompatibility there seem to lie three main issues. These are about **structure, strategy and relationships**. Agencies and clients need direction and knowledge in order that they can manage these three variables and in doing so reduce or at least minimise any gap in expectations and support.

13 AP Engineering

> **Tutorial note.** Under this syllabus, the intention in the mini-case is to direct candidates to specific parts of the scenario, and not use a marketing communications plan. The question is essentially about corporate branding and marketing communications strategy. Parts (c) and (e) are the most challenging. Part (c) requires some acknowledgement and understanding of the differences between emotional and rational messages for low and high involvement scenarios.
>
> Implementation issues for marketing communications planning are different from development issues, and should include aspects on budgeting, timetabling, managing, controlling and evaluating. Target audience choice and strategy development are not relevant at the implementation stage.

> To: Board of Directors
> From: Marketing Communications Consultant
>
> Date: June 2003
>
> **Communications Strategies: AP Engineering 2004 and Beyond**

This report assesses **suitable marketing communications strategies** that will enable AP Engineering (AP) to move forward with its new approach of total engineering solutions. The report is presented in six main sections, each addressing a specific aspect as follows.

(a)   Communications strategy for 2003/4
(b)   Justification and explanation for strategy
(c)   Suggested promotional tools
(d)   Core messages
(e)   Issues of implementation and integration
(f)   Conclusions

(a)   **Communications strategy for 2003/4**

Cultural and **organisational changes** at the company suggest that one of the first jobs that will be required of the communications is to pull together all areas of the business. This will enable an **integrated approach** and offering to be made, and suggests the importance of **internal communications**. In addition our company will need to tell its existing customers and other **stakeholders** about the new one-stop service now on offer.

The strategy that we should propose is initially one of **profile**. This is relevant when a number of different stakeholders need to be addressed, and the main aim of this strategy is to develop our corporate **brand** and **reputation** for providing a full solution for all engineering needs. A **pull** strategy, aimed at existing customers and new business, will then be used to **raise awareness** of specific services.

(b) **Justification and explanation for strategy**

The reasons for the suggestion of a profile strategy can be summarised as follows.

1   The reorganisation has pulled together **new staff** from a number of acquisitions and new alliances. Profile strategies cover **internal marketing** and this will be vital to ensure that all staff and associates work together, uniting to offer an integrated service.

Our **mission** and **vision** need to filter through the organisation, and a dialogue set up to ensure that any issues affecting **strategy implementation** are understood. Front line staff need to feel valued, particularly when they are new to AP- they may be feeling vulnerable and unsure of new roles in the enlarged organisation. It can be seen that internal marketing provides an essential role during this time of **change management**.

2   **External audiences** such as **customers** need to be told about our new services, and reassured that the changes will make things easier for them. **Suppliers** may also be an important audience. The combined approach of profile and push will ensure that our **corporate brand** is **repositioned** as an integrated service provider. The existing **core values** of credibility and value for money will be retained, but the **service** element will now be highlighted (generally higher margins for us).

3   **Profile strategies** are particularly important in service industries, where **people** are key to delivering the offering.

4   AP needs to maintain its **external visibility** to ensure that it is considered as a supplier by other influential audiences, such as specifiers and architects.

5   Profile strategies concentrate on building **reputation** and corporate **image**, to allow a later pull strategy to concentrate on specific markets with specific products.

6   Margins have been tight, and a profile strategy can be more **cost effective** in generating awareness.

(c) **Suggested promotional tools**

The primary tools that should be used for implementation of the strategy are as follows.

1   **Internal marketing communication** to include training, staff conferences, intranet facilities and newsletters. The flow of communication needs to be two-way. Employees should be encouraged, and even incentivised, to make suggestions, get involved with writing press releases about projects they have worked on and take part in external events.

2   **Video conference facilities** to bring relevant experts into the team when required for internal and external communication.

3   Corporate **website development** with areas for clients, suppliers, staff and other influential professionals, including the press. This should offer a range of useful information to help customers with their projects.

4   **Direct marketing** to existing customers will explain the changes. This will be highly **targeted**, and explain the impact that our new services will have upon ongoing business.

5   **Personal selling** and **key account management**. As a service industry, the new structure and vision can best be explained through personal contact. Key accounts might be invited to a road show.

6   **Key account management system**. Computer systems should be organised around customers, so that all aspects of the business focus on the customer and **integrate** all activity.

7   **Public relations**. This venture is newsworthy, and AP should encourage editorial coverage to get its corporate message out to customers, suppliers and influencers. AP may wish to set up a **reference programme** which encourages joint PR between the client and AP, using civil engineering and building **journals** and the client's **trade press**. Site visits and speaking on the conference circuit may boost AP's reputation as 'one stop' experts, and ensure that it is the first company that comes to mind when a business project is being considered.

8   **Trade shows** and **advertising** may be considered towards the end of the profile strategy.

A combination of the above tools will implement both profile and pull strategies and build the new corporate brand.

(d) **Core messages**

Although communicating with a number of different stakeholders, a single and **consistent message** will be required to show the simplicity of the new vision and the **benefits** that the integrated service will bring.

As the decision to use AP's service will tend to be **high involvement**, **rational product appeals** will often work best. This requires longer copy and complex messages. Some symbolism of the **brand** may be useful, to present the new ethos in an easy to remember way. This will be followed by more detailed message content, outlining the **features** and **benefits** of AP's combined services for different stakeholders.

 An **example** might be:

"AP - the best specialised staff, coming together for a total solution to engineering problems."

This will give a sense of belonging to staff, and functional benefits can be elaborated on in terms of features and benefits for customers. A new logo, showing parts of a jigsaw coming together, could be used to show this visually. This **branding instrument** could then be used on all marketing communications activity.

(e) **Issues of implementation and integration**

Before implanting an integrated marketing communications policy several key issues need to be addressed.

1   **Budgets** - without sufficient resource put behind the strategy, it cannot be implemented. The size of budget will depend on the availability of funds, and the attitude of top management towards seeing this as an **investment** rather than a cost. **Internal markets** must be dealt with first when **allocating** the budget, because we have already seen that the change management must be effective to make the service deliverable. Money spent on communicating the service to the

customer and other stakeholders will be wasted if the internal processes are not capable of delivering what is promised.

2 **Cultural differences** and methods of working between new and existing staff will need to be addressed. Training and development will be needed, as well as consultation with staff at all levels.

3 **Management of communications** - should this be undertaken **in house** or via an **agency**? Internal marketing communications is a specialised area and consultants could advise on implementation. A senior manager should be empowered with introducing the internal marketing communications changes necessary.

4 **Measurement and evaluation**. A decision needs to be made on how and when to measure the effectiveness of the campaign. A number of techniques will be used e.g. internal **focus groups** amongst staff to judge whether the change of culture is working, staff satisfaction **surveys**, editorial coverage assessed to judge whether favourable or not. The measurement will depend on the **objectives** set.

5 **Timing issues** - the project will start with internal marketing communications, and then follow through with the external strategies. Budgets will need to be spread, and therefore actions will need to be **prioritised.**

6 Identification of **key influencers** that will need to be brought on board to implement the change strategy eg unions, professional membership bodies.

7 Are **computer** and other **systems** capable of the necessary reorganisation around key account management?

8 Are all **managers and staff** behind the new changes? Are they **capable of delivering** the marketing communications strategy? What will we do if they will not or cannot implement the changes needed?

9 What is the **procedure** for ensuring that all aspects of the plan are **integrated**? Should a **corporate identity manual** be issued, to guide all areas of the business on the new approach? Are messages to all stakeholders **consistent**?

10 Does the plan **complement** and help achieve corporate and marketing **objectives**?

Conclusions

AP Engineering is entering an exciting new period in its evolution. The company has grown and we will need to become more participative in our approach, so that we can offer our customers a complete engineering service.

This requires a culture change and a mix of internal and external communications. Initially a profile strategy will be required, and this report has suggested several tools that might be used to implement this. This will be followed with a more specific pull strategy. A simple message has been suggested to portray the new service and, finally, a list of issues that will need to be considered before we implement the strategy. The future for AP Engineering is looking good, and now the role of marketing communications comes to the fore to achieve corporate goals.

Pilot paper

A plan of attack

If this were the actual exam paper in front of you right now, how would you react? Having read all the questions, would you be panicking, or feeling relieved because a favourite topic had come up? Would you be dreading all the work ahead of you over the next three hours?

What you should really do is spend a good **5 minutes looking through the paper**, working out which questions to do and the order in which to attempt them. A plan of attack for the whole paper is now needed. We'll consider two options.

Option 1 (if you're thinking 'Help!)

If you are a bit worried about the paper, do the questions in the order of how well you think you can answer them.

Question 1 must be attempted if you are going to pass this paper. However daunting it seems, take a calm look at it and break down the requirements. It concerns a relatively small domestic company. Read through the scenario and identify the key issues arising. Perhaps you would like to annotate the paragraphs of the scenario to help to focus your thoughts, as the question is quite broken up and you need to think carefully about each part. There is a lot to think about. Here are some potential areas for consideration.

- CSK's market share/profitability
- Privately owned
- Medium quality product
- Self assembly – cost conscious
- Direct and indirect channels
- High staff loyalty
- Old processes and systems
- Competition increasing
- Budget constraints

Marketing plan targeting growth
Needs a marketing communications plan
Promotional ideas need development
Conversion rates to be maintained
Press ads / brochures used
Sales team works on commission
Word of mouth important
Customer contact and trust is vital
Use of Internet and websites

Part (a) of the question deals with the current and future roles of promotional activity – what does CSK use now, and what could / should it use for the future, given its objectives? Part (b) brings in the concept of perceived risk – the customers of CSK are likely to attach a lot of importance to their choice of kitchen. Think about the types of perceived risk and how it can be alleviated. For example, performance risk leads the customer to ask questions like: "Will the kitchen be the one I really want, and will it work well for me, given the price that I can pay?" Communications need to specifically address this concern.

Part (c) concerns the use of the Internet and specifically its effect on relationships with distributors – CSK should think about the effect it could have on the timely supply of its products to distributors, dealing with queries, sending out product information etc. It is likely that the big budget competition will have Internet capabilities already, and distributors may even come to expect Internet capability as a standard facility offered by manufacturers. In part (d), you need to make your recommendations based on your previous analysis. Think about the primary tools:

- Personal selling
- Advertising
- Sales promotion
- Sponsorship

Publicity
Point of purchase
Direct mail

Exhibitions
Events
E-marketing

Which ones are best? Do not forget the budget constraints that CSK operates with.

Question 2 is a question about the promotional mix that also brings in some aspects of the agency / client relationship. In part (a) you are asked to discuss sales promotion and public relations, and then to apply your knowledge of the product life cycle concept in part (b). If you are familiar with the issues here (introduction, growth, maturity, decline) then this part is straightforward, but do not forget that it is only worth 5 marks. Remember too, that your answer must be set in the context of the food manufacturing industry and in briefing document format. Part (c) on improving trust between client and agencies calls on common sense to an extent, but do not overlook the importance of setting clear objectives and consistent communications.

Question 3 is again a dual aspect question. When choosing media opportunities to compare in part (a), make them appropriate choices for your report to an international electrical appliances manufacturer. Internet advertising and national newspapers are more likely to be used than the small ads. Part (b) represents an easy 8 marks – define, explain and provide an example for each. For part (c), refer to the headings identified by the syllabus when thinking about international markets – media availability, culture, religion, education and literacy.

Question 4 is a fairly challenging one on marketing channels in the car industry. The definitions in part (a) for 5 marks should cause few problems. Sources of conflict (part b) can usually come down to communication issues. As we saw in Chapter 9 of this text, Fill (2002) quotes the main reasons as follows:

- Failure to carry out the job as understood by all channel members
- Particular specific issues arising that cause disagreement, such as territories / margins
- Different ways of reaching the same objectives
- Inadequate communications

Part (c) calls upon your knowledge of differences between B2B and B2C markets – fundamentally, these derive from differences in the buying decision process (influenced by factors such as motivations and risk). Such differences will affect the choice of marketing communications.

Question 5 is a nice question about the agency relationship. Part (b) is more difficult than the straightforward definitions and explanations in part (a). The relationship marketing approach (using concepts such as trust, loyalty and commitment) is well documented, however, so it should not be too difficult to discuss its importance in the context of this particular agency / client partnership. The fact that the client has international operations adds to the complications in, as well as the importance of, developing a potentially lucrative relationship. Your documentation pack should reflect this.

Option 2 (if you are thinking 'No problem!')

Try not to be overconfident, but if you are feeling fairly comfortable, and relieved that the paper is not the nightmare that you are anticipating, then **turn straight to the Section A compulsory question**. It has to be done, and you need 90 minutes in which to have a good go at it, so why not tackle it while you are still relatively fresh, and at the height of your powers?

Once you've done the compulsory question, choose two of the questions from Section B.

Questions 2 and **3** are a mix of easy definitions and applied analysis. To make your answers relevant, it is supremely important that you constantly refer to the specific context of the organisations described in the question wording.

Question 4 on marketing channels draws heavily on the syllabus content. It is probably the most challenging question on the paper, but should present few problems if you have studied business-to-business marketing channels. The car industry is a key example of an industry where distribution channels have been subject to revision and regulation in the face of market pressures.

Question 5 on the agency relationship is another mixture of definitions and evaluation. The main challenge is to keep your answer relevant to the circumstances of the client, PEN, given that you are preparing specific documents for presentation to its staff.

No matter how may times we remind you...

Always, always allocate your time according to the marks for the question in total and then according to the parts of the question. And **always, always follow the question requirements exactly**.

You've got spare time at the end of the exam... ?

If you have allocated your time properly then you shouldn't have time on your hands, but if you do find yourself with a spare ten minutes, go back over the paper and check your work.

Finally...

Do not worry if you found the paper difficult. Others will have too. Forget about it and think about the next one!

BPP PROFESSIONAL EDUCATION

PART A

Country Style Kitchens

> Stakeholder analysis – no shareholders

> Large market

The general kitchen furniture market in the UK is worth over £900 million per annum. Country Style Kitchens (CSK) is a privately owned company located in a small west country town. The company makes medium quality kitchen furniture which has a strong country styling and design. The units are available in both finished and self-assembly format, and unit sales reflect a 35% and 65% split respectively. The move into the self-assembly market proved successful as it enabled the company to reach customers in a wider geographic area. An installation facility is available for the finished units but the trend appears to be in favour of self-assembly products.

> Scope here for quality improvements?

> Is this subject to fashion trends?

> Cost conscious customers

CSK's sales have grown steadily over their 45 years of trading and currently stand at £13.7 million per annum with net profit at 8.2%. Products are sold through both direct and indirect marketing channels. The indirect channels consist of a small number of appointed distributors who sell a range of kitchen and bathroom products from many different manufacturers. They hold limited stock but work from brochures and their own showrooms.

> % market share?

> How does CSK make sure its products are properly promoted?

Staff are very supportive of the company and appear to have a strong identification with the country style positioning. Over 50% have been with the company in excess of 15 years. It should be noted that many of the internal systems and procedures are old, slow and in need of updating, perhaps a reflection of the slower, rural culture that identifies the Country Style Kitchens company.

> Old fashioned – how to attract younger customers?

> How easy/expensive will this be? Internal marketing likely to be needed to get staff support

In addition to these internal challenges the company has begun to experience increased competition from major national kitchen furniture manufacturers. These companies either buy in prefabricated panels and apply a (rural) design template, or import them direct from overseas manufacturers. In addition, they have sufficient resources to use broadcast media and offer lower prices.

> Biggest challenge faced by CSK

> CSK at a big disadvantage here

In recognition of some of these problems facing the company, management have developed a marketing plan which seeks growth of 15% per annum achieved by market penetration and in particular the attraction of new customers. It now needs a marketing communication programme to deliver the marketing strategy.

> Can this be achieved with current range?

> Make sure that you understand the terms 'marketing plan', 'marketing communications programme' and 'marketing strategy'

The competition, as Country Style Kitchens see it, have huge resources which can be used to invest in promotional campaigns to drive awareness and action. For example, these companies have authentic websites, unlike Country Style Kitchens' website which is little

> An area for development

> Refer to theories of customer buying behaviour

than an online brochure. Many of the large, national standardised companies can produce promotional literature in large production runs and are happy to ignore wastage. Using expert photography of pretend kitchens the quality and impact of the literature is high. Country Style Kitchens' smaller budgets dictate that photographs of real customers' kitchens are used, which seldom look perfect and can appear amateurish. It costs £5 to produce each of the CSK brochures, so the vetting of each request for literature is important to avoid those people merely intent on collecting brochures. A high conversion rate is necessary, and although 50% of quotations are convert

Current promotional activities centre on small space advertising in the supplements of weekend newspapers to generate leads, and the use of brochures distributed via direct mail using bought in lists. In addition to this, a small number of largely commission-based sales consultants work in the geographic areas not covered by the distributors. This sales team is supported by a few office staff, who advise clients by telephone should they have any product assembly related problems. They also liaise with the distributors. Sales promotions are used seasonally to promote sales and to reduce any excess stock. Word of mouth is important although little is undertaken to manage or develop it.

Country Style Kitchens' customers want self-assembly country style kitchen units, but at mid to low range prices. Because they are bought direct there is little opportunity to inspect the quality before purchasing, so it is important that all customer contact is reassuring. For many price is key issue and a high degree of trust is necessary in order that a sale is completed.

Annotations:

- CSK cannot afford to do this
- How much effort is wasted having to do this vetting process?
- Are these lists sufficiently targeted at likely customers, or are they too general?
- Do customers trust their advice?
- Seems there is little scope for price increases
- Performance risk
- Need to find best way to use available resources
- Unlikely to attract significant numbers of new customers
- Unlikely to be eye catching
- A risk area, with price based competition and competitor promotion increasing
- This could be improved using an 'FAQ' section on a website
- This could also be done via the Internet
- Might not be able to rely on using the Internet for some customers
- How can this be developed?
- Does this affect brand image?

Part A

Question 1

You are a newly qualified Marketing Executive, and as a friend of one of the Directors, have agreed to advise CSK on their marketing communications. Prepare a report in response to the following:

What has happened to date?

What needs to happen now?

(a)   Evaluate the current and future roles of marketing communications at Country Style Kitchens.   **(15 marks)**

Define this. Why is it important?

(b)   Consider the importance of perceived risk to end user customers of CSK, and in the light of this knowledge make recommendations about how marketing communications might best be used.   **(10 marks)**

Don't sit on the fence

Think about the effects, not necessarily whether it is currently feasible for CSK

(c)   How might the development of Internet and digital-based technologies influence relationships with the distributors?   **(5 marks)**

Not customers

Must be suitable for CSK's budget

(d)   Recommend and justify a suitable co-ordinated marketing communications mix.

Select the most suitable elements

(20 marks)

(50 marks in total)

PART B – Answer TWO questions only

Question 2

As a newly appointed Marketing Assistant at a branded food manufacturing organisation your Marketing Manager has asked you to prepare a briefing document for her use at a forthcoming meeting with your current advertising agency. She is concerned that there is too much above-the-line activity and would like to see greater use of other promotional tools. Prepare your briefing document answering the following questions:

(a) Using appropriate criteria, compare and contrast the effectiveness of the following two promotional tools: sales promotion and public relations.   **(10 marks)**

(b) Explain how the tools of the promotional mix might be best used over the life of a product.   **(5 marks)**

(b) Recommend ways in which trust between clients and agencies might be improved.

(10 marks)

(25 marks in total)

Keep your answer in this context

What is this? Why might it not be appropriate?

Qualitative and quantitative

Key to the question

Apply the product life cycle phases

Just these, no more

This is a key syllabus term. Feel free to state the obvious, but it comes down to clear communication

Question 3

You are a Media Planner/Buyer working for a large media independent in a country of your choice. One of your clients, a consumer electrical appliances manufacturer, operating across a number of international markets, has asked you to provide a short report explaining key media concepts and the media opportunities that exist to support its promotional activities over the next five years. Write a short report setting out your response to the following questions:

(a) Discuss the advantages and disadvantages of any two media that you would recommend to your client.   **(10 marks)**

(b) Explain the media concepts reach, frequency and opportunities-to-see.   **(8 marks)**

(c) Describe the key factors that might influence the choice of media in (the client's) international markets.   **(7 marks)**

(25 marks in total)

Keep this context in your answer

Large resources

Emphasis on the future

Select two that are appropriate to this company

Easy marks

Might be limited in certain countries

Issues such as literacy, culture, education

Question 4

Car manufacturers have traditionally used dealer networks to distribute their cars to end-user consumers. Recent changes to EU regulations and developments in information technology have encouraged manufacturers to review their channels of distribution. For example, some have reduced the number of independently owned franchises, and some have introduced a direct sales operation via the Internet. Both initiatives have caused some dealer-based conflict and unrest.

As a Passenger Car Marketing Executive you have been requested to advise your colleagues about particular aspects of channel marketing. In anticipation of the meeting, you should prepare notes with regard to the following questions and the car market in a country of your choice.

(a)   What is the meaning of 'independence' and 'interdependence' when referring to the relationships between members of marketing channels?   **(5 marks)**

(b)   Appraise the main sources of conflict that can appear between members of marketing channels.   **(10 marks)**

(c)   Explain how marketing communications in marketing channels (b2b) are fundamentally different to those used in consumer markets.   **(10 marks)**

(25 marks in total)

Annotations:

- A question on marketing channels
- Context analysis
- Why?
- Why would dealers be unhappy with these developments?
- How does this benefit both manufacturer and customer?
- Important instruction re the context of your answer
- Easy marks for definitions
- Which ones are the most significant?
- Characterised by different risks – very personal communications often used

Question 5

The PEN company, an established manufacturer and distributor of personal electronic products, seeks an agency to help launch their new personal organiser. The advertising agency for whom you work has just been invited to pitch for PEN's international account following a successful credentials visit. As the potential Account Manager for this client you are required to organise a documentation pack that will be given to the client at the pitch. You are required to prepare the following:

(a)   An explanation of the role of the Account Manager and the nature and characteristics of the Client Brief.   **(15 marks)**

(b)   An evaluation of the importance of adopting a relationship marketing approach with clients.   **(10 marks)**

(25 marks in total)

Annotations:

- Answer the question from an agency perspective, not the client
- Define and apply

Answer plans

PART A

Question 1

(a) | *Current role* (5-6 marks) | *Future role* (9-10 marks) |
|---|---|
| Maintain market share | Grow market share by 15% |
| Maintain conversion rate | Increase conversion rate |
| Traditional media – small ads | Internet/website/word of mouth |
| Poor quality literature | Need to 'show off' the kitchens |
| Use of distributors | Increased use of direct selling? |
| Old processes | Coping with sophisticated competition |
| Budget constraints | Budget constraints |
| Little done to enhance brand | Promote brand more widely |
| Holding the customer's hand | Some customer contact to be maintained |
| Considerable staff loyalty | Use internal marketing to 'sell' changes |

(b) Define perceived risk - why it is important and how each type of risk can be addressed? (for 2 marks each):

- Performance
- Financial
- Physical
- Social
- Ego

(c) How might CSK develop its Internet capability to help its relationships with distributors? Examples for 1 - 2 marks each:

- A website could facilitate online ordering of stock by distributors
- Instant information on CSK's latest products
- Relationships would be improved by instant communication
- Saves having to employ dedicated office telephone staff

Make the point (for another mark) that this would need investment and CSK may need to analyse whether it is worthwhile – although it is highly likely that the competition will have Internet capability, and distributors may even come to expect it as a standard way of doing business for the future.

(d) Present the list of available tools and make recommendations as to which is suitable, given what you have already concluded re CSK's objectives and its limited budget. Divide answer into direct and indirect channels (as a guide, aim for 10 marks per channel for a total of 20 marks). Which of these would be appropriate in each?

■ Personal selling	Publicity	Exhibitions
■ Advertising	Point of purchase	Events
■ Sales promotion	Direct mail	E-marketing
■ Sponsorship		

PART B

Question 2

(a)   Directly compare sales promotion and public relations on measures such as (2 marks each):

- Cost
- Awareness building
- Conversion to sales
- Suitability for the market/target customer
- Suitability for the chosen distribution channel

(Measures need to be relevant for a food manufacturer)

(b)   Examine each stage of the product life cycle (PLC) – introduction, growth, maturity, decline - give example of relevant tool at each stage, and why, for 1-2 marks each:

Introduction   Intense TV campaign/direct mailings for awareness building

Growth   Continued press and TV coverage, over longer period. Stands at suitable events and shows

Maturity   Promotional coupons/POS to keep product in customer's mind

Decline   Decline in spend, maybe some limited in-store promotion

(c)   Why trust is important – unlikely to have a long term relationship without it. Five ways, for 10 marks:

- Communicate via regular briefings and updates
- Budget constraints made clear at outset
- Staff relationships fostered
- Share important market information/any concerns
- Appoint a team leader to co-ordinate

Question 3

(a)   The chosen media must represent future opportunities that are appropriate for an electrical appliance manufacturer – it is likely to have large resources as it is international. 5 marks available for each one chosen, listing 2 or 3 advantages and disadvantages for each. Suggest use TV and Internet advertising.

(b)   2/3 marks each – define/explain/example (see Chapter 6) up to a total of 8 marks.

(c)   Key factors are set out by the syllabus – media availability, culture, religion, education and literacy in local area – describe each one for 1 - 2 marks per factor up to a total of 7 marks (answer will consider the likely market for a consumer electrical appliances manufacturer, and therefore which factors will be more relevant than others).

Question 4

(a)   *Independence* - maintain own role and do own job and fulfil objectives in the marketing channel

Interdependence - activities impinge on others in the marketing channel.

(Apply both of these to the car market, for 2 - 3 marks each)

(b)   4 main sources of conflict per Chapter 9. 2 or 3 marks for each one up to a total of 10 marks, again as relevant to the car market. Explain why such conflict exist – ie why the dealers are not happy with the changes.

(c)   Set out key differences, for 10 marks. Explain each one, and why communications are affected. Possible inclusions:

- Buyer motivation
- Usually use rational appeals
- Technical/complex products
- Seeking information and reassurance
- Use of personal selling/demonstrations

Question 5

(a)   Role of account manager for 7 marks:

- 'Go between' for agency / client relationship
- Leads the team
- Co-ordinator
- Communicator
- Takes overall responsibility for agency work
- Seeks input from client to keep agency informed

Nature/characteristics of the client brief for 8 marks. Make it relevant to PEN, using the proforma from Chapter 12:

- Budget
- Key deadlines
- Company background
- Business objectives
- Background to the brief
- Communications objectives
- Target market and proposition

(b)   Relationship marketing:

- What it is (definition) for 2 marks
- How it applies in an advertising agency for 3 marks
- Why it is important in today's advertising industry for 3 marks
- Possible consequences of non-adoption of such an approach for 2 marks

List of Key Concepts and Index

A/S ratio, 99
Above-the-line promotion, 108
Adstock effect, 74
Advertising, 113, 157
Attitude, 23

Banner advertisement, 178
Belief, 23
Below-the-line promotion, 108
Brief, 316

Commitment, 250
Consumer buying behaviour, 15
Corporate strategy, 70
Culture, 16

Diffusion, 11, 31, 32
Direct marketing, 122

Ethical issues, 44
Exchange, 6

Frequency, 173, 181, 182
Full service, 309

Globalisation, 186

Independence, 242
Innovation, 10
Interdependence, 242

Key accounts, 148

Lifestyle, 19

Market positioning, 88
Marketing communications, 4
Media only, 309
Motivation, 19
Multinational corporations, 186

Noise, 8

Opinion leaders, 9

Perception, 22
Personal selling, 114
Positioning, 87
PR, 118
Psychological positioning, 89
Pull strategy, 140
Push Communication Strategy, 147

Ratings, 173, 181
Reach, 173, 181, 182
Relationship marketing, 294
Risk, 29

Sales promotion, 116
Share of voice, 100
Source credibility, 28
Stakeholder, 243, 257
Successful brand, 141, 153
Supply chain management, 242

Target Marketing Process (TMP), 79
Trust, 250

BPP
PROFESSIONAL EDUCATION

BPP
PROFESSIONAL EDUCATION

See overleaf for information on other
BPP products and how to order

CIM Order

To BPP Publishing Ltd, Aldine Place, London W12 8AA

Tel: 020 8740 2211. Fax: 020 8740 1184
email: publishing@bpp.com
online: www.bpp.com

Mr/Mrs/Ms (Full name) _____

Daytime delivery address _____

Postcode _____

Daytime Tel _____   Date of exam (month/year) _____

	6/03 Texts	9/03 Kits	Success Tapes	Passcards
CERTIFICATE (STAGE 1) NEW SYLLABUS				
1 Marketing Fundamentals	£19.95 ☐	£9.95 ☐	£12.95 ☐	£5.95 ☐
2 Marketing Environment	£19.95 ☐	£9.95 ☐	£12.95 ☐	£5.95 ☐
3 Customer Communications	£19.95 ☐	£9.95 ☐	£12.95 ☐	£5.95 ☐
4 Marketing in Practice	£19.95 ☐	£9.95 ☐	£12.95 ☐	£5.95 ☐
ADVANCED CERTIFICATE (STAGE 2) NEW SYLLABUS				
5 The Marketing Customer Interface	£19.95 ☐	£9.95 ☐	N/A	£5.95 ☐
6 Management Information for Marketing Decisions	£19.95 ☐	£9.95 ☐	N/A	£5.95 ☐
7 Effective Management for Marketing	£19.95 ☐	£9.95 ☐	N/A	£5.95 ☐
8 Marketing Operations	£19.95 ☐	£9.95 ☐	N/A	£5.95 ☐
DIPLOMA OLD SYLLABUS *				
9 Integrated Marketing Communications	£19.95 ☐	£9.95 ☐	£12.95 ☐	N/A
10 International Marketing Strategy	£19.95 ☐	£9.95 ☐	£12.95 ☐	N/A
11 Strategic Marketing Management: Planning and Control	£19.95 ☐	£9.95 ☐	£12.95 ☐	N/A
12 Strategic Marketing Management: Analysis and Decision (9/03)	£25.95 ☐	N/A	N/A	N/A
			SUBTOTAL	£ ☐

* Texts and kits for remaining new syllabus items will be available in the spring and summer of 2004.

POSTAGE & PACKING

Study Texts and Kits

	First	Each extra	
UK	£5.00	£2.00	£ ☐
Europe**	£6.00	£4.00	£ ☐
Rest of world	£20.00	£10.00	£ ☐

Success Tapes/Passcards

	First	Each extra	
UK	£2.00	£1.00	£ ☐
Europe**	£3.00	£2.00	£ ☐
Rest of world	£8.00	£8.00	£ ☐

Reduced postage rates apply if you **order online** at www.bpp.com

Grand Total (Cheques to *BPP Publishing*) I enclose a cheque for (incl. Postage)   £ ☐

Or charge to Access/Visa/Switch

Card Number ☐☐☐☐ ☐☐☐☐ ☐☐☐☐ ☐☐☐☐

Expiry date ☐☐☐☐   Start Date _____

Issue Number (Switch Only) ☐☐☐☐

Signature _____

We aim to deliver to all UK addresses inside 5 working days. A signature will be required. Orders to all EU addresses should be delivered within 6 working days.

All other orders to overseas addresses should be delivered within 8 working days.

** Europe includes the Republic of Ireland and the Channel Islands.

REVIEW FORM & FREE PRIZE DRAW

All original review forms from the entire BPP range, completed with genuine comments, will be entered into one of two draws on 31 January 2004 and 31 July 2004. The names on the first four forms picked out on each occasion will be sent a cheque for £50.

Name: _____   Address: _____

_____

_____

How have you used this Text?
(Tick one box only)

☐ Home study (book only)

☐ On a course: college _____

☐ With 'correspondence' package

☐ Other _____

Why did you decide to purchase this Text?
(Tick one box only)

☐ Have used companion Kit

☐ Have used BPP Texts in the past

☐ Recommendation by friend/colleague

☐ Recommendation by a lecturer at college

☐ Saw advertising

☐ Other _____

During the past six months do you recall seeing/receiving any of the following?
(Tick as many boxes as are relevant)

☐ Our advertisement in the *Marketing Success*

☐ Our advertisement in *Marketing Business*

☐ Our brochure with a letter through the post

☐ Our brochure with *Marketing Business*

Which (if any) aspects of our advertising do you find useful?
(Tick as many boxes as are relevant)

☐ Prices and publication dates of new editions

☐ Information on Text content

☐ Facility to order books off-the-page

☐ None of the above

Have you used the companion Practice & Revision Kit for this subject?   ☐ Yes   ☐ No

Your ratings, comments and suggestions would be appreciated on the following areas.

	Very useful	Useful	Not useful
Introductory section (How to use this text, study checklist, etc)	☐	☐	☐
Setting the Scene	☐	☐	☐
Syllabus coverage	☐	☐	☐
Action Programmes and Marketing at Work examples	☐	☐	☐
Chapter roundups	☐	☐	☐
Quick quizzes	☐	☐	☐
Illustrative questions	☐	☐	☐
Content of suggested answers	☐	☐	☐
Index	☐	☐	☐
Structure and presentation	☐	☐	☐

	Excellent	Good	Adequate	Poor
Overall opinion of this Text	☐	☐	☐	☐

Do you intend to continue using BPP Study Texts/Kits?   ☐ Yes   ☐ No

Please note any further comments and suggestions/errors on the reverse of this page.

Please return to: Glenn Haldane, BPP Professional Education, FREEPOST, London, W12 8BR

REVIEW FORM & FREE PRIZE DRAW (continued)

Please note any further comments and suggestions/errors below.

FREE PRIZE DRAW RULES

1 Closing date for 31 January 2004 draw is 31 December 2003. Closing date for 31 July 2004 draw is 30 June 2004.

2 Restricted to entries with UK and Eire addresses only. BPP employees, their families and business associates are excluded.

3 No purchase necessary. Entry forms are available upon request from BPP Professional Education. No more than one entry per title, per person. Draw restricted to persons aged 16 and over.

4 Winners will be notified by post and receive their cheques not later than 6 weeks after the relevant draw date. Lists of winners will be published in BPP's *focus* newsletter following the relevant draw.

5 The decision of the promoter in all matters is final and binding. No correspondence will be entered into.